(

ESSAYS ON SEVE RATURE

Cambridge Studies in French

General editor: MALCOLM BOWIE

Also in the series:

J. M. COCKING

Proust. Collected Essays on the Writer and his Art

LEO BERSANI

The Death of Stéphane Mallarmé

MARIAN HOBSON

The Object of Art. The Theory of Illusion in Eighteenth-Century France

LEO SPITZER

ESSAYS ON SEVENTEENTH-CENTURY FRENCH LITERATURE

Translated, edited and with an introduction by

DAVID BELLOS

Professor of French at the University of Southampton

CAMBRIDGE UNIVERSITY PRESS

CAMBRIDGE

LONDON NEW YORK NEW ROCHELLE

MELBOURNE SYDNEY

CAMBRIDGE UNIVERSITY PRESS
Cambridge, New York, Melbourne, Madrid, Cape Town, Singapore, São Paulo, Delhi

Cambridge University Press
The Edinburgh Building, Cambridge CB2 8RU, UK

Published in the United States of America by Cambridge University Press, New York

www.cambridge.org
Information on this title: www.cambridge.org/9780521289719

First published by Cambridge University Press 1983
This digitally printed version 2009

A catalogue record for this publication is available from the British Library

Library of Congress Catalogue Card Number: 82–14581

ISBN 978-0-521-24356-8 hardback
ISBN 978-0-521-28971-9 paperback

For my children

CONTENTS

ACKNOWLEDGMENTS

I should like to thank Princeton University Press for permission to reprint the essay 'The "Récit de Théramène" in Racine's *Phèdre*'; and Professor Mark Musa who, as Leo Spitzer's literary executor, has given permission for the translation and publication of all the other essays in this volume.

The original idea of producing this book was Malcolm Bowie's and I would like to thank him and Andrew Brown of C.U.P. for their encouragement and sensible advice. My own limited learning would not have allowed me to make these translations single-handed, but, having the good fortune to work in the large Arts Faculty of the University of Edinburgh, I was able to call on the knowledge and skills of many kind and willing helpers. Classical quotations were located for me by Allan Hood, Spanish queries answered by Donald Shaw and Italian mysteries clarified by Jonathan Usher. Philip Bennett helped me with medieval French and Tony Harper (at Strathclyde) with early German. Peter Allen, Andrew Barker, Brian Barron, Peter France, Nick Furness, Howard Gaskell and Peter Sharratt all took part in the hunt for locations and references of the most diverse kinds.

The bibliographies could not have been compiled without the resources of the University Library at Konstanz and the efficient help of its staff. I must thank also Professor Harri Meier at Bonn for information on Julius Schmidt. Most of all I must thank Hans-Robert Jauss for his recollections of Spitzer, for his advice, for the loan of personal copies of many otherwise unfindable items, and for his generous criticism of an earlier version of the Introduction.

I hope I have put the efforts of this army of distinguished helpers to a use that is worthy of them. Any remaining errors are mine – or Leo Spitzer's.

David Bellos
Paris 1981

A NOTE ON THIS EDITION

The articles which form the six chapters of this book were written in three different languages over four decades, and the originals use a variety of different conventions for quotations and references. Leo Spitzer wrote quickly, with a particular learned audience in mind, and paid little attention to presentation or to the difficulties later readers might have. Many of his sharpest insights are to be found in footnotes, which he used not for references but for second thoughts (often pages long) and themselves sometimes footnoted when he read through his piece a third time. A straightforward translation of Spitzer, such as that given in the French volume of *Etudes de style* (A41),* would thus remain difficult to read and to use, and would not be at all likely to win a new audience for this brilliant critic among the English-speaking students of French literature for whom this edition is intended. I have consequently taken the opportunity of translation to make the following quite substantial editorial changes to the originals:

1. *Footnotes and digressions.* All the material contained in footnotes in Spitzer's originals has been integrated into the running text of the chapters, except for points that have lost their relevance and have therefore been omitted. Manifest digressions from the main argument resulting from the 'raising' of footnotes have been enclosed in bold square brackets **[**thus**]**. A few transition sentences and phrases have been added to relink arguments disrupted by the insertion of footnote material.

2. *Additional footnotes* have been given by me where necessary for elucidation. All footnotes in this edition are mine, not Spitzer's.

3. *Quotations.* Spitzer quotes in eight languages and gives his references infrequently. I have located nearly all the quotations, and give them here in the form to be found in currently available editions of the relevant texts. I have translated all quotations except those in French, and omitted the original-language version except for Old French, Latin,

* See the Bibliography on pp. xxxi–xxxviii below.

and a few quotations of poetry in other languages. In some cases it has been possible to supply the French original where Spitzer quoted in German translation.

4. *References.* The List of References on pp. 285–90 below gives the bibliographic details of all books and articles quoted or referred to in the chapters, with certain exceptions. In the chapters, reference is made simply by the author's name and page number; where there is more than one entry for an author in the List of References, the relevant work is distinguished by a short title or by a date of publication. The exceptions are those few pieces, mostly articles in pre-war German periodicals, which I have been unable to locate. In these cases there are references in the chapters to authors and works which do not appear in the List of References; they are signalled in the text where they occur.

5. *Omissions.* I have left out appendices on Schiller's translation of Racine and Rilke's translation of Guilleragues, since their interest to readers with no German is not very great. Also omitted are some polemical onslaughts on now-forgotten colleagues and rivals.

6. *Recasting.* In some instances I have chosen to recast the order of Spitzer's paragraphs, particularly at the beginnings of the chapters and where substantial footnotes have been integrated into the text. Such reorderings are not signalled in the text.

7. To avoid tiresome repetition and also to make use of the publication of these essays together in one volume for the first time, I have represented all of Spitzer's internal cross-references within chapters, all of his cross-references between chapters, and a few new cross-references of my own by the symbol ⟶ followed by a page number.

8. In chapter 1, the division into sections, the section headings, and the choice of key-words printed in bold face are my own editorial inventions.

DB

INTRODUCTION

I

Leo Spitzer published his first book in 1910 (A1) and in the following fifty years produced a seemingly endless stream of scholarly and critical articles on the languages and literatures of Spain, France, Italy, Portugal, Romania, Germany, England and America – as many as 800 items in all, according to René Wellek (D9), and in the five languages which Spitzer wrote fluently if not with equal elegance. Yet he left no one great book; nor did he leave a theory or a method, or even (except perhaps in Italy) a school of imitators. Spitzer's place in the history of literary scholarship and criticism is thus difficult to pinpoint or to summarise in schematic terms; his practice is too diverse and too rich to be easily labelled with an '-ism' or a theory. By circumstance, by inclination but also by conscious choice, Spitzer ran the risk of being dismissed as an ultimately insignificant eccentric, a man of personal brilliance without the institutional weight of a theory or school to call his own. In recent years, however, Spitzer has been republished and retranslated in Spain, in Italy and in France, and even translated back into his native German; articles and essays inspired by or referring to his pioneering work in stylistics and literary criticism are surprisingly numerous; despite his difficulty, diversity and eccentricity, Spitzer cannot be regarded now, twenty years after his death, as an insignificant figure. The purpose of this edition is to bring him a new readership in the English-speaking world, and by the same token to bring scholars and students of French literature at every level into renewed contact with Spitzer's unique combination of erudition and insight that has often been built upon, but never surpassed.

I have chosen to present here not a faithful rendering of a representative sample of Spitzer's work, but a recast version of all his work on one particular area, the literature of seventeenth-century France (in which Saint-Simon's *Mémoires* are included by convention and in view of their subject, despite their later date of composition (1740–50) and even later date of publication (1829)). The mere fact of putting all of Spitzer's work on one area together produces the sort of book Spitzer never published and would not have wanted to publish. It gives these six very different essays the appearance of chapters in a comprehensive and definitive monograph or monologue. Spitzer believed passionately in the importance of dialogue in scholarship – indeed, believed that scholarship *was* dialogue, and that the only appropriate mode of publication was in articles in learned journals. But if dialogue with Spitzer is still possible and rewarding in the act of reading and testing his insights into Racine and La Fontaine, it is no longer possible in the literal sense in which Spitzer also intended it – in replies and rejoinders to his articles. If his work is to gain the new audience that it deserves, then it has to undergo not only translation but also a form of transposition into contemporary conventions of scholarship which makes it more like a monument than Spitzer would have wished. I have listed on pp. ix–x above the main kinds of changes that I have imposed on the originals and which make Spitzer appear in these chapters to be less quirky, more readable, less obscure and more monumental than he was in the original. For those readers familiar with the originals, I hope these versions appear no less brilliant and no less stimulating; but I hope most of all that these essays, because or in spite of the liberties taken with them in the process of translation, lead a new audience into reading the great literary texts of the past with the insight, the understanding and that special feeling for the unity of language, form and content which are Leo Spitzer's alone.

II

All of the essays brought together here are defences of individual writers, explanations of the *difference* of Racine, Corneille, Saint-Simon, La Fontaine and Guilleragues – of their difference from each other and more especially from us. This espousal of difference can be thought of quite properly as a philological understanding of literature – in contrast to a linguistic understanding in the modern sense, which tends to seek constants, similarities, and general structures. Philology is that science of language which studies the differences between tongues, and Spitzer was trained as a Romance philologist of the old school, of which he remained a wayward but unmistakable member all his life. At the same time, his application of the philological approach and of his philological knowledge to literary history and criticism was an act of revolt against his master at the University of Vienna, the Swiss linguist Wilhelm Meyer-Lübke, compiler of the monumental *Romanisches Etymologisches Wörterbuch*. What led Spitzer away from a well-established field for which he was so well equipped and in which he was already pre-eminent, towards the dangerous realm of criticism, where everything remained to be done? There was no doubt an element of youthful aggressiveness in Spitzer's choice (in the 1920s he came to be known as 'der rote Hahn', 'the red rooster' (c5, p. 219)) but there was also from the start a deeper quest which he was never to abandon. He wanted not simply to study Romance languages, but to justify that study by uncovering that which was different (from his own culture, from himself) in the characteristic uses to which the language was put. Meyer-Lübke's historical linguistics impressed Spitzer by its scientific sobriety and sheer erudition, but seemed supremely irrelevant and enclosed in a dry world of its own making, where 'on n'arrivait même pas à se demander si le problème en question valait tel traitement vétilleux' (c5, p. 213). He had come to the university to study French in order to discover what it was that made Frenchmen French, but in the positivistic literary history of Philip Becker he found only the pre-history of the great French texts, nothing that could be considered their 'living difference'. In one place, Spitzer attributes his dissatisfaction with his university courses to the very much more cosmopolitan and classical secondary education he had received at the Franz-Joseph-Gymnasium (c8, p. 579); elsewhere, to the open and international atmosphere of pre-war Vienna (c9); and in a very late article, to the influence of Sigmund Freud, whose prestige was high among the Jewish intellectual circles in which Spitzer moved (c14, repeated in c16, p. 26). However, Spitzer's grasp of Freud was neither profound nor adequate; and it is interesting to consider what separates these two minds that grew out of very much the same milieu.

Freud's theory of the human psyche, in all its different versions, assumes axiomatically that language, like dreams and behaviour, serves to hide the truth by distorting it (by condensation, displacement, etc.). Language is *opaque* for Freud, but for Spitzer it is – at least in those works of literary art on which he spent his creative and critical time – always, and absolutely, *transparent*. In 1954, Spitzer claimed he had taken from Freud the idea that a writer's language could be seen as the 'symptom' of his 'soul', but he also displays clearly a very shallow conception, not to say a complete misunderstanding, of psychoanalysis: '[I saw that] Freud's theory of the "complex", explaining morbid aberrations from the psychological norm in an individual as *systematic* and *constant* deviations, could be transferred to the particular language, or style, of the personality of a writer: the deviations (no longer morbid) of his style from the general linguistic norm would then emanate from a system located in the writer's psychic being' (c14). The crucial parenthesis 'no longer morbid' means that Spitzer never sought to disentangle the biological experience of the writer from his work, but treated the work and the writer as essentially coterminous and indeed interchangeable entities, both constituted and revealed by the forms of language used.

Although Spitzer's own accounts of his critical method changed over the years, his actual practice and his understanding of language and literature emerged virtually fully-fledged in his doctoral dissertation on neologisms in Rabelais and Balzac (A1, 1910) and remained constant throughout his long career. At this stage in pre-war Vienna, Meyer-Lübke was still great enough as a man and scholar to protect and encourage someone who was clearly in revolt against him, and who was also under constant threat from the antisemitic *Akademischer Verein deutscher Romanisten* ('University Union of German Romanists' – who were, in Spitzer's phrase, neither academic, nor German, nor Romanists). He was thus sent to Paris in 1911–12 where, as a pupil ('"ambassadeur", ricanait quelqu'un') of the Viennese school of Romance philology, he had introductions to all the great names of the day (Bédier, Roques, Gaston Paris, et al.) and conducted some etymological and philological research (A2, A3). He returned to Vienna as *Privatdozent* (teaching fellow) in 1912 and on the outbreak of the First World War was conscripted to work for the Austrian Censorship Office. He read the letters home from Italian prisoners of war, which provided him with the material for two fascinating books (A11, A14) – the first a philological study of circumlocutions for hunger (the prisoners were not allowed to say they were badly fed), the second a general linguistic study of the letters, now available in Italian translation (A14a). Meyer-Lübke moved to Bonn in 1915, believing that Austria would lose but that Germany would win the war (C5, p. 218); Spitzer, whose views and aspirations were quite different, none the less followed him in 1918, first as *Privatdozent*, then, from 1919, as *ausserordentlicher Professor* (non-statutory professor).

Spitzer left Vienna, it would seem, at least partly for straightforward self-advancement. He was still a very young and controversial man in a very hierarchical system, and – especially as a Jew – needed the backing of a great professor. (The obstacles to a career at that period in a German or Austrian university should not be underestimated: the brilliant philologist Elise Richter was never even an assistant at the University of Vienna, despite Meyer-Lübke's protection; she died at Theresienstadt concentration camp in 1944 (C9, p. 329).) In later years, however, Spitzer explained that he was glad to leave the heady but ultimately insubstantial intellectual atmosphere of Vienna. One part of Austrian culture was entirely cosmopolitan:

> Viennese life added to the classical basis of school education a passion for the culture of the west – French culture far more than German. The great theatrical events all came from abroad – Sarah Bernhardt, Duse, Reinhardt, d'Annunzio,

Tolstoy, Zola, Wilde belonged for us to the same cultural world as Hauptmann and Hofmannsthal.

The other side, particularly in evidence at the University, was petty, bourgeois and intolerant of the non-German peoples of the Austro-Hungarian monarchy, especially of Jews (C8, p. 579). Austria, Spitzer wrote in recollection, gave the young philologist 'the as-if world of language, the admiration of superior foreign cultures, but not a real or stable basis for the life of the mind' (C8, p. 580).

By the time of his move to Bonn, Spitzer was a pacifist, a left-winger, and an outspoken opponent of such barely hidden forms of renascent German nationalism as the movement for linguistic purity. His two 'politico-linguistic' tracts (A7 and A8) denounced the attempts to remove foreign words from German as xenophobic; and it was this public and polemical involvement which strained his relationship with Meyer-Lübke (who was moving steadily to the right) even more than his work on contemporary French literature.

It is perhaps hard now to imagine just how revolutionary it was for a German academic linguist to turn his attention in 1919–20 to the study of up-to-the-minute French novelists like Henri Barbusse or Charles-Louis Philippe (A10, B4). Spitzer recalled:

> Les étudiants voulaient apprendre le français moderne. Les étudiants revenant du front et qui avaient regardé la mort en face, ne pouvaient se résigner à étudier ni les formes verbales de la chanson d'Alexis ni les détails de la vie privée de Molière . . . Un spécialiste de la linguistique comme moi, que devait-il faire? D'abord brûler ses paperasses devenues inutiles . . . ensuite tâcher de trouver le joint entre la linguistique et *quelque chose d'autre*. (C4, pp. 583–4)

It is to Spitzer's credit that he responded to the demands of his post-war public, and of great significance that he did so by tackling contemporary writing, even if Barbusse and Philippe do not rank today as the most important writers of the war generation. Spitzer's responsiveness as a teacher and scholar was exemplary; his insistence in later writings on the dialogic nature of scholarly work was no empty posture.

Spitzer's relationship with Meyer-Lübke continued to decline, and he moved in 1925 to the ancient university of Marburg-an-der-Lahn as *Professor Ordinarius* (statutory professor), and then in 1930 to Cologne. The following eight years were the most productive of Spitzer's long career, especially as far as his study of post-medieval French literature is concerned. He had already practised his hand at traditional philology and medieval and modern literature, and at political polemic and writings on the language of personal emotion (A6, A17, works which deserve to be better known); and his academic position now seemed entirely secure. He wrote no books from this point on, but only articles – though some of them (e.g. chapter 1 below) are as long as many books by other people. It is in this period that Spitzer wrote his extraordinary study of Proust (composed virtually upon the appearance of the last volume of *Le Temps retrouvé* in 1927) and the pieces that form chapters I, II and III below.

These three chapters (and of course especially the first) constitute Spitzer's major attempt to grasp the difference of the French classical age, of 'le grand siècle', the central area of modern French culture. These chapters can be grasped, in the first place, as part of an enterprise rooted very much in the intellectual and political conditions of the Weimar Republic. In a general essay written in 1927, Spitzer regretted the new mood of inward-looking nationalism in Germany, the turning away from foreign cultures:

> It is certainly not to be regretted that we no longer [since the War] look up to everything French; but I think it is regrettable that together with the pain of separation we have lost the feeling of tension between ourselves and the otherness of the Romance world. (C3, p. 242)

The lack of this field of tension was an impoverishment of German intellectual life, and Spitzer saw his task as a 'Romanist' to be the reopening of German perspectives on a different way of thinking and feeling, the reanimation of the tension between the 'own' and the 'other'. The stress, in chapter I, on the 'distance' of Racine derives directly from this overall view of the scholar's task – a task serving essentially not 'la critique racinienne' in any universal sense and even less French criticism of Racine, but a need of the moment in German social and intellectual life.

Chapter I, Spitzer's longest and perhaps finest piece of criticism, has given rise to many misunderstandings, and it might be better to say at this point what it is not. It is not a comprehensive survey of Racinian language; nor is it a survey of *all* those aspects of Racine that make his plays distant from us. Spitzer does not proceed like a detective or a deductive scientist, identifying clues and traces that lead to the answer to the central question of what makes Racine different. Instead, he gives his answer in his very title, which is explicated on the first page of the study. Spitzer's movement is self-consciously circular and self-contained; he would like to believe that all he has to say is already contained in the object of study itself. That object of study is certainly not Racine in the sense of the historical person who wrote *Andromaque* etc.; nor is it the entirety of Racine's work; nor even the structure of what Barthes would call 'l'univers racinien'. The object of study, as Spitzer says on p. 3 quite clearly, is the essentially Racinian or the essence of Racine, the specific difference of Racine from anything and everything else. He does not even bother to consider whether that essential difference may lie (even in part) in subject-matter, stagecraft, characterisation or any other dimension of the plays. For Spitzer it must lie in the language of Racine, for it is through language alone that all dimensions of the text are constituted. What Spitzer then gives – as his demonstration of what it means to write like Racine – is in effect a list or enumeration of about a score of significant features of language, ranging from the microstylistic observation of *ce que* to the macrostylistic interpretation of the eye motif, which form as it were a constellation of luminous points around the central, initially given insight that Racine *is* modulation or, in my perhaps too precious translation of Spitzer's striking formula, classical *piano*.

Within 'style' Spitzer includes many features that others might attribute more easily to grammar, and some features that belong most certainly to rhetoric. Although he links much of what he describes to Latin models (thus giving substance to the traditional labelling of Racine as 'classical'), Spitzer cuts out entirely any linkage of Racine's style to that of his contemporaries and immediate predecessors. Subsequent critics have pointed out that a great deal of Spitzer's Racinian style is the more or less common property of all seventeenth-century writers of dramatic tragedy in France; thus Spitzer's claim to have described that which makes Racine different – and distant – falls to the ground. Spitzer's position is not as indefensible as it might seem, even if he never argued it out fully. Minor literature, that is to say literature of incomplete or uncertain artistic value, is simply not part of the object of study of Spitzerian stylistics. Of course Racine did not invent his style from top to bottom: but precisely because he is a great artist, he is still worth struggling with today, and it is Racine, not Pradon, who carries the seventeenth century to us now. It does not matter that Pradon is distant, for all that is second-rate can live but a day. It matters on the other hand very much that Racine is distant and difficult, for he demands to be conquered and possessed, if the task of the philologist (in the German sense), the communication between cultures, is to be achieved. That is a task which has to be carried out anew in every generation, and the lasting value of Spitzer's essay is that it explicitly sets up the requirement for criticism to confront 'otherness' ('alterity' in more modern theoretical parlance) from its own position in time, and without attempting to escape its own necessary historical limitations. The underlying importance of Spitzer's practice in the Racine essay has only really borne fruit in some branches of what are called reception aesthetics: it is in fact at the antipodes of most of what is called stylistic criticism in modern scholarship. It is in the end a logical circle or spiral, for if Spitzer returns from his journey with a huge amount of evidence of the linguistic forms of distantiating language, majestic language, attenuating language, it is because he set out to measure the distance, majesty and attenuation of a distant, but paradoxically very close, cultural entity.

Of course Spitzer's erudite confrontation of the 'own' with the 'other' in the linguistic forms of Racine had little weight in the altogether more sinister development of national self-concern and self-aggrandisement that was wrecking the Weimar Republic. Essays on Racine hardly counted for much against the tactics of the Nazi party, and on Hitler's seizure of power in 1933 Spitzer was ejected from his chair and fled the country. He found asylum in Istanbul, where he was joined later by his colleague Erich Auerbach, and where he was put in charge of an ambitious modern languages programme, housed in a magnificent palace overlooking the Sea of Marmara, with beadles at every door but no books (Wellek, D9). Spitzer stayed in Turkey for three years, writing mostly in French, and moved to the Johns Hopkins University in Baltimore in 1936. He remained there until he retired in 1956, when he moved to Forti dei Marmi on the Italian riviera. Apart from one semester as a visiting professor at Heidelberg in 1958 (his lectures there = A34), Spitzer never returned to a German-speaking environment between 1933 and his death in 1960, at the age of 73. None the less, Spitzer continued to engage with Romance languages and literatures from the firm ground of a Germanic cultural identity, and though he wrote in the American years in a variety of languages, his best work was composed in either German or French.

In the collection of articles published in book form in 1931 (A20, II.284–5) Spitzer included a brief concluding note entitled 'Schluss-aphorismen' (in French in Starobinski's essay, D17 and A41). These 'aphorisms' seem now to come much nearer the central values of Spitzer's work than the later and frequently reprinted English essay 'Linguistics and Literary History' (in A27). Scholarly work, Spitzer says, involves five concurrent levels of activity. The specialist level, in which some obscure part of a field of knowledge is clarified, is the lowest and least important. The methodological level, which seeks to enrich the method of the field of study, is the second in the hierarchy: 'material clarification without methodological clarification loses the momentum, the reaching-out-beyond-itself which is the property of all true scholarship'. The third level is that of 'knowledge of the world': the scholar must also clarify his own position in the world through his work, which should give him that kind of personal and metaphysical liberation which the work of art gives the artist. The fourth level is that of social engagement: all material scholarship, Spitzer says, is in a dialogic and dialectic relationship with some particular person – a colleague, a friend – to whose 'address' it is written; unaddressed scholarship is as pointless as an unaddressed letter. And finally, the fifth level is the metaphysical: scholarship should be on the edge of nothingness, clinging on to science and knowledge against *le néant*, written with self-irony and in self-defence – maybe written to escape *le néant*. Scholarly work is not a marble effigy, but a model of its creator's struggle, handing on to its reader the author's own imperative to struggle. Spitzer's concluding point is that it is less important to achieve completeness of knowledge or indeed to contribute to knowledge in the material sense than to maintain the much greater wholeness of the human stance of the scholar, that is to say, to operate on all five levels at once. To do that properly means *nicht allein sein*, to be not alone in the world.

These thoughts on the philosophy of scholarship explain a number of features of Spitzer's criticism, some obvious, some less so. The 'dialogic and dialectic' nature of Spitzer's manner, if not of all true scholarship, is abundantly clear in the many knuckle-rapping rejoinders to other (lesser) critics and the rather fewer tributes to individual colleagues in the chapters of this book. Five of these essays are written on some person-oriented pretext: chapter I is an answer to Vossler's suggestion on Racine's modulations, chapter III is written to put down Julius Schmidt, chapter IV to answer Ulrich Knoche, chapter V to H. C. Lancaster and C. Lynes, and chapter VI to show F. C. Green how much he missed. This type of 'addressing' is obviously more suited to articles in learned journals, circulating among a specific audience, than to 'well-formed' books published for the world at large. By attaching his essays to a particular dialogue in a particular time and place, Spitzer signalled the absence in his own work of any claim to permanent or universal validity. The conventions of modern British scholarship are quite the opposite: we tend to dress up far less significant thoughts as if they were 'marble effigies'. Beneath the surface, then, the 'dialogic' aspect of Spitzer's work (more marked in the original than in these translations) is not just a personal quirk nor simply a difference of the conventions of scholarly writing. It signals, paradoxically, the modesty of the scholar and expresses a firm view of the morality of scholarly writing, a question to which Spitzer returned, most notably in c8 and c11.

The one chapter of this book that is not addressed to a particular person is the study of Saint-Simon's portrait of the Sun-king, whom he saw as the first absolute monarch and the first systematic tyrant in history. Spitzer draws no facile parallels between the tyrant menacing Germany in 1931 and Louis XIV, in the way Pieter Geyl was to do somewhat later in his parallel between Hitler and Napoleon. None the less, chapter II is unmistakably involved in the politics of its own time, and the critical metaphors of 'enclaves' (if one may read Spitzer in a Spitzerian manner) give away the underlying purpose of the piece. Saint-Simon's study allows Spitzer to look upon a tyrant as from after his passing, and thus affords that kind of release from the oppression of the present that artistic achievement might afford the artist. It is not the scholar's escape-route from reality, but a way of confronting the absolute evil of tyranny through the application of scholarship. It is no coincidence if chapter II is the one where Spitzer approaches most nearly the ideal of purely immanent criticism. His own position gives him all he needs to struggle with Saint-Simon's ultimately 'very modern' perception of the nothingness to which the abuse of power must lead.

Another point to draw from these 'aphorisms' concerns the place of learning in Spitzer's writing. By the standards of today (and only a little less so by the standards of his own day) Spitzer was phenomenally knowledgeable, and he experienced no embarrassment about using whatever piece of knowledge that seemed relevant, in whatever language. Consequently his writings (in the original) seem to demand an almost impossible range of competences in his reader. Quotations are given in any one of eight languages without translation, references are made to lines in Cicero and Shakespeare, Seneca and Gide, Béroul and Goethe without any indication of their location, as if the reader *knew* where they came from. Yet despite this show of knowledge, Spitzer is not only unconcerned about knowledge for its own sake (and frequently quotes inaccurately from memory); his concern is to go beyond 'material scholarship' ('footnote learning') so far as to abandon it entirely. Chapter I was written in first draft without access to any secondary sources other than Vossler's little book; chapter II concludes with the exhortation to younger scholars *not* to read any secondary literature. This is, of course, a further expression of Spitzer's revolt against the positivism of Meyer-Lübke and against the general over-valuation of pedantic learning in German academic life. None the less, Spitzer's low ranking of mere knowledge has a peculiar and paradoxical authority in coming from one of the most knowledgeable minds of the century.

The impression of erudition made by Spitzer's work of the German period is partly due to the fact that he brings together knowledge from literary history and from diachronic linguistics, two fields in which few people have equal competence. Spitzer maintained that they were a single field and no more to be distinguished from each other 'than bread and cheese from cheese and bread' (C3, p. 260). Fifty years on, academic syllabuses in Britain as in Germany continue to reflect this conviction, but few modern linguists really succeed in uniting the two fields in their own practice as teachers. Spitzer is certainly not the source of the seemingly inseparable conjunction of language and literature in what undergraduates are expected to learn but teachers not expected to teach; but he is one of the very few people who can claim justifiably to have made full sense of that combination.

He was able to do this at least in part because he held a very particular notion of language, and a restricted view of what was literature. In Spitzer's understanding of language we do not find a Saussurean distinction between *langue* (the general system of a language) and *parole* (linguistic acts or utterances within that system). Spitzer's intellectual development was more or less complete before the ideas of Saussure gained any currency outside Geneva, and the tradition in which he stands is quite clearly that of the German Romantics, whose ideas on language go back, ultimately, to Wilhelm von Humboldt. The important distinction here is between standard or ordinary language and creative, deviant, special language (not between 'system' and 'acts' of language). Poets are not simply users of language, but the creators of it; conversely, language is not a smooth and rounded system, but is marked by bumps and dents which speak the history of its creation. The study of these excrescences or particularities was called *Stilistik* in German as early as 1837, seventy years before Charles Bally published his *Précis de stylistique*, which is mistakenly regarded as the origin of both the term and the subject of stylistics (cf. C12, pp. 167–8). Spitzer was obviously influenced directly in this by Karl Vossler, who was himself a pupil of the Italian aesthetician Benedetto Croce. Spitzer's own version of romantic linguistic idealism was however far more solidly grounded in linguistic knowledge and far more empirically oriented than those of his mentors. It can also be seen as a parallel to the development at the same time in Russia of the Formalists' notion of 'literariness', the essential difference of literary from ordinary language. Spitzer did not discover Formalism, it would seem, until the publication of Victor Erlich's book in 1956,* but he paid a handsome tribute to Shklovsky in particular in the last conference paper of his life, given at Liège in August 1960 (C18). There can be no question of a filiation of Spitzerian stylistics and Russian formalism; the coincidence of their views on literary language is for that reason a stronger confirmation that both schools of thought were responding to the central problem (at least of literary scholarship) of their time, namely the collapse of positivism into irrelevance and routine.

Characteristically, Spitzer tended to refer to his subject as *Stilforschung* ('stylistic research', the activity) rather than *Stilistik* (the entity 'stylistics') and he divided its field into two complementary parts: the study of significant details in the standard language, termed *Stilsprachen*, and the study of significant deviant languages, i.e. the language of great writers, termed *Sprachstilen*. Both parts of the field bear a fruit for which there is no other term than 'soul' – historical etymologies of words like the German *Stimmung* (A38) or English *conundrum* and *quandary*† describe and explain particular features of 'Germanness' and 'Englishness', just as close and comprehensive study of the particular language of Racine reveals 'the essentially Racinian', a constitutive

* *Russian Formalism. History – Doctrine* (The Hague: Mouton, 1956).

† In *Journal of English and Germanic Philology* 42 (1943) 405; see also A27, pp. 4–6.

element of 'Frenchness'. There are obvious pitfalls into which this kind of national idealism can fall, and Spitzer was one of the most outspoken critics of simplistic, overhasty generalisations on the subject of 'Frenchness' (see C3 for a very effective demolition of Klemperer's and Wechssler's notions of 'the eternal French soul'). All the same, his own work is based on a conception of language that is national, romantic, and idealist. He escapes the more obvious traps of that conception because of his immense learning; and he transcends it by bringing to the romantic perception of differences a hermeneutic awareness that difference is always measured from, and as a dimension of, the self.

Where Spitzer does seem much closer to more familiar critical orthodoxies is in his insistence on treating the work of a writer as 'an internally stable cosmos', as an autonomous whole. The similarity with modern theories of autonomous art is however more apparent than real. The autonomy Spitzer speaks of is certainly not autonomy from the world of lived experience and history, but the right of the reader, the linguist and the critic to interrogate a scene of Corneille's *Polyeucte*, a chapter of Saint-Simon, or the language of Racine without reference in the first place to the writer's biography, the material genesis of the text, or the sources that may or may not have been used: in other words to ask not 'how did this text come to be?' but to ask 'what is the shape and meaning of this text in itself?'. The language of the great works of the Romance literatures is not the ultimate object of Spitzer's inquiry (not an entity referring to itself) but a perfectly polished and transparent lens, through which the true reader may glimpse the ineffable individuality of the writer's 'soul', a part, inevitably, of the 'soul' of his language and of his nation.

Spitzer's critical method is thus linguistic only in the sense that it examines the language of literature, and it is 'immanent' only in the sense that it puts external knowledge about history and the genesis of texts in the background. On the other hand, what is left in the background is none the less absolutely crucial to the readings Spitzer gives. Whether he likes it or not (and his feelings varied on this point) Spitzer's idealist position draws upon and contributes to a literary-historical interpretation. The long essay on Racine (chapter I) was criticised for failing to place the dramatist's language in the context of the language of his period. Yet it is easy to see (perhaps because of our own historical perspective) that this essay draws on a particular literary-historical conception of classicism, which it seeks to modify to that of 'baroque'. Indeed, the dialogue or dialectic between the period-concepts of 'medieval', 'renaissance', 'baroque', 'classical', and 'romantic' runs through and under all the chapters of this book – and there is nothing less 'immanent' to the works themselves than these art-historical terms of academic invention! One might say that Spitzer's marriage of language and literature in his critical practice is achieved ultimately at the expense of linguistic and literary history. It is obvious in the chapters of this book that Spitzer not only needs but is constantly drawn towards the great schemas of intellectual and literary history, yet just as constantly draws back from any extended discussion of them, preferring (in the originals) to put such matters in parentheses or footnotes, or to quote other scholars rather than take full responsibility for them himself. This is, I think, a blemish in Spitzer's work, and one that is not a necessary blemish determined either by his cast of mind or by his in any case very flexible method. Spitzer had a rich and subtle historical mind, and his hesitation to indulge it explicitly derives most of all from his quite comprehensible reluctance to engage with one of the least savoury aspects of German academic life in the Weimar Republic. Historical thought had enormous prestige in the universities, and new synthetic schemes of universal history, history of art, history of ideas (*Geistesgeschichte*) and so forth abounded. German historical generalisations of this period now seem laughably hollow when they are not combined – as they are in the works of Spitzer's colleagues E. R. Curtius and Erich Auerbach – with real erudition and wide experience. Spitzer saw the dangers of such lofty and insubstantial concerns as the definition of 'medieval' versus 'modern', 'classical' versus 'romantic': they could lead to disengagement from real works of literature, and disengagement from the scholar's own situation in the here-and-now. (The latter was indeed the fate of Curtius, who remained in Germany throughout the Nazi period, engaged in medieval research to avoid any political conflict (c8, p. 591) and continued to dress in a frock-coat and bow-tie amidst the rubble of defeated Germany.) Above all, Spitzer was wary of oversimplifications, of rigid schemes, of all-encompassing ideas which left no space for the creative impact of the individual writer: 'Too much trivialised history-of-ideas is evidently as unhealthy for a nation as too much Muzak' (c8, p. 593). Under the Nazi regime, the worst examples of nationalistic pseudo-scholarship were to be found in history-of-ideas, which was often nothing more than blatant propaganda; literary history also lent itself to this kind of betrayal. Spitzer's evasion of history is the unfortunate result (but no doubt the only possible healthy result) of the kind of literary history practised by those around him. One guesses he would have had a much more fruitful dialogue with modern historical writing in the manner of Richard Cobb or Le Roy Ladurie.

In a characteristically paradoxical move, Spitzer came to the defence of German *Geistesgeschichte* in his American years, against the 'History of Ideas' of A. O. Lovejoy. The issue was of some personal importance to Spitzer, since Lovejoy had implied that Hitlerism was the ultimate fruit of German romanticism; but in this polemic (c7), as in others with the linguist Bloomfield (c6), one feels that Spitzer is out of his element, struggling in a culture which is not his own and which forces him to adopt a simplified stance as a representative of all things European – whereas his real position was far more complex.

Even after many years in America Spitzer complained of being 'echolos', without an audience to answer him back (Wellek, D9), and there is a huge difference in the quality and subtlety of his theoretical pronouncements in English and the piece he wrote in 1945 for the first issue of the first German modern languages periodical to be published after the Allied victory. 'Das Eigene und das Fremde' (c8) is a survey of Romance scholarship in Europe in the first half of this century and a blueprint for a new German modern languages movement. It was the fundamental text for Hans-Robert Jauss and his generation, the text which made sense of their position and of the project of studying a foreign literature.

Philology is defined from the start as that branch of knowledge 'which seeks to understand man in so far as he expresses himself in words', and it puts the philologist in a double or forked position: 'he has to consider a foreign nation and his own, and to compare them'. All understanding of language, whether it be foreign *or one's own*, is essentially comparative, a movement from what is distant to what is close and back again: '*Amor de lonh* – the saying of the Provençal troubadours – is the philologist's motto' (p. 576). The student of a foreign culture, Spitzer writes, must feel the temptation of betraying his own (of 'going native', we might say) but not give way to it: 'without the readiness to lose oneself entirely, there can be no philology; but however adaptable he may be, the philologist must stop short of becoming a butterfly' (p. 577). These exhortations are consistent with Spitzer's own practice as a critic: in his exemplary sympathy with the literature of the Romance world he never loses points of contact and comparison in German culture. (For reasons given above, I have omitted from these chapters passages on Rilke's German translation of the *Lettres portugaises* and Schiller's translations of Racine.) There is an obvious lesson here also for British students of foreign languages, whose position is much more comparable to that of Spitzer than to that of (e.g.) French or English critics of their own literatures: philologists (in the German sense) should assume their own double position as intermediaries in their own practice and seek neither an impossible assimilation into the foreign culture, nor a rigidly national view of their subject. The business of philology is a constant tension between 'das Eigene' ('one's own') and 'das Fremde' ('the other' or 'foreignness').

Some of the sharpest paragraphs of this 1945 article concern the double standards of scholarship. In pre-war Germany, Spitzer writes, 'the eminent professor and unfettered researcher could be a philistine in everyday life – a chauvinist and hater of Frenchmen' (p. 590). The popularity of medieval studies was partly due to the possibility it offered of avoiding all contact with living, modern Frenchmen. In the new Germany of 1945, Spitzer calls for human integrity from students of modern languages, for a type of scholarship based on their own position in the world as cultural intermediaries and based not on scorn but on love for their subject.

Spitzer is not an evaluative critic in the British manner, declaring his greater taste for this work and his lesser liking for that. His essays contain no explicit declarations of love or hate, because the very fact of devoting his time to an article on a given work is to be understood as a declaration that he has already been entirely seduced. His submission to the loved one is total: the text is, axiomatically, a perfect work of art, the scholar's task is only to understand and demonstrate how it is perfect in all its parts (see for example, p. 166 below: 'every line is in its right place'). When used by a man of wide erudition and brilliant insight like Spitzer, this basic axiom is a powerful tool or, rather, a liberating key to much that remains hidden to readers less willing to give their entire assent to a work of art. It is no doubt this ability to be seduced again and again that allowed Spitzer his brilliant 'discovery' of the artistry of *Les Lettres portugaises* in chapter VI: but it would be impossible to describe this open submission as a method or a theory, or even as a model of literary criticism. It is a personal trait (not unrelated to other personal traits of a more down-to-earth kind) and the particular mark of Spitzer's genius. Spitzer's scholarly and critical work is in effect an implementation, quite untainted by other considerations, of the programme launched by Victor Hugo in the *Préface de Cromwell*: 'On quittera, et c'est M. de Chateaubriand qui parle ici, *la critique mesquine des défauts pour la grande et féconde critique des beautés*' (p. 107).

What Hugo meant by *la critique des défauts* is that kind of normative criticism, more or less learned, more or less schoolmasterly, which selects parts of the work as being good, others as less good, and which can be summed up as a report: 'shows talent but could try harder'. It is the criticism of a La Harpe, and it still has a role in the control mechanisms of modern publishing, that is to say in newspaper reviews and the like. The task of romantic criticism, on the other hand, is not to control but to display. *La critique des beautés* is that form of criticism which seeks only to lead the reader towards the beauty and ineffable individuality of the work in hand, assumed by the act of the critic's choice to be a perfect work of art. In a nineteenth-century romantic critic like Sainte-Beuve the tradition of normative criticism remained not only present but extremely active beneath a quite unartistic submission to contemporary models of natural science. In later generations of romantics, the 'criticism of beauties' could disintegrate, as in the writings of Paul Flat, into mere paraphrase and imbecile 'vibrations'.

Creative critics like Proust and Valéry (whom Spitzer frequently quotes) came nearer to the ideal of openness and sensitivity contained in Hugo's striking formula; but it is in Spitzer, and perhaps in Spitzer alone, that *la critique des beautés*, enriched by a vast erudition in language as well as literature, and shorn of any creator's involvement with literary fashion, shows all its greatness and fertility.

Spitzer thus only ever wrote about texts that were *admirable* – and, with the exception of the essay on Racine and very few others, only about individual texts or parts of texts*. Over the course of fifty years he thus constituted as it were his own canon of 'admirable' literature which is of some interest in its own right. As can be seen from the Bibliography, stage comedy is entirely absent from Spitzer's French canon, and theatre is generally under-represented. Some early twentieth-century prose-writers (Péguy, Philippe, Barbusse) can hardly be said to have kept the place allotted to them, whilst others (Malherbe, Diderot, Saint-Simon, La Fontaine and especially Guilleragues) owe their present place in the literary canon in large part to Spitzer's insights. Spitzer did not tackle texts because they were there in a preexisting tradition and institution, as Roland Barthes (for example) seems to have done. Even when he takes central and established figures as his subject, one feels that he has reinvented them as writers, just as his opus as a whole invents a French literary canon that is to some degree unbalanced, and profoundly personal.

It is of course true that the axiomatic belief that a work of literature is a 'perfect work of art' produces a logically circular critical argument (i.e. if perfection is the precondition for critical attention, then critical study cannot *prove* that perfection, but serves only to demonstrate what was assumed in the first place). The same circularity exists in all types of interpretation and *explication de texte*, from Biblical exegesis to practical criticism; Spitzer certainly saw his own method in a distant but definite relation to these disciplines.

> Oui, en effet, c'est l'explication de texte française – mais d'abord, pratiquée ou plutôt: conquise par un Allemand prenant son point de départ dans sa sensibilité allemande. Et ensuite [c'est une] explication tâchant de trouver un principe unitaire auquel tout dans un texte, le style, le tour d'idées, la composition, le contenu peut être ramené, s'efforçant de chercher l'essence fondamentale . . . peut-être dernier reste laïcisé d'une spéculation théologique. *Omnis pulchritudinis forma unitas est*,† disait saint-Augustin. (C4, p. 585)

* 'Spitzer's axiomatic consideration of the poetic text as perfect *a limine* (once it has been separated from the imperfect) corresponds to Gadamer's "presumption of perfection" (a presumption which for Gadamer, as for Heidegger, was to be tested against a close reading of the text itself)' (H.-R. Jauss).

† 'Unity is the form of all beauty'.

Now the 'prejudice for unity' is not just the presupposition of Spitzer's method, it is also the basis of the aesthetic judgment of the French seventeenth century, which is one of the reasons why I have brought together here Spitzer's work on the classical period rather than any other. However, Spitzer's love of paradox and contradiction leads him in all these essays to discover beneath the smooth surface of classical verse and prose not a fundamental unity, but sets of polarities. In the case of La Fontaine, of course, the demonstration of the artistry and cleverness of the transitions can only be made the stronger by stressing the contradictions between the different parts of the fable reunited by style alone. In the case of Saint-Simon, it is precisely the absence of transitions between radically different attitudes that constitutes the style. In Corneille, the presence of both faith and love in the same scene is not a problem that Spitzer wants to solve or reduce to a unity, for the sense of *Polyeucte* is to deal with both faith and love in a single work of art. The analysis of Racine in chapter I is conducted throughout in terms of an irreducible polarity between 'lyrical self-expression' and 'formal restraint', between which the linguistic devices of attenuation negotiate as it were a superficial appearance of smoothness. Spitzer pushes the analysis to the point where it dismantles the presupposition of unity, just as he says Marianne's passion (in the *Lettres portugaises*) ends up by destroying its own object, *le chevalier*. The result is put most bluntly in chapter V: French classicism is not classical at all, it is 'baroque'; its aesthetic is not one of unity, but one of unresolved contradictions held in tension by subtly modulated and formal language. Some of Spitzer's critics find this reversal of literary-historical terms simply perverse (e.g. Auerbach, D2): but whether the term 'baroque' is well chosen or not seems to me a less important matter than Spitzer's determination to push his reading to the edge of collapse – or as he says in the 'Closing Aphorisms' of A20 (1931), to the edge of nothingness.

Spitzer's description of the language of Racine (or of Proust, or Butor) is far from exhaustive and makes no use of statistics or any other 'objective' or 'scientific' paraphernalia. His manner looks, and in a sense is, impressionistic, subjective and lacking in rigour. Part of the discredit into which Spitzer fell in the 1950s in France and elsewhere was due to sharp attacks on his lack of scientific method by, among others, Charles Bruneau. Spitzer's less well-known counter-attack to these objections is still worth quoting:

> La stylistique appliquée à la langue littéraire que M. Bruneau appelle 'scientifique' me semble tout bonnement une stylistique ennuyeuse, parce que banale . . . Cette sorte de 'science appliquée' est plutôt 'appliquée' (aux exercices d'école) que 'science' – si science est la poursuite de vérités nouvelles. (C12, p. 167)

Reading is not, Spitzer maintains, a linear process of deduction, such as might be amenable to the linear-deductive tools of the natural sciences. Reading is a circle, as is all true understanding, a constant interpenetration and reintegration of the detail with the whole, of the new with the known. Within this circular movement of the mind (elsewhere he calls it a 'to-ing and fro-ing' from self to text and from detail to whole (A27, pp. 18–19 etc.)) the sense of a text emerges, as do those details which are significant or somehow close to the centre of meaning. In the last analysis, the emergence of meaning and significance in the reader's mind is a mysterious and ineffable occurrence which can be learnt but not taught, experienced but not forced: the closing of the circle (*das Zirkelschluss*) is simply a 'click' that happens.

Many glib objections were made to Spitzer's description of his method by American behaviourists and logical positivists; for example, 'it is a vicious circle to intuit the nature of the author's personality from his writings and then to interpret those writings in accordance with the "inner necessity" of that intuited personality' (H. Cherniss, 'The Biographical Fashion in Literary Criticism', *Classical Philology* 12 (1917) 288). Spitzer sought to defend himself by invoking the names and arguments of the German philosophers Schleiermacher and Dilthey, in which he had more justification than in his later invocation of Freud, but in which he was none the less grasping at straws. Spitzer's awareness of hermeneutics follows and does not precede chapters I–IV of this book: although his manner can certainly be accounted for in terms of the hermeneutic circle (the theory is at least good enough for that!), it does not *derive* from any consciously worked-out philosophical basis, but from a particular personality and a particular place. A later generation of German scholars, most notably Hans-Robert Jauss (who was, incidentally, Spitzer's assistant at Heidelberg in 1958), made hermeneutics the starting point for a theory and practice of literary criticism (see Jauss, 'Limits and Tasks of Literary Hermeneutics', *Diogenes* 109 (1981) 92–119, and Bellos, 'Reception Aesthetics', *Strathclyde Modern Language Studies*, no. 2, 1982). Although Spitzer was not unaware of the philosophical problems of the act of interpretation, he was not concerned overmuch with theory and devoted the best part of his formidable energy to practical criticism, concrete interpretation, and empirical studies of language.

Spitzer's personality stands out far less in my translations than it does in the originals, of course, and less in these essays on 'le grand siècle' than in the extraordinary article on Diderot's style (in A27), where Spitzer seems almost to be talking about his own style of writing. Spitzer's prose is all jolts and starts; it is the language of excitement rising and falling in the arduous conquest of a fortress or of a mistress: victory comes at the end of a long period broken by half a dozen nested subordinations in one of Spitzer's celebrated 'nutshell' formulae – 'klassische Dämpfung', 'enumeración caótica', 'pseudoobjektive Motivierung', 'inszenierende Adverbialbestimmung' and so forth. As Starobinski has said, Spitzer's aggression towards other critics is rather like the jealousy of a lover: there is certainly a complementary balance between the critic's submission to the work of art and his energetic attacks on any understanding of it other than his own. Far from being faults these personal features constitute the special value of Spitzer's work: 'on cherchait une méthode, et l'on trouve un homme!' Spitzer's critical essays are written not as by a disembodied spirit claiming objective knowledge, but by a man engaged in his own historical and social world and performing a function within it, that of the intermediary between cultures. He writes as himself, with all that that implies, producing provisional, time-restricted interpretations intended to have a meaning for the public or person to whom they are addressed. The right of an academic to do this was not widely accepted in Germany in the 1920s and 1930s; not many British scholars nowadays have the courage to lay themselves open in that way to the accusation of 'subjectivity'. Spitzer's criticism offers a model of scholarship that is truly modest (renouncing claims to anything more than provisional validity;⟶206–7) and at the same time truly demanding, less on library time than on human resources. Spitzer's criticism, in the end, contains beneath its rich layer of instruction in language and literature a moral lesson of greater import than any of the particular lessons given on Racine or La Fontaine. When Spitzer defends his right to read the French classics as a *geniessender Leser* (⟶112–13), that is to say 'as a person contemplating his own enjoyment of the work of art', he is appealing to the moral integrity of a scholarship conscious of its own necessary limits, and incorporating history (his own position in history) into the heart of his work. He was indeed much better at putting this fundamental honesty into practice than he was at explaining or theorising about it; that is something which is not easily accepted in Germany or France, but which will not prove an obstacle, I hope, to a renewed interest in this remarkable scholar in the English-speaking world, and through him in the literature of France which remains for us, as for Spitzer, tantalisingly familiar yet profoundly distant.

David Bellos
Paris 1981

BIBLIOGRAPHY

I have not attempted to compile an exhaustive bibiliography of Leo Spitzer's writings, scattered as they are in scores of learned journals published over half a century in nearly every European country and many others. Spitzer himself did not have copies of all his own publications, many of which were lost on his departure from Germany in 1933 and others in a fire at Istanbul. I have compiled (under A) a full list of all of Spitzer's publications in book form held in the University Library at Konstanz, the British Library and the Bibliothèque nationale, together with other titles listed by Wellek (D9). Because this volume is addressed mainly to students of French, I give (under B) as full a list as I could make of all Spitzer's publications in periodicals on French literature from Villon to Butor. Under C I have listed those autobiographical and general pieces used for the Introduction, and under D all the pieces on Spitzer I have come across.

It must be stressed that modern French literature was by no means Spitzer's principal concern. His contributions to French and Provençal medieval literature have at least equal weight; his work on Spanish and on Italian literature is also very substantial and has played a more important role within recent scholarly study of those literatures than his work on French. A full Spitzer bibliography would also include, alongside hundreds of reviews and philological–etymological notes, substantial sections on German, Portuguese, Romanian, English and American literature and language, as well as the first linguistic study of the sign-system of advertising. Readers wishing to explore Spitzer's work in other fields can begin by consulting Wellek's selective but wide-ranging list in D9; beyond that, there are the usual general bibliographies (Dietrich–*IBZ*, etc.) but enthusiasts should be warned that the indexers of the bibliographic supplement to the *Zeitschrift für romanische Philologie* in the 1920s gave up on Spitzer and entered opposite his name not a single number but a simple word: *passim*.

Bibliography

A: *Books and collections of articles published as books*

A1 *Die Wortbildung als stilistisches Mittel exemplifiziert an Rabelais, nebst einem Anhang über die Wortbildung bei Balzac in seinen 'Contes drolatiques'* (Habilitationsschrift). Beihefte zur *Zeitschrift für romanische Philologie*, no. 19. Halle, 1910.

A2 *Die Namengebung bei neuen Kulturpflanzen im Französischen.* Halle, 1912.

A3 (collab. E. Gamillscheg) *Die Bezeichnungen der 'Klette' im Galloromanischen.* Halle: Niemeyer, 1915.

A4 *Aufsätze zur romanischen Syntax und Stilistik.* Halle: Niemeyer, 1918.

A4a Reprint of 4. Darmstadt, 1967.

A5 (collab. H. Sperber) *Motiv und Wort.* Leipzig, 1918. (Contains essay on Christian Morgenstern)

A6 *Über einige Wörter der Liebessprache. Vier Aufsätze.* Leipzig: Reisland, 1918.

A7 *Betrachtungen eines Linguisten über Houston Stewart Chamberlains Kriegaufsätze und die Sprachbewertung im allgemeinen.* Leipzig, 1918.

A8 *Fremdwörterhatz und Fremdvölkerhass, eine Streitschrift gegen Sprachreinigung.* Vienna, 1918.

A9 *Katalanische Etymologien.* Hamburg: Meissner, 1918.

A10 *Studien zu Henri Barbusse.* Bonn: F. Cohen, 1920.

A11 *Die Umschreibungen des Begriffes 'Hunger' im Italienischen.* Halle: Niemeyer, 1921.

A12 *Lexikalisches aus dem Katalanischen und den übrigen ibero-romanischen Sprachen.* Geneva: Olschki, 1921.

A13 (collab. E. Gamillscheg) *Beiträge zur romanischen Wortbildung.* Geneva: Olschki, 1921.

A14 *Italienische Kriegsgefangenenbriefe.* Bonn: Hanstein, 1921.

A14a *Lettere di prigioni di guerra italiani, 1915–1918*, transl. Renato Solmi. Turin: Boringhieri, 1976.

A15 *Italienische Umgangssprache.* Bonn: Schroeder, 1922.

A16 *Hugo-Schuchardt-Brevier. Ein Vademecum der allgemeinen Sprachwissenschaft.* Halle: Niemeyer, 1922.

A17 *Puxi: eine kleine studie zur Sprache einer Mutter.* Munich: Hueber, 1927.

A18 *Stilstudien*, 2 vols. Munich: Hueber, 1928.

A18a Reprint of 18. Darmstadt, 1961.

A18b Reprint of 18. Munich, 1961.

A19 *Meisterwerke der romanischen Sprachwissenschaften*, 2 vols. Munich: 1929, 1930.

A20 *Romanische Stil- und Literaturstudien*, 2 vols. Marburg: Elwert, 1931.

A21 *Die Literarisierung des Lebens in Lopes 'Dorotea'.* Bonn, 1932.

A21a Reprint of 21. New York: Russell & Russell, 1968.

A22 (collab. K. Vossler, H. Hatzfeld) *Introducción a la estilística romance*, transl. and notes by Amado Alonso and Raimundo Lida. Buenos Aires: Impr. de la Universidad, 1932.

A23 *Quelques remarques sur J. Coromines 'El parlar de Cardos i Vall Ferrera'*. Barcelona: Imp. de la Casa d'Assistencia P. Macia, 1937.

A24 *L'Amour lointain de Jaufré Rudel et le sens de la poésie des troubadours*. University of North Carolina Studies in Romance Languages and Literature, no. 5. Chapel Hill: University of North Carolina Press, 1944. Reprinted in A32, A41.

A25 *La enumeración caótica en la poesía moderna*, Colección de estudios estilísticos, Anejo 1. Buenos Aires, 1945. Reprinted in A30.

A26 *Essays in Historical Semantics. Testimonial Volume in Honor of Leo Spitzer on the Occasion of his Sixtieth Birthday*. Privately printed, 1947.

A26a Reprint of 26. New York: Russell & Russell, 1968.

A27 *Linguistics and Literary History. Essays in Stylistics*. Princeton University Press, 1948.

A27a Reprint of 27. New York: Russell & Russell, 1962.

A27b Paperback reprint of 27. Princeton University Press, 1967.

A28 *A Method of Interpreting Literature*. Northampton (Mass.), 1949.

A28a *Eine Methode, Literatur zu interpretieren*, transl. Gerd Wagner. Munich: Hanser, 1966.

A28b Reprint of 28. New York: Russell & Russell, 1967.

A29 *Critica stilistica e semantica storica*. Bari: Laterza, 1954.

A29a Reprint of 29. Bari: Laterza, 1966.

A30 *Lingüística e historia litteraria*. Madrid: Gredos, 1955.

A30a Second edn of 30. Madrid: Gredos, 1961.

A31 *Studia philologica et litteraria in honorem Leo Spitzer*, ed. Anna Hatcher and C. Selig. Bern: Francke, 1958.

A32 *Romanische Literaturstudien, 1936–56*. Tübingen: Niemeyer, 1959.

A33 *Marcel Proust e altri saggi di letteratura francese moderna*, ed. P. Citati. Turin, 1959.

A34 *Interpretationen zur Geschichte der französischen Lyrik*, ed. Helga Jauss-Meyer and Peter Schunk. Heidelberg: C. Winter, 1961.

A35 *Essays on English and American Literature*, ed. Anna Hatcher. Princeton University Press, 1962.

A36 *Sobre antigua poesía española*. Buenos Aires, 1962.

A37 *Cinque saggi di Ispanistica*. Turin: Ed. Bertini, 1962.

A38 *Classical and Christian Ideas of World Harmony: Prologomena to an Interpretation of the Word 'Stimmung'*. Baltimore: Johns Hopkins University Press, 1963.

A39 *L'armonia del mondo. Storia semantica di un'idea*. Bologna, 1967.

A40 *Texterklärungen*, ed. K. Henninger. Munich, 1969.

A41 *Etudes de style*, ed. J. Starobinski. Paris: Gallimard, 1970.

A41a Paperback reprint of 41. Paris: Collection TEL, 1980.

A42 *L'Art de Quevedo dans le 'Buscón'*. Paris: Ediciones hispano-americanas, 1972.

A43 *Studi italiani*, ed. Claudio Scarpati. Milan: Vita e Pensiero, 1976. (Includes a bibliography)

A44 *Approches textuelles des 'Mémoires' de Saint-Simon*. Par Leo Spitzer et Jules Brody. Tübingen: Gunter Narr / Paris: J.-M. Place, 1980.

B: *Spitzer's articles on French literature from Villon to Michel Butor* (Items B13, B18, B26, B38, B44 and B53 are included in this volume.)

B1 'Die syntaktischen Errungenschaften der französischen Symbolisten' (1918). In A4.

B2 'Inszenierende Adverbialbestimmung im neueren französischen', *Die Neuren Sprachen* 28 (1920) 1–30. Repr. in A18.

B3 'Über zeitliche Perspektive in der neueren französischen Lyrik' (on Verhaeren and others), *Die Neueren Sprachen* 31 (1923) 241–66. Repr. in A18.

B4 'Pseudoobjektive Motivierung' (on Charles-Louis Philippe), *Zeitschrift für französische Sprache und Literatur* 46 (1923) 359–85. Repr. in A18.

B5 'Rabelaisiana', *Zeitschrift für romanische Philologie* 43 (1923) 611–14, and 44 (1924) 101–2.

B6 'Der Unanimismus Jules Romains im Spiegel seiner Sprache', *Archivum Romanicum* 8 (1924) 59ff. Repr. in A18.

B7 'Zu Charles Peguys Stil' in Wahle and Klemperer (eds.) *Vom Geiste der neueren Literaturforschung. Festschrift für Oskar Walzel*. Potsdam: Athenaion, 1924. Repr. in A18.

B8 'Ehrenrettung von Malherbes "Consolation à M. du Périer"', *Die Neueren Sprachen* 34 (1926) 191–6. Repr. in A18; see also A34.

B9 'Umkehrbare Lyrik'. Original publication not found. Repr. in A18.

B10 'Zum Stil Marcel Prousts' (1928). In A18. Italian translation in A33. French translation in A41.

B11 'Vigny's *Le Cor*. Ein Versuch immanenter Stilerklärung', *Germanisch-romanische Monatshefte* 16 (1928) 399–414.

B12 'Zur Auffassung Rabelais' (1931). In A20.

B13 'Die klassische Dämpfung in Racines Stil', *Archivum Romanicum* 12 (1928) 361–472, and 13 (1929) 398–9. Repr. in A20 with additions. French translation in A41. Partly translated in R. C. Knight (ed.) *Racine: Modern Judgements*, London: Macmillan, 1969. Translated as chapter 1 of this volume.

B14 'Notiz zu Peguys Stil', *Die Neueren Sprachen* 37 (1929) 503ff.

B15 'Zu einer Stelle bei Eustache Deschamps' (1931). In A20.

B16 'Einige Voltaire-Interpretationen' (1931). In A20. Italian translation in A29. French translation in A41.

B17 'Saint-Simons Porträt Ludwigs XIV' (1931). In A20, II. 1–47. French translation in *Cahiers Saint-Simon* 7 (1979) 37–67. Repr. in A44. Translated as chapter II of this volume.

B18 'Erhellung des "Polyeucte" durch das Alexiuslied', *Archivum Romanicum* 16 (1932) 473–500. Translated as chapter III of this volume.

B19 'Racine et Goethe', *Revue d'histoire de la philosophie et d'histoire générale de la civilisation* 1 (1933) 58–75.

B20 'Explication linguistique et littéraire de deux textes français'. Inaugural lecture, Istanbul, 1933. Pub. *Le français moderne* 3 (1935) 316–23 (Romains, *La Mort de quelqu'un*), and 4 (1936) 37–48 (Ronsard, 'Sur la Mort de Marie').

B21 'Zum Kommentar Villons ("Quand de ce monde voult partir")', *Neuphilologische Mitteilungen* 36 (1935) 207–11.

B22 'Une Habitude de style (le rappel) chez M. Céline', *Le Français moderne* 3 (1935) 193–208.

B23 'Zu Victor Hugos *Le Rouet d'Omphale'*, *Neuphilologische Mitteilungen* 37 (1936) 98–107, 160. Repr. in A32.

B24 'Au sujet de la répétition distinctive', *Le Français moderne* 4 (1936) 129–35.

B25 'A Linguistic and Literary Interpretation of Claudel's *Ballade*', Conference paper, 1937. Pub. *French Review* 16 (1942/3) 134–43.

B26 'Die Kunst des Übergangs bei La Fontaine', *Proceedings of the Modern Languages Association* 53 (1938) 393–437. Repub. in A32. French translation in A41. Italian translation in A29. Translated as chapter IV of this volume.

B27 'Etude ahistorique d'un texte. Villon, *Ballade des dames du temps jadis*'. Lecture, Bryn Mawr, 1938. Pub. *Modern Language Quarterly* 1 (1940) 7–22. Repr. in A32.

B28 'Pour le commentaire de Villon (*Testament*, v. 447)', *Romania* 64 (1938) 522–3.

B29 'Le Lion arbitre moral de l'homme', *Romania* 64 (1938) 525–30.

B30 'Verlebendigende direkte Rede als Mittel der Charakterisierung' (on Montherlant), *Vox Romanica* 4 (1939) 65–86.

B31 'Le "Bel Aubépin" de Ronsard. Nouvel Essai d'explication', *Le Français moderne* 8 (1940) 223–36.

B32 'Le Prétendu Réalisme de Rabelais', *Modern Philology* 37 (1940) 139–50.

B33 'Le Style circulaire', *Modern Language Notes* 56 (1941) 110–13. Repr. in A32.

B34 'L'Etymologie d'un cri de Paris (chez Proust)', *Romanic Review* 35 (1944) 244–50. Repr. in A32, A41.

B35 'Patterns of Thought in the Style of Albert Thibaudet', *Modern Language Quarterly* 9 (1948) 259–72 and 478–91.

B36 'Interpretation of an Ode by Paul Claudel'. In A27.

B37 'The Style of Diderot' (1948). In A27. Italian translation in A29. German translation in A40.

B38 'The "Récit de Théramène"' (1948). In A27. Italian translation in A29. German translation in D. Steland (ed.) *Französische Literatur von Ronsard bis Rousseau.* Frankfurt: Fischer, 1968, pp. 114–55; and in Theile (see D18). Reprinted as chapter V of this volume.

B39 '*Explication de texte* as applied to Voltaire' (1949). In A28, 64–101.

B40 'Ronsard's *Sur la Mort de Marie', The Explicator* 10 (1951) 1–4.

B41 'La *Vie de Marianne*. Lettre ouverte à M. Georges Poulet', *Romanic Review* 44 (1953) 102–26. Repr. in A32 and A41. German translation in A40.

B42 'Balzac and Flaubert Again', *Modern Language Notes* 68 (1953) 583–90.

B43 'The Works of Rabelais' in F. Horn (ed.) *Literary Masterpieces of the Western World*. Baltimore: Johns Hopkins University Press, 1953, pp. 126–47.

B44 'Les Lettres portugaises', *Romanische Forschungen* 65 (1954) 94–135. Repr. in A32. Translated as chapter VI of this volume.

B45 'The Poetic Treatment of a Platonic–Christian theme. Du Bellay's Sonnet of the Idea', *Comparative Literature* 6 (1954) 193–217. Revised version in *Traditio*. Repr. in A32. Expanded in A38, A39.

B46 'Stylistique et critique littéraire' (review of R. A. Sayce, *Style in French Prose*, with digression on Bossuet). *Critique* 11 (1955) 557–609.

B47 'La genèse d'une poésie de Paul Valéry', *Renaissance* (New York) 2 (1944) 311–21. Repr. in A32.

B48 'Le Style chez Ch.-F. Ramuz: le raccourci mystique', *Agonía* 6, pp. 12–26. Repr. in A32.

B49 'Baudelaire's "Spleen"', *The Hopkins Review* 6 (1953) 33–9. Repr. in A32.

B50 'A New Synthetic Treatment of Contemporary Western Lyricism' (review article on Hugo Friedrich, *Struktur der modernen Lyrik*), *Modern Language Notes* 72 (1957) 523–37.

B51 (collab. Wolfgang Spitzer) 'Zu Ronsards Sonnett, "Je voudray bien richement jaunissant"', *Romanistisches Jahrbuch* 9 (1958) 194–8.

B52 'Zu Marots *Eglogue au Roy soubs les noms de Pan et Robin*', *Romanistisches Jahrbuch* 9 (1958) 161–73.

B53 'Nota sulla favola di La Fontaine "Les Deux Pigeons"', *Studi Francesi* no. 7 (1958) 86–8. Repr. in A32. See pp. 195–6 below.

B54 Review of M. Riffaterre, *Le Style des 'Pléiades' de Gobineau, Modern Language Notes* 73 (1958) 68–74.

B55 Review of Stephen Ullmann, *Style in the French Novel, Comparative Literature* 10 (1958) 368–71.

B56 'La particella 'si' davanti all'aggetivo nel romanzo stendhaliano *Armance*', *Studi francesi* 8 (1958) 199–213.

B57 'Quelques aspects de la technique de Michel Butor', *Archivum linguisticum* 13 (1961) 171–95 and 14 (1962) 49–76. Repr. in A41.

B58 'Rabelais et les "Rabelaisants"', *Studi francesi* 4 (1960) 401ff. Repr. in A41.

B59 'Ancora sul prologo al primo libro del *Gargantua* di Rabelais', *Studi francesi* 27 (1965) 423–4.

C: *Articles by Leo Spitzer on his own life, on his method, and on general topics*

C1 'Die Romanistischen Zeitschriften im deutschen Reich'. Location and date unknown (post-1936).*

C2 'Schopenhauer und die Sprachwissenschaft', *Germanisch–romanische Monatshefte* 8 (1920) 258–2.

C3 'Der Romanist an der deutschen Hochschule', *Die Neueren Sprachen* 35 (1927) 241–60.

C4 'L'Etat actuel des études romanes en Allemagne', *Revue d'Allemagne et des pays de langue allemande* 6 (1932) 572–95.

C5 'Mes Souvenirs de Meyer-Lübke', *Le Français moderne* 6 (1938) 213–24.

C6 'Answer to Mr. Bloomfield', *Language* 20 (1944) 245–51.

C7 '*Geistesgeschichte* vs History of Ideas as applied to Hitlerism', *Journal of the History of Ideas* 5 (1944) 191–203.

C8 'Das Eigene und das Fremde. Über Philologie und Nationalismus', *Die Wandlung* 1 (1945/6) 566–94.

C9 'In Memoriam Elise Richter', *Romance Philology* 1 (1948) 329–38.

C10 'Linguistics and Literary History' in A27, 1–39.

C11 'The Formation of an American Humanist', *Proceedings of the Modern Languages Association* 46 (1951) 39–48.

C12 'Les Théories de la stylistique', *Le Français moderne* 20 (1953) 160–8.

C13 'Language – The Basis of Science, Philosophy and Poetry' in G. Boas (ed.) *Studies in Intellectual History*. Baltimore: Johns Hopkins University Press, 1953, pp. 67–93.

C14 'La mia stilistica', *La cultura moderna* (Bari) no. 17 (December 1954) 17–19. (Includes a photograph of L.S.)

C15 'Lo sviluppo di un metodo', *Ulisse* 13 (1960) 26–33; a fuller version in *Cultura neolatina* 20 (1960) 109–28.

C16 'Les Etudes de style dans les différents pays' in *Langue et littérature. Actes du VIIe Congrès de la fédération internationale des langues et littératures modernes*. Paris: Les Belles Lettres, 1961, pp. 23–38.

* Professor Jauss was kind enough to lend me his own copies of this item and of several others in this list.

D: *Articles concerning Leo Spitzer*

D1 Pedro Salinas, 'Esquicio de Leo Spitzer' in A26, i–iv.

D2 Erich Auerbach, review of A27, *Romanische Forschungen* 61 (1948) 393–6.

D3 Jean Hytier, 'La Méthode de M. Spitzer', *Romanic Review* XLI (1950) 42–59.

D4 Gustav Siebenmann, *'Leo Spitzer', Vox Romanica* XIX (1960) 409–18. (Includes a photograph of L.S.)

D5 Charles Bruneau, 'La Stylistique', *Romance Philology* 6 (1951) 1–17.

D6 Erich Köhler, 'Zur Bibliographie Leo Spitzers', *Romanistisches Jahrbuch* V (1952) 38–40.

D7 Anon., 'Leo Spitzer', *The Johns Hopkins Magazine* 3 (1952) 19–21 and 26–7.

D8 Henri Peyre, 'Avant-propos' in A31.

D9 René Wellek, 'Leo Spitzer 1887–1960', *Comparative Literature* 12 (1960) 310–34; additions in 13 (1961) 378–9. Reprinted in R. Wellek, *Discriminations*. New Haven: Yale University Press, 1970, pp. 187–224. (Contains a bibliography)

D10 Angela Bianchini, 'Gli ultimi anni italiani di Leo Spitzer', *L'Europa letteraria* I (1960) 167–9.

D11 Gianfranco Contini, 'Tombeau de Leo Spitzer', *Paragone* 12 (1961) 3–12.

D12 Yakov Malkiel, 'Necrology: Leo Spitzer', *Romance Philology* 14 (1961) 362–4.

D13 Emerico Giacherey, 'Leo Spitzer (1887–1960)', *Belfagor* 16 (1961) 441–63.

D14 Fritz Schalk, 'In Memoriam Leo Spitzer', *Romanische Forschungen* 73 (1961) 132–5. (Contains a list of L.S.'s contributions to *RF*)

D15 Helmut Hatzfeld, 'Necrology: Leo Spitzer 1887–1960', *Hispanic Review* 29 (1961) 54–7.

D16 Michel Baraz, review article on A32, *Modern Language Notes* 78 (1963) 60–74.

D17 Jean Starobinski, 'Leo Spitzer et la lecture stylistique', *Critique*, July 1964. Revised version in A41, 7–39.

D18 Jürgen von Stackelberg, 'Racine, Pradon und Spitzers Methode', *Germanisch-romanische Monatsschrift* 19 (1969) 413–34. Also in W. Theile (ed.) *Racine*. Darmstadt: Wissenschaftliche Buchgesellschaft, 1976, pp. 385–415.

D19 Helmut Hatzfeld, 'Leo Spitzer's and Stephen Ullmann's Stylistic Criticism' in T. E. Hope, T. W. B. Reid, Roy Harris, Glanville Price (eds.) *Language, Meaning and Style. Essays in Memory of Stephen Ullmann*. University of Leeds, 1981.

I

RACINE'S CLASSICAL *PIANO*

(1928, WITH ADDITIONAL MATERIAL FIRST PUBLISHED IN 1931)

This study of Racine's style continues to be recognised as the best treatment of the subject yet written. It argues that 'attenuation' or 'modulation', the toning-down of direct emotion by the particular devices of the 'majestic' style, is the hallmark of Racinian language and constitutes the distant beauty of his poetry. Although this view is not universally shared, Spitzer's demonstration of the rhetoric of attenuation remains a milestone both in Racine criticism and in the study of style. A more recent approach is Peter France, *Racine's Rhetoric* (Oxford University Press, 1965), which contains a useful bibliography and also takes issue with a number of points made by Spitzer.

Spitzer says that he wrote the first draft of this study without consulting any secondary sources other than Vossler's book and without using the only Racine lexicon then available, Charles Marty-Laveaux's *Lexique de la langue de Jean Racine* (1873). He added examples and further material from Marty-Laveaux to his own in the second draft, but was dissatisfied with the *Lexique* for a variety of reasons. Since we now possess much better tools, most notably J.-G. Cahen, *Le Vocabulaire de Racine* (1946) and Bryant C. Freeman and Alan Bateson's computer-assisted *Concordance du Théâtre et des Poésies de Jean Racine* (Ithaca: Cornell University Press, 1968), I have omitted Spitzer's references to and many of his criticisms of Marty-Laveaux's *Lexique*. Also omitted are all references to the secondary sources from which Spitzer obtained many of his Latin examples; and some of the copious quotations from Racine have been reduced to line-references to shorten slightly this very long article. The division into sections and the section-headings are also my own.

All quotations from Racine are given from the current *Nouveaux Classiques Larousse* editions.

DB

Il rase la prose, mais avec des ailes.*

Racine's style is not easy for the modern reader, especially if he is not French. Direct access to the heart of Racine's work, deeply embedded in its language, is inhibited and made difficult by the sober attenuation, the cold rationality, the almost formulaic quality of his style which – often quite suddenly and without warning – bursts into moments of song and living form, snuffed out just as quickly by a cold rationality which puts down any lyrical excitement the reader may have timidly permitted himself. Racine – the essentially Racinian – is neither simply formulaic nor simply lyrical song, but precisely the sequence and intertwining of both elements. As Karl Vossler rightly said:

> The ideal of [Racine's] style is to follow established usage and to appear unmarked, which is a negative and indeed a prosaic aim. Racine's poetic language has no 'strong' features. It is a secularised style modelled on polite conversation, reaching its moments of high solemnity essentially through the renunciation of sensual, direct or colourful language. The renunciation of sensual happiness is the guiding star of Racine's work, and of his language. An unequalled closedness and modesty that is both secular and transcendent, an inwardness and restraint that appear boring and poor to the vulgar, but noble to the educated taste . . . After the strained flights [of Corneille's images] Racine's language brought a calm serenity, a gliding and gentle descent towards earth . . . In Racine, word-order, rhyme and rhythm are all made to help create a flowing harmony in the concrete, modest conversational language of the characters. From the point of view of a history of style, Racine took these devices from Corneille, and to a degree from Rotrou . . . It would be attractive, perhaps, to pursue in detail these discrete attenuations and to illustrate them with comparisons. (Vossler, *Racine*, pp. 149–50, 154, 157)

In this essay I should like to pursue the attenuations in Racine's style, but not simply in his word-order, rhymes and rhythms, and not with reference to the poet's predecessors as Vossler urges, since that would

* This unattributed epigraph seems to be a rephrasing of Sainte-Beuve's comment in *Port-Royal*, p. 608: 'Racine . . . rase volontiers la prose, sauf l'élégance toujours observée du contour.'

make Racine appear too much like a satellite of other planets. As is my custom in style studies, I shall take Racine as a star in himself, as an entire, internally stable cosmos. I leave to other scholars the task of presenting these attenuations, taken here as it were absolutely, in terms of their relationships to pre-existing models, that is to say historically. I have joined the all-purpose term 'classical' to the '*piano*' of my title because the attenuation of Racine's style creates precisely that effect of distinguished restraint, of self-enclosure, which is described – in German literature as well, as in the case of Goethe's *Iphigenie auf Tauris* – as classical. The word '*piano*' is meant to suggest the soft pedal on the pianoforte, not the one that lengthens and strengthens the note (the *forte*, the one meant in the well-known saying that the French language is 'un piano sans pédale'): Racine's language is a language with a *piano* pedal.

1. The Indefinite Article

The first of the *piano* effects or attenuations in Racine's style is what I shall call **de-individualisation by the indefinite article** (in the plural by *des*). For example, in *Andromaque* I.iv, Andromaque wishes to reject the amorous advances of the king, Pyrrhus:

> Captive, toujours triste, importune à moi-même,
> Pouvez-vous souhaiter qu'Andromaque vous aime?
> Quels charmes ont pour vous *des* yeux infortunés
> Qu'à *des* pleurs éternels vous avez condamnés?
> Non, non, d'*un* ennemi respecter la misère,
> Sauver *des* malheureux, rendre *un* fils à sa mère,
> De cent peuples pour lui combattre la rigueur,
> Sans me faire payer son salut de mon cœur,
> Malgré moi, s'il le faut, lui donner un asile:
> Seigneur, voilà *des* soins dignes du fils d'Achille. 301–10

In this passage, Andromaque tries to obliterate her own self as much as possible. After a fleeting appearance of the 'lyrical I' of the widow of Hector in the triple apposition of l.301 (*captive . . . triste . . . importune*), an atmosphere of distance is established in l.302 when Andromaque names herself (⟶ 17). From this point on, everything is said as if there were no particular case but only general principles involved: it is no longer about Andromaque, but about *an* enemy (*un ennemi*, l.305) whose misfortune Pyrrhus should respect, about unfortunate people (*des malheureux*, l.306), not about the particular Astyanax but about *a* son (*un fils*, l.306) to be returned to his mother – or so it might seem, as if it were not a matter of an actual case. However, the hearer knows that it has to do with Andromaque and with her son's fate not only because of the context but also because the speaker returns to the first person with *malgré moi* in l.309. Andromaque speaks here both personally and generally at the same time. Her emotion is deeply buried within her, we can feel it in her turmoil and rage, but through her lips comes only the general, one could almost say only the legalistic, aspect of her case: here is *an* enemy (in the masculine) whose misery commands respect, here is *a* son with a right to his mother. This is an attenuated, unlyrical manner of expression. [Note also the use of *autre* in the masculine or, more properly, neuter gender to refer to a woman in *Andromaque* IV.vi, l.1377–8: 'Ton cœur, impatient de revoir ta Troyenne / Ne souffre qu'à regret qu'*un autre* t'entretienne'.] On the other hand, the suppressed emotion invades the linguistic expression and gives new strength to the dynamic of those general and soulless articles *un* and *des*: under their modesty and restraint can be heard a tone of declamation and rhetoric, an appeal and an insistence on one's rights. Unsaid emotion takes its revenge by energising its verbal expression, by exercising a counterpressure on the words that repress it. So we have a *piano* strung with tension – and a demonstration that Racine's language is not 'dead', but animated by subterranean, bottled-up life. To show that this feature is characteristic of Racine, I need only give some further illustrations from *Andromaque* and the later plays. For example, in *Andromaque* III.i Oreste retreats behind the general features of his own situation:

> J'abuse, cher ami, de ton trop d'amitié;
> Mais pardonne à *des* maux dont toi seul as pitié;
> Excuse *un* malheureux qui perd tout ce qu'il aime,
> Que tout le monde hait, et qui se hait lui-même. 795–8

With this use of the indefinite article there arises a degree of strangeness and distantiation between the speaker and his addressee. [My colleague P. Friedländer has pointed out a comparison with Seneca's *Medea*, l.503, where Medea says to Jason *Tibi innocens sit quisquis est pro te nocens*, 'You should consider innocent anyone who has done wrong on your behalf'. The *quisquis* has the literal meaning 'anyone who, whosoever' but refers to a particular 'who', namely Medea. It suggests some kind of game of linguistic deceit; Friedländer calls it a 'dialectical movement' between general and particular meanings.] The device is all the more remarkable when the distance is constantly being closed and opened up again within the same speech, as is mostly the case for Racine's regal characters who move in a special atmosphere, now coming down close to their interlocutors, now estranging themselves from them.

> A de moindres faveurs *des* malheureux prétendent,
> Seigneur; c'est *un* exil que *mes* pleurs vous demandent.
> *Andromaque* I.iv, 337–8

First Andromaque insists with pride on the rights of the unfortunate in general; but with the vocative *Seigneur*, l.338, she addresses Pyrrhus as the master of her fate in personal terms, marking the transition to a more intimate manner in which her personal wishes can be voiced (. . . *mes pleurs vous demandent*, l.338). The alternation of pride and humility in Andromaque's character is mirrored by the alternation of individual and de-individualised modes of expression. [E. Winkler, *Grundlegung der Stilistik*, p. 113, argues rather differently that the indefinite article in l.103 of Molière's *Les Femmes savantes* has the effect of making the word *mérite* more concrete:

> Et l'on peut pour époux refuser un mérite
> Que pour adorateur on veut bien à sa suite.

The indefinite article, he says, withdraws so much 'intellectual energy' from the word *mérite* that 'the abstract core of meaning can leave the word and allow the external appearance of a meritorious thing or person to take its place'. On the other hand, *mérite* is more abstract than what it replaces, i.e. 'la personne qui mérite notre amour'; the notion that 'love can only favour true merit' is left unstressed as something perfectly obvious (an example of how a high culture reveals itself in what it takes for granted). Winkler emphasises the outward show of the article; I stress the indefiniteness of the indefinite article.]

On of the finest examples of the attitude both modest and determined communicated by the use of *un* is to be found in Monime's speech to Mithridate:

> Et le tombeau, Seigneur, est moins triste pour moi
> Que le lit d'un époux qui m'a fait cet outrage,
> Qui s'est acquis sur moi ce cruel avantage,
> Et qui me préparant un éternal ennui,
> M'a fait rougir d'*un* feu qui n'était pas pour lui.
>
> *Mithridate* IV.iv, 1350–4

D'un feu means *de mon amour* – but the appended relative clause makes it possible to accommodate a definite refusal (of Mithridate's offer) almost incidentally and as if it went without saying, to conceal a dagger beneath the elegantly gathered skirt of a long sentence. A more perfidious grace, a more graceful perfidy would be hard to imagine.

The de-individualising indefinite article with its *piano* of emotion – if one may put it thus – occurs especially, of course, where the speaking 'I' seeks both to obscure itself and yet to claim its rights:

> Le croirai-je, seigneur, qu'un reste de tendresse
> Vous fasse ici chercher *une* triste princesse?
>
> Hermione, in *Andromaque* II.ii, 477–8

Also, to foreground the absolute as against the contingent nature of the speaker's relationship to a husband, or any other kith and kin:

> Voilà de mon amour l'innocent stratagème:
> Voilà ce qu'*un* époux m'a commandé lui-même.
> *Andromaque* IV.i, 1097–8

Hector is meant here, but is referred to only as '*a* spouse': he had commanded in virtue of his marital status. Even where the relative is the object of discussion, he is referred to by the kinship role which dignifies him, as in *Andromaque* II.i:

> CLÉONE: Mais vous ne dites point ce que vous mande *un* père.
> HERMIONE: *Mon* père avec les Grecs m'ordonne de partir. 405, 408

Or in *Bajazet* II.i:

> Ne désespérez point *une* amante en furie,
> S'il m'échappait un mot, c'est fait de votre vie. 541–2

This is a very concise way of saying 'do not make me despair, for I am a lover gone mad'. One suspects that behind the *furioso* of the expression there lies a general experience, some sort of maxim along the lines 'A lover made mad must not be made to despair'. Racine individualises or 'degeneralises' maxims in that he characteristically forges them into human form; whereas Corneille, as is well known, delights in autonomous *sententiae* intended to be quoted as maxims. However, maxims do sometimes occur explicitly in Racine:

> Est-ce qu'en holocauste aujourd'hui présenté
> Je dois, comme autrefois la fille de Jephté,
> Du Seigneur par ma mort apaiser la colère?
> Hélas! *un fils n'a rien qui ne soit à son père.* *Athalie* IV.i, 1259–62

This could have become directly *Est-ce qu'en holocauste . . . un fils doit apaiser* . . . [Gabriel Des Hons, pp. 206, 174 has pointed out the Racinian allusion in a passage from Anatole France's *La Révolte des Anges* (1914): 'Maurice . . . lança tout d'une haleine des paroles qu'une mère n'aurait jamais dû entendre' (p. 250); cf. *Phèdre* III.i, 742: *J'ai dit ce que jamais on ne devait entendre.* The alteration France makes to the line from Racine remains Racinian: 'une mère'. Incidentally, the passage which this critic calls 'véritable André Chénier' should more properly also be compared to Racine: 'Elle couve, elle est mère: une mère est craintive', A. France; *Elle flotte, elle hésite; en un mot elle est femme, Athalie* III.iii, 876.]

It is worth noting here the importance of kinship terms in Racine's plays dealing with kings and the high-born, for they make these potentates closer to us, and more human. Nothing is more unjust than to reproach French classical tragedy with 'title-mania'. As Marmontel said in 1763 (repeated by Lessing, p. 58):

> C'est faire injure au cœur humain et méconnoitre la Nature, que de croire qu'elle ait besoin de titres pour nous émouvoir et nous attendrir. Les noms sacrés d'ami, de père, d'amant, d'époux, de fils, de mère, d'homme enfin: voilà les qualités pathétiques: leurs droits ne périront jamais. (Marmontel, II.147)

Racine perceived the note of pathos in the names of universal human relationships.

Note how in the following passage from *Mithridate* III.v the referring expressions come in three stages of definiteness:

> Pourvu que vous vouliez qu'*une main* qui m'est chère,
> *Un fils*, le digne objet de l'amour de son père,
> *Xipharès*, en un mot, devenant votre époux,
> Me venge de Pharnace, et m'acquitte envers vous. 1059–62

The speaker, Mithridate, creeps up like a cunning animal, from the distant *une main*, then *un fils* a little nearer, to the definite article *le digne* . . . and finally the proper name *Xipharès*. (Cf. Rudler, p. 149, where this point is not brought out adequately.) Another instance where the proper name marks the climax of a clarification is to be found in Œnone's speech in *Phèdre* I.iii:

> . . . au *fils de l'étrangère*,
> A *ce fier ennemi* de vous, de votre sang,
> *Ce* fils qu'une Amazone a porté dans son flanc,
> Cet *Hippolyte* . . . 202–5

[Note that our evidence on the indefinite article and the use of kinship terms supports the reading given by Mesnard and older editions for *Mithridate* I.iii, 306: 'Ce roi . . . / N'accuse point le ciel qui le laisse outrager / Et *des* indignes fils qui n'osent le venger?' where Louis Racine, Boileau and Brossette require *deux. Des indignes fils* is entirely appropriate to the reticence of Racinian characters.]

Another case of explicit maxim occurs in *Bajazet* III.v:

> Votre mort (pardonnez aux fureurs des amants)
> Ne me paraissait pas le plus grand des tourments. 687–8

Here the extraordinary nature of what is said (that the jealous lover could acquiesce even in the death of the loved one) has to be softened by the parenthetic appeal to the general experience of lovers. This is how one should understand the use of the plural in place of the singular, to allow the individual to dissolve in a multiplicity of experiences:

> Pardonnez, Acomat, je plains avec sujet
> Des cœurs dont les bontés, trop mal récompensées,

M'avaient pris pour objet de toutes leurs pensées.
Bajazet II.iii, 616–18

In reality only one quite particular heart is meant here by *des cœurs*. The plural-indefinite expression simulates a general stance which obviates the need for an individual *prise de position*. An especially elegant version of this type of expression is *des* + (plural) noun + relative clause, because the 'principled' point of view can be put especially discreetly in the final relative. An example has already been quoted: *des maux dont toi seul as pitié,* connected with a polite recognition of the addressee, *un malheureux qui perd tout ce qu'il aime* (*Andromaque* III.i). A similar example from *Phèdre* II.ii:

HIPPOLYTE: Je révoque *des lois* dont j'ai plaint la rigueur . . .
ARICIE: Modérez *des bontés* dont l'excès m'embarasse. 475, 481

Hippolyte is referring here to laws handed down by Thésée; Aricie means '*vos* bontés'. The de-individualising effect is particularly strong when *un* is put before parts of the body; they become tools, so to speak, that could be replaced by other ones, and they come into consideration only in respect of whatever activity they can perform. For example:

N'êtes-vous pas ici sur la montagne sainte
Où le père des Juifs sur son fils innocent
Leva sans murmurer *un* bras obéissant . . . *Athalie* IV.v, 1438–40

Abraham's arm was an obedient arm, it might have been disobedient – there is, as it were, nothing noteworthy about the arm other than its obedience. It is not Abraham's arm, not *his* (individual) arm, but any arm *x* such that *x* has the function *obedience*. [Cf. Lerch (1919), pp. 246–7, on La Fontaine's 'impressionistic' *ouvre un large bec* (*Fables* I/2, 'Le Corbeau et le Renard', l.12). See also *Athalie* V.ii, 1593–6, *une main téméraire*.]

Since Latin and Greek do not have articles as such, Racine's use of *un* and *des* is not based on any classical model. However, it might be thought that it was precisely the absence of the article in Latin that Racine sought to imitate through the indefinite. Consider the parallel between Terence's sentence in *The Girl from Andros* and Racine's version of it: *Pro peccato magno paulum supplicii satis est patri, Andria* V.iii ('Though the offence be great / A father may the punishment abate', trans. F. Perry; or, more literally, 'For (a) great crime (a) little punishment suffices for (a) father'); *Un père, en punissant, Madame, est toujours père: / Un supplice léger suffit à sa colère, Phèdre* III.iii, 901–2. [Vossler sees indefinite article + proper name, e.g. *un Ovide, des Mécènes* as 'the heightening of the individual to universal significance, so characteristic of the renaissance' (*Frankreichs Kultur*, p. 279). It could simply be the continuation of Latin *Maecenas*, 'a Maecenas',

Maecenates, 'givers of favour'. Elsewhere Vossler makes much the same comment on *un* + noun, as in *un prince dans un livre apprend mal son devoir*. He is quite right to connect *un prince* with *un Ovide*, i.e. with the use of the proper name as the name of a type, for proper names originally conferred upon their holders the obligations of the values they referred to. *Un Ovide* means 'one who is worthy to be named Ovid'. *Un prince* and *un Ovide* are expressions of pride in intellectual nobility.]

Under the heading of de-individualisation we must also put **impersonal expressions** such as:

> Hé quoi! votre courroux n'a-t-il pas eu son cours?
> Peut-*on* haïr sans cesse? et punit-*on* toujours?
> *Andromaque* I.iv, 311–12

Here the speaker invokes a general mode of behaviour which he wishes his addressee to adopt ('one cannot hate for ever, thus *you too* should not always hate'). But often *on* replaces a reference to a definite person:

> Quel est l'étrange accueil qu'on fait à votre père,
> Mon fils? *Phèdre* III.v, 921–2

'The reception prepared for your father' (by Phèdre in fact): Thésée sees the general principle that a poor reception has been arranged on his return home, but by whom it has been arranged is for the moment of no importance. Similarly, when Œnone returns all too soon from her errand to Hippolyte, Phèdre cries out:

> Mais déjà tu reviens sur tes pas,
> Œnone? On me déteste, on ne t'écoute pas. *Phèdre* III.ii, 823–4

A certain kind of modesty, and a superstitious fear of conjuring fate by naming it, an awareness of falling prey to an unavoidable fate (the fate, precisely, of not being heard), all these things stop Phèdre from speaking aloud the brutal sentence she really means: *Hippolyte me déteste, Hippolyte ne m'écoute pas*. Another case occurs in *Andromaque* III.vii when Pyrrhus addresses Andromaque:

> Madame, demeurez.
> On peut vous rendre encor ce fils que vous pleurez.
> Oui, je sens à regret . . . 947–9

Here the reader senses how, in order to stop the worried mother from leaving, Pyrrhus first puts in her view the return of her son without stressing his own action (*on peut vous rendre*), and only then reveals his own self as suitor, which is what the return depends upon. Here the Racinian art of attenuation converges with the necessary attenuation of the character of the unsuccessful suitor.

[Cf. Elmire's ambiguous use of *on* in *Le Tartuffe* IV.v. Also the point made by Jean-Jacques Rousseau, *La Nouvelle Héloïse*, p. 253: 'Le *je* est presque aussi scrupuleusement banni de la scène française que des écrits de Port-Royal, et les passions humaines, aussi modestes que l'humilité Chrétienne, n'y parlent jamais que par *on*.']

2. The Demonstrative

The *piano* effect, the attenuation of sensibility, is also the result of what I should like to call the **distantiating use of the demonstrative.** Now a very basic and involuntary movement of any speaker wishing to direct the attention of his hearer towards some thing or state of affairs is to point to it. Racine grasped how to introduce a certain distance between the pointing subject and the thing pointed to, and turned physical deixis into an intellectual indicativeness. In a Racinian demonstrative pronoun there is not so much a finger pointing to something proximate as a direction sign leading to the far distance. How does that come about? It comes from Racine's direction of deixis to things that are already there – which serves to put them in the far distance. Whoever says 'this son' instead of 'your son' suppresses with the suppressed possessive all the human warmth of the physical connection of mother-and-son, and transforms the son into an autonomous phenomenon disconnected, as it were, from the mother:

> . . . je viendrai vous prendre
> Pour vous mener au temple où *ce fils* doit m'attendre;
> Et là vous me verrez, soumis ou furieux,
> Vous couronner, madame, ou le perdre à vos yeux.
>
> *Andromaque* III.vii, 973–6

In this scene Pyrrhus leaves his attitude towards Astyanax open: he will only take account of him when Andromaque shows her submission to the king; for the time being the boy is just 'that son' who can perfectly well be slaughtered. All the hard-heartedness of Andromaque's barbarous suitor hangs on the cold neutrality of the demonstrative adjective with its abstract and official tone. [Cf. *La Chanson de Roland*, ed. Whitehead, l.1031: *Luisent cil elme, ki ad or sunt gemmez* ('These helmets shine, studded with gold'), which prompts Lommatzsch, p. 208* to mention 'linguistic reflexes of vague, rhetorical gestures'. I would stress the vagueness. Deixis originally contained the kind of manifest indicativeness necessary in legal matters, e.g. *Par mon chief, ço dist Charles, oreindreit leur direz / O jo vos ferai ja cele teste colper,* 'Upon my head, said Charles, you will tell them directly, or I shall have this (your) head cut off', *Le Voyage de Charlemagne à Jérusalem et à Constantinople*, ed. Aebischer, l.41–2. The coolness of this legal expression has an effect of stylistic coolness in later non-legal usage.]

* I have been unable to identify this reference.

Confidants are more likely to see 'objectively' than heroines: passionlessness is often in Racine the doubtful privilege of servant characters. The following lines, which could only come from the sceptical Ismène, almost sound as though they were in ironical quotation marks:

> Je sais de ses froideurs tout ce que l'on récite;
> Mais j'ai vu près de vous *ce superbe Hippolyte* . . .
>
> *Phèdre* II.i, 405–6

It is hardly surprising that in the narration of the sacrifice of Isaac, from which we have already quoted, Abraham is presented through the demonstrative:

> Leva sans murmurer un bras obéissant,
> Et mit sur un bûcher *ce* fruit de sa vieillesse . . .
> Et lui sacrifiant, avec *ce* fils aimé,
> Tout l'espoir de sa race, en lui seul renfermé . . .
>
> *Athalie* IV.v, 1440–4

In the son we are shown only the filial relationship; the intimacy and natural closeness of father and son are suspended by the distancing demonstrative. This Isaac is almost more the *fruit de la vieillesse d'Abraham* than he is a *fils aimé*! The demonstrative elevates characters and actions to the non-human sphere of History. One might recall at this point those portraits, much favoured in seventeenth- and eighteenth-century painting, which show their subjects pointing in some way – for example, Philippe de Champaigne's *Richelieu* (1635) or Jean-Marc Nattier's *Mesdames Henriette d'Angleterre et Adelaide de France* (1742). Racine the king's historiographer himself indicates the historical dimension:

> Faut-il vous rappeler . . .
> Près de *ce* champ fatal Jézabel immolée,
> Sous les pieds des chevaux *cette* reine foulée? *Athalie* I.i, 109–16
>
> Nous regardions tous deux *cette* reine cruelle . . . *Athalie* II.ii, 416

Athalie has here become a 'spectacle', an object of historical contemplation, and distant from us. Perhaps this use of the demonstrative derives from historical writing (or memoir literature; cf. the frequent *ce prince* in Madame de la Fayette): there is something necessarily abstract about references to distant happenings and figures in a written representation. *Ce prince* died out with the French monarchy; it can still be found, though, in the preface to Raynouard's *Lexique roman*: '. . . le ministre de la maison du Roi m'invita à lui exposer en détail le plan de mes travaux projetés; je rédigeai, à cet effet, un Mémoire qu'il mit sous les yeux de *ce prince* que les Muses avaient consolé dans son exil . . .' (i.e. Louis-Philippe).

In the mouth of a ruler or diplomat, the demonstrative can give a cutting edge to the dispassionate great man who treats people and men as political tools:

> D'ailleurs, un bruit confus, par mes soins confirmé
> Fait croire heureusement à *ce* peuple alarmé
> Qu'Amurat le dédaigne . . .
> Surtout qu'il se déclare et se montre lui-même,
> Et fasse voir *ce* front digne du diadème.
>
> *Bajazet* I.ii, 243–5, 249–50

The possessive would have suggested some degree of empathy (*notre peuple, son front*); the demonstrative remains cool, cautious, neutral. Where a character speaks of himself (of his body, etc.) using the demonstrative, he becomes alien to himself, with an effect that is either sincerely modest or coldly objective:

> Mais, hélas! il peut bien penser avec justice
> Que, si j'ai pu lui faire un si grand sacrifice,
> *Ce cœur*, qui de ses jours prend ce funeste soin,
> L'aime trop pour vouloir en être le témoin.
>
> *Bajazet* III.i, 837–40

> Fuis; et si tu ne veux qu'un châtiment soudain
> T'ajoute aux scélérats qu'a punis *cette main* . . .
>
> *Phèdre* IV.ii, 1059–60

Here too, as with the indefinite article, there is a perceptible tone of entreaty and protestation, a note of rhetorical pathos in the use of the demonstrative: '*This* heart that has suffered so much', '*this* hand that has punished too much'. Racine has the ability to distantiate and nonetheless to call up a 'subterranean movement'. [Recently Thibaudet has made fun of the habit of French politicians of referring to their country as *ce pays*, using a demonstrative 'qui m'a toujours paru bizarre et qui doit appartenir, comme les *ille* et *iste* du barreau romain, à la mimique professionnelle de l'avocat' ('Réflexions sur la politique', p. 436). The distantiating *ce* was originally solemn and oratorical; it signified that the orator was not at that moment considering France as 'his' country but as 'this country' that has this or that right to etc., and which is so to speak present in the parliament chamber. Cf. the lawyer Cicero, *vobis atque huic urbi ferro flammaque minitans*, 'threatening you and *this city* with sword and fire', *Catilina*, 2.1.1.]

The periphrastic *en ces lieux* for *ici, en ce jour* for *aujourd'hui*, should be connected to this device. The periphrases are not only less usual and conventional than the everyday expressions: they contain a certain notion of distance, a strangeness, so to speak, with respect to the indicated place and time. *Ces lieux* (in the uncontoured plural) is not the natural and physically perceptible residence of Racine's characters; *ces lieux* hangs together with the 'unity of place', or rather non-place, of

Racinian theatre. The palace that might be shown by the stage set is not at all the characters' real residence; all roots in a given terrain or *terroir* are suspended. The unlimiting *où* is also related to the immateriality of place;⟶ 31.

I should also mention here the classical *il est* for *il y a*. Its frequency is not due solely to the rule of hiatus, but also to the more abstract colouring and less exact localisation that it has. The limiting deictic *y* is missing; *il est* asserts only mere existence.

Ici is relatively infrequent in Racine (an example: *Je ne viens point ici . . ., Andromaque* III.iv, 861); expressions such as the following are much more common:

> Vous savez qu'*en ces lieux* mon devoir m'a conduite . . .
> *Andromaque* II.ii, 582

> Je croyais apporter plus de haine *en ces lieux*.
> *Andromaque* III.vii, 951

In this last example, *ces lieux* becomes as it were the residence of hatred; the nuance would not be possible with *ici*.

> Qui t'amène *en des lieux* où l'on fuit ta présence?
> *Andromaque* V.iii, 1554

The direct connection of a relative clause is possible only with *lieux*.

> Et depuis quand, seigneur, entre-t-on *dans ces lieux*
> Dont l'accès était même interdit à nos yeux? *Bajazet* I.i, 3–4

This refers to the hidden secrets of the harem.

> Que vois-je? Quelle horreur *dans ces lieux* répandue
> Fait fuir devant mes yeux ma famille éperdue?
> *Phèdre* III.v, 953–4

Cf. *Andromaque* l.951 quoted above.

> Prends garde que jamais l'astre qui nous éclaire
> Ne te voie *en ces lieux* mettre un pied téméraire.
> *Phèdre* IV.iii, 1061–2

Un pied dematerialises this sentence as much as *ces lieux*.

It is interesting to note that in *Phèdre* Racine felt the need to replace *en ces lieux* generally by the 'maritime' expression *sur ces bords*, 'on these shores', which perhaps conjures up the far horizon of the sea without giving any precise limits or contours to it:

> Depuis que *sur ces bords* les Dieux ont envoyé
> La fille de Minos et de Pasiphaé. I.i, 35–6

> Ariane, ma sœur, de quel amour blessée
> Vous mourûtes aux bords où vous fûtes laissée! I.iii, 253–4

Further examples: I.v, 358; II.i, 391; II.v, 600, etc.

One wonders whether the source of this expression is not the Latin *ripa* ('bank'), as in Virgil's *Evaditque celer ripam irremeabilis undae*, 'He quickly escaped the bank of the river that could never be crossed twice', *Aeneid* VI.425, on which II.i, 388 *Et repasser les bords qu'on passe sans retour* is modelled. In La Fontaine *bords* clearly has a dramatic tone, as in 'Sur les humides bords du royaume du vent' (*Fables* I/2, 'Le Chêne et le roseau', l.16). Note that Propertius I, 19.12 uses the plural *litora* ('shores'): *Trajicit et fati litora magnus amor*, 'A great love crosses even the shores of fate'. Another model for the line quoted from Racine is Catullus III.12, *illuc unde negant redire quemquam*, 'The place whence they say no one returns', which Lanson cites in connection with Chretien de Troyes's *le reaume dont nus estranges ne retorne*, 'the kingdom whence no stranger returns'. All these expressions cast a veil of uncertainty, of intentional imprecision: the Old French poet gives the most extreme ('estranges'!), the Latin the most obscured, and Racine the most paradoxical version – he lays more stress on the boundary and the impossibility of return by the repetition of the radical *passer*.

There is an instance where the formulaic *ces lieux* becomes a new creation:

> Hé! depuis quand, Seigneur, craignez-vous *la présence*
> *De ces* paisibles *lieux*, si chers à votre enfance . . .
>
> *Phèdre* I.i, 29–30

Contemporaries objected: 'Whenever did you hear of *places* having a *presence*?'* In Virgil, *Aeneid* VI.638 we find the expression *devenere locos laetos*, literally 'they came to fortunate places', i.e. 'to the abode of the fortunate'.

The periphrasis *ce jour* is somewhat rarer: examples include *Andromaque* IV.iii, 1213, *ce jour, il épouse Andromaque*; IV.v, 1295, *jusques à ce jour*; *Bajazet* II.i, 423, *et je puis dès ce jour / Accomplir le dessein qu'a formé mon amour*; II.v, 701, *dès cette journée*. *Jour(née)* could not give the same sense of extension as *en ces lieux*: hence its less frequent use. [On *aujourd'hui* as an expression of natural feeling, cf. Spitzer (1930).]

To the distantiating use of the demonstrative we can also connect the ***si* and *tant* of asseveration**. The use of *si* in the sense 'so (. . . as it really is, as you can see)' calls on the addressee as witness, and ought to produce a particularly 'warm' effect. In Racine it seems to me that the opposite effect is achieved: his *si* has something cool and modulating to it, which clearly derives from the frequent formulaic use of this

* The criticism seems to go back to the author of the *Dissertation sur les deux tragédies de Phèdre*, p. 367, quoted in Mesnard, III.306n: 'avez-vous jamais ouï dire que les lieux aient une présence?'. In chapter V below, Spitzer attributes the point also to A. W. Schlegel (⟶ p. 224). In current editions of *Phèdre*, *présence* in l.29 is glossed as 'aspect'.

expression in e.g. letter-writing: *Je vous remercie de votre si charmante lettre*, which originally meant something like 'your letter . . . of *such* charm *as* I cannot express', '*as* I had not expected', etc. There are lines in Racine that seem to have precisely that tepid emotional temperature of the formal openings of letters. For example:

> Et ne profanez point des transports *si* charmants.
>
> *Phèdre* III.iv, 915

The line would almost have more emotional impact without that *si* which, in its appeal to witness and its assumption of another's judgment, is too clearly rational. (When Phèdre's passion is described as *une flamme si noire*, I.iii, 310, the *si* transforms the personal image of the black flame into an *asseveration*, an expression of outrage dependent on a code of moral values.) Further instances:

> . . . le forçant de rompre un nœud *si* solennel,
> Aux yeux de tous les Grecs rendons-le criminel.
>
> *Andromaque* II.i, 443–4

> Peut-être en ce moment Amurat en furie
> S'approche pour trancher une *si* belle vie. *Bajazet* I.iii, 265–6

> Que dis-je? Cet aveu que je te viens de faire,
> Cet aveu *si* honteux, le crois-tu volontaire? *Phèdre* II.v, 693–4

In *Britannicus* IV.iv, 1391, *Seigneur, j'ai tout prévu pour une mort si juste*, the *si* is used by Narcisse in exactly the same way as the indefinite article (*une mort*) to permit a hypocritical appeal to the necessity and justice of the contemplated act of murder – 'a death *as* justified (as this one)'.

The soft harmony of repeated *si* perhaps increases the fading effect:

> Ah! crois-tu . . . que . . .
> D'une si douce erreur si longtemps possédée,
> Je puisse désormais souffrir une autre idée . . .?
>
> *Bajazet* II.i, 547–50

The repetition of the sound suggests the untiring assertion of an error dear to the speaker's heart.

Tant is less grammaticalised (in contrast to Italian *tanto* in *tante grazie* or Spanish *tan* in *¡cosa tan rara!*) and thus has a 'warmer' effect:

> Astyanax, d'Hector jeune et malheureux fils,
> Reste de *tant* de rois sous Troie ensevelis.
>
> *Andromaque* I.i, 71–2

> L'auriez-vous cru, Madame, et qu'un si prompt retour
> Fît à *tant* de fureur succéder tant d'amour?
>
> *Bajazet* III.v, 1019–20

[Also: *Bajazet* I.i, 97–9.] The importance of the reversal in the example from *Bajazet* is represented by the triple deixis directed towards the addressee (*Madame*, 1019); but what is being referred to is the plot, and what is presented are relations between the knowledge of the speaker and the hearer. In other words, we have here representation and information, not an expression of the lyrical 'I', and therefore we have classical attenuation. The line is reminiscent of classical models, e.g. *Aeneid* I.9–11, where the queen has urged on Aeneas . . . *tot volvere casus, / tot adire labores / Tantaene animis celestibus irae*?, '. . . to face *so* many adventures, to face *so* many trials . . . gods capable of *such* rancour'. (The comparison was suggested by P. Friedländer.)

3. Third-Person Expressions

Racine takes care not to let the self sing out too freely. He likes to place an **objectivising third-person expression** (noun, proper name or pronoun) in his characters' speech, where it alternates with the first person: that is to say, his characters are made to refer to themselves by their own names. This device does not only facilitate the initial presentation of a character to the audience, as in e.g. *Athalie* IV.iv, 1419–20, where Eliacin is proclaimed king and acknowledges his own official name of Joas by using it of himself, creating thereby a continuity between his existence as Eliacin and as Joas. Also in *Andromaque* I.i Oreste opens the play with the words *Oui, puisque je retrouve un ami si fidèle* and goes on to acquaint the audience with the two characters on stage by saying:

> Qui l'eût dit qu'un rivage à mes vœux si funeste
> Présenterait d'abord Pylade aux yeux d'Oreste? 5–6

Here the device is of course also an invocation of the legend in which Orestes is a known figure; it names also what lies outside of the play as much as those uses of *si* which presuppose the listener's familiarity with the situation: *un ami si fidèle* implies 'as is Pylades', *un rivage à mes vœux si funeste* implies 'as is this one'. By speaking of himself, Oreste appeals to the Orestes of the legend, he sees himself as he speaks as a figure on a stage; he thus acquire an aura of majestic nobility on which he can draw. He can even use the *epitheta constantia* ('Homeric epithets') of himself, i.e. those adjectives which are always attached to a character in 'objective' epic narration:

> Je te vis à regret, en cet état funeste,
> Prêt à suivre partout le déplorable Oreste . . .
> *Andromaque* I.i, 45–6

[Note that Oreste is to a certain extent designated by the frequent rhyming of his name with *funeste*, which could be called a 'rhyme-epithet'. Cf. Péguy, 'Victor Marie, comte Hugo', p. 715:⟶ 68. On the degeneration of the Racinian use of proper names as rhyme-words in Voltaire, see Köster, p. 240.] It is no coincidence that Oreste, pursued by fate and knowing himself to be pursued, often sees himself *sub specie fati* – from the point of view of destiny – or that his sense of identity is altered to the point of referring to himself more as 'Oreste' than as 'I':

> . . . et le destin d'*Oreste*
> Est de venir sans cesse adorer vos attraits,
> Et de jurer toujours qu'il n'y viendra jamais.
>
> *Andromaque* II.ii, 482–4

> Mais, de grâce, est-ce à *moi* que ce discours s'adresse?
> Ouvrez vos yeux: songez qu'*Oreste* est devant vous,
> *Oreste*, si longtemps l'objet de leur courroux!
>
> *Andromaque* II.ii, 530–2

> Ah! madame, est-il vrai qu'une fois
> *Oreste* en vous cherchant obéisse à vos lois?
>
> *Andromaque* IV.iii, 1147–8

But it is not only Oreste with the plague of madness upon him who exhibits this feature; all of Racine's characters slip easily out of the Nessus's cloak of first-person pronoun into the ceremonial toga of their official proper names. We have already quoted this example:

> Captive, toujours triste, importune à moi-même,
> Pouvez-vous souhaiter qu'*Andromaque* vous aime?
>
> *Andromaque* I.iv, 301–2

Here the name *Andromaque* signifies the figure of Hector's widow in its entirety: in the proper name the personality of Andromache in all its individual resolutions is summarised and compressed into a single entity, into the obligatory nobility of the character. We could almost translate this instance by 'an Andromache': Andromaque herself has been dissolved into the general principle. She can be an 'I' (*moi-même*, l.301) only incidentally and in passing, after which she must rise again immediately to the grandeur of classical self-control. This 'recovery of the self' has some precedents in antiquity. P. Friedländer has pointed out the following examples in Seneca's *Medea*, where Medea is talking to herself: *Perge nunc, aude, incipe / quicquid potest Medea, quicquid non potest*, 'Go on, now, be daring and try everything, Medea, what's possible and what's not', l.566–7. Where the character considers her own strength, she sees herself non-subjectively, as from the outside. Similarly in *Medea* l.171 where the nurse says *Medea . . .*, the heroine replies *Fiam*, 'I shall become (a) Medea'; and in l.910, *Medea nunc sum*, 'I am now Medea'. I suspect that this mode of speech arose particularly easily in characters which were present in the mythical awareness of the ancients: Seneca's Medea thus appeared to the audience as *a* Medea, as the figure already known to the public from other sources. One can grant Racine's public a certain degree of active familiarity with the classics, but not an active mythical imagination; but in any case the self-naming device gives to the character using it a self-conscious majesty, or rather a majesty conscious of its selfhood, that points out beyond the individual play.

The name signifies, as a consequence, the categorical imperative of the character – but this moral imperative has a didactic, unlyrical, pondered and attenuated quality: it is a Racinian *piano*. Andromaque looks upon herself as upon her image; cf. her words in III. viii:

> Peins-toi dans ces horreurs Andromaque éperdue. 1005

But Andromaque is not alone in having this kind of limiting self-consciousness; her rival Hermione is just as much subject to it:

> Ne vous suffit-il pas que *ma* gloire offensée
> Demande une victime *à moi* seule adressée;
> Qu'*Hermione* est le prix d'un tyran opprimé;
> Que *je* le hais . . . IV.iii, 1189–92

> Hé quoi? c'est donc *moi* qui l'ordonne?
> Sa mort sera l'effet de l'amour d'*Hermione*? V.i, 1421–2

This outside view of the empirical 'I' is especially effective when the speaker contrasts him- or herself with other characters, and designates him- or herself with the same impartial and objective proper names as the others:

> HERMIONE: . . . quel que soit Pyrrhus,
> Hermione est sensible, Oreste a des vertus
> *Andromaque* II.i, 471–2

> PYRRHUS: Elle est veuve d'Hector, et je suis fils d'Achille;
> Trop de haine sépare Andromaque et Pyrrhus
> *Andromaque* II.v, 662–3

In these examples, as in e.g. *Phèdre* II.v, 703, *La veuve de Thésée ose aimer Hippolyte!*, the situation is seen as through the eyes of an epic narrator.

Racine can subtly raise or lower the majestic veil of the proper name. Phèdre speaks here in II.v of a thread such as Ariadne's:

> Un fil n'eût point assez rassuré votre amante.
> Compagne du péril qu'il vous fallait chercher,
> *Moi-même* devant vous j'aurais voulu marcher;
> Et *Phèdre au Labyrinthe* avec vous descendue
> Se serait avec vous retrouvée, ou perdue. 658–62

Phèdre is lost but does not yet wish to admit she is lost: her oscillation between amour-propre and self-sacrifice is what corresponds to the alternation between the periphrasis *votre amante* (l.658) and the protestation *moi-même* (l.660), which rises further to the surprising image of *Phèdre au Labyrinthe* (l.661) – only Ariadne has been heard of in the labyrinth before! In Hippolyte's mouth the naming device has a different sound: as if excluded from the civilised world by his own actions, he is and remains the barbarian, *le rebelle Hippolyte*:

> Tout retrace à mes yeux les charmes que j'évite;
> Tout vous livre à l'envi *le rebelle Hippolyte*. *Phèdre* II.ii, 545–6

> Songez que je vous parle une langue étrangère;
> Et ne rejetez pas des vœux mal exprimés,
> Qu'Hippolyte sans vous n'aurait jamais formés. *Phèdre* II.ii, 558–60

And in the speech of the grand vizier Acomat we can hear the amour-propre of the accomplished diplomat:

> Bajazet vit encor: pourquoi nous étonner?
> Acomat de plus loin a su le ramener. *Bajazet* IV.vii, 1403–4

Less frequently, Racinian characters are addressed by their proper names (instead of by *vous*), and this too produces a sense of distance. (This also has classical precedents, e.g. Seneca, *Medea*, l.496, where Jason says to Medea, *Medea amores obicit?*, 'Medea reproaches me for my love-affairs?') In these words to Oreste, Hermione sounds almost mocking:

> J'ai voulu vous donner les moyens de me plaire,
> Rendre *Oreste* content; mais enfin je vois bien
> Qu'il veut toujours se plaindre et ne mériter rien.
> *Andromaque* IV.iii, 1234–6

Abner's words to Joad are more respectful:

> Pensez-vous être saint et juste impunément?
> Dès longtemps elle hait cette fermeté rare
> Qui rehausse en *Joad* l'éclat de la tiare. *Athalie* I.i, 26–8

And the picture of Hermione's emotional state given by Pylade to Oreste in *Andromaque* I.i seems completely objective:

> Toujours prête à partir, et demeurant toujours,
> Quelquefois elle appelle Oreste à son secours. 131–2

This actually brings the dialogue to an end, for Pylade seems to be speaking of an *absent* Oreste.

4. Verbs of Display

I come now to that use of the verb *montrer* which points to a spectacle within the play, revealing the situation in its world-historical significance – as when the curtain is drawn back before the kneeling Habsburg in Grillparzer's play *King Ottocar. His Rise and Fall* (1825):

> *Montrer aux nations* Mithridate détruit . . . *Mithridate* III.i, 921

Nations are watching! In III.v, Mithridate says to Monime:

> C'est faire à vos beautés un triste sacrifice,
> Que de vous *présenter*, Madame, avec ma foi,
> Tout l'âge et le malheur que je traine avec moi. 1036–8

Rudler comments quite correctly that *présenter* 'seems a little more majestic, a little more emphatic and a little more concrete' than *offrir* (Rudler, p. 135). I would say that *présenter* here is one of the ceremonial obligations of a ruler.

In this connection one should also note the use of the intrinsically 'spectacular' verb *éclater*, a use which comes not simply from the special vocabulary of love (*Pour la veuve d'Hector ses feux ont éclaté, Andromaque* I.i, 108), but from the religious language of the baroque; it is commonly found in Racine and his contemporaries (and as late as Saint-Simon;⟶ 120) for anything remarkable or majestic, anything that 'makes a show of itself': *faire éclater sa gloire, Athalie* I.i, 127; *va de son bras . . . faire éclater l'appui, Esther* I.i, 21; *Dis-lui par quels exploits leurs noms ont éclaté, Andromaque* IV.i, 1115. When Hippolyte uses *éclater* of himself in the following lines, it sounds perhaps too much like self-advertisement:

> Seigneur, je crois surtout avoir fait *éclater*
> La haine des forfaits qu'on ose m'imputer *Phèdre* IV.ii, 1107–8

One should also not forget that for Racine the theatre is a moral institution that must give a teaching and 'show' some lesson. Almost as if he had wanted to prepare the ground for me, Brémond has listed some (but not all!) of the expressions in the *Préface* to *Phèdre* indicating a didactic intention:

> Ce que je puis assurer, c'est que je n'en ai point fait [de tragédie] où la vertu soit plus *mise en jour* que dans celle-ci. Les moindres fautes y sont sévèrement punies. La seule pensée du crime y est regardée avec autant d'horreur que le crime même. Les faiblesses de l'amour *y passent* pour de vraies faiblesses; les passions n'y sont présentées aux yeux que pour *montrer* tout le désordre dont elles sont cause; et le vice y est peint partout avec des couleurs qui en font *connaitre* et haïr la difformité. (Quoted in Brémond, p. 181)

It has been suggested that this feature can be traced back to the French requirements of *gloire* and social existence. '*Seigneur* and *Madame* never felt alone, but that all their *transports* were observed by *tous les humains* or *l'Univers'*, says Köster, p. 239. Of course it was the rule even in lyrical poetry from the time of the Pléiade on not to make a secret, but to show one's inclination *coram publico* – as for example in François Maynard's *A la belle vieille* (1646):

> Chloris, que dans mon cœur j'ai si longtemps servie
> Et que ma passion montre à tout l'univers . . .

The loved one is usually in this kind of poetry a natural phenomenon – a sun or dawn – that shines upon all humanity.

5. Figures of Majesty

Speech is also rendered impersonal by the **royal plural**. The self-naming device brings in its wake the categorical obligations of a historical or legendary persona; the royal plural, on the other hand, allows the speaker to stay covered by the office he exercises for the community. This plural also occurs principally in connection with decisions, deliberations and self-exhortations, where Racine again has his speaking characters oscillate between their private singular selves and their 'governing' plural pronouns. The mediating 'I' disintegrates into a plurality of persons, but can reintegrate, 'pull itself together', at any moment:

> Tu veux que je le fuie? Hé bien! rien ne m'arrête:
> Allons, *n'envions* plus son indigne conquête . . .
> Fuyons . . . Mais si l'ingrat rentrait dans son devoir . . .
> Si sous mes lois, Amour, tu pouvais l'engager!
> S'il voulait . . . Mais l'ingrat ne veut que m'outrager.
> *Demeurons* toutefois pour troubler leur fortune;
> *Prenons* quelque plaisir à leur être *importune*;
> Ou, le forçant de rompre un nœud si solennel,
> Aux yeux de tous les Grecs *rendons-le* criminel.
> J'ai déjà sur le fils attiré leur colère;
> Je veux qu'on vienne encor lui demander la mère.
> Rendons-lui les tourments qu'elle me fait souffrir . . .
>
> *Andromaque* II.i, 433–47

The 'I' now steps forward, threatening and domineering (*je veux que*, l.436), now creeps back behind a counselling 'we', and finally shows through from beneath the official mask thanks to a grammatical loophole – *Prenons quelque plaisir à . . . être importune*, l.440 (singular agreement). Similarly in *Bajazet* IV.iv:

> Sur tout ce que j'ai vu *fermons* plutôt les yeux;
> *Laissons* de leur amour la recherche importune;
> *Poussons* à bout l'ingrat, et *tentons* la fortune;

Voyons si, par *mes* soins sur le trône élevé,
Il osera trahir l'amour qui l'a sauvé,
Et si, de *mes bienfaits lâchement libérale,*
Sa main en osera couronner *ma* rivale.
Je saurai bien toujours retrouver le moment
De punir, s'il le faut, la rivale et l'amant:
Dans *ma* juste fureur, observant le perfide,
Je saurai le surprendre avec son Atalide . . .
Voilà, n'en *doutons* point, le parti qu'il faut prendre.
Je veux tout ignorer. 1236–50

It is striking that the first person plural *possessive* is not used. *Notre* would perhaps destroy the fictitiousness of the plural expression and suggest a real plural subject. The point is especially clear in this line from *Andromaque* v.ii: *Non, ne révoquons point l'arrêt de mon courroux*, l.1407, and contrasts with Latin models which also mix singular and plural in the first person but in reverse order, e.g. Catullus 68.17, *multa satis lusi: non est dea nescia nostri,* '*I* have played well enough: the goddess is not ignorant of *us*'. The instance of plural possessive in *Phèdre* v.vii, 1647–8, is doubtful:

Allons, de mon erreur, hélas! trop éclaircis,
Mêler *nos* pleurs au sang de *mon* malheureux fils.

According to Brunot, the royal plural is a purely literary device which never passed into everyday usage, but was explicitly recommended by theoreticians as appropriate to tragic diction (Brunot, iv.1, 378). In model sentences demonstrating the transition from singular to plural and vice versa, such as *Ne délibérons plus, allons droit à la mort; / La tristesse m'appelle à ce dernier effort* (*Iphigénie* iv.vii, 1429–30), the 'deliberative' shading of this device is very apparent.

Behind his monarchs and rulers Racine often shows the land of their dominion, but only as the power which the monarch embodies. The king's domain is at the same time an enhancement and an objective correlative of the king's personality, so that we have as it were a *terra majestatis* (royal domain) parallel to the *plural majestatis* (royal plural). And so this passage from *Bérénice* i.v, 234–6

Dans l'Orient désert quel devint mon ennui!
Je demeurai longtemps errant dans Césarée,
Lieux charmants où mon cœur vous avait adorée.

prompts Mesnard to comment that '*Lieux charmants* . . . n'est pas un trait moins exquis que *l'Orient désert*' (Mesnard, iii.xxxiv). In *Andromaque* i.ii, Pyrrhus ends a long speech with the conclusive line:

> *L'Epire* sauvera ce que *Troie* a sauvé. 220

That is to say, 'I, Pyrrhus, will save what the Trojans saved from Troy'; the king identifies himself with his land, rather as in Shakespeare the king of France is referred to as 'France'. In III.v, Céphise says to Andromaque:

> Un regard confondrait Hermione et *la Grèce* . . . 889

One could say that the unity of place itself permits the spectator of Racinian drama to imagine infinite spaces. Distant and endless realms are suggested by lines like *Dans l'Orient désert quel devint mon ennui*, and also when the name of a country or other geographical term serves as witness to a deed. For example:

> Pensez-vous avoir seul éprouvé des alarmes?
> Que *l'Epire* jamais n'ait vu couler mes larmes?
> *Andromaque* II.ii, 525–6

> Le *Jourdain* ne *voit* plus l'Arabe vagabond,
> Ni l'altier Philistin, par d'éternels ravages,
> Comme au temps de vos rois, désoler ses rivages . . .
> *Athalie* II.v, 474–6

The evocation of a character's geographical domain by the use of a proper name in Racine has been well brought out by Fubini, commenting on the line *Le Pont vous reconnaît dès longtemps pour sa reine* (*Mithridate*, I.iii, 231):

> The whole line is in its first and last words, *Le Pont* and *reine*: the graceful queen is seen against the background of her oriental domain. Phèdre does not say, 'I saw Hippolyte in Athens', but:
>
> *Athènes* me montra mon superbe ennemi *Phèdre* I.iii, 272
>
> The image of the handsome young man is distanced from the character and from the reader by the luminous backcloth of the immortal city. (Fubini, p. 67)

The universe itself can also just about serve as the backcloth for a Racinian character:

> Avec tout l'univers j'honorais vos vertus . . . *Bérénice* I.iv, 269

'The world is watching!' Or again the closing lines of *Mithridate*, where Xipharès calls on the whole world to take up arms to avenge the king:

> Ah! Madame, unissons nos douleurs
> Et par tout l'univers cherchons-lui des vengeurs. V.v, 1697–8

6. Personification

The retreat from the personal to the general is nowhere more fully realised than by the **personification of abstract qualities** which figure in the place of characters. In Racine, it is less the characters who act than abstract forces, by which they are moved and innervated. It has been demonstrated by others already that for the classical writer the individual is only conceivable 'as a sum of ethical and intellectual qualities, only one of which is usually given a dramatic formulation; the body and the organs of a character are made to act as if they were tools dependent on these abstract qualities' (Neubert, p. 171). The numerous uses of *mon âme, mon cœur, mon esprit, la vertu, la haine, la constance, l'amour, la faiblesse, la raison* would be, in this argument, much more than mere circumlocutions for the concept of the self. The type of metonymic personification found in e.g. 'those honours deep and broad, wherewith / *Your majesty* loads our house' (*Macbeth* I.vi, 17–18)* can be shown a dozen times in any text of Racine, so a single example will suffice:

> Hermione . . .
> Semble de son amant dédaigner l'*inconstance*
> Et croit que, trop heureux de fléchir sa rigueur,
> Il la viendra presser de reprendre son cœur. *Andromaque* I.i, 125–8

The expression avoids direct and immediate reference to its subject (which would give something like 'Hermione scorns her inconstant suitor', 'happy to sway her') and contains in its formulation a kind of general justification: *Hermione dédaigne l'inconstant parce qu'il faut dédaigner l'inconstance*, etc. An attitude towards a human being has given way here to a view about human qualities.

> Ah! seigneur, vous entendiez assez
> Des soupirs qui craignaient de se voir repoussés.
> Pardonnez à l'éclat d'une illustre fortune
> Ce reste de fierté qui craint d'être importune.
> *Andromaque* III.vi, 911–14

Even in this scene where she uses all her self-control to negotiate with Pyrrhus, Andromaque does not allow the man to whom she is speaking to make any step towards her. His effort and will must run into the wall of personified abstractions – *éclat, fortune, fierté*: it is not Andromaque who 'fears' to be importunate', but her 'pride'; not she who begs forgiveness, but 'the splendour of her fate', *l'éclat de sa fortune*. Even her own human expression, sighs (not *my* sighs;⟶ 6), are made abstract and personified as the grammatical subject of *craignaient de se voir repoussés*. Similarly in the following passage Phèdre is portrayed not as a suffering woman, but as the incarnation of various forces of passion that act on her behalf. (Likewise the confidante Œnone, who acts independently, is but the incarnation of one of Phèdre's disembodied desires.)

* Spitzer's example was the opening of Schiller's 'Der Graf von Habsburg': 'Zu Aachen in seiner Kaiserpracht / Im altertümlichen Saale / Sass König Rudolfs *heilige Macht* / Beim festlichen Königsmahle.'

Un désordre éternel règne dans son esprit.
Son chagrin inquiet l'arrache de son lit.
Elle veut voir le jour; et *sa douleur profonde*
M'ordonne toutefois d'écarter tout le monde . . .

Phèdre I.ii, 147–50

In *Andromaque* II.ii an unspecified force is explicitly designated as the origin of Pyrrhus's action:

Madame: il me renvoie; et quelque autre puissance
Lui fait du fils d'Hector embrasser la défense. 513–14

Not 'he defends Hector's son' but 'a (dark) force makes him assume the defence of . . .'.

All this produces in the end a periphrastic pomp, a ceremonial of circumlocutions which drown the individual in abstractions:

Oui, *mes vœux* ont trop loin poussé leur violence
Pour ne plus s'arrêter que dans l'indifférence.

Andromaque I.iv, 365–6

Il se souvient toujours que son *inimitié*
Voulut de ce grand corps retrancher la moitié . . . *Bajazet* I.i, 39–40

Je crois que *votre haine*, épargnant ses vertus,
Ecoute sans regret ces noms qui lui sont dus. *Phèdre* II.ii, 471–2

Cependant je rends grâce au *zèle officieux*
Qui sur tous mes périls vous fait ouvrir les yeux. *Athalie* I.i, 65–6

[Other examples include *Andromaque* III.vi, 909–10; *Bajazet* I.i, 49–50; *Athalie* III.v, 1004–6.] There are classical models in plenty: Racine transforms Virgil's *divum inclementia* ('mercilessness of the gods') into *pour fléchir l'inclémence des dieux* (*Iphigénie* I.ii, 187; see Mesnard III.60). Cicero writes: *suffragiis offendebatur saepe eorum voluntas,* 'their will often ran up against people's votes', *Pro Sestio*, 105. Silver Age Latin provides even more extravagant abstract circumlocutions, e.g. *ubertas lactei roris*, literally 'richness of milky dew', for 'mother's milk'.

Modern styles of address like *Your Majesty, Your Excellency* etc. have a derivation similar to that of *leur valeur* in *Bajazet* I.i, 50, in the sense that a laudatory abstraction stands for a concrete person. But a process of personification can be observed in these styles of address as in Racine's abstract formulations: they are not completely abstract expressions but are halfway to being designations of persons. We have here another of the forms of majestic language, lying somewhere between personal and official diction, not yet set in lifeless formulae but encasing the charcter's soul in an armour of abstraction and unapproachability.

Even a locality or a day can appear as the source of an action without it being implied that these mere witnesses are really responsible for the actions. It is not the day or the place that is 'to blame' for this or that, but this or that happens on a particular day, at a particular place. In the ancient world, with its local gods and its deities for each day and hour, the personification of place- and time-indications corresponded to ideas that were genuinely held; but in Racine's day such devices could only work as almost formulaic abstractions, at best as the dim reflection of an incomprehensible force of destiny.

> Qui l'eût dit qu'*un rivage* à mes vœux si funeste
> Présenterait d'abord Pylade aux yeux d'Oreste?
> *Andromaque* I.i, 5–6

> *Le jour* qui de leurs rois vit éteindre la race
> Eteignit tout le feu de leur antique audace. *Athalie* I.i, 95–6

[See also above the quotations where *Epire* and *Jourdain* are the witnesses of actions.] Racine does indeed frequently personify the forces of destiny, but in general he only hints very gently at the role of fate as an actor in the drama: its personification is almost but not entirely formalised.

> Jusqu'ici *la fortune et la victoire mêmes*
> Cachaient mes cheveux blancs sous trente diadèmes.
> *Mithridate* III.v, 1039–40

[The mythical character of these forces of fortune and victory is hinted at by *mêmes*, used just like Latin *ipsae* (cf. Rudler, p. 138).]

7. Blurring

We have already seen in the use of *soupirs, désirs* instances of the **blurring plural** of abstract nouns which allows characters to avoid precision and sharp outlines in their self-expression. The specifically Racinian plurals of *amours, fureurs, flammes* are of course well known. Here are some examples:

> N'allez point par vos pleurs déclarer *vos amours*. *Bajazet* I.iv, 411

> Je connais *mes fureurs*, je les rappelle toutes. *Phèdre* III.iii, 853

However, many other emotional states are also presented in unrestricted plurality:

> Apprend donc à son tour à souffrir *des mépris*!
> *Andromaque* II.i, 400

> . . Dissipez *ces indignes alarmes*!
> *Andromaque* II.i, 401

Dans *ses retardements* si Pyrrhus persévère . . .
Andromaque II.i, 406

In this last example, note that the simpler *retard*, which cannot be put into the vague plural, is not used. The verbal noun usually has a more concrete sense than forms in *-ment*; see Wackernagel I.99 on Latin models, e.g. use of *gaudia* for *gaudium*.

Les refus de Pyrrhus m'ont assez dégagé . . . *Andromaque* II.ii, 512

Tous mes ressentiments lui seraient asservis. *Andromaque* III.viii, 1011

N'achève enfin sur vous *ses vengeances funestes*,
Et d'un respect forcé ne dépouille les restes. *Athalie* I.i, 23–4

Where a metaphor or figurative image is used the plural attenuates the concreteness of the content; the plural of vagueness blurs the physical contour of the image. The plural in the following example raised objections in the eighteenth century:

Il n'a plus aspiré qu'à s'ouvrir *des chemins*
Pour éviter l'affront de tomber dans leurs mains.
Mithridate V.iv, 1569–70

Gonzague Truc, p. 285, puts the objection thus: 'un seul chemin tout ouvert suffisait pour éviter l'affront'. The point is that *un chemin* would be taken in its proper sense, one would *see* a way in front, whereas 'way' has here the sense of 'means'. Similarly a singular *soin* would be a too palpable care: the plural *soins* gives a particularly blurred and unlimited extension, in e.g.

Déjà, trompant *ses soins*, j'ai su vous rassembler.
Athalie IV.iii, 1344

Ses soins here means in effect 'her'. Compare the meaning of the singular:

Aurais-je perdu tout le soin de ma gloire? *Phèdre* II.v, 666

And there is the celebrated instance in *Britannicus* where plural *soins* refers to distilling a poison:

La fameuse Locuste
A redoublé pour moi ses soins officieux . . . IV.iv, 1392–3

As Truc says (p. 125), '*soins officieux* disent tout sans rien préciser et laissent dans une manière d'ombre la noire besogne'. Behind Narcisse, who says these lines, the audience can glimpse a whole crowd of obscure accomplices; the emptiness of the Racinian stage is balanced by figures we sense dimly in the shadows.

Plural *charmes* also has a less precise effect than the singular. 'Charms', usually a woman's, set us dreaming of a variety of things, whilst 'her charm' would sound too definitional. [Hugo von Hofmannsthal noted that 'the advantage of the French language is its freedom to form plurals of physical abstract nouns – *les fatigues, les vides, les noirs*' (*Das Buch der Freunde*, p. 89). Racine even used *charmes* of a man (*Bajazet* I.i, 138): physical reference is sufficiently obscured by the plural to allow this.]

The plural expressions of emotion or emotional states also reduce the character in question to the particular emotion or state mentioned. *N'allez point par vos pleurs déclarer vos amours* makes the character nothing other than the tears of love. The plural extends, so to speak, the field of tears; a single feature is enlarged at the expense of the rest of the character, which becomes at this point 'all tears'.

The blurring of contours can serve to express a modest attitude:

> De mes faibles attraits le Roi parut frappé. *Esther* I.i, 70

[Note here also the modesty of *parut*.] On the other hand, the greater the expansion and inclusiveness of the personality, the more distant it appears. The Racinian hero can wander through the halls without end of his inner palace; but no critic with any psychological training would be bold enough to claim *Nourri dans le sérail, j'en connais les détours* (*Bajazet* IV.vii, 1424). Rudler felt how in the line *D'ailleurs mille desseins partagent mes esprits* (*Mithridate* III.v, 1045), *mille* as much as *esprits* is there 'to magnify Mithridate'. I would add: as befits the nature of this cunning, inscrutable oriental diplomat.

One should add to the blurring plurals Racine's **blurring vocabulary**. Cases like *sein* or *flanc* instead of *ventre* belong here. [See Brunot IV.303; one should add to his comments the point made by Mesnard III.75, that *élevé dans son sein* is a Latinism modelled on *gremio ac sinu matris educabatur*.] However, in these kinds of expression one should not see only the 'mot noble'. Of course it is polite to be not too precise; but the vague and the imprecise are also the hallmarks of literary art focussed on the spiritual and the ideal.

Brunot has pointed out that Racine divides the words for parts of the body into two groups: the noble, which includes *bouche, bras, chair, cheveux, cœur, front, genou, gorge, joue, main, oreille, os, veine*; and the non-noble, which either disappear or are used with contempt, including *barbe, cerveau, cervelle, cuisse, dent, dos* (literal sense), *épaule, foie, jambe, mollet, nerf, peau, poitrine, poumon, ventre,* etc. It is immediately clear that apart from 'objectionable' parts of the body like *cuisse*, *ventre*, *poitrine*, those that are avoided are the ones that delimit too sharply, e.g. *dent, barbe, cerveau, peau,* or which cannot be given any 'higher' colouring. Shoulders and backs can only bend under the whip, but knees may be gracefully bent; veins are invisible, muscles are visible, so Phèdre may feel love *dans ses veines*.

Even words like *lien, hymen, courroux* (for *relation, mariage, colère*) are not just 'nobler' or 'less realistic', but also much vaguer than their corresponding normal terms. Brunot shares Victor Hugo's view (in the *Préface de Cromwell*, p. 93) that the famous *lit* in *Britannicus* IV.ii, 1137 – *Mit Claude dans mon lit et Rome à mes genoux* – is an instance of daring realism in Racine. I think that on the contrary *lit* is used here as a vaguer and more majestic expression for 'marriage' (as the Romans would say *thalamus* or *torus*). The King's Bed – an expression with a legal origin – is not the piece of furniture the middle classes hide in an alcove, but in the age of Louis XIV something as mystical and radiant as the Throne. Thus *lit* is often paired with *trône* in Racine (e.g. *A son trône, à son lit, daigna l'associer, Bajazet* II.i, 468). Nor do I agree with Brunot (IV.303) that the familiar circumlocutions of Racine 'voilent de leur noblesse l'expression exacte des objets'. When Racine writes *dans le simple appareil / D'une beauté qu'on vient d'arracher au sommeil* (*Britannicus* II.ii, 389–90) he does not exactly mean 'en chemise': first, because Roman women did not have 'chemises' of the sort worn in the seventeenth century; secondly, just as the clothing worn by Romans was not so close-fitting nor so tailored as ours, so the words used for it fitted more loosely. *Le simple appareil* is more than a chemise; it is a costume, a night-dress. The proper term, had it been used, could only have torn away the delicate veil that covers the subdued eroticism of Racine's language.

The neutral **unlimiting pronoun** *ce que*, an essentially quantitative but actually unquantified expression, gives to the ungraspable and incomprehensible both absolute clarity and complete indefiniteness. (⟶ 18, Seneca, *Medea* 567, for Latin precedents). Some examples:

> L'Epire sauvera *ce que* Troie a sauvé. *Andromaque* I.ii, 220

What is meant is in fact Astyanax.

> Il peut, seigneur, il peut, dans ce désordre extrême,
> Epouser *ce qu*'il hait et punir *ce qu*'il aime.
> *Andromaque* I.i, 121–2

These lines refer to the two women with whom Pyrrhus is involved.

People are transformed by this device into abstract and ideal properties. Expansion through this unlimiting linguistic device is particularly powerful where the subject is emotional and irrational:

> Vous pouvez sur Pyrrhus *ce que* j'ai pu sur lui.
> *Andromaque* III.iv, 876

By such non-intervention in the souls of others, by keeping their distance in this way, Racine's characters drape themselves in their own special aura of nobility. The threatening insinuations of Narcisse are hidden beneath the ambiguous euphemisms of this line:

> Mais peut-être il fera *ce que* vous n'osez faire.
>
> *Britannicus* IV.iv, 1408

[Heiss (1928) p. 671, has pointed out the 'self-betraying neuter pronoun, which Argan [in Molière's *Le Malade imaginaire*] lets slip in the quarrel in Act I, sc.v over the liberator of his daughter: *Une fille de bon naturel doit être ravie d'épouser ce qui est utile à son père*. This *ce qui* is one of Molière's most brilliant *trouvailles*. It is well prepared and, at the end of the short fuse where it explodes, it captures Argan in his entirety in a burnished mirror. The selfishness of this medically obsessed domestic despot has become so insatiable that he reduces people – the liberator and the daughter who should free herself – to things which he assesses only according to their suitability to his own health.' Molière's originality (and Heiss's excellent point) can be appreciated all the more when one realises that this comically characterising *ce qui* is a parody of the defining-impersonal *ce que* of tragedy.]

The **unlimiting *où*** also contributes to the blurring of outlines. It occurs particularly with abstract nouns that do not obviously suggest any kind of localisation or circumscribed space to which the *où* could refer; I count *cœur* of course as an abstract noun, not to be taken in its physical sense of cardiac muscle or as the red symbol of playing cards.

> Je ne viens point ici . . .
> Vous envier un cœur qui se rend à vos charmes.
> Par une main cruelle, hélas! j'ai vu percer
> *Le seul où* mes regards prétendaient s'adresser.
>
> *Andromaque* III.iv, 861–4

Certainly, *percer le cœur* has an originally concrete sense and is thus halfway to becoming a formula. That is shown by the following: the heart (the organ) cannot be seen! The verb *s'adresser*, which has low directional–local force, also prevents one from taking 'heart' in any physically visible sense, as does the uncontoured *où*, which suggests an abstract and self-enclosed sphere of the heart.

Gentleness is to be seen in the eyes of King Asuérus. Racine expresses this point in *Esther* by phrases like *avec des yeux où régnait la douceur*. One imagines a calm and even sea ruled by a stable climate of gentleness. The king also gives a token of his gentle rule:

> . . . avec des yeux où régnait la douceur:
> 'Soyez reine', dit-il; et dès ce moment même
> De sa main sur mon front posa son diadème. *Esther* I.i, 74–6

This use of *où* is not yet formulaic because *régner* is also not yet entirely a formula. Now some other borderline cases:

> . . . pour avancer *cette mort où* je cours . . .
>
> *Andromaque* II.ii, 499

That does not quite mean 'that death to which I run': death becomes here a dark realm without a frontier.

> Tous ceux qui . . .
> Des princes malheureux nourrissent les faiblesses,
> Les poussent *au penchant où* leur cœur est enclin . . .
>
> *Phèdre* IV.vi, 1321–3

Here again *penchant* has a concrete sense of 'slope' and *enclin* strengthens the image of a falling gradient; on the other hand, *enclin* is also abstract (in the sense of 'subject to') and the *où* has to be understood as an uncontoured abstract. Now some purely abstract examples:

> . . . cette mélancolie
> Où j'ai vu si longtemps votre âme ensevelie.
>
> *Andromaque* I.i, 17–18

> O toi, qui vois la honte où je suis descendue . . . *Phèdre* III.ii, 813

> Joas les touchera par sa noble pudeur,
> Où semble de son sang reluire la splendeur . . . *Athalie* I.ii, 273–4

[See also *Andromaque* IV.i, 1109; and *Andromaque* I.i, 81, II.i, 454, where unlimiting *où* follows, as is frequently the case, the blurring plural of abstract nouns.]

8. Auxiliary Verbs

To the linguistic devices which give Racine's characters their stature and majesty but at the same time attenuate their direct self-expression belong the **phraseological verbs** which allow actions to be expressed indirectly, in their psychological layering. By these verbs actions are referred back to their motives, to the modal qualities of *will, can, may, ought.* What is important in actions in Racine is not the active or dramatic element, but their psychological value, exclusively. There is a perceptible withdrawal from action-in-the-world and a retreat into inwardness. One might expect language steeped to that extent in the soul to serve an intensely lyrical self-expressivity. The opposite happens, because the verbs *savoir, vouloir, oser, daigner* have too much of a rational colouring: the attitude of Racinian characters is conditioned by acts of judgment and choice. What is heightened is the discernment, responsibility and decisiveness of the characters, not their soulfulness. A remnant of Corneille in Racine's language! (The obsolete positioning of personal pronouns before the modal with dependent infinitive underlines the formulaic quality of the phraseological verbs in Racine, e.g. *Où ma raison se va-t-elle égarer? Phèdre* IV.vi, 1264.)

The coolest of all these verbs is the majestic ***daigner***, 'to deign', originally 'to consider worthy'. [Cf. Virgil, *Aeneid* IV.192, *cui se pulchra* *viro dignetur iungere Dido*, 'whom the fair Dido deigned to take as a lover'.]

> Et votre bouche encor, muette à tant d'ennui,
> N'a pas *daigné* s'ouvrir pour se plaindre de lui?
> *Andromaque* IV.ii, 1139–40

Of course a part of the body, a mouth, does not *deign* to do anything; the mouth has here become mentalised and the action dissociated from the soul; all this serves only to clothe the addressee in the armour of majesty. In the next example, the Virgilian phrase *cui non risere parentes* ('on whom no parents smiled', i.e. 'who was an orphan'; *Eclogues* IV.62) is transformed by a Racinian *daigner* to present Eriphile's fate as her parents' fault:

> Je reçus et je vois le jour que je respire
> Sans que père ni mère ait *daigné* me sourire. *Iphigénie* II.i, 425–6

Or in *Athalie*, Eliacin

> . . . se croit quelque enfant rejeté par sa mère
> A qui j'ai par pitié *daigné* servir de père. I.ii, 183–4

Joad, the high priest who speaks these words, puts himself into what he takes to be Eliacin's thoughts, but he is himself so walled in by his own highness that he cannot grant Eliacin any other manner of thought than that he, Joad, 'deigned' to take him for his own child. *Daigner* has become nowadays in modern democratic thinking a monarchical cliché. Mesnard, in his 'Etude' (VIII.xl, note 1), feels that the *daigner* in Iphigénie's cry to her father before she is to be sacrificed, *Daignez m'ouvrir vos bras pour la dernière fois* (V.iii, 1664), is no more authentic than period costume.

Vouloir does not connote condescension but often marks the force of an explicitly regal will:

> Vous qui sans désespoir ne pouviez endurer
> Que Pyrrhus d'un regard la *voulût* honorer?
> *Andromaque* IV.ii, 1135–6

> Car on dit qu'elle seule a fixé son amour;
> Et même il a *voulu* que l'heureuse Roxane,
> Avant qu'elle eût un fils, prît le nom de Sultane.
> *Bajazet* I.i, 100–3

[See also *Andromaque* IV.v, 1288–9; *Bajazet* I.i, 104–5.] *Vouloir* can also bring an intellectual tone to a brutally physical and drastic situation:

> Je l'ai vu dans leurs mains quelque temps se débattre,
> Tout sanglant à leurs coups *vouloir* se dérober;
> Mais enfin à l'autel il est allé tomber.
> *Andromaque* V.iii, 1518–20

The act of willing is 'seen' – we are here on an intellectual plane. Phèdre, on the other hand, 'wants' the end she has chosen as punishment for the passion she has fought in full self-awareness:

> *J'ai voulu*, devant vous exposant mes remords,
> Par un chemin plus lent descendre chez les morts.
>
> *Phèdre* v.vii, 1635–6

Prétendre retains some of the sense of a legal claim. It does not express a frank and heartfelt wanting but a rationally motivated willing:

> A ma table, partout, à mes côtés assis,
> Je *prétends* vous traiter comme mon propre fils
>
> *Athalie* II.vii, 697–8

> . . . j'ai vu percer
> Le seul où mes regards *prétendaient* s'adresser.
>
> *Andromaque* III.iv, 863–4

Boastfulness belongs to heroic ceremoniousness. In the Christian milieu of Racine, where boasting would be an act of pride before God, *se vanter* + infinitive can only be used as a formula, a phrase. Such unchristian hubris thus has to be named and branded with the modal verb *oser*:

> Noble et brillant auteur d'une triste famille,
> Toi, dont ma mère *osait se vanter d'être* fille . . .
> Soleil, je te viens voir pour la dernière fois.
>
> *Phèdre* I.iii, 169–72

Oser marks the will overstepping barriers, the will that a great lord may allow himself on earth. Phèdre's tragedy is that her desires are *osés*, that she knows even whilst being a queen that her will is dangerous and daring.

> Mes fureurs au dehors ont *osé* se répandre. III.i, 741

She can feel here how her passions have escaped from her control and have 'acted' , so to speak, on their own account; she has not the courage to act in her own name, and thus Œnone, the revelation and embodiment of Phèdre's secret desires, acts for her and to imbue her with the courage of action. It is to good purpose that the diabolical plan which Œnone puts to Phèdre is pointed up by a rhythmically stressed *oser* and thereby subjected to a rational attenuation, to a *piano* effect:

> Pourquoi donc lui céder une victoire entière?
> Vous le craignez. *Osez l'accuser* la première
> Du crime dont il peut vous charger aujourd'hui.
>
> *Phèdre* III.iii, 885–7

And Phèdre, shaken, repeats: *Moi, que j'ose opprimer et noircir l'innocence*? (l.893). It must be granted of course that this use of *oser* is not merely modal and that it has a poetic value, in that the 'daring' of a particular emotion, as I said, forms the cornerstone of the tragedy. Nonetheless, in the modulation of the verb by a modal there remains a quality of indirection and attenuation that would be lost entirely in a direct, explicit imperative: *accusez-le la première*! The impression given in Racine is that everything is measured on a scale of moral values, that nothing can burst forth directly or freely.

The circumlocutory ***savoir*** has a nuance of excessive rationality, of convoluted intrigue and calculation:

> Je ne m'en cache point: l'ingrat m'*avait su plaire* . . .
> *Andromaque* IV.iii, 1193

> Pour moi, *j'ai su* déjà par mes brigues secrètes
> *Gagner* de notre loi les sacrés interprètes . . . *Bajazet* I.ii, 233–4

[Other examples: *Andromaque* IV.iii, 1234–5; *Bajazet* I.i, 92–3; I.iii, 323–4. Cf. also *Bajazet* II.i, 524 *Rentre dans le néant dont je t'ai fait sortir* for similar sense expressed without circumlocution.] This kind of speech is used not only by byzantine schemers like Acomat (in the example quoted from *Bajazet* I.ii), nor only by those made acute and devious by the force of passion (Hermione, in *Andromaque* IV.iii), but also by the lovelorn Roxane (*Bajazet* I.iii). *Savoir* suggests self-satisfaction and congratulation, it stresses one's success, performance and personal worth, and it destroys any possibility of a lyrical atmosphere. Thus *savoir* can also acquire an ironic tone when the performance is questioned:

> Voilà comme Pyrrhus vint s'offrir à ma vue;
> Voilà par quels exploits *il sut* se couronner . . .
> *Andromaque* III.viii, 1006–7

Pouvoir and its synonyms displace action into the sphere of potentiality; they turn real deeds into only possible, contemplated, less direct ones:

> Puis-je vous demander quel funeste nuage,
> Seigneur, *a pu* troubler votre auguste visage? *Phèdre* IV.ii, 1041–2

> Oui, je tiens tout de vous; et *j'avais lieu de* croire
> Que c'était pour vous-même une assez grande gloire . . .
> *Bajazet* II.i, 513–14

> Je n'ai point oublié quelle reconnaissance,
> Seigneur, *m'a dû* ranger sous votre obéissance.
> *Mithridate* IV.iv, 1323–4

With *devoir*, Monime, in the last example, stresses not only her own gratitude and submission towards Mithridate but also the *necessity* for her to be grateful and submissive; her emotion is not as it were entirely in her own name but is a semi-detached property, so to speak. This manner of speech is as polite as it is cold – indeed, Monime wants to 'cool down' Mithridate and reject his advances.

Finally, ***aller* + infinitive** gives the dependent verb fuller meaning by making it less automatic. We have already seen this passage from *Andromaque:*

> Je l'ai vu dans leurs mains quelque temps se débattre,
> Tout sanglant à leurs coups vouloir se dérober;
> Mais enfin à l'autel *il est allé tomber.* v.iii, 1518–20

Il est tombé would have given the event as taking place; *il est allé tomber* makes the action more striking and urgent, but also less direct. In it we hear as it were not a corpse falling to the ground, but the falling logic of a predictable sequence ('he wanted to break free but finally he had to fall'); it is an attenuation and a modulation of the overdramatic. Another instance:

> Vous veniez de mon front observer la pâleur,
> Pour *aller* dans ses bras *rire* de ma douleur.
> *Andromaque* IV.v, 1327–8

Without *aller* the vulgar and heartless conduct that is denounced in these lines would remain uncriticised; the speaker's judgment is contained in the *aller* which enters into the depths of a hostile soul. *Aller* is of course a verb that expresses physical movement, but in Racine it is reduced to an intellectual–automatic sense; and in the gap between the original physical sense and the intellectual there is space for the play of meaning. In the next example, phraseological *aller* becomes the incarnation of bodily movement:

> Je ne te retiens plus, sauve-toi de ces lieux;
> *Va* lui jurer la foi que tu m'avais jurée;
> *Va* profaner des dieux la majesté sacrée . . .
> Porte aux pieds des autels ce cœur qui m'abandonne;
> *Va, cours*; mais crains encor d'y trouver Hermione.
> *Andromaque* IV.v, 1380–6

Va jurer, va profaner are ironic exhortations to swear and profanate, but the *va* which rises to *cours* has the meaning 'go away', 'get out of my sight', already prepared by the nobler form, *sauve-toi de ces lieux*; Hermione demands here a passionately desired direct action. Cf. in Malherbe's 'Ode au roi Louis XIII allant châtier les Rochelois', *Marche, va les détruire* . . . There is an example of the reverse process in *Andromaque* II.v, where the verb of movement has the sense of a spiritual wager:

> PYRRHUS: Retournons-y. Je veux la braver à sa vue . . .
> *Allons.*

PHŒNIX: *Allez*, seigneur, vous jeter à ses pieds;
Allez, en lui jurant que votre âme l'adore,
A de nouveaux mépris l'encourager encore. 677–82

The innocent *allons*, 'let's go', of the first speaker is returned with crushing irony by the confidant. By restoring on occasion the original sense to words in moments of high passion, Racine keeps the formula free from stylistic sclerosis.

I should add remarks here on the circumlocution with ***voir***. Instead of saying *j'ai / il a fait*, Racine often puts *tu m'as / il m'a vu faire*. The speaker gives his or another's experience or action not directly as an experience or action of the self (of the other) but as it is seen by or reflected in the mind of a hearer. It is an expressive device which is admittedly social, highly suited to dialogue (it involves the hearer in the speaker's language), and occasionally rhetorically and persuasively effective through its appeal to the hearer's testimony; but on the other hand it is an attenuation and puts a *piano* on the personal experience of life.

Tu vis naître ma flamme et mes premiers soupirs . . .
Tu vis mon désespoir; et *tu m'as vu* depuis
Traîner de mers en mers ma chaîne et mes ennuis.
Andromaque I.i, 40, 43–4

The repetition of *voir* indicates the importance placed by the speaker on his hearer's testimony. *Voir* does not have here quite the sense of physical seeing, but means something like 'experience', or rather it is halfway from 'seeing' to 'knowing'. [Perhaps one might mention here the well-known French predisposition to eidetic or visual presentation, as in *Je ne vois pas Monsieur X faisant cette conférence*, 'I can't imagine X . . .'; it is probably based on Latin constructions, e.g. Caesar, *suos fugere et concidi videbat,* 'he saw his own men fleeing and being slain', *Bellum civile*, 2.34.]
Here are some examples in first-person report:

J'ai vu mon père mort et nos murs embrasés;
J'ai vu trancher les jours de ma famille entière,
Et mon époux sanglant traîné sur la poussière,
Son fils seul avec moi, réservé pour les fers.
Andromaque III.vi, 928–31

J'ai vu, Seigneur, *j'ai vu* votre malheureux fils
Traîné par les chevaux que sa main a nourris *Phèdre* V.vi, 1547–8

It is even here not possible to imagine Hector or Hippolyte bleeding and rolling in the dust, and so the repeated *j'ai vu* suggests something like 'that is what my eyes had to see', 'that is what I learnt'. Compare these with *Phèdre* V.vi, 1542–3:

. . . L'intrépide Hippolyte
Voit voler en éclats tout son char fracassé . . .

But *voir*, like *aller*, can also be very formulaic, serving perhaps only to highlight the exceptional nature of the action:

Mais je l'ai *vue* enfin me confier ses larmes.
Andromaque I.i, 129

Racine's *voir* is neither entirely concrete nor entirely mental, and in this sense it is perfectly characteristic of an art that is neither coarsely material nor entirely devoid of physicality. Let us now look at some further instances:

Et là *vous me verrez*, soumis ou furieux,
Vous couronner, Madame, ou le perdre à vos yeux.
Andromaque III.vii, 975–6

Vous les verrez, soumis, rapporter dans Byzance
L'exemple d'une aveugle et basse obéissance. *Bajazet* I.i, 61–2

There is something passive, almost stoical, in the special force of this *voir*, 'to know by seeing': man becomes a spectator of his own fate. It is not surprising that *voir* tends to occur in the place of passive constructions:

Il a pour tout le sexe une haine fatale.
Je ne me verrai point préférer de rivale. *Phèdre* III.i, 789–90

That is to say, 'no rival will be preferred to me'.

. . . Ah! Seigneur, vous entendiez assez
Des soupirs qui craignaient de *se voir* repoussés.
Andromaque III.vi, 911–12

De se voir repoussés = *d'être repoussés*; *se voir*, used of sighs, effects a personification of the sighs;⟶ 25. This avoids the lifelessness of the passive. The act of seeing can itself be made passive, but not lifeless, when used in this way:

Mais de ce souvenir mon âme possédée
A deux fois en dormant revu la même idée;
Deux fois mes tristes yeux *se sont vu retracer*
Ce même enfant toujours tout prêt à me percer.
Athalie II.v, 519–22

One might also say that *voir* is an appropriate construction for a work destined for the theatre, a work to be seen; Racine's language often alludes to the spectacle which his plays offer–*Montrer aux nations Mithridate détruit*, etc.,⟶ 21.

It is often hard to say whether personification or formalisation is the predominant effect:

Hermione elle-même *a vu* plus de cent fois
Cet amant irrité revenir sous ses lois . . .

Andromaque I.i, 115–16

Grammatically, Hermione is the subject, although emotionally she is the object or destination of the return of her lover. Cf. similar usage in *Andromaque* I.i, 123–4. Often, *voir* introduces a wider circle of witnesses to express a mood:

. . . *la Grèce* avec douleur
Vous voit du sang troyen relever le malheur . . .

Andromaque I.ii, 151–2

Pensez-vous avoir seul éprouvé des alarmes?
Que *l'Epire* jamais n'*ait vu* couler mes larmes?

Andromaque II.ii, 525–6

The 'spectacle' may be explicitly mentioned:

N'est-ce pas à vos yeux un spectacle assez doux
Que la veuve d'Hector pleurante à vos genoux?

Andromaque III.iv, 859–60

I find this use of *entendre*, 'to hear', in *Phèdre* parallel to the construction with *voir*:

Respectez votre sang, j'ose vous en prier.
Sauvez-moi de l'horreur de l'*entendre* crier . . . IV.iv, 1171–2

The biblical sentence *Vox sanguinis fratris tui clamat ad me de terra*, 'The voice of thy brother's blood crieth unto me from the ground' (Genesis IV.10; see Des Hons, p. 180) must have undergone its transformation in the personality of the speaker, Phèdre. [Perhaps Racine's pleonastic *voir* is an imitation of the Ciceronian *videri* ('to be seen') in the subordinate clause, e.g. *restat ut de imperatore ad id bellum deligendo . . . dicendum esse videatur,* 'it remains that it is seen to be necessary to speak about the choice of a commander for this war . . .', *De Imperio Pompei* 27. See Laurand, II. 191.]

This is where the periphrastic expression of the verb should be mentioned, for example the use of *porter ses pas* instead of *aller*, corresponding to the Latin *vestigia* (*gressus*) *ferre* (cf. Mesnard, p. xxxviii). Walking is replaced by majestic stepping; the more dignified it becomes, the less obviously is it walking, as in the German *die Schritte lenken*, 'to direct one's steps' – as if the steps had to obey a command from the brain: an essentially cerebral expression of a cerebral attitude. As early as the eighteenth century, Moncrif offered this construction as an example of the monstrosities of classical style: *Cet exemple de cruauté alla porter la terreur dans tous les esprits*, instead of *cette cruauté terrifia tous les espirits* (quoted in Boulenger–Thérive, p. 165). As this example shows, circumlocutions with *aller* avoiding a direct transitive verb always suggest an aversion to violent action and active effects, and are characterised by locational imprecision.

9. Evaluating Terms

The modal verbs accompanying the effective verb of action are value-judgments of the latter; that is to say, action subordinated to e.g. an obligation, will, wager, claim etc. is, in the moment of its enunciation, already ranked on a psychological scale of values, already evaluated. Such modal verbs thus attenuate the lyrical force of the expression. The same effect of 'cooling' or *piano* can be achieved by the **adjectives and adverbs of value** which give a moral judgment of general validity on the thing or action thus qualified, and tend to rob the characters' speech of personal impulsion; through such value-terms characters refer beyond themselves to a trans-subjective scale of values.

> Déjà pour satisfaire à votre *juste* crainte
> J'ai couru les deux mers . . . *Phèdre* I.i, 9–10

With ***juste***, the speaker Théramène certainly pays due respect to Hippolyte's apprehension, but in its generalised validity *juste* also kills off all the lyrical force of *crainte*. [A. Schmidt has pointed out that the *à* contributes as much as *juste* to the glorification and personification of *crainte*.] The moral viewpoint endangers the aesthetic efficacy of this sentence – or rather, the aesthetic effect contains a moral component.

The word *juste* is characteristic of an age that considered itself unproblematically stable and able to distinguish the right and the just from the wrong and the unjust. Later on phrases like *une juste hyménée* were to be criticised (Mesnard, p. xxxvii). It is characteristic of French attitudes to stability that Anatole France, a writer confident and conscious of his nationality to the extent of adopting his nom-de-plume, read Racine almost every day in order to find 'le secret des justes pensées et des paroles limpides' (Des Hons). So there *are* 'right' thoughts!

The external reference of *juste* is even more marked when a dramatic character uses it of himself or herself:

> J'ai conçu pour mon crime une *juste* terreur . . . *Phèdre* I.iii, 307

Juste serves here to seal off the power of terror and to switch it onto a moral track: all the danger of that dramatic, elemental force disappears. Similarly, in Phèdre's words to Hippolyte in II.v:

> Je tremble que sur lui votre *juste* colère
> Ne poursuive bientôt une odieuse mère. 593–4

Cf. *Bajazet* IV.iv, 1245–6:

> Dans ma *juste* fureur, observant le perfide,
> Je saurai le surprendre avec son Atalide . . .

Avec sujet has the same meaning and the same effect:

> je plains *avec sujet*
> Des cœurs dont les bontés, trop mal récompensées,
> M'avaient pris pour objet de toutes leurs pensées.
> *Bajazet* II.iii, 616–18

Anger is softened and de-poeticised by the acknowledgment of its legitimacy.

> C'est moi, prince, c'est moi dont l'*utile* secours
> Vous eût du labyrinthe enseigné les détours. *Phèdre* II.v, 655–6

In describing her help as 'useful' Phèdre is not showing her amour-propre but giving her speech a stable moral ground to counterbalance the extreme and all too personal nature of what she is saying. Compare the effect of the adjective *heureuse* in the sense of 'opportune' when coupled with *audace*, 'boldness':

> Et vous avez montré, par une *heureuse audace*,
> Que le fils seul d'Achille a pu remplir sa place.
> *Andromaque* I.ii, 149–50

In the next example from *Phèdre*, Hippolyte is certainly giving his own moral judgment of his life up to that point, but the quantity of morally evaluative epithets used acts as a counterweight to his self-expression: the self-condemnation is so substantial that it seems that Hippolyte is looking at himself from above, or that the poet is speaking through him:

> Assez dans les forêts mon *oisive* jeunesse
> Sur de *vils* ennemis a montré son adresse.
> Ne pourrai-je, en fuyant un *indigne* repos,
> D'un sang plus glorieux teindre mes javelots? III.v, 933–6

> D'un mensonge si noir *justement* irrité,
> Je devrais faire ici parler la vérité . . . IV.ii, 1087–8

If the objectivising adjective (and the *un* and the *si* as well!) were left out of the last example, the line would be more 'felt': *Du noir mensonge irrité* . . . Obviously the adverb performs for the verb the same filling-out function that the adjective has for the noun, e.g. in *Bajazet* I.ii, 244, [*un bruit*] / *Fait croire heureusement à ce peuple alarmé*. Let us now consider these lines from *Athalie*:

> Du Dieu que j'ai quitté l'*importune* mémoire
> Jette encore en mon âme un reste de terreur;
> Et c'est ce qui redouble et nourrit ma fureur. III.iii, 956–8

Racine makes Mathan explain his rage by his awareness of a suppressed (today we should say: repressed) fear. In fact this self-characterisation expresses the poet's view of Mathan, and so the word *importune* is an instance of objective exposition. Racine forces the view upon his reader that Mathan is hostile to the Jewish God only because the memory of his renunciation of that faith 'importunes' him.

In Racine the word ***triste*** also carries a value-judgment. Rudler, p. 136, quotes the entry from the *Dictionnaire de l'Académie*: 'TRISTE. Se dit aussi pour dire petit, léger, médiocre, peu considérable.' An example:

> C'est faire à vos beautés un *triste* sacrifice . . .
>
> *Mithridate* III.v, 1036

Racine uses Homeric ***epitheta ornantia*** (Homeric epithets;⟶ 17). They give an aesthetic elevation to the work as a whole and have an epic rather than a dramatic effect – e.g. *déplorable*, which Anatole France translated back into Latin as *tristis Orestes* (cf. Des Hons, p. 242). Now Brunot sees the Homeric epithets of the French classical period as a stylistic failure, and his attitude derives very obviously from the preference of nineteenth-century stylisticians for the *épithète rare*. These linguistic impressionists, however, aimed to reproduce the particular effect made by a particular object, not to impose a unified order upon material things. According to Brunot, the adjectives of even the greatest French classical writers are 'cold' and 'banal':

> 'Son *heureuse* fécondité', dit Bossuet, 'redoublait tous les jours les sacrés liens de leur amour mutuelle . . .' La périphrase est déjà un peu noble pour dire que 'tous les ans' sinon 'tous les jours' il leur naissait un enfant! mais elle était nécessaire. Soit. Les mots *heureuse* et *sacrés* ne la relèvent guère, même si on donne au premier son sens latin, au second sa valeur religieuse. Dans *Esther*, dans *Athalie*, si on rencontre de-ci de-là quelques adjectifs évocateurs, la plupart du temps on peut annoncer, avant de les avoir entendus, ceux que les substantifs traîneront par la main . . . Il convient de reconnaître dans ces faiblesses moins une négligence des auteurs qu'un effect des théories qui n'avaient cesse de réduire le vocabulaire.
>
> Quoi qu'il en soit, en pleins chefs-d'œuvre, il nous faut, à nous, un réel effort pour nous accommoder de ce vocabulaire pauvre, stérile, où les mêmes expressions, les mêmes ornements surtout sont répétées à satiété. (Brunot, IV.2.261)

Brunot really sees as a 'weakness' what a Racine or a Bossuet would have seen as a strength. The classical poets sought not striking effects but an even elevation of style. It was as if the entire stage was to be raised a level by the elevation of the tragic vocabulary: *colère* becomes *courroux, mariage* becomes *hymen, chien* becomes *chien dévorant* and *fécondité* is raised to *heureuse fécondité*. It is no coincidence that Brunot can find *two* style-raising effects in a single sentence from Bossuet, nor is it a coincidence that he finds them used to describe a queen, that is to say a person who for Bossuet was not quite the same as an ordinary mortal. The repetition of the same epithet is no more objectionable to a seventeenth-century author than the repetition of *Your Majesty* was until recently for us* in letters written to a reigning monarch. The colourlessness of the epithets goes well with majesty: majesty calls for calm, rather than impact, for permanence, rather than brilliance. We can no longer write like that if only because we have lost the spiritual category of majesty.

Brunot himself raises the point that the epithets of the classics are mostly of a psychological variety (cf. Bossuet's description of the battle of Rocroi in the *Oraison funèbre du prince de Condé*). But why then does he criticise the 'nakedness and negativity' of *Hippolyte étendu, sans forme et sans couleur* – the description of Hippolyte's corpse after his accidental death in *Phèdre* v.vi – when all of Théramène's interest, and all of ours, is in Hippolyte's bride Aricie, and in the way she reacts to his death?

> *Elle* approche: *elle* voit l'herbe rouge et fumante;
> *Elle* voit (quel objet pour les yeux d'une amante!)
> Hippolyte étendu, sans forme et sans couleur.
> *Elle* veut quelque temps douter de son malheur;
> Et ne connaissant plus ce héros qu'*elle* adore,
> *Elle* voit Hippolyte, et le demande encore.
> Mais trop sûre à la fin qu'il est devant ses yeux,
> Par un triste regard *elle* accuse les Dieux,
> Et froide, gémissante, et presque inanimée,
> Aux pieds de son amant *elle* tombe pâmée. 1577–86

What is portrayed is not the impression that the corpse would make on anyone, or on us, but the impression it makes on Aricie: shapelessness and colourlessness are the details seen by Aricie alone, it is they that convince her that the man she thought to be alive is dead. Racine is concerned with the psychological and not, as Zola might have been, with the visual image of a corpse. The corpse is seen through Aricie's (and Racine's) temperament, not through Zola's. One can thus only make a criticism out of the intellectual set of Racine's vocabulary if one rejects the whole literary output of a society 'dont la littérature était', in Brunot's own words, 'toute d'observation intérieure et de fine analyse'. But what sense can there be in accepting the clear and simple syntax and the somewhat monotonous verse-forms of the French classics, whilst rejecting the vocabulary chosen by these writers, as Brunot seems to do (p. 622)? One could just as easily wish for more turbulent syntax and

* Spitzer's native Austria became a republic in 1920; Germany lost its Kaiser in 1919.

verse-forms (for a German that would actually be more natural): there would be nothing particularly natural or logical in having a wilder stream of words rushing down a regular syntactic bed, as in Victor Hugo.

In Giraudoux's *Siegfried von Kleist* the word *ravissant* (as in e.g. *la main ravissante* of a woman) is the only thing that Siegfried has rescued from his French existence in his new German life, and it is supposed to harmonise also with Goethe's use of language (of *reizend*?):

C'est le type de l'épithète banale, commode, presque vulgaire, mais il est ma famille, mon passé . . . Des gens le disent parfois le soir sans s'en douter dans la rue. Pour moi ils jonglent avec des flammes. (Giraudoux, *Siegfried*, pp. 99, 100)

The scholar can confirm the poet's observation, for it goes to the heart of the French use of the epithet to damp down the flames of irrationality. With its line of descent from the language of the mystics and its recoinage as a term of sociability and likeableness, *ravissant* does make play of chaotic–destructive forces, and 'juggles with flames'.

Racine's Homeric epithets create a stable order hovering over his characters (not produced by them), an order in which particular attributes are consistently paired with particular things or beings. In this world there is for example an unbreakable connection between the leader and his friendliness: *Je me laissais conduire à cet aimable guide* (*Iphigénie* II.i, 501). In the ideal world of Racine's language there are no unfriendly guides.

Brunot argues that Racine did not dare to use the word *chien* on its own without 'softening' it with an epithet, and quoted the well-known passage from *Athalie* II.v to prove it (though here the epithet seems in fact to have more of a heightening effect):

. . . des membres affreux
Que des chiens dévorants se disputaient entre eux. 505–6

But we also find this:

Les chiens, à qui son bras a livré Jézabel . . .
Déjà sont à ta porte . . . *Athalie* III.v, 1038–40

So the *dévorants* of II.v becomes the elevation of the intrinsically admissible term *chiens*; the epithet is the means of relating things and beings to a higher plane of existence. Here is a similar case from *Athalie* II.v, referring to a dream:

Moi-même quelque temps, honteuse de ma peur,
Je l'ai pris pour l'effet d'une sombre vapeur. 517–18

It is true that here *vapeur* on its own, a term in vogue for describing bodily conditions (cf. Boileau, *Le Lutrin* IV.40, 'Girot . . . / Nomme sa vision l'effet d'une vapeur'), would have been inadmissible. And

Roxane, in *Bajazet* IV.v, can only describe a hangman's noose in the following manner:

> ces *nœuds infortunés*
> Par qui de ses pareils les jours sont terminés. 1279–80

The word *infortunés* when transferred to an object does make the object more animated. One should perhaps consider the circumlocutions applied to concrete objects not as instances of preciosity and artifice; the periphrasis *nœuds infortunés* fits Roxane's vengeance-speech extremely well, as Lytton Strachey has shown (p. 23).

Avantage is a word belonging to both the moral and the commercial spheres; qualified by *noble*, it becomes unambiguously attributable to the former.

> Et mon front, dépouillé d'un si *noble avantage* . . .
> *Mithridate* III.v, 1043

[Cf. *Bajazet* I.i, 117, *la noble expérience*; II.i, 449. *le nœud sacré d'un heureux hyménée.*] These are pieces of adjectival padding and rounding-off, but they do also ennoble the tone of pathetic discourse; through them, all phenomena are coloured either black or white. Moral good and evil are foregrounded even when the context leaves no doubt possible about the value-judgment:

> Mathan, de nos autels *infâme* déserteur
> Et de toute vertu *zélé* persécuteur. *Athalie* I.i, 37–8

> Je reconnus Vénus et ses feux *redoutables*
> D'un sang qu'elle poursuit tourments inévitables!
> *Phèdre* I.iii, 277–8

> Moi seule, j'ai tissu le lien *malheureux*
> Dont tu viens d'éprouver les *détestables* nœuds.
> *Bajazet* V.xii, 1731–2

The metaphors contained in the accompanying nouns are entirely divested of concrete suggestiveness by the morally evaluative adjectives, e.g. above, *redoutables feux, détestables nœuds*. Even when the adjectives themselves have a poetic ring (like *funeste, redoutable*), their evaluative use attenuates and silences all passion: a word like *extrême*, which designates something as extreme after all, has a quite remarkable ability to produce an effect that is the opposite of 'extreme'. The fact that a thing is named as being 'on the limit' shows that the speaker is calm enough to have a table of measurement in his mind; 'extreme' is not a word of primary emotion, but a term of calm, and one which thus communicates calm. It is characteristic that Racine often pairs *extrême* with *désordre* because he composes on the basis of a position of calm, of *ordre*, and banishes disorder by naming it:

Il peut, Seigneur, il peut, dans ce *désordre extrême*,
Epouser ce qu'il hait et punir ce qu'il aime.

Andromaque I.i, 121–2

Cf. *Bajazet* II.iii, 633 for a similar case. Also with *funeste*:

Et venais vous conter ce *désordre funeste*. *Athalie* II.ii, 420

Perhaps the everyday word *désordre* is ennobled and poeticised by the epithets *extrême, funeste. Extrême* is frequently attracted to nouns of emotion, where it exorcises all *extremidades* of feeling, as one says in Spanish; it becomes in such usages a formula for pathos.

Modérez donc, Seigneur, cette fureur *extrême*.

Andromaque III.i, 709

Seigneur, qu'ai-je entendu? quelle surprise *extrême*!

Bajazet II.iii, 573

Danger appears less dangerous when described as *extreme* danger:

Quoi? vous pouvez vous taire en ce péril *extrême*?

Phèdre V.i, 1329

'Extreme' signifies excess, overload. It will now be no surprise to find in Racine excess reduced to reasonable measure by an explicit *trop*:

Roxane . . .
Ne put voir sans amour ce héros *trop* aimable . . .

Bajazet I.iv, 367–9

The meaning is admittedly something like 'this hero too lovable [for her not to fall in love with him]', but *trop* has here also a socially oriented connotation of reasonable measurement which downgrades the heroic in favour of the *aimable*. Even more sociable and polite is where a character himself says 'too much' and uses an explicit *trop* to highlight the extent of his performance or sensibility:

Et soudain à leurs yeux je me suis dérobé:
Trop heureux d'avoir pu, par un récit fidèle,
De leur paix, en passant, vous conter la nouvelle . . .

Bajazet III.ii, 896–8

Trop here marks the courtliness and affability of a messenger: 'I am only too happy to announce . . .' Similar uses of *trop* as a formula for stressing excessive devotion to duty:

Et c'est moi, qui, du sien ministre *trop fidèle,*
Semble depuis six mois ne veiller que pour elle . . .

Bajazet IV.iv, 1213–14

Tu vois combien son cœur, prêt à le protéger
A retenu mon bras *trop prompt* à la venger? *Bajazet* IV.viii, 1407–8

In fact this use of *trop* (familiar enough in common expression of politeness like *vous êtres trop aimable*) should perhaps have been dealt with in the section on the formal use of *si* and *tant* above. In the next example, *trop* could perfectly well be replaced by formal *si*:

> Tandis qu'à mes périls Atalide sensible,
> Et *trop digne* du sang qui lui donna le jour
> Veut me sacrifier jusques à son amour? *Bajazet* II.v, 722–4

A descendant cannot after all be really 'too' worthy of his forefathers. The measurement and measuredness of the adverb *trop* has a rather icy effect.

Racine can also give depth to formal language. In the next set of examples, *trop* can be glossed as 'unfortunately all too . . .' (cf. *hélas! trop véritable*), that is to say the adverb contains a restrained protest at what is being told, at the order of the world, and this repressed sob does in the end produce a 'lyrical' effect:

> Lui montrer à la fois, et l'ordre de son frère,
> Et de sa trahison ce gage *trop sincère.* *Bajazet* IV.v, 1317–18

(The *gage* is a letter.)

> . . . pardonnez aux larmes
> Que m'arrachent pour vous de *trop justes* alarmes.
> *Athalie* IV.iii, 1385–6

> Je tremble qu'un discours, hélas! *trop véritable*,
> Un jour ne leur reproche une mère coupable. *Phèdre* III.iii, 865–6

[Cf. also *Andromaque* I.ii, 226, *Il a par trop de sang acheté leur colère*. Note that here *trop* is associated with a verb of 'measurement', *acheter*, just as *vendre cher* is a verb of measurement in e.g. *Bajazet* IV.i, 1443; cf. also IV.v, 1328, *Me payer les plaisirs que je leur ai prêtés*. These terms are certainly *précieux* (transference of commercial terminology, elsewhere of military and hunting terms) and have a peculiarly attenuating effect. 'Ce sont souvent les scènes d'ironie, si fréquentes dans les tragédies de Racine, qui les amènent et font passer', wrote Marty-Laveaux of these and similar expressions (*Lexique*, p. xiv).]

Racine is also able to rob the other evaluative adjectives of their stabilising function in two different ways. The first is by applying these epithets of stability to intended actions, where in the moment of utterance the epithets are not yet applicable; they would only be applicable were the action or event to take place, and the notional assumption of the *fait accompli* makes the epithet sound somewhat unreal. For example:

> Et même il a voulu que l'*heureuse Roxane*
> Avant qu'elle eût un fils, prît le nom de Sultane.
> *Bajazet* I.i, 101–2

Now in the speaker's view Roxane only deserves the description *heureuse* after the decision of the Sultan, which is what is being reported here.

> Et moi-même, à mon tour, je me verrais lié?
> Et les dieux jusque-là m'auraient humilié?
> Dans mes *lâches* soupirs d'autant plus méprisable . . .
> Ne souviendrait-il plus à mes sens *égarés*
> De l'obstacle éternel qui nous a séparés? *Phèdre* I.i, 95–104

The whole sentence is in the conditional – Hippolyte still does not believe he is caught in the net of love. The description of himself as a 'coward', as 'lost' (*lâches, égarés*) would be appropriate only if the presupposition of his being 'caught by love' were correct; yet even at the moment of utterance these epithets of condemnation cast around themselves a deep spell of moral judgment.

> Ne pense pas qu'au moment que je t'aime,
> Innocente à mes yeux, je m'approuve moi-même,
> Ni que du fol amour qui trouble ma raison
> Ma *lâche complaisance* ait nourri le poison. *Phèdre* II.v, 673–6

Phèdre actually show no 'lâche complaisance' towards herself, yet her moral self-criticism is carried here so far as to make cowardice thinkable.

> On craint que de la sœur les flammes *téméraires*
> Ne raniment un jour la cendre de ses frères.
> *Phèdre* II.i, 429–30

Téméraires is not yet true as it is said, since Aricie is speaking here; it is she who is the sister of six brothers and who might find in her lover an avenger for them. *Téméraires* is thus spoken by Aricie on behalf of her enemies who fear her: it is a kind of free indirect or semi-reported thought, and it stands on the same level of discourse as *ne raniment.* Aricie's full meaning is 'they fear: let not one day the "daring" love – as they would say – etc.'. The evaluating adjective has its stabilising effect somewhat undermined by its being conceived as a supposition and by empathy.

One could also consider such adjectives as a kind of consecutive-proleptic device: *les flammes téméraires* are 'the flames which would then deserve to be called daring'. The judging and interpreting speaker inserts him- or herself in advance into the understanding the hearer must acquire. Victor Hugo made fun of this line from *Iphigénie*:

> et la rame inutile
> Fatigua vainement une mer immobile. I.i, 49–50

'C'est justement quand la mer est immobile que la rame est utile', he objected (quoted by Mesnard, p. xliii). But he mistook *inutile* for a Homeric epithet, whereas it is what I call a consecutive-proleptic adjective, a presupposition of a consequence – 'the oar which [by being rowed in vain] becomes useless'. Victor Hugo reacted against the underlying tone of judgment in this expression.

The second way in which objectivising epithets can be given new life by Racine is by the idealisation of objects. I shall mention just two famous lines from *Phèdre*. First:

> Que ces vains ornements, que ces voiles me pèsent! I.iii, 158

It is always pointed out how Racine empathises here with his heroine, down to her physical sensations – especially in the following couplet where even the burden of her coiffure is described:

> Quelle importune main, en formant tous ces nœuds,
> A pris soin sur mon front d'assembler mes cheveux? 159–60

However, it seems to me that it is not a physical notation, but much more clearly an idealisation of feminine ornaments into an immaterial veil (*voiles*) and indeed a condemnation of ornament from the point of view of the vanity of earthly things: *vain* is a very moral epithet for a woman's dress! Dust is idealised in a similar fashion in I.iii:

> Quand pourrai-je, au travers d'une *noble poussière*,
> Suivre de l'œil un char fuyant dans la carrière? 177–8

What is meant is 'the dust in which the noble charioteer can prove himself [to be noble]' and the device used is an archaising **hypallage**. Other instances from *Phèdre* of this rhetorical figure (reversal of the natural relation of two elements):

> . . . respecte Thésée.
> De ses *jeunes erreurs* désormais revenu . . . I.i, 22–3

> Implacable ennemi des *amoureuses lois* . . . I.i, 59

> Et s'est montré vivant aux *infernales ombres* . . . II.i, 386

Just as *jeunes erreurs* makes the errors seem more youthful, more human then e.g. the literal expression *erreurs de la jeunesse,* so in *noble poussière* the word 'dust' is made to seem something which like man is subject to a moral scale of values. Anatole France explained why Phèdre's *J'ai voulu . . . Par un chemin plus lent descendre chez les morts* (V.vii, 1636) produces its peaceful effect:

> Tout ce charme venait du mot *lent*, qui donnait au chemin des morts une sorte de vie mystérieuse, insaisissable, profonde. Il y a en poésie de grandes beautés qui sont en même temps des beautés délicates. (Quoted in Des Hons, p. 117)

The same kind of animation, that is to say the attribution of animate adjectives to otherwise inanimate nouns, occurs with those expressions like *peuple adorateur* (*Bérénice* I,iii, 53), *parricides mains* (*Thébaïde* IV.iii, 1201), *fille meurtrière* (*Athalie* IV.iii, 1329) which stand on the borderline between noun and adjective and which could be termed *substantivoids** or *quasi-nouns* (based on the type of Latin usage in *exercitus victor* 'the victorious' or 'the victors' army'). These quasi-nouns have an effect as synthetic and concise as abbreviations of sentences: 'the people who pray' ⟶ 'the adoration-people'. The quasi-noun *parricides mains* has a particularly condensed effect as the word-order (adjective + noun) relegates the epithet to the class of banal adjectives.

A similarly subterranean animation of external objects occurs also in *des routes toutes prêtes* (*Mithridate* II.iv, 560) or *D'un camp prêt à partir vous entendez les cris* (ibid. III.v, 1046). The camp is half a tented field, half a living army; the roads have become travellers. Cf. Virgil, *Georgics* III.249, *heu! male tum Libyae solis erratus in agris*, 'Woe betide him who gets lost in Libya's lonely fields', quoted in Meillet, *Esquisse*, p. 224.

10. Figures of Contrast

If the judgment that underlies the evaluative epithets destroys the lyrical immediacy of the expression of emotion, then the *piano* of moral evaluation reaches a *pianissimo* when the judgment underlying the epithet is unexpected because it does not normally go with the noun in question – that is to say, when we have one of Racine's frequent oxymorons. Notwithstanding the wit and surprise-effect that they have, they betray the disengagement of the speaker from the content of his speech. Lucidity and wit are not qualities of language bursting out from passionate feelings. Note that couplings of noun + adjective with contradictory meanings constitute a particularly effective way of stressing a point frequently used by Racine, e.g. *Faisons de sa ruine une juste conquête* (*Andromaque* IV.iii, 1181); *Mes malheurs font encor toute ma renommée* (*Bajazet* II.i, 482). A comparable figure is the use of two contradictory adjectives, e.g. *Britannicus* I.i:

> Et que, derrière un voile, *invisible et présente*,
> J'étais de ce grand corps l'âme toute-puissante. 95–6

The more obvious it is made to seem, the more cutting the oxymoron, just as a striking claim is the more effective for being made in an imperturbably calm voice.

> Oui, je bénis, Seigneur, l'*heureuse cruauté* . . .
> *Andromaque* II.v, 643

Here it is the confidant who has the ability to make such a strikingly

* Spitzer's term.

unruffled evaluation of cruelty; but Andromaque herself uses the same kind of language:

> Voilà de mon amour l'*innocent stratagème* . . . IV.i, 1097

This aperçu might be expected to come from someone in judgment on Andromaque rather than from the loving subject herself. The notation here is still a personal one; inevitably, though, it spreads out into a general sentence: *l'amour se sert d'innocents stratagèmes*. And that often happens:

> Conduisez ou suivez une *fureur si belle* . . .
> *Andromaque* IV.iii, 1229

> Voilà de ton amour le *détestable fruit* . . .
> *Andromaque* V.iii, 1555

> Il me laisse exercer un *pouvoir inutile*. *Bajazet* I.i, 90

> Peut-être je saurai, dans ce désordre extrême,
> Par un *beau désespoir* me secourir moi-même . . .
> *Bajazet* II.iii, 633–4

'Beautiful despair' sounds like play-acting, self-dramatisation, exhibitionism (or, as Erich Auerbach would say, the aristocratic cult of emotion), but it was surely meant by Racine (who is here transposing l. 1022 of Corneille's *Horace, Ou qu'un beau désespoir alors le secourût*) as an objective evaluation: a beautiful, as it were a Roman despair, leading to heroic deeds.

> Vos pleurs vous trahiraient: cachez-les à ses yeux;
> Et ne prolongez point de *dangereux adieux*.
> *Bajazet* II.v, 675–6

A complex state of affairs is compressed here into *dangereux adieux*, its surprising word-order emphasising the inappropriateness of a tender farewell in the prevailing situation.

There is a great number of other examples that could be quoted: *funeste soin* (*Bajazet* III.i, 839); *funeste plaisir* (*Phèdre* IV.vi, 1248); *tranquille fureur* (*Bajazet* IV.v, 1276); *orgueilleuse faiblesse* (*Iphigénie* I.i, 82); *heureuse rigueur* (*Phèdre* II.i, 435); and from *Athalie*, *heureux larcin* (I.ii, 166), *charme empoisonneur* (IV. iii, 1388) and *saintement homicides* (IV.iii, 1365). Vossler has commented on those of the examples that come from the speeches of the high priest Joad in *Athalie*:

> There cannot be the slightest doubt that Racine has given this Joad the ugly trait of moral two-facedness. Does he not put in his mouth expressions like *heureux larcin* . . . *saintement homicide* . . .? The lines of this rigid theocrat and God-fearing murderer are bathed in bloody vengeance and in loving kindness. One would be quite wrong to regard Joad as a hero after Racine's heart. But the poet had no intention of making him small, suspect or unworthy. Approval and

disapproval are inapplicable to an absolute phenomenon like Joad. (Vossler, *Racine*, p. 112)

However, the 'double illumination' of phenomena is to be observed not only in the words of the high priest Joad, not only in the play *Athalie* (where even God is said to be *fidèle en toutes ses menaces,* I.1, 112) but also, as my collection of examples shows, in all the heroes of Racine. Des Hons also lists examples of this kind, and he comments:

Tous le commentateurs de Racine signalent comme hardiesses lui appartenant en propre ou, du moins, caractéristiques de sa manière, certaines alliances de mots formant entre eux des antithèses ou accouplés contrairement à l'usage, telles que *instruire dans l'ignorance* (*Britannicus* I.ii, 183), *entendre un regard* (*Britannicus* II.iii, 682), *boire la joie* (*Esther* II.viii, 789), *funestes bienfaits* (*Phèdre* V.v, 1483), *tranquille fureur* (*Bajazet* IV.v, 1276), *saintement homicide* (*Athalie* IV.iii, 1365). (Des Hons, p. 185)

I believe that these oxymorons are the essence of Racinian tragedy, for through them the poet shows the antinomies in which man's life is constricted, the pain and the pleasure of passion. Phèdre's line *Je goûtais en tremblant ce funeste plaisir*, constituted by two paradoxical pairings, characterises precisely the fearful joys of passion which the heroine courts, as do Racine's heroines generally. Racine sees Phèdre in a double light: he empathises with her emotion, and also measures her by the eternal scales of morality – just as he sees in Joad a *passionate* theocrat, who in his passion has recourse to *stratagèmes* that are far from innocent, and who justifies 'happy', i.e. godly, thefts and holy murders. What is different about the tragedy of *Athalie* is that the paradoxicality of passion is transposed to the highest service on this earth, the service of God, and this daring constitutes the peculiar greatness of the believer Racine. In the representation of godliness he remains objective; he sees human imperfection in man's devotion to his God. The oxymorons which run through the whole theatre of Racine are the stylistic reflections of a double understanding of man, an understanding made of empathy and evaluation, and which acknowledges conflicts between *what is* and *what ought to be*. But as the moral themes are subtly introduced within the expression of what is, they have a muting, *piano* effect on the latter. The oxymorons have too much acid sharpness in them not to corrode the lyrical immediacy of the poetry.

The oxymoron is a figure too elaborate, too well turned, too ingenious in the manner of Petrarch, to have any affective force. The same can be said of Racine's frequent **antitheses** which, like oxymorons, establish a contradiction, an antimony (cf. the line from Seneca's *Medea* quoted above, *Tibi innocens sit quisquis est pro te nocens?*):

Toujours *prête à partir* et, *demeurant* toujours,
Quelquefois elle appelle Oreste à son secours.

Andromaque I.i, 131–2

Tel est mon partage funeste:
Le *cœur* est pour Pyrrhus, et *les vœux* pour Oreste.
Andromaque II.ii, 537–8

Et, tout ingrat qu'il est, il me sera plus doux
De *mourir* avec lui que de *vivre* avec vous.
Andromaque IV.iii, 1247–8

Consequently I do not think Mesnard is right to say that one rarely finds lines in *Andromaque* where the artifice is insufficiently hidden, as perhaps l.148, *Hector tombe sous lui, Troie expira sous vous* (Mesnard, 'Etude', p. xxvii). Such devices are on the contrary quite usual in Racine – Fubini also talked of expressions which 'smack of scholastic rhetoric' (Fubini, p. 206). For example:

Mon unique espérance est dans mon désespoir. *Bajazet* I.iv, 336

[Think of Oronte's sonnet in Moliere's *Le Misanthrope*!]

L'auriez-vous cru, madame, et qu'un si prompt retour
Fît à tant de fureur succéder tant d'amour?
Bajazet III.v, 1019–20

Mais de faire fléchir un courage inflexible
De porter la douleur dans une âme insensible
D'enchaîner un captif de ses fers étonné
Contre un joug qui lui plaît vainement mutiné,
C'est là ce que je veux, c'est là ce qui m'irrite.
Phèdre II.i, 449–53

Présente, je vous fuis; absente, je vous trouve . . .
Phèdre II.ii, 542

Cf. the Latinate construction of *Je vous entends absente, je vous oy* in the sonnet *Que dites-vous, que faites-vous mignonne* (Ronsard I.95).

Vous l'osâtes bannir, vous n'osez l'éviter. *Phèdre* III.i, 764

Je l'évite partout, partout il me poursuit. *Athalie* II.v, 489

Chargé d'indignes fers vos généreuses mains. *Athalie* V.ii, 1566

(See also *Phèdre* II.ii, 555; II.v, 687–8; IV.v, 1203; *Athalie* II.iii, 437–8; IV.iii, 1391–2.) Most of these cases are concerned with revealing the paradox of a passion or delusion: Hermione, Roxane, Aricie, Phèdre, Athalie, Hippolyte and Joas parade before us their problematical contradictions; and it is not surprising that it is especially the female characters, since women are supposed to be full of contradictions anyway, that are represented antithetically. [Racine's use of antithesis is essentially moderate and moderating. Compare these examples from Esprit Fléchier (1632–1710) where the oppositions are carried through at length: *j'envisage non pas sa fortune, mais sa vertu; les services* . . .

non pas les places . . ., les dons . . . non pas les honneurs, etc., quoted by Norden, p. 797, as an example of the antithetical style of the French humanists, which goes back ultimately to Isocrates and Cicero. Recently Charles Péguy has taken up the type of antitheses seen in Fléchier.*]

Antithetical shaping appeals to intellect and rationality, it brings with it the domination of the mind. A binary division as watertight as in the line *Le cœur est pour Pyrrhus, et les vœux pour Oreste* is, in the context of the intricate movements of the human heart, startling: the paradoxical attitude of Aricie, trying to achieve the impossible (*fléchir un courage inflexible*), justifies suspicions about antithesis; it does not reconcile the opposition or break down the incompatibility. It offers a self-analysis, not an outpouring, of emotion; it reveals irrationality in the mirror of reason, it is a self-definition of a split feeling. [See F. Neubert, p. 153, on dualism and the polarity of *raison/passion* in Corneille and Racine.] And so the breaking of the alexandrine into two halves matches the disintegration of the ego to the left and the right of the caesura: *Fit à tant de fureur / succéder tant d'amour*. Linguistic linkages (*tant . . . tant, vous l'osâtes . . . vous l'osez*, etc.) cannot restore the fragmented unity but manage only to hold in tension a situation taken to its limits. The poetry of many of these linked antitheses lies perhaps in the use of *et*, a restrained expression of a bleakly definitive, intolerable coexistence:

> Hippolyte est sensible, *et* ne sent rien pour moi! *Phèdre* IV.v, 1203
>
> Le cœur est pour Pyrrhus, *et* les vœux pour Oreste!
> *Andromaque* II.ii, 538

The asyndetic cases, with their abrupt compounding of intolerable states of affairs (without explicit linkage), sound to me more rational as statements of the illogical:

> Vous l'osâtes bannir, vous n'osez l'éviter. *Phèdre* III.i, 764
>
> Tu me haïssais plus, je ne t'aimais pas moins. *Phèdre* II.v, 688

Racine frequently exploits the division of the alexandrine or of a couplet to portray a two-sided action, or two alternative actions which betray the oscillation of the character or at least his hesitation between differing impulses. This is particularly effective at the end of an act; for example at the end of *Andromaque* IV, Pyrrhus coolly and meanly sets Andromaque and Astyanax against each other like two pieces in a game of chess, the pawn in his hand against the queen he is after:

> Andromaque m'attend. Phœnix, garde son fils. 1392

Other examples:

> Bajazet interdit! Atalide étonnée! *Bajazet* III.vii, 1069

* See Spitzer's articles on Péguy, B7 and A18, and B14.

J'aurai soin de ma mort; prenez soin de sa vie.
Bajazet v.vi, 1618

Sa mort vous laisse un fils à qui vous vous devez
Esclave s'il vous perd, et roi si vous vivez.
Phèdre I.v, 343–4

The either/or of desperation:

J'aime: je viens chercher Hermione en ces lieux,
La fléchir, l'enlever, ou mourir à ses yeux.
Andromaque I.i, 99–100

Et Phèdre au Labyrinthe avec vous descendue
Se serait avec vous retrouvée, ou perdue. *Phèdre* II.v, 661–2

(Cf. also *Bajazet* III.viii, 1115–16, 1121–2; *Andromaque* III.vii, 974–5.)

On other occasions, an elegantly pointed opposition of two groups or of two persons is made, e.g. Andromaque and Hermione:

Le sort vous y voulut l'une et l'autre amener
Vous, pour porter des fers, elle pour en donner . . .
Et ne dirait-on pas, en voyant au contraire
Vos charmes tout-puissants, et les siens dédaignés,
Qu'elle est ici captive, et que vous y régnez?
Andromaque I.iv, 347–52

Or in *Athalie*:

Roi, voilà vos vengeurs contre vos ennemis.
Prêtres, voilà le roi que je vous ai promis. IV.iii, 1307–8

The closer the syntactic parallelism between the two members of the antithetical pair, the sharper the point of the otherwise unmotivated opposition:

. . . finissant là sa haine et nos misères . . .
Andromaque III.vi, 945

Prenons, en signalant mon bras et votre nom,
Vous, la place d'Hélène, et moi, d'Agamemnon.
Andromaque IV.iii, 1159–60

Le ciel punit ma feinte et confond votre adresse. *Bajazet* II.v, 666

Et plaignant à la fois son trouble et vos alarmes . . .
Phèdre IV.i, 1021

(See also *Bajazet* II.i, 486 and v.xii, 1738.) The rapid mental switches demanded by these possessive pronouns and adjectives detract from the reader's empathy. This line from *Iphigénie: Mettons en liberté ma tristesse et leur joie* (II.i, 398) makes Mesnard, 'Etude', p. xli, express admiration for 'ces beautés de diction, ces expressions aussi originales que justes' – but we would comment, 'trop justes', 'trop originales' to be really and effectively poetic. An intellectual effort is necessary when reading Racine to separate out two figures, two sentences that are presented in a single, seamless weld:

> une loi moins sévère
> Mit Claude dans mon lit, et Rome à mes genoux.
>
> *Britannicus* IV.ii, 1136–7

And this intellectual effort spoils the pleasurable enjoyment of poetry.

Racine developed his own special variety of antithesis which opens an **unforeseen perspective**. The tide of speech carries us on and suddenly we find ourselves on the edge of an abyss into which we may glance fearfully. At such moments all the vibrating passion of Racine's forms and figures is revealed as if in a flash of lightning (Hatzfeld thus refers to the technique of 'final lightning'):

> Hé bien, madame, hé bien, il faut vous obéir:
> Il faut vous oublier, ou *plutôt vous haïr.*
> Oui, mes vœux ont trop loin poussé leur violence
> Pour ne plus s'arrêter que dans l'indifférence.
>
> *Andromaque* I.iv, 363–6

The listener is lulled by the first one and a half lines of Pyrrhus's speech, but then suddenly the flame of his tortured spirit shoots forth with *ou plutôt vous haïr*. Pyrrhus himself realises how unexpectedly this brutal movement welled up from the depths of his being, and he feels the need to justify himself: *Oui, mes vœux . . .*

> Ne vous suffit-il pas que ma gloire offensée
> Demande une victime à moi seule adressée;
> Qu'Hermione est le prix d'un tyran opprimé;
> Que je le hais; enfin, seigneur, *que je l'aimai*?
>
> *Andromaque* IV.iii, 1189–92

Love suddenly bursts forth from Hermione's hatred: Freud's term *Hassliebe* ('the love–hate relationship') described this moment perfectly. (Later on, Hermione puts her feelings for Pyrrhus thus: *S'il ne meurt aujourd'hui, je puis l'aimer demain*, IV.iii, 1200.) Similarly, after the murder of Pyrrhus, the illogicality of Hermione's passions can be seen breaking the surface of her words to Oreste in the contradictory wishes she expresses:

> N'as-tu pas dû cent fois te le faire redire?
> Toi-même avant le coup me venir consulter
> Y revenir encore, ou plutôt m'éviter? V.iii, 1550–2

Roxane expresses contradictory emotions rather differently in *Bajazet* II.i:

Mais avez-vous prévu, si vous ne m'épousez
Les périls plus certains où vous vous exposez?
Songez-vous que sans moi tout vous devient contraire?
Que c'est à moi surtout qu'il importe de plaire?
Songez-vous que je tiens les portes du palais?
Que je puis vous l'ouvrir ou fermer pour jamais;
Que j'ai sur votre vie un empire suprême;
Que vous ne respirez qu'autant que je vous aime?
Et, sans ce même amour, qu'offensent vos refus,
Songez-vous, en un mot, que vous ne seriez plus? 503–12

Like a tiger slowly creeping up, Roxane come gradually closer, and finally claws into her prey with a well-prepared effect of surprise. Although the *en un mot* in l.512 leads one to expect a summing-up of the preceding content, *que vous ne seriez plus* remains quite unforeseen. Note the psychological development of love and concern for another into hatred and death-wish. With his uncanny perception of the unity of all emotions, Racine manages to compress that whole development into ten lines!

There is of course also Phèdre's celebrated declaration of her love for Hippolyte, surfacing as it were from underneath her impassioned panegyric of Thésée, as if the god of love were subverting her very words:

Oui, prince, je languis, je brûle pour Thésée:
Je l'aime . . .
Mais fidèle, mais fier, et même un peu farouche,
Charmant, jeune, traînant tous les cœurs après soi,
Tel qu'on dépeint nos dieux, *ou tel que je vous voi.*
Phèdre II.v, 634–40

Phèdre switches track only in the last hemistich. In the preceding lines she adorns Thésée with the attributes of his son (there is a particularly perceptible transference from Hippolyte's appearance in l.636, *et même un peu farouche*) and she likens him to the gods; but only at the end does she direct her impassioned eyes to the young man standing before her, to grasp and consume him. The whole passage acquires a new meaning retrospectively from this final shift.

Further examples of antitheses which open unforeseen perspectives:

. . . pour sauver votre honneur combattu,
Il faut immoler tout, et *même la vertu.* *Phèdre* III.iii, 907–8

Non, non, j'ai trop de soin de votre renommée.
Un plus noble dessein m'amène devant vous:
Fuyez vos ennemis, et *suivez votre époux.* *Phèdre* V.i, 1386–8

The last hemistich containing the second member of the antithesis brings Hippolyte's unexpected proposal for the hand of Aricie, and his decision to flee with her only after their marriage.

In such antitheses, symmetrically built like the triumphal arches of classical Rome, Racine opens up as it were a lateral view, from which one can gaze into the unimagined depths of the human heart.

The division of the alexandrine into two hemistiches lends itself naturally enough to stichomythia, where the two half-lines are attributed to different speakers and clash against each other like weapons in an oratorical combat. There are classical models, and of course Corneille used the device; but my impression is that in Racine these direct, conflictual sequences of hemistiches are less frequent and, when used, less harsh than in Corneille. Battles over principles, as between Athalie and Joas in the passage quoted below, are rare; more typical uses of stichomythia are for contradictions based on a character's feelings, and for the correction of another character's words.

PYLADE: Vous me trompiez, seigneur.
ORESTE: Je me trompais moi-même.
Andromaque I.i, 37

HERMIONE: Ah! ne souhaitez pas le destin de Pyrrhus.
Je vous haïrais trop.
ORESTE: Vous m'en aimeriez plus.
Andromaque II.ii, 539–40

BAJAZET: Mais enfin voulez-vous . . .
ROXANE: Non, je ne veux plus rien.
Bajazet II.i, 520

ŒNONE: Ils ne se verront plus
PHÈDRE: Ils s'aimeront toujours.
Phèdre IV.vi, 1251

JOAS: Moi! des bienfaits de Dieu je perdrais la mémoire!
ATHALIE: Non! je ne vous veux pas contraindre à l'oublier.
JOAS: Vous ne le priez point.
ATHALIE: Vous le pourrez prier.
JOAS: Je verrais cependant en invoquer un autre.
ATHALIE: J'ai mon Dieu que je sers; vous servirez le vôtre:
Ce sont deux puissants dieux.
JOAS: Il faut craindre le mien.
Lui seul est Dieu, madame, et le vôtre n'est rien.
Athalie II.vii, 680–6

The two voices merge into a single unity, as in a musical duet two soloists produce a single harmony; and the score of the Chorus in e.g. *Athalie* III.viii consists of pure voice-music:

PREMIÈRE [VOIX]: Je vois tout son éclat disparaitre à mes yeux.
LA SECONDE: Je vois de toutes parts sa clarté répandue.
LA PREMIÈRE: Dans un gouffre profond Sion est descendue.
LA SECONDE: Sion a son front dans les Cieux!

LA PREMIÈRE: Quel triste abaissement!
LA SECONDE: Quelle immortelle gloire!
LA PREMIÈRE: Que de cris de douleur!
LA SECONDE: Que de chants de victoire!
1220–5

Racine undeniably indulged his liking for formal antithesis to excess, particularly in the early tragedies; that is to say, he took pleasure in the intellectual play of oppositions in the Petrarchan manner even when no justification for binary antithesis was present, e.g. in the principle of a character's construction, the structure of a scene, a philosophical dualism to be expressed, etc. A line such as Andromaque's *J'ai cru que sa prison deviendrait son asile* (III.vi, 937), which means in effect that she had hoped Pyrrhus would release Astyanax, is well put to the point of wittiness, and seems almost a *jeu d'esprit*. Hippolyte's *Quand je suis tout de feu, d'où vous vient cette glace* (*Phèdre* V.i, 1374) is utterly Petrarchan in its conceit. In the celebrated 'récit de Théramène' in *Phèdre* V.vi, the monster's emergence from the sea is described in an antithetical figure that is much more a piece of literary cleverness than a felt opposition:

Cependant sur le dos de la *plaine liquide*
S'élève à gros bouillons une *montagne humide* 1513–14

(Marty-Laveaux, p. vi, finds 'un peu d'emphase' in these lines.)

Antithetical cleverness makes the modern reader uneasy, especially when it hangs on mere appearance or on word-meanings, or where a term is taken in two different senses to make in effect a punning opposition. Accustomed as we are to measuring the word by its meaning and content (perhaps excessively), we tend to withdraw our assent to meaningless and empty word-play by describing it as 'precious'. Racine's precious antithetical figures have often been listed: here are some examples, with the hinge-word (having a double metaphorical function) highlighted:

Brûlé de plus de *feux* que je n'en allumai . . .
Andromaque I.iv, 320

Je percerai le *cœur* que je n'ai pu toucher
Andromaque IV.iii, 1244

On craint que de la sœur les *flammes* téméraires
Ne raniment un jour la cendre de ses frères *Phèdre* II.i, 429–30

Voilà mon *cœur*. C'est là que ta main doit frapper.
Impatient déjà d'expier son offense
Au-devant de ton bras je le sens qui s'avance. *Phèdre* II.v, 704–6

The metaphoric elaboration of the heart as the object of striking in opposition to the striking hand ('arm' in *Phèdre* II.v, 706) is effected in the mode of *préciosité*. As in the example from *Andromaque* IV.iv above, the heart is here not only the physical organ but also the seat of the emotions, that which is 'already impatient'; conversely, the impatience of the (figurative) heart is so great that the (physical) heart beats in advance of the blow. This is a precious figure, comparable to Théophile de Viau's *il en rougit, le traistre* (*Pyrame et Thisbée*, v.iii, 1228). This particular word-play recurs several times in Racine, e.g. *Phèdre* I.iii:

> Noble et brillant auteur d'une triste famille
> Toi, dont ma mère osait se vanter d'être fille,
> Qui peut-être *rougis* du trouble où tu me vois
> Soleil . . . 169–72

i.e. the sun blushes/dawns with shame. The pun on *rougir* is *précieux*, whatever else has been said about it, and even if Racine took seriously Phèdre's invocation of the sun's mythical status as her ancestor.

In the examples listed above, the poet plays on the two meanings, literal and figurative, of a single word–*feux, flammes, cœur,* etc. Another type of *préciosité* involves the pairing of two words, the one having a simple and the other a metaphorical reading, so that a potentially figurative reading accrues to the simple term. There is a well-known example from *La Thébaïde*:

> Pour couronner ma tête et ma flamme en ce jour . . . v.iv, 1427

Other examples:

> Mon rival porte ailleurs son *cœur* et sa *couronne* . . .
> *Andromaque* I.i, 78

('Crown' acquires the meaning 'power'.)

> Traîner de mers en mers ma chaine et mes ennuis.
> *Andromaque* I.i, 44

> Dans sa cour, dans son cœur, dis-moi ce qui se passe.
> *Andromaque* I.i, 102

> Je viens mettre mon cœur et mon crime à vos pieds.
> *Bajazet* v.vi, 1576

Hence we find–admittedly only in the comedy *Les Plaideurs*–the 'congruence of the incongruous', that is to say a presentation of an incongruity between what is mentally necessary and what actually is, which is tantamount to a revelation of hypocrisy:

> Et j'ai toujours été nourri par feu mon père
> Dans la crainte de Dieu, Monsieur, et des *sergents*.
> *Les Plaideurs* II.iv, 436–7

Many antitheses in Racine seem to turn on oppositions between linguistic elements, between the words that are used, e.g.:

Je m'*abhorre* encor plus que tu ne me *détestes.* *Phèdre* II.v, 678

This certainly makes a very fine distinction between the moral *abhorrence* that Phèdre feels for herself and the total *detestation* in which Hippolyte holds her. This subtle differentiation attenuates the passage in a rational manner; naked emotion has neither time nor calm enough for semantic niceties! Such exquisite calculations of the *mot juste* correspond precisely to the propriety of language, to the elevated style which is the intention and achievement of Racinian tragedy.

Je vous *cède*, ou plutôt je vous *rends* une place
Un sceptre que jadis vos aïeux ont reçu . . .
Phèdre II.ii, 494–5

Est-ce Phèdre qui *fuit*, ou plutôt qu'on *entraîne*?
Phèdre II.vi, 714

Etrangère . . . que dis-je? *esclave* dans l'Epire . . .
Andromaque II.v, 689

Que dis-je, *souhaiter*? Je *me flatte*, j'espère . . .
Athalie V.vi, 1784

Quelle raison subite
Presse votre *départ*, ou plutôt votre *fuite*? *Bérénice* III.i, 667–8

The kind of self-correction in speech illustrated by these examples certainly suggests that the initial word used was the wrong one, but it simulates a rhetorical climax too coolly and calmly for the reader to be taken in by it. It has in the end the same general effect as Pyrrhus's words to Andromaque:

Pour la dernière fois, *sauvez-le, sauvez-nous.*
Andromaque III.vii, 960

Plutôt signals the presence of an **artificial correction**, as can be seen from the actual disparity of the things that are notionally brought together by this device:

. . . le jour que son courage
Lui fit chercher *Achille*, ou plutôt le *trépas* . . .
Andromaque III.viii, 1018–19

This particular way of putting it is constructed nonetheless from the underlying *mot*, 'Achille was death for Hector'. Finally, we can also count asyndetic juxtapositions as self-corrections, e.g.:

J'ai pris, j'ai fait couler dans mes brûlantes veines
Un poison . . . *Phèdre* V.vii, 1637–8

J'aime, je prise en lui de plus nobles richesses . . .
Phèdre II.i, 441

II. Figures of Association

It is possible that my whole section on Racinian antithesis has overstressed the rational side, the mental machinery; to do justice to the poetry one ought always to keep its living flesh on the intellectual skeleton, and it is precisely the much-vaunted 'music' of Racine's language that softens his mechanical clatter. The 'poignant epigrams' from which Racine's language is made (Lytton Strachey's term) are nonetheless given a spiritual function. Let us take a passage from *Bajazet*:

> Infortuné, proscrit, incertain de régner,
> Dois-je irriter les cœurs au lieu de les gagner?
> Témoins de nos plaisirs, plaindront-ils nos misères? II.i, 483–5

These lines are indisputably based on antithetical patterning. However, the gentle musicality of the last line, with its sequence of 'dark' and 'light' vowels that only Grammont's method could analyse properly (e - oẽ - $_{e}$ - o - e - i/ /ẽ - õ - i - o - i - e), its alternation of masculine and feminine words to close the hemistiches, its combination of an interrogative intonation with the affirmation of a contrast – this line, like many of those I have quoted, has an overall effect that escapes the sort of analysis used up to now. Paul Valéry was right to point to 'Racine's doubly organised sentences', 'dont la syntaxe, d'une part, la prosodie, de l'autre, composent une substance sonore et spirituelle, engendrent savamment une forme pleine de vie' ('Discours de la diction des vers' (1926), quoted in Des Hons, p. 263). In the famous line from *Andromaque, Je l'aimais inconstant, qu'aurais-je fait fidèle?*, the syntactic ellipsis of *fidèle* (= 'si tu avais été fidèle') sharpens the edge of the contrast. Linguistic compression of this order does not merely express oppression, it embodies it. To take another case from *Phèdre* II.i:

> Le nom d'amant peut-être offense son courage;
> Mais il en a *les yeux,* s'il n'en a *le langage*. 413–14

Here the striking quality of Racine's observation of the ways human love can be expressed draws our attention away from the (not entirely rigorous) opposition of eyes and language. The whole turmoil of the lover, whose eyes betray what his tongue dares not say, infects the reader who is left to ponder on the contrast Racine has pointed out. Racine has the art of adding reverie to the rational, or as Des Hons puts it from the opposite standpoint, 'de penser les sentiments'.

We have already met several kinds of **twinning**. Close linkage of this sort imposes patterning of great compression. Racine likes to use 'as . . . as . . .' constructions, which strike German readers as utterly pedantic and professorial; but the French *et . . . et . . .*, modelled on Latin *et . . . et . . .*, exudes calm superiority, muted control (as do *ou . . . ou . . .*, *ni . . . ni . . .*). To pattern things so clearly implies a high degree of assurance and self-confidence (that is why these structures are not typical of popular language):

> Vous connaissez, Madame, *et* la lettre *et* le sein.*
>
> *Bajazet* IV.iii, 1183

> Lui montrer à la fois, *et* l'ordre de son frère,
> *Et* de sa trahison ce gage trop sincère. *Bajazet* IV.v, 1317–18

> Je sentis tout mon corps *et* transir *et* brûler. *Phèdre* I.iii, 276

> Je mets sous son pouvoir *et* le fils *et* la mère. *Phèdre* III.i, 806

> Une pitié secrète *et* m'afflige *et* m'étonne. *Phèdre* IV.iv, 1457

> Et tout ce que des mains de cette reine avare
> Vous avez pu sauver *et* de riche *et* de rare,
> Donnez-le. *Athalie* V.ii, 1591–3

> Quelquefois à l'autel
> Je présente au grande-prêtre *ou* l'encens *ou* le sel.
>
> *Athalie* II.vii, 673–4

> La frayeur les emporte; et sourds à cette fois,
> Ils ne connaissent plus *ni* le frein *ni* la voix. *Phèdre* V.vi, 1535–6

(See also *Bajazet* V.iv, 1497; *Athalie* II.v, 477; III.iii, 913; IV.iii, 1361.) Very often also two words, sometimes semantically quite distant from each other, are tied together in a taut, concise pairing without the reduplicated *et . . . et . . .*:

> Mais le sultan, surprise d'une trop longue absence,
> En cherchera bientôt *la cause et la vengeance.*
>
> *Bajazet* I.i, 81–2

> . . . il fallait, comblant ta perfidie,
> Lui ravir tout d'un coup *la parole et la vie.* *Phèdre* IV.ii, 1085–6

> Autant que je le puis j'évite sa présence.
> De peur qu'en le voyant quelque trouble indiscret
> Ne fasse *avec mes pleurs* échapper *mon secret.*
>
> *Athalie* I.ii, 192–4

Note how in the last example the psychological element *tears* is reduced to an accessory by the preposition *avec* (the subject of the main verb being the duller and socially oriented *trouble*). Cf.*Mithridate* III.v:

> C'est faire à vos beautés un triste sacrifice
> Que de vous présenter, Madame, avec ma foi,
> Tout l'âge et le malheur que je traîne avec moi. 1036–8

The sentence is modelled on the type of closing formulae for letters found in e.g. *permettez-moi de vous présenter, avec l'assurance de mon*

* For *seing*.

dévouement, mes hommages . . ., and allows the king's faith (*foi*, l. 1037) to be presented discreetly, as an accessory, not a principal. [Although Rudler (pp. 135–6) commented on the 'impression d'une tristesse d'autant plus sincère qu'elle est plus digne, plus réservée' made by this passage, he did not notice the grammatical point.]

In the next example, the twinning is made even tighter by the singular verb (criticised by Racine's contemporaries):

> Reine, sors, a-t-il dit, de ce lieu redoutable
> D'où te bannit ton sexe et ton impiété. *Athalie* II.ii, 404–5

Other examples of close twinning can be cited (e.g. *Athalie* II.v, 595, or v.i, 1519–20), but Racine can also loosen these tightly joined groups by adding a third member:

> Mais tout dort, et l'armée, et les vents, et Neptune.
> *Iphigénie* I.i, 9

Shakespeare, said Lytton Strachey, would have used a *single* detail to describe a silent night; Virgil would have given several points or features. As for Racine:

> What a flat and feeble set of expressions! is the Englishman's first thought – with the conventional 'Neptune', and the vague 'armée' and the commonplace 'vents'. And he forgets to notice the total impression which these words produce – the atmosphere of darkness and emptiness and vastness and ominous hush. (Lytton Strachey, p. 16)

The interesting point is that Racine manages to dispose his words and compose his sentences in such a way as to suggest an unbounded horizon and yet to imply order and limitation as well. The triple repetition loosens the twinning, the *et* . . . *et* . . . *et* tightens the thread that ties the elements together again. The 'vague' collective noun *armée* draws the eye to an unbounded vista, as does the plural *vents*. But *Neptune* is not merely conventional, as Strachey says, it is the name of a particular personality – albeit a capricious, inscrutably mysterious personality. Neptune establishes a boundary line not only because he is the third term in the list, but because he is a single, and divine, entity, whilst being in himself a multiplicity of impenetrable caprices.

The twinning is especially tightly drawn when the sentence forks, as it were, from a common verb in the 'trunk' clause (the rhetorical term for this is **isocolon**).

> Princes . . .
> Votre devoir ici n'a point dû vous conduire,
> Ni vous faire quitter, en de si grands besoins,
> *Vous le Pont, vous Colchos*, confiés à vos soins.
> *Mithridate* II.ii, 423–6

Traditionally, *Vous le Pont* is spoken to Pharnace in a cold, magisterial voice and *vous Colchos* to Xipharès with a fond, fatherly tone. A single line spans two opposite attitudes.

The line *une loi moins sévère / Mit Claude dans mon lit, et Rome à mes genoux* (*Britannicus* IV.ii, 1136–7) is built on the same forking pattern, which here comes close to the classical rhetorical device of **zeugma.** [Cf. Sallust, *pacem an bellum gerens,* 'waging peace or war', *Jugurtha* 46.8; Tacitus, *manus ac supplices voces ad Tiberium tendens*, 'stretching out hands and pleading voices to Tiberius', *Annals* 2,29.6.]

Another linking device signifying an ingathering and control of the content is the repetition of the radical. This classical stylistic figure, perpetuated by Malherbe in e.g. *Rose, elle a vécu ce que vivent les roses* ('Consolation à Monsieur du Périer')* occurs again in Racine:

> *Mortelle*, subissez le sort d'une *mortelle.* *Phèdre* IV.vi, 1302

In emphatic discourse repetition is a device for giving stress to a particular word, but the linking of ideas by the repetition of the radical produces an attenuation, a *piano* effect: Hatzfeld talks of an 'echo technique'.

> J'aime à voie que . . .
> Vous vous abandonniez *au crime en criminel.*
> *Andromaque* IV.v, 1310–12

> Je l'ai vu vers le temple . . .
> Mener en *conquérant* sa nouvelle *conquête* . . .
> *Andromaque* V.ii, 1433–4

> Bajazet est aimable: il vit que son salut
> Dépendait de lui *plaire*, et bientôt il lui *plut.* *Bajazet* I.i, 155–6

[Cf. Ovid, *Tristia* 4.3.37: *Fleque meos casus: est quaedam flere voluptas*, 'Weep for my sad plight: there is some pleasure in weeping'.]

> . . . ma joie est extrême
> Que le *traître*, une fois, se soit *trahi* lui-même.
> *Bajazet* IV.v, 1273–4

By appearing to be forced, this kind of repetition often evokes a sense of stoical self-control. Just as the line seems artificially held down, so does the attitude of Mithridate, when he demands *Quand je me fais justice, il faut qu'on se la fasse* (III.v, 1052). Louis Racine criticised the *la* which refers, despite Vaugelas's prohibition, to *justice* used in a fixed phrase; but it serves nonetheless to hold down the lid, so to speak, even more firmly.

When only pronouns or pronominal adjectives are repeated, the

* See Spitzer's articles on Malherbe, B8 and A18, and also A34.

effect is often to establish parallels, to give a sense of evenness and stylisation:

> Thésée à *tes* fureurs connaîtra *tes* bontés. *Phèdre* IV.ii, 1076
>
> Chaque mot sur *mon* front fait dresser *mes* cheveux.
> *Phèdre* IV.vi, 1268
>
> Et tous, devant l'autel avec ordre introduits,
> De *leurs* champs dans *leurs* mains portant les nouveaux fruits,
> Au Dieu de l'univers consacraient ces prémices
> *Athalie* I.i, 9–11
>
> Grâce aux dieux! *Mon* malheur passe *mon* espérance.
> *Andromaque* V.v, 1613

12. Expansions

The use of attenuating adverbial phrases, appositions and parentheses to fill 'empty' hemistiches also contributes to the impression left by Racine's characters of speaking a language intentionally shaped and blunted. In his essay on Molière, Brunetière rejected the attacks made on the playwright's *chevilles* – the half-lines which add nothing to the content – on the grounds that they afford agreeable relief to the listener's attention (Brunetière, *Etudes critiques*, VII.91). In *Le Misanthrope* I.i, Molière began with:

> On sait que ce pied plat . . .
> Par de sales emplois s'est poussé dans le monde.

Only subsequently was the waffle of *digne qu'on le confonde* inserted into the preexisting model to make the definitive l.129. The couplet thereby acquired an element of padding which, by suggesting copiousness, also suggests a stable evenness. It is significant that what was used for padding out lines consisted of those stable *evaluations* of things and people which correspond entirely to the spirit of an age which believed itself set up for all eternity. Racine's padding consists less of conditional clauses which, by positing a possible alternative set of circumstances, cannot serve to undermine what is said than of determiners which define a situation, establish a value, and thus serve the same stylistic function as the evaluating epithets dealt with above. Thus in the first example below, Oreste's spontaneous exclamation *heureux si je pouvais au lieu d'Astyanax lui ravir ma princesse* (i.e. seize Hermione from Pyrrhus) is modulated by an inserted *dans l'ardeur qui me presse*: the half-line establishes that Oreste is aware of his situation, of an *ardeur qui le presse*, and by thus defining his state the line ceases to be spontaneous:

> Heureux si je pouvais, *dans l'ardeur qui me presse,*
> Au lieu d'Astyanax lui ravir ma princesse.
> *Andromaque* I.i, 93–4

Il peut, seigneur, il peut, *dans ce désordre extrême,*
Epouser ce qu'il hait et punir ce qu'il aime.

Andromaque I.i, 121–2

The first half of l.121 sounds threatening and imploring at the same time; the attenuating adverbial phrase that follows restores calm and expresses an evaluation.

. . . Qu'aucun par un zèle imprudent
Découvrant mes desseins, soit prêtre, soit lévite,
Ne sorte avant le temps et ne se précipite;
Et que chacun enfin, *d'un même esprit poussé,*
Garde en mourant le poste où je l'aurai placé.

Athalie IV.v, 1448–52

Appositions are used to similar effect:

Je ne viens point, *armé d'un indigne artifice,*
D'un voile d'équité couvrir mon injustice.

Andromaque IV.v, 1277–8

Et là vous me verrez, *soumis ou furieux,*
Vous couronner, madame, ou le perdre à vos yeux.

Andromaque III.vii, 975–6

The two adjectives in the first line imply an *either/or*, and presuppose that alternatives will be given in the second line.

Et que, derrière un voile, *invisible et présente,*
J'étais de ce grand corps l'âme toute-puissante.

Britannicus I.i, 95–6

The veil that conceals but does not abolish is a kind of theatrical curtain which rises to reveal the drama of the second line: the soul which shines through the body. The oxymoron *invisible et présente* intimates that the soul itself is 'invisibly present'.

Je saurai, s'il le faut, *victime obéissante,*
Tendre au fer de Calchas une tête innocente . . .

Iphigénie IV.iv, 1181–2

The whole sense of this scene is formulated in *victime . . . innocente*: the phrase anticipates the dramatic action; it is the abstract formula to which the ensuing visible drama can be reduced. Racine does not leave us to watch his play; he hastens to talk us into his interpretation of it, to guide us rationally, almost to lead us by the hand or nose. Before we see Iphigénie gracefully bow her head to the sacrifice, we hear the moral formula which appropriately encapsulates the meaning of her action (and which also remains rhythmically subordinated to the 'spectacle' which has precedence on stage).

Mesnard, 'Etude', p. xxxviii, points out the elegance of Racine's appositional formulae, but one should also distinguish between the 'front' and 'back' versions of the device, i.e. as between

> Esclave couronnée,
> Je partis . . . *Mithridate* I.iii, 255–6

and

> Prêts à vous recevoir, mes vaisseaux vous attendent:
> Et du pied de l'autel vous y pouvez monter
> Souveraine des mers qui vous doivent porter.
> *Mithridate* I.ii, 240–2

There is majesty in this gracefully flowing train of words; according to Lytton Strachey, the last line presents 'the radiant spectacle of a triumphant flotilla riding the dancing waves' (Strachey, p. 17). The finest example of apposition is perhaps this passage from *Mithridate* II.iv:

> Ah! pour tenter encor de nouvelles conquêtes,
> Quand je ne verrais pas des routes toutes prêtes,
> Quand le sort ennemi m'aurait jeté plus bas,
> *Vaincu, persécuté, sans secours, sans Etats,*
> *Errant de mers en mers, et moins roi que pirate,*
> *Conservant pour tous biens le nom de Mithridate,*
> Apprenez que suivi d'un nom si glorieux,
> Partout de l'univers j'attacherais les yeux. 559–66

The hypothetical adjectival phrases in apposition, falling step by step to ever deeper misfortune and reaching their nadir in the supposition of piracy, depict the whole psychological movement of Mithridate, who springs back to superhuman grandeur from the contempt which he feels to be contained in his defeat. It is the name *Mithridate* which points back to the heights and unleashes the *Apprenez que* . . . The rhyme on *pirate*/*Mithridate* firmly links the lowest and highest points in the king's psychological course. As Péguy remarked:

> Il est extrêmement remarquable . . . combien Racine met les noms propres à la rime, ce qui est une droite et grande et brave et directe façon de quarrer le vers . . . Cela donne au vers une facture délibérée, complète, un achèvement plein carré, une absence d'hésitation, une volonté d'emplir. (Péguy, p. 715)

The figure of Mithridate takes on the same *carrure* as he rises from, and in the face of, the deepest misfortune. Without excitement, the old war-horse lets the 'appositions of misfortune' file past until, after we are utterly downcast, and after he has trumpeted his return with *Apprenez que*, he appears as a world-conquering ego: *j'attacherais* . . . [At the same time, these appositions are purely literary imitations of the Latin poets. Virgil, *Aeneid* VI.268: *Ibant obscuri sola sub nocte per umbram*, 'They went darkly on a lonely night through the shadows', uses what was already in Latin an archaic turn restricted to poetic language. Cf. Meillet, *Esquisse*, p. 223. See also *Phèdre* IV.ii, 1055–7, IV.vi, 1271–2, V.vi, 1527–8, for further examples of apposition.]

Parentheses also have the same effect of attenuating in advance:

J'épouserais, et qui (s'il faut que je le die)?
Une esclave attachée à ses seuls intérêts . . .

Bajazet II.v, 718–19

Votre mort (pardonnez aux fureurs des amants)
Ne me paraissait pas le plus grand des tourments.

Bajazet II.v, 687–8

[Cf. Ovid, *Heroides* 18.110: *Omnia sed vereor (quis enim securus amavit) / Cogit et absentes plura timere locus*, 'I am afraid of everything (for whoever loved without anxiety?) and the situation forces absent lovers to fear even more'.] Racine's representation of passionate love recognises the awesome fact that the lover will accept the destruction of the object of love rather than yield possession to anyone else. *Votre mort* begins the line as if a dagger were raised; the parenthetical self-assessment *pardonnez aux fureurs* . . . softens the impact of the frightenly logical maxim, which follows in l.688. (Note the plural *fureurs*,⟶ 27). The madness of love, at its cruellest in these lines, is justified by being ordered into a series of similar *fureurs*.) In other instances, the insertion of a phrase standing outside the normal construction of the sentence gives rise to disturbance:

Je n'ai pu vous cacher, *jugez si je vous aime*,
Tout ce que je voulais me cacher à moi-même.

Phèdre V.i, 1345–6

Ses prêtres toutefois, *mais il faut se hâter*,
A deux conditions peuvent se racheter. *Athalie* V.ii, 1581–2

A parenthetic insertion can allow a realistic image, on the limit of what was possible in the theatre in Racine's time, to be prepared, spiritualised and judged as a situation:

Elle approche: elle voit l'herbe rouge et fumante;
Elle voit (quel objet pour les yeux d'une amante!)
Hippolyte étendu, sans forme et sans couleur.

Phèdre V.vi, 1577–9

At the same time, this parenthesis draws together the picture painted in the following line and sets it in a frame.

Racine's use of parenthesis shows once again how he can endow a device inherited from classical styles with a wide range of nuances. [Cf. Ovid, *Metamorphoses* III.106: *inde, fide majus, glaebae coepere movere*, 'and then, incredibly, the earth began to move', where the insertion similarly points forward to prepare an unprecedented statement.] All these insertions create tension; they restrain and delay the listener who wants to hurry to the end of the sentence. The tension increases as does the impression of artifice when a poetic word-order is used, following a latinate pattern with inversion and retardation. Some instances are relatively harmless:

> Je ne fais *contre moi* que vous donner des armes.
> *Andromaque* III.vii, 950

> Je sais *à son retour* l'accueil qu'il me destine. *Bajazet* I.i, 86

But in the later plays the tension seems to be higher:

> De cette nuit, Phénice, as-tu vu la splendeur? *Bérénice* I.v, 301

First the dark night sky, which then suddenly shines forth in splendour!

> Il n'est point de rois . . .
> Qui, sur le trône assis, n'enviassent peut-être
> Au-dessus de leur gloire un naufrage élevé.
> *Mithridate* II.iv, 567–9

Mithridate means to say something like 'my going down might make other kings with all their glory envy me': his paradoxical thought is mirrored by the paradoxical image and the paradoxical word-order.

> Il faut de mon époux
> Contre un sang odieux réveiller le courroux
> *Phèdre* IV.vi, 1259–60

> Du temple, orné partout de festons magnifiques,
> Le peuple saint en foule inondait les portiques . . .
> *Athalie* I.i, 7–8

This last instance is reminiscent of the Latin figure of **hyperbaton,** as in *aequam memento rebus in arduis servare mentem*, 'Remember to maintain a calm mind in difficult circumstances', Horace, *Odes* 2.3.1–2, where all disturbance is held down by a rule which is also the source of the linguistic tension. Vossler has commented on *Esther* I.i, 64, *De mes larmes au ciel j'offrais le sacrifice*:

> The outline of a supplicant is visible but the details of her sacrificial action do not arrest the eye, for the affectivity of the words thus combined envelops and transfigures the vision. (Vossler, pp. 155–6)

One should add, however, that the word-order tension symbolises dynamically, so to speak, the state of tension of a character performing a sacrificial act. A similar instance in *Athalie* I.i:

> Et du temple déjà l'aube blanchit le faîte. 160

The temple comes into view before the explanation, *l'aube blanchit*; yet the temple is but a ghostly vision, since apart from its spire it remains entirely in the darkness.

On other occasions the speaker does not wish to make his meaning too open or obvious, and the synthetic word-order helps him to 'enfold' his thought:

> Et mon front, dépouillé d'un si noble avantage,
> Du temps qui l'a flétri, laisse voir tout l'outrage.
> *Mithridate* III.v, 1043–4

Rudler comments: 'la périphrase embellit et adoucit avec beaucoup d'art la chose, qui est douloureuse à dire' (Rudler, p. 140), but the synthetic word-order works towards the same effect as the circumlocution. Cf. the convoluted turn of phrase in the celebrated line *C'est Vénus toute entière à sa proie attachée* (*Phèdre* I.iii, 306). The word-order alone makes the 'attachment to the prey' a bodily entanglement and convolution.

13. Emphases

One does of course find in Racine many impassioned speeches where the speaker seems to give free rein to his sensibility. On closer inspection, however, one may recognise quite specific technical devices which constantly recur when excitement is to be portrayed. They are the rhetorical devices inherited from classical writing, which when applied systematically formalise and stylise speech. Racinian excitement is an excitement that does not forget to fold its garb of eloquence along tried and trusted lines! First, there is *solemn repetition* of threatening prophecies, anxious questions and insistent assertions:

> Il peut, seigneur, *il peut*, dans ce désordre extrême,
> Epouser ce qu'il hait . . . *Andromaque* I.i, 121–2

> Votre amour contre nous allume trop de haine:
> *Retournez, retournez* à la fille d'Hélène.
> *Andromaque* I.iv, 341–2

> *Quittez*, seigneur, *quittez* ce funeste langage.
> *Andromaque* II.ii, 505

> *Songe, songe,* Céphise, à cette nuit cruelle,
> Qui fut pour tout un peuple une nuit éternelle;
> Figure-toi . . .
> *Songe* aux cris des vainqueurs, *songe* aux cris des mourants . . .
> *Andromaque* III.viii, 997–1003

> *Qui sait* même, *qui sait* si le roi votre père
> Veut que de son absence on sache le mystère? *Phèdre* I.i, 17–18

Et toi, Neptune, *et toi*, si jadis mon courage
D'infâmes assassins nettoya ton rivage — *Phèdre* IV.ii, 1065–7
Souviens-toi . . .

Craignez, Seigneur, *craignez* que le ciel rigoureux
Ne vous haïsse assez pour exaucer vos vœux.
Phèdre V.iii, 1435–6

Mais j'en crois des témoins certains, irréprochables:
J'ai vu, j'ai vu couler des larmes véritables.
Phèdre V.iii, 1441–2

Excusez ma douleur. Cette image cruelle
Sera pour moi de pleurs une source éternelle.
J'ai vu, Seigneur, *j'ai vu* votre malheureux fils
Traînés par les chevaux que sa main a nourris.
Phèdre V.vi, 1545–8

Rompez, rompez tout pacte avec l'impiété . . . — *Athalie* I.i, 90

Faut-il, Abner, *faut-il* vous rappeler le cours
Des prodiges fameux accomplis en nos jours? — *Athalie* I.i, 109–10

Here are some examples of the device in Latin authors: *o pater, pater mi, salve*, 'o father, my father, greetings', Plautus, *Trinummus* (*The Three Pieces of Money*), l.1180; *sine sine fruatur*, 'allow him to enjoy it!', Apuleius, *Metamorphoses* 1.7.i; *Eheu fugaces, Postume Postume, labuntur anni*, 'Alas, the fleeting years pass by, Postumus', Horace, *Odes* II.14, 11.1–2; *Fuit, fuit ista quondam in hac re publica virtus*, 'Once, once, long ago there was that virtue in this state', Cicero, *Catilina*, 1.1.3; *nos, nos, dico aperte, consules desumus*, 'I say openly, it is we consuls who are wanting', Cicero, *Catilina*, 2.1.1. The French type *craignez, seigneur, craignez* combines repetition and insistent appeal. But Racine cannot cut up his line in the same bold way as the Latins could (at least in verse: the device was contrary to ordinary conversational usage). Component but not particularly independent parts of the sentence can often, by repetition, be elevated to ominous isolation: *j'ai vu, j'ai vu . . .* arouses our expectation, and the question, 'well what did you see?' becomes more pressing; similarly with *qui sait, qui sait*; *songe, songe*; *craignez, craignez*; *il peut, il peut* (increasing the power of 'being able', and the unpredictability of the one who 'is able').

Secondly, there is **augmentative asyndeton**, admittedly softened by Racine's delicate handling. Note the unison of the lines already quoted from *Andromaque*:

Captive, toujours triste, importune à moi-même,
Pouvez-vous souhaiter qu'Andromaque vous aime?
Andromaque I.iv, 301–2

with Bajazet's question:

> Infortuné, proscrit, incertain de régner,
> Dois-je irriter les cœurs au lieu de les gagner?
>
> *Bajazet* II.i, 483–4

Other lines with the same melody:

> Charmant, jeune, traînant tous les cœurs après soi . . .
>
> *Phèdre* II.v, 639

> Muet, chargé de soins, et les larmes aux yeux . . .
>
> *Bérénice* I.iv, 157

> Belle, sans ornements, dans le simple appareil
> D'une beauté qu'on vient d'arracher au sommeil.
>
> *Britannicus* II.ii, 389–90

Waves of sweet sadness, reminiscent perhaps of Virgil, roll from these triple repetitions to an emotional crescendo. The third leg does not bring a triumphant closure to the line, but ends it rather on uncertainty and contradiction (*importune à moi-même, incertain de régner*), and in any case with something that is transitory (*les larmes aux yeux, dans le simple appareil*, the gerundive *traînant*). It is weakness rather than strength that is multiply articulated in these asyndetons, problematic awareness rather than the clear formulation of problems. Even the following example from *Phèdre* is more insistent than grandiloquent:

> Les dieux livrent enfin à la Parque homicide
> L'ami, le compagnon, le successeur d'Alcide. II.ii, 469–70

[Alcide = Hercules; the line refers to Theseus.] The use of the present shows the intensive as opposed to an extensive import of the device:

> Mais le fer, le bandeau, la flamme est toute prête . . .
>
> *Iphigenie* III.v, 905

These are not three different menaces but a *single* danger triply articulated.

Where verbs are juxtaposed in this way, even forms as pressing as imperatives become something closer to expressions of pained sympathy than to real commands; they are *suggestive* rather than categorical imperatives:

> *Presse, pleure, gémis*; peins-lui Phèdre mourante . . .
>
> *Phèdre* III.i, 809

And in the narrative tenses of the verb Racine avoids the unreflecting, youthful flamboyance of *veni, vidi, vici* ('I came, I saw, I conquered', Suetonius, *Life of Caesar*, 37) as he avoids the theatrical repetition of *Catilina abiit, excessit, evasit, erupit* ('Catiline went out, went away, escaped, burst out', Cicero, *Catilina*, 2.1.1). Phèdre's confession is downcast, overcome:

> Je le vis, je rougis, je pâlis à sa vue . . . I.iii, 273

What is portrayed here is more a progressive centripetal collapse than a rhetorical self-aggrandisement: the stylistic *crescendo* matches a *piano* of the character's strength. To adapt Hatzfeld's terminology, we have a veni - vidi - victus sum device! Racine adopts the stylistic form from the classics, but attenuates and spiritualises it. He absorbs, as it were, all the sound and fury of the formula for excitement and retains only its stylising shape. When the listener for once really does hang on breathlessly to a narration of actual events, asyndeton does not occur: in the 'récit de Théramène', the sea-monster appears thus:

> L'onde approche, se brise, et vomit à nos yeux,
> Parmi des flots d'écume, un monstre furieux.
>
> *Phèdre* V.vi, 1515–16

(Similarly a little later, *l'essieu crie et se rompt*, where the sharp sound of the *i* is softened by the connective *et*.)

The classical use of asyndeton to depict and excuse chaotic involvement and promiscuity (e.g. in Terence, *Adelphoe*, l.470–1, *Persuasit nox amor vinum adolescentia. Humanum est*, 'There was the night, the wine, his youth, to persuade him. It's only human') seems quite foreign to Racine. He thus uses *tout* for the **compression of various attributes or ingredients**, to bring different nouns or noun-phrases into a single entity. The device expresses an ordered and all-seeing mind, in complete control of the contingent; it is the stylistic form 'd'un cœur toujours maître de soi' (*Andromaque* IV.v, 1323)!

The prototype of the *tout* device brings all the ingredients of a single line together, as in *Beauté, gloire, vertu, je trouve tout en elle* (*Bérénice* II.ii, 544), but the full form stretches over much longer passages:

> Quoi? sans que ni serment ni devoir vous retienne,
> Rechercher une Grecque, amant d'une Troyenne?
> Me quitter, me reprendre, et retourner encor
> De la fille d'Hélène à la veuve d'Hector?
> Couronner tour à tour l'esclave et la princesse;
> Immoler Troie aux Grecs, au fils d'Hector la Grèce?
> *Tout cela* part d'un cœur toujours maître de soi.
>
> *Andromaque* IV.v, 1317–23

> *Tout* conspirait pour lui. Ses soins, sa complaisance,
> Ce secret découvert, et cette intelligence,
> Soupirs d'autant plus doux qu'il les fallait celer,
> L'embarras irritant de ne s'oser parler,
> Même témérité, périls, craintes communes,
> Lièrent pour jamais leurs cœurs et leurs fortunes.
>
> *Bajazet* I.i, 157–162

(There is a very similar passage beginning *Tout conspirait pour lui* in *Andromaque* II.i, 464–70.)

> Quoi, madame! les soins qu'il a pris pour vous plaire,
> Ce que vous avez fait, ce que vous pouvez faire
> Ses périls, ses respects et surtout vos appas
> *Tout cela* de son cœur ne vous répond-il pas?
>
> *Bajazet* I.iii, 269–272

> Quoi! cet amour si tendre, et né dans votre enfance,
> Dont les feux avec nous ont crû dans le silence;
> Vos larmes que ma main pouvait seule arrêter;
> Mes serments redoublés de ne vous point quitter:
> *Tout cela* finirait par une perfidie? *Bajazet* II.v, 713–17

> *Tout* parle contre lui:
> Son épée en vos mains heureusement laissée,
> Votre trouble présent, votre douleur passée,
> Son père par vos cris dès longtemps prévenu,
> Et déjà son exil par vous-même obtenu. *Phèdre* III.iii, 888–92

Voilà can present a résumé in the same manner as *tout cela*:

> Sauver des malheureux, rendre un fils à sa mère,
> De cent peuples pour lui combattre la rigueur . . .
> Malgré moi, s'il le faut, lui donner un asile:
> Seigneur, *voilà* des soins dignes du fils d'Achille.
>
> *Andromaque* I.iv, 306–10

The breath-control required to speak a sentence of so many separate phrases corresponds to the overcoming of the 'tasks' which are here sketched out for Pyrrhus to perform; as the speaker reaches *voilà*, she has already scored a notional and respirational victory. [Des Hons quotes classical precedents here, though they are much less angled towards declamation and copiousness: *Scortum adducere, apparare de die convivium, Non mediocris hominis haec sunt officia*, 'procuring girls, preparing a banquet in the daytime: these are not the services of an ordinary man', Terence, *Adelphoe* I.965.]

14. Narration

The **listing of noun-phrases** alone constitutes a triumph over the contingent. To represent events by nouns overrides their happening; and the device is most appropriate in the portrayal of situations such as these:

> Solyman jouissait *d'une pleine puissance*:
> L'Egypte ramenée à son obéissance;
> Rhodes, des Ottomans ce redoutable écueil,

De tous ses défenseurs devenu le cercueil;
Du Danube asservi les rives désolées;
De l'empire persan les bornes reculées;
Dans leurs climats brûlants les Africains domptés,
Faisaient taire les lois devant ses volontés.

Bajazet II.i, 473–80

This is the right form for a poet describing an Augustan age, or who feels he was born into one. Disorder is banished, all is bathed in the fortune and fulfilment of being. Significantly Racine often puts narrative in the form *c'est son rêve accompli*, i.e. noun + participle for an event that happened. This use of the past participle is often rather paradoxical, e.g. *A ce mot, ce héros expiré / N'a laissé dans mes bras qu'un corps défiguré* (*Phèdre* V.vi, 1567–8) – an 'expired hero' can hardly be the real 'subject' of a sentence; it is a wittily contradictory and Latinate manner of expression. Cf. also in *Athalie* V.iii

De Joas conservé l'étonnante merveille. 1688

The active 'saving' of Joas is avoided – Racine gives a more personalised presentation of the process. Roustan, p. 259, commented on this example from *Britannicus* IV.iv:

Quoi? pour Britannicus votre haine affaiblie
Me défend . . . 1399–1400

'Le poète a ramassé dans un tour bref [*haine affaiblie* for *l'affaiblissement de votre haine*] une idée que la précipitation de Narcisse a vivement expliquée.' Lerch has given Latin models for this use of noun + participle, e.g. *Duo consules interfecti terrebant*, 'The death of two consuls caused terror' (literally, 'two dead consuls'), Livy 27.44.5; *In nova fert animus mutatas dicere formas corpora*, 'My mind urges me to speak of shapes metamorphosed', Ovid, *Metamorphoses* I.1. He also offers the explanation that 'the Romans' effort to keep a personal subject (object, etc.) in the sentence' plays a role in this device; he establishes in a 'stylistic interpretation' that the construction is not 'as abstract or cold' as others; and finally, to the question of whether its use in French is a Latinism or not, he answers *non liquet* (Lerch, *Prädikative Partizipia*, pp. 19, 31, 98, etc.). He gives a very fine demonstration that Voltaire, though he condemned Corneille's *après un sceptre acquis* as illogical, says himself (like Racine, see below!): *L'Angleterre ravagée par la peste, Londres réduit en cendres . . . mettaient la France en sûreté.* As Lerch admits elsewhere, the whole question needed to be looked at again less as a formula or logical problem than in terms of the history of style; stylistic interpretation and 'explanation' of the device must obviously be put together into a 'style-historical explanation and interpretation'.

Noun + participle replaces the becoming by a situation that has already come to be, replaces the individual stages of happening by listable facts: it gives us instead of the flow of history a string of individual pearls. Thus historical becoming is always made dependent on the dramatic character observing or recalling the history in question; Racine makes it obvious that he finds narration undramatic and forces himself 'd'en abréger le cours':

> Tu sais combien mon âme, attentive à ta voix,
> S'échauffait aux récits de ses nobles exploits,
> Quand tu me dépeignais *ce héros intrépide*
> Consolant les mortels de l'absence d'Alcide,
> *Les monstres étouffés*, et *les brigands punis*
> *Procuste, Cercyon*, et *Scirron*, et *Sinnis*
> Et *les os dispersés* du géant d'Epidaure
> Et *la Crète fumant* du sang du Minotaure.
> Mais quand tu récitais des faits moins glorieux
> *Sa foi partout offerte*, et reçue en cent lieux;
> *Hélène* à ses parents dans Sparte *dérobée*
> *Salamine témoin* des pleurs de Péribée;
> Tant d'autres, dont les noms lui sont même échappés,
> Trop crédules esprits que sa flamme a trompés!
> *Ariane* aux rochers contant ses injustices;
> *Phèdre enlevée* enfin sous de meilleurs auspices;
> Tu sais comme, à regret écoutant ce discours,
> Je te pressais souvent d'en abréger le cours . . .

Phèdre I.i, 75–92

Participial narration of this kind, dissolving history into medallions and summary terms, is familiar to us from classical sources, e.g. Seneca, *Troades* 229–31: *Haec tanta clades ac tantus pavor, / sparsae tot urbes turbinis vasti modo, alterius esset gloria . . .*, 'This great disaster to nations, this great terror, so many cities wrecked as though by a huge whirlwind, would be someone else's glory'. It permits all kinds of learned allusions to be elegantly worked into classical poetry and prose. Rapid movement from one medallion to the next allows the high points and splendours of the narrated situations to be put next to each other, and through allusive devices whole myth-cycles can be evoked. Compare the line *Et la Crète fumant du sang du Minotaure*, achieving its effect through its surface meaning, with l.80, *Procuste, Cercyon, et Scirron, et Sinnis* which impresses the ear with its *s*-sounds and its foreign accents, reminiscent of the Parnassian poets. In the following passage from the exposition of *Athalie*, spoken by the high priest Joad, the whole purpose of the noun + participle device is to highlight the *traits éclatants* extracted from the course of history:

> Faut-il, Abner, faut-il vous *rappeler* le cours
> Des prodiges fameux accomplis en nos jours?

Des tyrans d'Israël les célèbres disgrâces,
Et Dieu trouvé fidèle en toutes ses menaces;
L'impie Achab détruit et de son sang trempé
Le champ que par le meurtre il avait usurpé;
Près de ce champ fatal Jézabel immolée,
Sous les pieds des chevaux cette reine foulée,
Dans son sang inhumain les chiens désaltérés,
Et de son corps hideux les membres déchirés;
Des prophètes menteurs la troupe confondue,
Et la flamme du ciel sur l'autel descendue;
Elie aux éléments parlant en souverain,
Les cieux par lui fermés et devenus d'airain,
Et la terre trois ans sans pluie et sans rosée;
Les morts se ranimant à la voix d'Elisée:
Reconnaissez, Abner, à ces traits éclatants,
Un Dieu tel aujourd'hui qu'il fut dans tous les temps.

Athalie I.i, 109–126

The two long passages quoted both deal with *events* happening before the beginning of the dramatic action of the respective plays. Now I shall give an example of how a *character* is represented in a similarly prior situation (significantly, there is a predominance of participles):

Songe, songe, Céphise, à cette nuit cruelle
Qui fut pour tout un peuple une nuit éternelle;
Figure-toi Pyrrhus, les yeux étincelants,
Entrant à la lueur de nos palais brûlants,
Sur tous mes frères morts se faisant un passage,
Et, de sang tout couvert, échauffant le carnage;
Songe aux cris des vainqueurs, songe aux cris des mourants,
Dans la flamme étouffés, sous le fer expirants;
Peins-toi dans ces horreurs Andromaque éperdue:
Voilà comme Pyrrhus vint s'offrir à ma vue.

Andromaque III.viii, 997–1006

This portrait too is enclosed, framed by the *figure-toi . . . voilà . . .* The story is presented ominously, eerily (*songe, songe . . . figure-toi . . . peins-toi*), but it is seen throughout through the eyes of a character on stage, and so in some sense humanly contained. No overflowing of the stream of life! The word *peindre* is noteworthy: to paint is to fix in still form the movement of becoming. Cf. the medallion in the line from *Phèdre, Presse, pleure, gémis; peins-lui Phèdre mourante*, later altered to *plains-lui* (III.i, 809). And now a passage where a character is presented independently from his situation, like a figure in relief, as it were – but, significantly, a *gentle* relief (*douceurs*):

Je ne sais si cette négligence,
Les ombres, les flambeaux, les cris et le silence,

Et le farouche aspect de ses fiers ravisseurs,
Relevaient de ses yeux les timides douceurs.

Britannicus II.ii, 391–4

The description is structured antithetically (*ombres/flambeaux, cris/silence, farouche/timides*) but the antitheses are blunted by the attenuated formulation; Mesnard noted the 'beau désordre' of these lines and commented:

La peinture la plus achevée et la plus frappante n'est peut-être pas celle de la scène elle-même si vivement mise sous nos yeux, c'est plutôt . . . celle de l'âme de Néron.

15. Inner Depth

Racine often uses **aposiopesis**, the device of self-interruption in speech, to indicate that emotion does not permit the speaker to continue. This rhetorical device is of course also one that is familiar from Greek and Latin sources (e.g. Neptune's threat to the winds in *Aeneid* I.135, *quos ego*! . . ., 'I'll show you!', transl. Jackson Knight). Racine once again removes its tone of austerity and command, its harshness and violence, and interiorises the device. Usually, he gives, with a sentence constructed in rhetorical terms, a simpler, more directly emotional expression to natural feeling. Racine's economy of language and psychological discretion makes it quite natural for him to slow down the verbal flow from time to time, to allow a 'felt tone' to sound as from the heart:

Considère, Phœnix, les troubles que j'évite,
Quelle foule de maux l'amour traîne à sa suite,
Que d'amis, de devoirs, j'allais sacrifier,
Quels périls . . . Un regard m'eût tout fait oublier.

Andromaque II.v, 637–40

Pyrrhus interrupts his fine enumeration of the sufferings brought by love in order to give his assent to the power of a love which willingly accepts all these sufferings: the simple, inward-looking sentence that follows the aposiopesis reveals totally the inner turmoil of the character. Sometimes aposiopesis can save the poet a wearisome enumeration:

Sais-tu quel est Pyrrhus? T'es-tu fait raconter
Le nombre des exploits . . . Mais qui les peut compter!

Andromaque III.iii, 851–2

The instance that comes closest to the Latin model of *quos ego*! . . . seems to be in Roxane's speech to Bajazet:

Et ta mort suffira pour me justifier.
N'en doute point, j'y cours, et dès ce moment même . . .
Bajazet, écoutez: je sens que je vous aime.

Bajazet II.i, 536–8

However, in this instance (most editions do not actually print the . . . at the end of l.537) we have a speaker interrupting her threats not just because she cannot put all her rage into words, but because her inner self forbids her to use threatening words, but turns them for her into words of love; like Balaam (Numbers 24.10) she was 'called to curse' and yet must bless. It is also significant that Roxane, having presumed too much of her own anger, has to abandon the vindictive *tu* for the more measured and reasonable *vous*. The language of these lines follows as faithfully as can be imagined the running course of Roxane's emotions, and the breaking-off of speech corresponds to the point where her feelings switch. Cf. Athalie's words spoken in front of Joas:

> Quel prodige nouveau me trouble et m'embarrasse?
> La douceur de sa voix, son enfance, sa grâce,
> Font insensiblement à mon inimitié
> Succéder . . . Je serais sensible à la pitié?
>
> *Athalie* II.vii, 651–4

Athalie can literally say no more, express nothing further in words. There is a particularly famous passage in *Phèdre* I.iii where the heroine's reticence clashes with Œnone's impatient expectation to produce an edgy dialogue that catches at and finally extracts the sought-after name:

> PHÈDRE: Tu vas ouïr le comble des horreurs.
> J'aime . . . A ce nom fatal, je tremble, je frissonne.
> J'aime . . .
> ŒNONE: Qui?
> PHÈDRE: Tu connais ce fils de l'Amazone,
> Ce prince si longtemps par moi-même opprimé?
> ŒNONE: Hippolyte? grands dieux!
> PHÈDRE: C'est toi qui l'as nommé. 261–4

Further instances of aposiopesis from *Phèdre*:

> Théràmene, fuyons. Ma surprise est extrême.
> Je ne puis sans horreur me regarder moi-même.
> Phèdre . . . Mais non, grands dieux! qu'en un profond oubli
> Cet horrible secret demeure enseveli! II.vi, 717–20

> . . . vos invincibles mains
> Ont de monstres sans nombre affranchi les humains;
> Mais tout n'est pas détruit; et vous en laissez vivre
> Un . . . Votre fils, seigneur, me défend de poursuivre.
> Instruite du respect qu'il veut vous conserver,
> Je l'affligerais trop si j'osais achever.
> J'imite sa pudeur, et fuis votre présence
> Pour n'être pas forcée à rompre le silence. V.iii, 1443–50

The *enjambement* of *laissez vivre/Un* in l.1445–6 stretches the verse-form to its very limits. Racine probably never took his almost impressionistic imitations of the movement of feelings further than this. In any case, this example is the clumsiest and coarsest of all the cases quoted from the entire seventeenth century by Grammont, p. 36; see also ibid. p. 41 on voice-pitch indications. Aricie is here unable to name the 'monster' (Phèdre) to Thésée's face; she sets up a barrage or block for him to clear. The linguistic blockage symbolises the obstacle inherent in the situation. It is significant that although Racine is familiar with self-interruption he moderates the use he makes of it: as Vossler indicates, Aricie sketches out a 'perfectly regular' passionately excited speech, but Thésée later refers to it, saying *que cache un discours/ Commencé tant de fois, interrompu toujours*? (v.iv, 1451–2):

> It is palpably obvious here that Racine has sought to create a psychological interruption whilst avoiding any grammatical break. However much the soul may falter, the construction of the speech may not be allowed to crumble. That is commanded by the sustained style (*style soutenu*), as by the Franco-Grecian ideal of courtly comportment. (Vossler, *Sprachphilosophie*, p. 162).

By the same token, the lines spoken by Thésée are a good stage-direction to the actress playing Aricie, telling her that she has to make the 'psychological interruptions' dramatically perceptible, and break the grammatically faultless passage with pauses and hesitations.

If aposiopesis is seen as a way of returning to the inner depths and to the source of a character's speech, then Racine possesses yet another means of modelling speech on inner life. He can break off not simply as an aposiopesis, but in order to reduce the speech to its absolute minimum form, to compress and to abbreviate it. Every reader of Racine is familiar with **perfectly simple lines** and hemistiches which follow a high-flown passage and give a definitive closure to the speech in a brief, simple, and authentic form. It is characteristic of a poet opposed to crude effect that he should have such negative climaxes, so to speak, where rhetoric reaches its apotheosis in simplicity.

> Je passais jusqu'aux lieux où l'on garde mon fils.
> Puisqu'une fois le jour vous souffrez que je voie
> Le seul bien qui me reste et d'Hector et de Troie,
> J'allais, seigneur, pleurer un moment avec lui:
> *Je ne l'ai point encore embrassé d'aujourd'hui*!
>
> *Andromaque* I.iv, 260–4

It is tempting to take the last line out of context, and to quote it as an explosive expression of basic maternal feelings; but one should not forget to read it also in its connection with the pathos of the preceding lines and to feel how Racine makes a mother's cry emerge from a well-formed speech like natural spring water from a constructed fountain.

Mesnard gives examples of this feature of Racine's style, though he is wrong not to quote passages at length. He comments correctly:

> Mais Racine n'abaisse le ton que pour arriver à quelque effet, soit d'agréable naïveté, soit d'énergie; et quand il l'a abaissé, il le relève si promptement que l'impression d'une dignité soutenue demeure. (Mesnard, p. xxxi)

Concision after grandiloquence is more effective than concision upon concision. Racine could have cribbed even this from the classics: Laurand, II.39, mentions the alternation of long and short sentences in Cicero. 'Les petites phrases sont de deux sortes, tantôt familières, tantôt véhémentes. Souvent elles ont pour but de donner à la phrase plus de simplicité, de naturel . . .'

Let us consider now another famous passage from *Andromaque*:

> Avec quelle furie
> As-tu tranché le cours d'une si belle vie!
> Avez-vous pu, cruels, l'immoler aujourd'hui,
> Sans que tout votre sang se soulevât pour lui?
> Mais parle: de son sort qui t'a rendu l'arbitre?
> Pourquoi l'assassiner? Qu'a-t-il fait? A quel titre?
> *Qui te l'a dit*? v.iii, 1537–43

The last short line is well known; but it is worth pointing out how that pointed and imperious apostrophe emerges from customary pathetic declamation (*le cours d'une si belle vie, l'immoler, votre sang se soulevât*). Hermione begins by reproaching Oreste generally with the murder of Pyrrhus, and only in the *mot de nature* of the last line does she show that she – the instigator of the deed – has forgotten her own culpable role. A further example from *Mithridate*:

> . . . de vous présenter, Madame, avec ma foi,
> Tout l'âge et le malheur que je traîne avec moi.
> Jusqu'ici la fortune et la victoire mêmes
> Cachaient mes cheveux blancs sous trente diadèmes.
> *Mais ce temps-là n'est plus*. Je régnais, et je fuis. III.v, 1037–41

The staccato sounds of l.1041 give to the utter destruction of Mithridate's power the ring of a funeral announcement. One is reminded here of the short lines of Malherbe's lamentation, 'Consolation à Monsieur Du Périer' (1607); both have a laconic stoicism, or stoical laconism, facing the inescapable with words that are contained and limited; the awakening from dream to cold reality is matched by the stylistic change from abundance to sober brevity. Cf. this line from *Iphigénie*:

> Si ma fille une fois met le pied dans l'Aulide,
> *Elle est morte* . . . I.i, 134–5

> Seigneur, m'est-il permis d'expliquer votre fuite?
> Pourriez-vous n'être plus ce superbe Hippolyte,

Implacable ennemi des amoureuses lois
Et d'un joug que Thésée a subi tant de fois?
Vénus, par votre orgueil si longtemps méprisée,
Voudrait-elle à la fin justifier Thésée?
Et vous mettant au rang du reste des mortels,
Vous a-t-elle forcé d'encenser ses autels?
Aimeriez-vous, seigneur? *Phèdre* I.i, 57–65

The myth-telling (long-winded verbiage to the modern reader) is concluded by a hemistich giving a straightforward diagnosis of the whole situation in a nutshell, as if a tutor had seen through layers of deception into his pupil's soul.

Frappe. Ou si tu le crois indigne de tes coups,
Si ta haine m'envie un supplice si doux,
Ou si d'un sang trop vil ta main serait trempée,
Au défaut de ton bras prête-moi ton épée.
Donne. *Phèdre* II.v, 707–11

Imperatives which form one-word sentences, and which, like this one, draw the final consequence from a state of affairs and feelings, are often found at the head of a line:

Partez, séparez-vous de la triste Aricie.
Mais du moins en partant assurez votre vie.
Défendez votre honneur d'un reproche honteux,
Et forcez votre père à révoquer ses vœux.
Il en est temps encor. Pourquoi, par quel caprice,
Laissez-vous le champ libre à votre accusatrice?
Eclaircissez Thésée. *Phèdre* V.i, 1333–9

Je sais que, dès l'enfance élevé dans les armes,
Abner a le cœur noble, et qu'il rend à la fois
Ce qu'il doit à son dieu, ce qu'il doit à ses rois.
Demeurez. *Athalie* II.iv, 456–9

Mais je sens que bientôt ma douceur est à bout.
Que Joad mette un frein à son zèle sauvage,
Et ne m'irrite point par un second outrage.
Allez. *Athalie* II.v, 598–601

Initial imperatives of this kind were to develop into the short lines of La Fontaine's and Molière's *vers libre*. Racine uses a short (octosyllabic) line for the words of the oracle reported by Agamemnon in *Iphigénie* I.i; one of them contains a decisive imperative: *Sacrifiez Iphigénie*, l.62. [Cf. Grammont, p. 116.] Often in Racine a word is given first in rhetorical periphrasis and then in its simple form:

Moi, régner! Moi, ranger un Etat sous ma loi,
Quand ma faible raison ne règne plus sur moi!

> Lorsque j'ai de mes sens abandonné l'empire!
> Quand sous un joug honteux à peine je respire!
> *Quand je me meurs*! *Phèdre* III.i, 759–63

Quand je me meurs hits the reader like a thunderbolt. If I may adopt a phrase frequently used in histories of French literature: *Racine a enseigné la force du mot propre*. Similar examples from other plays:

> Car enfin n'attends pas que mes feux redoublés
> Des périls les plus grands puissent être troublés.
> Puisqu'après tant d'efforts ma résistance est vaine,
> Je me livre en aveugle au transport qui m'entraîne;
> *J'aime*. *Andromaque* I.i, 95–9

> Mais si, dans le combat, le destin plus puissant
> Marque de quelque affront son empire naissant,
> *S'il fuit*, ne doutez point que . . . *Bajazet* I.i, 63–5

In all these examples there is certainly a warm, felt, natural expressiveness, but the jewel sparkles from within an elaborate, 'precious' linguistic setting. Racine's 'felt tone' is simply a (heightened) variant of the ornate style.

Another device, in one way the contrary of aposiopesis, is the **post-amplification of a speech**, which leads to structural asymmetry. We might have expected such a device to produce an impression of spontaneity – as a speech bursts its original banks – had Racine not turned it, as was his wont, into a recipe or formula. Marty-Laveaux, p. cxv, gives examples, including these four parallel lines hitched on to *tant d'alarmes*:

> Bérénice, Seigneur, ne vaut point tant d'alarmes,
> Ni que par votre amour l'univers malheureux,
> Dans le temps que Titus attire tous ses vœux
> Et que de vos vertus il goûte les prémices,
> Se voie en un moment enlever ses délices. *Bérénice* V.vii, 1484–8

Cf. *Phèdre* I.i,

> Il veut avec leur sœur ensevelir leur nom,
> Et que . . .
> Jamais les feux d'hymen ne s'allument pour elle. 108–10

Cf. Terence, *missat ancilla ilico obstetricem accersitum ad eam et puerum ut adferret*, 'straight she sends a maid, to fetch the midwife – and a child as well', *Andria* 515 / *The Girl from Andros* III.ii, transl. Perry. There is a rather different kind of asymmetry in *Athalie* I.iv:

> Vous voulez que ce Dieu vous comble de bienfaits,
> Et ne l'aimer jamais? 369–70

The infinitive turns the speech right round in an ironical thrust, underlining the contradiction in the attitude that is being attacked.

This is also the place to put another typically Racinian stylistic figure, the **sequences of subordinate clauses** presenting a list of arguments or assertions. They are designed to give an impression of disorder, but linguistically they are of course exquisitely ordered: *beau désordre.*

> Elle s'en est vantée assez publiquement.
> . . . Qu'elle n'avait qu'à vous voir un moment;
> Qu'à tout ce grand éclat, qu'à ce courroux funeste,
> On verrait succéder un silence modeste;
> Que vous-même à la paix souscririez le premier,
> Heureux que sa bonté daignât tout oublier.
>
> *Britannicus* IV.iv, 1417–22

It is perhaps tempting to see Racine's numerous exclamatory sentences as vivid, direct expressions of emotion. There are certainly a great number of interjections to be found, especially *ah!* and *hélas!* (The celebrated closing sigh of *Bérénice* – Antiochus's *hélas!* – is perhaps the model for Goethe's ending of *Iphigenie auf Tauris* with *Lebt wohl!*, 'farewell'.)* However, Racine's interjections are very frequently counterbalanced in their effect by the rationality of the speeches in which they occur, e.g. by the clear antithetical patterning in *Ah! je l'ai trop aimé pour ne le point haïr* (*Andromaque* II.i, 416), or by the nomothetic force of the following:

> La plus sainte des lois, ah! c'est de vous sauver. *Bajazet* II.iii, 592
>
> Mais, hélas! de l'amour ignorons-nous l'empire? *Bajazet* II.vii, 1085
>
> Hélas! un fils n'a rien qui ne soit à son père. *Athalie* IV.i, 1262
>
> Loin du trône nourri, de ce fatal honneur,
> Hélas, vous ignorez le charme empoisonneur. *Athalie* IV.iii, 1387–8

Impersonal maxims like these acquire a warmth of individuality from the insertion of the 'voice of sensibility' in the interjection; a soft, stoical, passive tone of renunciation, of patient acceptance of mortal suffering, can also be heard in those formulations, as if their *ah!* and *hélas!* were the despairing cries of all humanity in its pain and suffering. Here too Racine's art can make these sounds of pain express the deepest level of meaning which his well-ordered sentences conceal:

> Crois que je n'aime plus, vante-moi ma victoire;
> Crois que dans son dépit mon cœur est endurci;
> Hélas! et, s'il se peut, fais-le-moi croire aussi.
>
> *Andromaque* II.i, 430–2

* Spitzer says that *Iphigenie auf Tauris* ends with 'Ach!' He is perhaps confusing it with Hölderlin's *Amphitryon*, which does indeed end thus.

In this *hélas!* (as in *s'il se peut*), Hermione betrays her utter despair that she could possibly believe in the hardening of her heart.

16. Apostrophe

The vocative use of styles of address is sometimes comparable in effect to interjections, e.g. *Un père, en punissant, Madame, est toujours père* (*Phèdre* III.iii, 901). I simply cannot understand why German and even French critics have taken exception to Racine's use of *Madame, Seigneur* etc. for classical or oriental characters. Just because these were the official styles of address of French lords and ladies of the seventeenth century does not mean, to a Frenchman, that they are applicable *only* to his own time and place. Would a German object if in a French translation of Goethe's *Faust* Gretchen were addressed as *mademoiselle* instead of *Fräulein*?

In Racine's time, as to some extent in modern France, it was impolite to address someone without using his title. According to Vaugelas, one had to say, 'Il n'appartient qu'à vous, *Seigneur* . . .' (quoted by Rudler, p. 136); nowadays children who say 'bonjour' without adding 'monsieur', etc., still sometimes get the ironical reply, 'Bonjour, chien!' Consequently it was quite impossible to put impolite or uncourtly expressions in the mouths of the historical, larger-than-life characters of the classical stage. The use of courtly styles of address within the family heightens the characters' majesty, e.g. when Néron says *Madame* to his mother Agrippine in *Britannicus* or when Joad addresses his wife as *princesse* (*Athalie*): the characters are seen not only in their mutual relations but also in relation to the world and to us. Politeness of this sort adds a special horror when terrible things are told with the utmost urbanity:

AGRIPPINE: Je connais l'assassin.
NÉRON: Et qui, madame?
AGRIPPINE: Vous.
Britannicus V.vi, 1650

Racine could work into these words the changes of his characters' souls: he saw that appelations and exclamations were in closer contact with emotion than other words, and he put into society's titular terminology emotional values ranging from pain to anger and joy. The best-known example is the *Seigneur* in Monime's speech to Mithridate:

Nous nous aimions . . . Seigneur, vous changez de visage.
Mithridate III.v, 1112

Grammont comments:

Ce mot 'seigneur' vient comme un cri couper et interrompre son récit jusque-là paisible . . . En prononçant les mots 'nous nous aimions' elle remarque dans la physionomie de Mithridate un mouvement subite qui lui arrache instantanément et comme malgré elle ce cri 'seigneur', et c'est en poussant ce cri qu'elle comprend la ruse dont elle a été dupe et embrasse les conséquences de sa crédulité. (Grammont, p. 75)

The cry *Seigneur* is the switchpoint also from narration to emotional outburst: *Seigneur* stands on the border between the two, for it is both a social form of address and a discharge of contained emotion. The line-initial *Seigneur* in the following passage from *Andromaque* is a different kind of switchpoint:

La Grèce en ma faveur est trop inquiétée:
De soins plus importants je l'ai crue agitée,
Seigneur; et sur le nom de son ambassadeur,
J'avais dans ses projects conçu plus de grandeur. I.ii, 173–6

Seigneur vents Pyrrhus's irony not on Greece but on its ambassador Oreste, who stands before him. The *s*-sounds, expressing 'un sifflement d'ironie' according to Grammont, p. 305, are unleashed by the ironic appellative *seigneur*!

Incomplete sentences used as exclamations fall with striking regularity into that well-groomed, classical-sounding two-part mould which became a 'fixed form' of Racine's style:

Bajazet interdit! Atalide étonnée! *Bajazet* III.vii, 1069

Quel coup de foudre, ô ciel! et quel funeste avis!
Phèdre IV.v, 1195

Vaines précautions! cruelle destinée! *Phèdre* I.iii, 301

O tendresse! ô bonté trop mal récompensée!
Project audacieux! détestable pensée! *Phèdre* IV.i, 1005–6

O soins tardifs et superflus!
Inutile tendresse! Hippolyte n'est plus. *Phèdre* V.vi, 1491–2

Pendant qu'il me parlait, ô surprise! ô terreur!
J'ai vu ce même enfant dont je suis menacée. *Athalie* II.v, 534–5

[Cf. Cicero, *O nomen dulce libertatis! o jus eximium nostrae civitatis!* 'O sweet name of freedom! exquisite right of our city-state!' *In Verrem* V.163.]

Apostrophes of higher powers – as a speaker in the midst of dialogue suddenly raises his eyes to heaven and moves from conversation into reading off an inner vision, as it were – constitute a further archaistic stylisation of pathos in Racine's plays. In classical times, when tragedy was still close to its roots in religious ritual, it was quite natural for dramatic characters to cast their eyes towards the gods that were not far away. For a Christian writer whose God lives nowhere and least of all around the *fauteuils* 'where the young bloods sit', such invocations are formal. That is why Racine also apostrophises places to bear witness, and internalises the inherited formula by having characters address their own souls or abilities; thus the glance originally directed to the gods above turns down to question the divinely inhabited inner depths of man.

> Seigneur, tant de grandeurs ne nous touchent plus guère:
> Je les lui promettais tant qu'a vécu son père.
> Non, vous n'espérez plus de nous revoir encor,
> *Sacrés murs,* que n'a pu conserver mon Hector!
>
> *Andromaque* I.iv, 333–6

> . . . Mais si l'ingrat rentrait dans son devoir!
> Si la foi dans son cœur retrouvait quelque place!
> S'il venait à mes pieds me demander sa grâce!
> Si sous mes lois, *Amour*, tu pouvais l'engager!
>
> *Andromaque* II.i, 436–9

Here, Andromaque is in conversation with Pyrrhus but calls upon the absent father Hector to witness the actions of his son and 'enemy':

> J'attendais de son fils encor plus de bonté.
> Pardonne, *cher Hector*, à ma crédulité!
> Je n'ai pu soupçonner ton ennemi d'un crime;
> Malgré lui-même enfin je l'ai cru magnanime
>
> *Andromaque* III.vi, 939–42

> Non, non: il ne fera que ce qu'il a dû faire.
> *Sentiments trop jaloux*, c'est à vous de vous taire:
> Si Bajazet l'épouse, il suit mes volontés;
> Respectez ma vertu qui vous a surmontés;
> A ces nobles conseils ne mêlez point le vôtre;
> Et, loin de me le peindre entre les bras d'une autre,
> Laissez-moi sans regrets me le représenter
> Au trône où mon amour l'a forcé de monter.
>
> *Bajazet* III.i, 817–24

> Noble et brillant auteur d'une triste famille . . .
> *Soleil*, je te viens voir pour la dernière fois. *Phèdre* I.iii, 169–72

> . . . mon père y tient l'urne fatale;
> Le sort, dit-on, l'a mise en ses sévères mains:
> Minos juge aux enfers tous les pâles humains.
> Ah! combien frémira son ombre épouvantée,
> Lorsqu'il verra sa fille à ses yeux présentée . . .
> Que diras-tu, *mon père*, à ce spectacle horrible?
> Je crois voir de ta main tomber l'urne terrible;
> Je crois te voir, cherchant un supplice nouveau,
> Toi-même de ton sang devenir le bourreau.
> Pardonne . . . *Phèdre* IV.vi, 1278–89

Invocations of abstract qualities, as in the example above from *Bajazet* III.i, are much favoured by Corneille and are common also in Spanish drama. Cf. Emilie's speech at the opening of *Cinna*:

> Impatients désirs d'une illustre vengeance
> Dont la mort de mon père a formé la naissance,
> Enfants impétueux de mon ressentiment,
> Que ma douleur séduite embrasse aveuglément,
> Vous prenez sur mon âme un trop puissant empire; 1–5

It seems to me that Racine uses this admittedly rather stiff stylistic device less often than Corneille. In *Phèdre* III.ii, where Corneille offers the model of *Souverains protecteurs des lois de l'hyménée*, Racine prefers to have his heroine appeal to Venus:

> Déesse, venge-toi: nos causes sont pareilles. *Phèdre* III.ii, 822

Mesnard fails to understand how Voltaire could contrast the 'beauté de poésie' of Corneille with the 'beauté de sentiment' of Racine. It must be because Voltaire was sensitive to the more emotional, more intimate manner of Racine – in *Phèdre* mortal woman turns to the divine Venus *as a woman*, so to speak, as her sister.

In the passage given above from *Phèdre* IV.vi, talking *about* an absent person turns into a speech *to* a person made present.

In the passage from *Phèdre* I.iii also quoted, the emphatic placing of vocative *Soleil* at the head of the line and the *enjambement* are obvious features. This is a characteristic mark of Racine's style, to make the preceding line on which the vocative of supplication hangs particularly long and thereby striking. Cf. further examples:

> A de moindres faveurs des malheureux prétendent,
> *Seigneur.* *Andromaque* I.iv, 337–8

> Et sur quoi jugez-vous que j'en perds la mémoire,
> *Prince*? *Phèdre* II.v, 665–6

Or the speech of the apparition to Jézabel in *Athalie*:

> 'Le cruel Dieu des Juifs l'emporte aussi sur toi.
> Je te plains de tomber dans ses mains redoutables,
> *Ma fille*.' En achevant ces mots épouvantables . . . II.v, 498–500

Also from *Athalie*:

> Vous m'avez commandé de vous parler sans feinte,
> *Madame.* II.v, 579–80

> Quelque monstre naissant dans ce temple s'élève,
> *Reine*: n'attendez pas que le nuage crève. II.vi, 603–4

These vocatives release emotional containment in the same way as Racine's interjections. One feels in the *Reine* of the last example a necessary discharge of tension, so to speak. The last word of the line, *crève*, is spoken from the soul!

17. Figures of Confidence

There is no lack in Racine of rhetorical **assertions in anaphoric form**, that is to say, sentences built up of a large number of parallel clauses each very much like the others, whose sheer quantity (like the storeys of a skyscraper) is what makes the effect an imposing one. This formal model of declamatory self-assurance matches the energy of a speaker confident of his own position, or seeking to establish his own confidence.

> Mais, de grâce, est-ce à moi que ce discours s'adresse? . . .
> Oui, c'est vous dont l'amour, naissant avec leurs charmes,
> Leur apprit le premier le pouvoir de leurs armes;
> Vous que mille vertus me forçaient d'estimer;
> Vous que j'ai plaint, enfin que je voudrais aimer.
>
> *Andromaque* II.ii, 530–6

[Cf. Cicero, *te imitere oportet, tecum ipse certes*, 'you should emulate yourself, compete with yourself', *Ep. ad familiares*, 9.14.6. The pointing finger penetrates into what is pointed at: *At! at! hoc illud est, Hinc illae lacrimae, haec illa est miseria,* 'Why, look you, here it is! Hence flowed those tears! This was the pitying heart!' Terence, *Andria* l.126 / *The Girl from Andros*, transl. Perry, I.i.] In the next example from *Andromaque*, Pyrrhus pleads with Andromaque to soften her refusal for the sake of Astyanax, and asks rhetorically:

> Faut-il que mes soupirs vous demandent sa vie?
> Faut-il qu'en sa faveur j'embrasse vos genoux?
>
> III.vii, 958–9

In the next scene, Céphise asks Andromaque whether she thinks Hector would blush at Pyrrhus's actions:

> Pensez-vous qu'après tout ses mânes en rougissent?
> Qu'il meprisât, madame, un roi victorieux
> Qui vous fait remonter au rang de vos aïeux,
> Qui foule aux pieds pour vous vos vainqueurs en colère,
> Qui ne se souvient plus qu'Achille était son père,
> Qui dément ses exploits et les rend superflus? III.viii, 986–91

Further examples:

> Songez-vous que sans moi tout vous devient contraire?
> Que c'est à moi surtout qu'il importe de plaire?
> Songez-vous que je tiens les portes du palais?
> Que je puis vous l'ouvrir ou fermer pour jamais;

Que j'ai sur votre vie un empire suprême;
Que vous ne respirez qu'autant que je vous aime?
Et, sans ce même amour, qu'offensent vos refus,
Songez-vous, en un mot, que vous ne seriez plus?

Bajazet II.i, 505–12

Cependant croyais-tu, quand, jaloux de sa foi,
Il s'allait plein d'amour sacrifier pour moi;
Lorsque son cœur, tantôt m'exprimant sa tendresse,
Refusait à Roxane une simple promesse;
Quand mes larmes en vain tâchaient de l'émouvoir;
Quand je m'applaudissais de leur peu de pouvoir,
Croyais-tu que son cœur, contre toute apparence,
Pour la persuader trouvât tant d'éloquence?

Bajazet III.iii, 907–14

Et comptez-vous pour rien Dieu, qui combat pour nous?
Dieu, qui de l'orphelin protège l'innocence
Et fait dans la faiblesse éclater sa puissance;
Dieu qui hait les tyrans et qui dans Jezraël
Jura d'exterminer Achab et Jézabel;
Dieu, qui frappant Joram, le mari de leur fille,
A jusque sur son fils poursuivi leur famille;
Dieu, dont le bras vengeur, pour un temps suspendu,
Sur cette race impie est toujours étendu?

Athalie I.ii, 226–34

Racine possesses a regular means of giving expression to the growth of a speaker's self-confidence in the course of speaking, namely the **self-confirming *oui*** which usually introduces formulations of a stronger kind than the ones quoted above, e.g.

Souffrez que j'ose ici me flatter de leur choix
Et qu'à vos yeux, seigneur, je montre quelque joie,
De voir le fils d'Achille et le vainqueur de Troie.
Oui, comme ses exploits nous admirons vos coups.

Andromaque I.ii, 144–7

Ce n'est pas les Troyens, c'est Hector qu'on poursuit.
Oui, les Grecs sur le fils persécutent le père . . .

Andromaque I.ii, 224–5

Madame, demeurez.
On peut vous rendre encor ce fils que vous pleurez.
Oui, je sens à regret qu'en excitant vos larmes
Je ne fais contre moi que vous donner des armes.

Andromaque III.vii, 947–50

The characteristic use of *oui* in the opening line of a play, intended to make the listener believe he is entering the middle of a conversation, shows to what extent the device was a formalisation of primary affective language.

> *Oui*, puisque je retrouve un ami si fidèle
> Ma fortune va prendre une face nouvelle.
>
> *Andromaque* I.i, 1–2

> *Oui*, c'est Agamemnon, c'est ton roi qui t'éveille.
>
> *Iphigénie* I.i, 1

> *Oui*, je viens dans son temple adorer l'Eternel. *Athalie* I.i, 1

In subsequent lines the neutral tone of initial *oui* is made even plainer by the regular anapaestic structure of the verse, which possesses, according to Grammont, p. 15, 'un effect de régularité ou de monotonie' or indeed no effect at all.

Similar remarks can be made on the **self-confirming *non*** in negative utterances:

> Seigneur, tant de grandeurs ne nous touchent plus guère:
> Je les lui promettais tant qu'a vécu son père.
> *Non*, vous n'espérez plus de nous revoir encor.
>
> *Andromaque* I.iv, 333–5

And finally, *que dis-je* (on artificial self-corrections, ⟶ 61).

> Des ennemis de Dieu la coupable insolence,
> Abusant contre lui de ce profond silence,
> Accuse trop longtemps ses promesses d'erreur.
> *Que dis-je*? Le succès animant leur fureur,
> Jusque sur notre autel votre injuste marâtre
> Veut offrir à Baal un encens idolâtre. *Athalie* I.ii, 167–72

Parallel to the *oui* at the opening of a play, indicating some extended preceding speech or thought or a preexisting situation, is the *enfin* with which *Mithridate* III.v begins. Rudler comments, p. 134:

> Mithridate semble sortir d'un long combat intérieur. Ce mot est comme un dernier soupir de douleur, un dernier écho de ces luttes intimes.

The plays and scenes of Racine rise up as if from silence; some fall back into silence with muted closing lines, e.g. *Bérénice*, ⟶ 85. This is quite the opposite of Corneille's direct opening lines: *Elvire, m'as-tu fait un rapport bien sincère?* (*Le Cid*), *Impatients déjà d'une illustre vengeance* (*Cinna*), etc; even Malherbe opens his *Ode au roi Louis XIII* with a direct attack:

> Donc un nouveau labeur à tes armes s'apprête . . .

The actor Baron is said to have delivered the first line of *Iphigénie* in a very low voice (Mesnard III.149): as Arcas, Agamemnon's confidant, awakes, the play itself wakes from the sleep of not-being.

A related device is that of **perseverating repetition**, where a speaker returns again and again to a word he (or his interlocutor) has used to emotional effect. In French one would say *il bat sur le même clou*, he drives the word in because the effect it arouses cannot be got rid of. This is Hermione, speaking to her confidante:

> De tout ce que tu vois tâche de ne rien *croire*;
> *Crois* que je n'aime plus, vante-moi ma victoire;
> *Crois* que dans son dépit mon cœur est endurci;
> Hélas! et, s'il se peut, fais-le-moi *croire* aussi.
>
> *Andromaque* II.i, 429–32

Other examples of perseverating repetition:

> PYRRHUS: Retournons-y. Je veux la braver à sa vue . . .
> *Allons.*
> PHŒNIX: *Allez*, seigneur, vous jeter à ses pieds;
> *Allez*, en lui jurant que votre âme l'adore,
> A de nouveaux mépris l'encourager encore.
>
> *Andromaque* II.v, 677–82

> PHÈDRE: Œnone, la *rougeur* me couvre le visage . . .
> ŒNONE: Ah! s'il vous fait *rougir, rougissez* d'un silence . . .
>
> *Phèdre* I.iii, 182–5

> ŒNONE: Ne vaudrait-il pas mieux . . .
> *Régner*, et de l'Etat embrasser la conduite?
> PHÈDRE: Moi, *régner*! Moi, ranger un Etat sous ma loi,
> Quand ma faible raison ne *règne* plus sur moi!
> Lorsque j'ai de mes sens abandonné l'empire!
> Quand sous un joug honteux à peine je respire!
> Quand je me meurs! *Phèdre* III.i, 755–63

[Amman, II.25, talks of 'raw blocks of words' in such cases and sees here a 'movement of tension between the two [characters]'.]

The use of exaggerated **round numbers** looks at first glance like an expression of affectivity; but when one has got used to the constantly recurring thousands, hundreds and scores, the figures have more the effect of a dull formula, corresponding to the Latin *sescenti* ('six hundreds' = 'a large number'). Racine also imitated the ancient usage of repeating the same round number twice over in an action of several parts, e.g.

> . . . Vingt fois, depuis huit jours,
> J'ai voulu devant elle en ouvrir le discours;
> Et, dès le premier mot, ma langue embarrassée
> Dans ma bouche vingt fois a demeuré glacée.
>
> *Bérénice* II.ii, 473–6

Similarly in *Phèdre* I.iii, 191–3, *Les ombres par trois fois . . . Et le jour a trois fois* . . . Malherbe's ironical prohibition had no influence on French classical writers in this respect.

> Et mon cœur, soulevant *mille* secrets témoins,
> M'en dira d'autant plus que vous m'en direz moins.
> *Andromaque* IV.V, 1307–8

> Andromaque, au travers de *mille* cris de joie,
> Porte jusqu'aux autels le souvenir de Troie.
> *Andromaque* V.ii, 1437–8

> Oreste vous adore;
> Mais de *mille* remords son esprit combattu
> Croit tantôt son amour et tantôt sa vertu.
> *Andromaque* V.ii, 1462–4

> Amurat à mes yeux l'a *vingt* fois présentée. *Bajazet* II.iii, 613

> Pensez-vous que *cent* fois, en vous faisant parler,
> Ma rougeur ne fut pas prête à me déceler? *Bajazet* II.V, 771–2

> Je sortais par votre ordre, et cherchais Hippolyte,
> Lorsque jusques au ciel *mille* cris élancés . . .
> *Phèdre* III.iii, 830–1

> Tremblante comme vous, j'en sens quelque remords.
> Vous me verriez plus prompte affronter *mille* morts.
> Mais puisque je vous perds sans ce triste remède,
> Votre vie est pour moi d'un prix à qui tout cède.
> *Phèdre* III.iii, 895–8

> Et retrancher des jours qu'aurait dû *mille* fois
> Terminer la douleur de survivre à mes rois. *Athalie* V.ii, 1573–4

The thousands and hundreds are obviously exaggerated numbers, but in as much as they are round numbers they serve to spread a mood of calm and lucid orderliness. Racine must have been aware of the formality of *mille fois* himself, as he gives a special shading to it by an unusual place in the sentence:

> Cet amour est ardent, il le faut confesser,
> Plus ardent mille fois que tu ne peux penser. *Bérénice* II.ii, 421–2

Also, when he wants to achieve a special effect, he uses different round numbers, e.g.:

> Jusqu'ici la fortune et la victoire mêmes
> Cachaient mes cheveux blancs sous *trente* diadèmes.
> *Mithridate* III.V, 1039–40

'Never, surely, before or since, was a simple numeral put to such a use – to conjure up triumphantly such mysterious grandeurs', comments Lytton Strachey, p. 14.

Of course, one also finds frequently in Racine the figure three attached to symbolic or significant actions, as in Greek and Latin authors: e.g. Euripides's Phaedra, like Racine's Phèdre, takes no food for three days (I.iii, 194). Consequently I take Monime's expression in *Mithridate* IV.ii below in a purely conventional sense:

> Les Dieux qui m'inspiraient, et que j'ai mal suivis
> M'ont fait taire trois fois par de secrets avis. 1237–8

However, the corresponding scene in III.v indicates only two 'reticences' on Monime's part. According to Mesnard, the actress Mlle Clairon introduced a third hesitation, at least gesturally, in the earlier scene. This is not another contribution to the study of mental arithmetic in art; the point is the predominance in Racine of conventional numbers.

18. Closeness and Distance

The **alternation of *vous* and *tu*** expresses the changing emotional rapport between characters. In one and the same scene, *vous* can give way to an intimate *tu* or its use as an aggressive form of address, only to be displaced again by a moderating *vous*, according to the undulations of the characters' sensibilities. The distinction has of course long been lost in English; in German, the *Du/Sie* distinction is far more fixed. The instability of Racinian *tu* corresponds to an instability of feeling. The alternations of the pronoun may indeed seem irritating in most of the *scènes à faire* of Racine's plays: it constitutes a kind of standard prop, already exploited to the full in Corneille (Roustan, *Précis*, p. 158). What comes off particularly well in Racine are the sudden, vehement explosions of a long-held-back *tu*, as e.g. when Hermione says to Pyrrhus in a scene begun with *vous, Je ne t'ai point aimé, cruel?* (*Andromaque* IV.v, 1356); she returns to *vous* in l.1371, *Achevez votre hymen* as she attempts to reach a solution, but as jealousy once again moves her in her attack on the man she loves she switches with the words:

> . . . Perfide, je le voi
> Tu comptes les moments que tu perds avec moi! 1375–6

Or in *Bajazet* II.i, Roxane's tirade (520–42) begins with an outburst in *tu* forms:

> Non, je ne veux plus rien,
> Ne m'importune plus de *tes* raisons forcées.

but moves to more civil and supplicating forms in l.538, *Bajazet, écoutez; je sens que je vous aime*. In her next speech, however, Roxane gives herself up to despair: *Ah! crois-tu . . .*, l.547. Note of course that immediately before the transition to *vous* in l.538 Roxane had threatened her lover with death:

Et ta mort suffira pour me justifier.
N'en doute point, j'y cours, et dès ce moment même . . . 536–7

With the *vous* of l.538 Racine hints that Roxane's love is too strong to allow her to carry out her murderous intention: by recognising this fact about herself the heroine gains distance and the ability to reflect upon her own feelings (*je sens que je vous aime*). Between *ta mort* and *je vous aime* a thought is thought through and shattered as it comes into conflict with a basic emotion. Precisely in so far as it is purely formal, the *tu*/*vous* transition acts as a linguistic reflex of instantaneous experience.

Similarly, Phèdre's declaration of love to Hippolyte in *Phèdre* II.v begins with *vous*, and then suddenly switches:

Ah cruel, tu m'as trop entendue.
Je t'en ai dit assez pour te tirer d'erreur.
Hé bien! connais donc Phèdre et toute sa fureur. 670–2

The *tu* form, here, delivers up the heroine's ultimate, intimate and deepest secret.

19. Figures of Meaning

Most of what needs saying about Racine's metaphors has been said already. For Vossler, Racine's principal characteristic, in contrast to Corneille, lies 'less in the transcendence of the physical than in the reincarnation of the intellectual meaning of words', in that his language 'is as much to be *thought* as to be *seen* through' (Vossler, *Racine*, p. 185). Note nonetheless the heightening of physical reference in a line like *Dieu tient le cœur des rois entre ses mains puissantes* (*Esther* I.i, 67) in comparison to its source in the Latin bible, *Cor regis in manu domini*, 'The king's heart is in the hand of the Lord' (Proverbs XXI.1). *Tient entre*, spoken from the heart, gives us a visual image and ranks as one of those 'alliances de mots inusités' for which Racine was notorious even in his own day (cf. Truc, p. 114). But one should really avoid this phrase coined by Racine's son Louis, for it assumes, in the manner of an instruction manual in rhetoric, that poetry is the *putting* together of *words*; it leaves out of account the fact that in metaphoric expressions *things* are *seen* together. Only the *listener*, testing a new expression against existing convention, gets the impression of words 'put together in new ways', and even he gets that impression only so long as he is not carried away by the poetry, not yet ready to take it on its own terms. Unfortunately Marty-Laveaux built his collection of Racine's stylistic traits on this theory of poetry as the putting-together of words, as if words were the pieces of a mosaic; for him, metaphor is all too often just a matter of a 'choix habile'.

Valéry speaks in a similar vein to Vossler of the 'équilibre admirable

. . . entre la force sensuelle et la force intellectuelle du langage' in Racine (quoted in Des Hons, p. 263) and it is primarily to the imagery that this refers. One might also say that Racine adopts conventional metaphoric formulae but revitalises them, restoring the etymological meaning of the word (cf. Des Hons, p. 116, on Anatole France's admiration for Racine's 'restoration' of the word *reliques*). Of course, some of the conventional formulae are fresher for Racine than for us, for whom some expressions have as a result become extremely obscure. For example:

> Et la plus prompte mort, dans ce moment sévère,
> Devient de leur amour la marque la plus chère.
>
> *Bajazet* IV.v, 1293–4

which has the approximate meaning, 'the most precious sign or mark of the love [of people like that], when they are deceived, is to wish for the immediate death of the person they love'.

> . . . votre amour, si j'ose vous le dire,
> Consultant vos bienfaits, les crut, et sur leur foi
> De tous mes sentiments vous répondit pour moi.
>
> *Bajazet* V.iv, 1498–1500

'Love took counsel from kind acts': i.e. because she was treated kindly by Bajazet, Roxane believed she had won his love. Cf. also *Britannicus* II.ii, 472, *D'aucun gage, Narcisse, ils n'honorent sa couche*, where, as Marty-Laveaux notes, *gage* in the sense of 'offspring' is a calque of Latin *pignus*.

We have already looked at cases like *Traîner de mers en mers ma chaîne et mes ennuis* (*Andromaque* I.i, 44), where the formulaic *traîner des chaînes* is returned to its original, concrete meaning by the addition of *et mes ennuis*. Cf. Malherbe, *Paraphrase du Psaume CXLVI*: 'Nous passons près des rois tout le temps de nos vies / A souffrir des mépris et ployer les genoux', where plural *genoux* has a retroactive effect on *mépris*, making it almost a concrete term. Racine prefers to remain on the border between the intellectual and the physical, the abstract and the concrete. Where his source or model is too intellectual or abstract, he adds a physical dimension (cf. above *Esther* I.i, 67); if his source is too concrete, he makes it more abstract, e.g. *respirer le jour* for *haurire lucem*, 'to breathe the light' (Mesnard, p. xlii; also in Corneille). In spite of all traditionalistic critical nonsense, even a contemporary of Racine's could perceive the 'newness' of turns such as *Il a par trop de sang acheté leur colère, Andromaque* I.ii, 226. 'J'avoue pourtant qu'*acheté* a quelque chose de plus nouveau et de plus brillant qu'*attiré*', wrote Subligny in 1668 (quoted in Truc, p. 106). Racine's use of conventional metaphors can thus also be considered as a classical *piano*, an instance of that same will to form which gives not a direct but a stylised and traditional reproduction of things; and yet the formulae adopted are not left as barren soil, but mellowed and fructified as La Fontaine's *vigneron* would have wished: *Creusez, fouillez, bêchez!* Racine works with conventional metaphors but his rule is: Keep off the conventional!

All that I can really add to existing observations on Racine's conventional formulae is the point that consistent use of traditional expression in the same play raises these elements to the status of leitmotivs. For example, there is nothing more ordinary than describing the effect of eyes or glances upon the object of a character's love; but Racine has the art of reducing his figures as it were to nothing beyond their glance and eye – certainly the most intellectual expression of love, as the medieval troubadours well knew. Here are some (not all!) of the passages in *Andromaque* where the power of eyes is mentioned. (Although the same eye-motif runs through all of Racine's plays, e.g. *Britannicus* V.i, 1501,* my point is to show the *density* of eye-allusions in a single play. The spectator cannot escape eyes that are also cast on him throughout an entire evening.)

Act I, sc.iv

PYRRHUS: Me refuserez-vous un *regard* moins sévère? 290
ANDROMAQUE: Quels charmes ont pour vous des *yeux* infortunés
Qu'à des pleurs éternels vous avez condamnés? 303–4
PYRRHUS: Mais que vos *yeux* sur moi se sont bien exercés!
Qu'ils m'ont vendu bien cher les pleurs qu'ils ont versés! 315–16
PYRRHUS: Animé d'un *regard*, je puis tout entreprendre: 329

Act II, sc.i

CLÉONE: Vous pensez que des *yeux* toujours ouverts aux larmes
Se plaisent à troubler le pouvoir de vos charmes . . .? 449–50

Act II, sc.ii

ORESTE: Je sais que vos *regards* vont rouvrir mes blessures . . . 485
Enfin je viens à vous, et je me vois réduit
A chercher dans vos *yeux* une mort qui me fuit.
Mon désespoir n'attend que leur indifférence:
Ils n'ont qu'à m'interdire un reste d'espérance;
Ils n'ont, pour avancer cette mort où je cours,
Qu'à me dire une fois ce qu'ils m'ont dit toujours. 495–500
Ouvrez vos *yeux*: songez qu'Oreste est devant vous . . . 531

* Spitzer's point is amply confirmed by later computer-assisted concordances: *œil/yeux* occur no less than 546 times in Racine's theatre and poetry.

HERMIONE: Oui, c'est vous dont l'amour, naissant avec leurs charmes,
Leur apprit le premier le pouvoir de leurs armes . . . 533–4

ORESTE: Vos *yeux* n'ont pas assez éprouvé ma constance?
Je suis donc un témoin de leur peu de puissance?
Je les ai méprisés? Ah! qu'ils voudraient bien voir
Mon rival comme moi mépriser leur pouvoir! 557–60
Venez dans tous les cœurs faire parler vos *yeux*. 568

Act III, sc.ii

HERMIONE: Que mes *yeux* sur votre âme étaient plus absolus. 815
ORESTE: Vos *yeux* ne font-ils pas tout ce qu'ils veulent faire? 817

Act III, sc.iv

HERMIONE: Vos *yeux* assez longtemps ont régné sur son âme. 885

Act III, sc.v

CÉPHISE: Je croirais ses conseils et je verrais Pyrrhus.
Un *regard* confondrait Hermione et la Grèce . . . 888–9

Act III, sc.vii

PYRRHUS: Mais, madame, du moins tournez vers moi les *yeux*:
Voyez si mes *regards* sont d'un juge sévère . . . 952–3

Act IV, sc.ii

CLÉONE: Vos *yeux* ne sont que trop assurés de lui plaire. 1146

Act IV, sc.iii

ORESTE: Croirai-je que vos *yeux*, à la fin désarmés,
Veulent . . . 1151–2

Act IV, sc.v

PYRRHUS: Et quoique d'un autre *œil* l'éclat victorieux
Eût déjà prévenu le pouvoir de vos *yeux* . . . 1291–2
HERMIONE: . . . si le ciel en colère
Réserve à d'autres *yeux* la gloire de vous plaire,
Achevez votre hymen, j'y consens; mais du moins
Ne forcez pas mes *yeux* d'en être les témoins. 1369–72

Act V, sc.ii

CLÉONE: Je l'ai *vu* . . .
Et d'un *œil* où brillaient sa joie et son espoir
S'enivrer en marchant du plaisir de la *voir*. 1433–6

Sometimes the eye or glance is physical – as when a gesture is indicated (*ouvrez vos yeux, tournez vers moi les yeux*); sometimes the eye is the mirror of the soul (*d'un œil où brillaient sa joie et son espoir, si mes regards sont d'un juge sévère*); sometimes eyes are autonomous beings which govern (*mes yeux . . . sur votre âme . . . absolus, vos yeux . . . ont régné sur son âme*) or speak (*ils n'ont . . . qu'à me dire, dans tous les cœurs faire parler vos yeux*) or act (*ils m'ont vendu bien cher*); and, finally, they are sometimes formulaic expressions for 'I', 'you', 'he', etc. (*quoique d'un autre œil l'éclat victorieux eût . . . prévenu le pouvoir de vos yeux*). Ocular omnipotence, proclaimed throughout the play, raises love to the level of an unphysical, intellectual essence, reflected dimly in the gleam of eye or glance.

Note that the *précieux* image of a battle of eyes (e.g. *Bérénice* IV.iv, 995, *les yeux armés de tous les charmes*) seems to be softened to a less turbulent power of the eye. In my view Mesnard is wrong to criticise in *Andromaque* 'l'abus que Racine a fait de l'*œil, des yeux*, quelquefois dans des phrases où ces mots sont employés improprement'.

After the troubadours, after Petrarchism, after Corneille, nothing could be commoner than the image of love as flame. [It has classical sources as well, though not exclusively as a metaphor for love; Cicero says *exardescit sive amor sive amicitia*, 'whether love or friendship flames up', *De Amicitia*, 27.100.] However, in *Phèdre*, and perhaps because of the etymological meaning of his heroine's name (Greek *phaedra* = 'the shining one'), Racine made fire the symbol of Phèdre's passion. Fire gives (i) light and (ii) warmth: Phèdre, daughter of Minos god of the underworld, tormented by dark forces, strives towards light, towards her ancestor the sun; in the first place she wants to see the light of day, though she is condemned to night and to death; in the second place she burns with love whilst she feels the warmth of life ebbing away. Darkness and light, heat and cold fight a constant battle in her. She is an oxymoron incarnate (⟶ 52), a dying light and a cooling flame, *une flamme noire*. Racine's shining Phèdre is a torch that flames only for a moment before going cold; a child of her 'brilliant' family, she takes after Helios (the sun-god) as much as she resembles Minos. And the black/light opposition is symbolic on the one hand simply for good/evil and on the other for conscious/unconscious. As this symbolic system has not previously been brought out, as far as I know, I give as the last piece of my evidence some of the relevant passages in *Phèdre*.

First I must mention however that I cannot accept Marty-Laveaux's simple identification of *flamme noire* with Racine's conventional use of the 'langage particulier de la galanterie'. The expression may be historically conditioned, but it is also elevated to a peculiarly Racinian symbol.

My colleagues Dornseift and Friedländer have pointed out a passage from Pindar, *Fragments* 108 (Bowra text): 'he who can look upon the light from Theoxenos's eyes and not feel longing surge up within him, his *black* heart has been forged over a cold *flame* from adamant or steel'. It is quite possible that Racine combined 'black heart' + 'cold flame' to make *une flamme si noire*, but such borrowing and combination leaves unexplained the symbolism of Racine's phrase, to which the elements 'black'and 'flame' are both necessary.

Finally, Mauriac does at least mention the role of light and dark in *Phèdre*:

> Le soleil pour elle seule, contre elle seule. Les autres humains n'existent pas. Hippolyte même n'apparait que dans la fulguration du désir de Phèdre . . . La face étonnée de Phèdre attire toute la lumière: à l'entour, des ombres s'agitent. (Mauriac, p. 130)

Since Mauriac goes on to say 'Le miracle de Phèdre est d'exprimer . . . les deux aspects du même amour qui tourmente les humains' – love as natural instinct, love as criminal instinct – he could have made clear the opposition between the light over Phèdre and the darkness before her eyes.

Act I, sc.i

THÉRAMÈNE: Et d'ailleurs quels périls vous peut faire courir
Une femme mourante, et qui cherche à mourir?
Phèdre, atteinte d'un mal qu'elle s'obstine à taire,
Lasse enfin d'elle-même et du jour qui l'éclaire,
Peut-elle contre vous former quelques desseins? 43–7
Chargés d'un feu secret, vos yeux s'appesantissent.
Il n'en faut point douter: vous aimez, vous brûlez . . .
134–5

Act I,sc.ii

ŒNONE: Son chagrin inquiet l'arrache de son lit:
Elle veut voir le jour: et sa douleur profonde
M'ordonne toutefois d'écarter tout le monde. 148–50

Act II, sc.ii

PHÈDRE: Mes yeux sont éblouis du jour que je revoi . . . 155
ŒNONE: Vous vouliez vous montrer et revoir la lumière.
Vous la voyez, Madame; et prête à vous cacher,
Vous haïssez le jour que vous veniez chercher?
PHÈDRE: Noble et brillant auteur d'une triste famille . . . 166–9
Soleil, je te viens voir pour la dernière fois! 172
ŒNONE: Les ombres par trois fois ont obscurci les cieux
Depuis que le sommeil n'est entré dans vos yeux;
Et le jour a trois fois chassé la nuit obscure
Depuis que votre corps languit sans nourriture . . . 191–4
Réparez promptement votre force abattue,
Tandis que de vos jours, prêts à se consumer,
Le flambeau dure encore, et peut se rallumer. 214–16
PHÈDRE: Je le vis, je rougis, je pâlis à sa vue . . . 273
Je sentis tout mon corps et transir et brûler.

Je reconnus Vénus et ses feux redoutables . . . 276–7
En vain sur les autels ma main brûlait l'encens . . . 284
Ce n'est plus une ardeur dans mes veines cachée:
C'est Vénus toute entière à sa proie attachée . . . 305–6
J'ai pris la vie en haine, et ma flamme en horreur.
Je voulais en mourant prendre soin de ma gloire,
Et dérober au jour une flamme si noire . . . 308–10
Et que tes vains secours cessent de rappeler
Un reste de chaleur tout prêt à s'exhaler. 315–16

Act I, sc.v

Et si l'amour d'un fils en ce moment funeste
De mes faibles esprits peut ranimer le reste. 365–6

Act II, sc.v

ces dieux qui dans mon flanc
Ont allumé le feu fatal à tout mon sang . . . 679–80
J'ai langui, j'ai séché, dans les feux, dans les larmes. 690

Act III, sc.i

ŒNONE: Vous nourrissez un feu qu'il vous faudrait éteindre. 754

Act III, sc.iii

PHÈDRE: ma flamme adultère . . . 841
Penses-tu que, sensible à l'honneur de Thésée,
Il lui cache l'ardeur dont je suis embrasée? 845–6

Act IV, sc.i

ŒNONE: Honteuse du dessein d'un amant furieux
Et du feu criminel qu'il a pris dans ses yeux,
Phèdre mourait, Seigneur, et sa main meurtrière
Eteignait de ses yeux l'innocente lumière. 1015–18
THÉSÉE: Et ce feu dans Trézène a donc recommencé? 1031

Act IV, sc.vi

PHÈDRE: Mon époux est vivant, et moi je brûle encore! . . . 1266
Misérable! et je vis? et je soutiens la vue
De ce sacré soleil dont je suis descendue? 1273–4

Act V, sc.vii

Le ciel mit dans mon sein une flamme funeste . . . 1625
Elle a craint qu'Hippolyte . . .
Ne découvrît un feu qui lui faisait horreur. 1627–8
J'ai pris, j'ai fait couler dans mes brûlantes veines
Un poison . . .
Déjà jusqu'à mon cœur le venin parvenu
Dans ce cœur expirant jette un froid inconnu;

Déjà je ne vois plus qu'à travers un nuage
Et le ciel et l'époux que ma présence outrage;
Et la mort, à mes yeux dérobant la clarté,
Rend au jour, qu'ils souillaient, toute sa pureté . . .
THÉSÉE: . . . D'une action si noire
Que ne peut avec elle expirer la mémoire!
Allons, de mon erreur, hélas! trop éclaircis,
Mêler nos pleurs au sang de mon malheureux fils. 1637–48

20. Conclusions

The material presented in this long essay adequately demonstrates, I think, why, in spite of Racine's underlying lyricism and psychological profundity, his poetry always makes on us an impression of something muted, distanced and icy; and why it takes full maturity, and a special understanding of the stylistic expressions of modesty and restraint, in order even to feel the hidden ardour of Racine. It will have become obvious to every reader of Racine that individual lines quoted out of context make a much greater impact than when they are left in the even rhythm of the full dialogue: look for example at Des Hons's collection of quotations (put together only at the instigation of Des Hons's master, Anatole France). The reason for this is that the sheer mass of attenuating devices piled on top of each other in the speeches of Racine's characters has its own powerful effect on the reader or hearer, an effect which is absent when individual 'jewels' of tested emotional value are presented in isolation. The objection that might be made to all this would be that I have analysed *only* the unpoetical and rebarbative elements of Racine's style, and that the infinitely great and ageless beauty of his poetry, like the dust on a butterfly's wings, has fallen through the holes in my stylistic and grammatical butterfly-net.

My reply is (a) yes! and (b) no! The objection holds, in so far as I could not (as I pointed out) decompose the *composite* beauty of musical, syntactic, lexical, rhythmical and intellectual elements without damage (the limits of the analytic method are precisely that it isolates components which have their specific effect only in combination with all these others); and the objection does not hold, in so far as the stoical Racine himself attached at least as much importance to the attenuating devices of his classical poetry as he did to the lyrical, elegiac, direct or musical outpouring of his inner self, a project so much more in accordance with our modern but still romantic artistic tastes. As Fubini rightly says, Racine was 'one of the serenest poets to have sung in any age'. Sainte-Beuve made the same point in 1840: 'Il y a le calme de l'âme supérieure et divine même au travers et au-dessus de tous les pleurs et de toutes les tendresses' (*Port-Royal*, p. 600).

It does not seem easy to do justice both to Racine and to Victor Hugo at the same time. This is how Maurras puts it:

> Lorsque j'aimais Hugo en brute, il me souvient que j'entendais mal le divin Racine; et depuis que j'entends Racine, il me semble que, désormais forcé de n'aimer plus Hugo qu'avec mesure, j'en viens à l'aimer beaucoup mieux.

Mesnard, on the other hand, is a Racinian who is quite unfair to the romantics. Comparing Racine's line *Je suis un malheureux que le destin poursuit (Mithridate* IV.ii, 1218) with Hugo's *Je suis une force qui va* (*Hernani* IV.iii), he exclaims: 'de quel côté est l'emphase et la déclamation, de quel côté est la simplicité et la nature!' But that is not the point: the contrast is not between simplicity and bombast, but between closed and open representation. *Je suis une force qui va* opens onto the infinite with its uncomplemented verb, whilst *je suis un malheureux que le destin poursuit* is a self-enclosed affirmative sentence, its speaker shut in as it were in the doorless vault of an implacable destiny.

Another misleading comparison from Maurras:

> Il y a, quoi qu'on dise, une hiérarchie des plaisirs, une noblesse et une plèbe des sentiments . . . Quand vous aurez relu Racine et que les jolis vers d'Aymerillot vous tintinnabuleront à l'oreille:
>
> Deux liards couvriraient fort bien toutes mes terres
> Mais tout le grand ciel bleu n'emplirait pas mon cœur*
>
> une céleste voix aura vite couvert cette rumeur qui ne manque d'ailleurs pas d'agrément. Vous entendrez les monosyllabes incomparables:
>
> Le ciel n'est pas plus pur que le fond de mon cœur
>
> et vous sentirez la différence de ces deux arts. Et vous comprendrez qu'il n'y en a qu'un. (Maurras, p. 70)

Ill-will makes Maurras unjust and, what is worse, incorrect. When one compares two artistic practices, one should at least give accurate quotations. Racine's Hippolyte says in fact 'Le *jour* n'est pas plus pur que le fond de mon cœur' (*Phèdre* IV.ii, 1112). However, that makes the comparison invalid. In Hugo there is a rising heart full of sky, and thus the sequence of monosyllables can be broken by a broad-bellied *emplirait* – the expanse of the sky is felt in physical terms; in Racine we have a serene assertion of spiritual purity, in which the *light of day* functions only as a measure of that purity: no rising, but a stable essence. Skyward space versus clear daylight! The unending versus perfection! Apart from that, the two lines must be seen in their respective contexts. Aymerillot is something of a boaster and an artful dodger; despite his somewhat effeminate appearance he does not renounce Hugolian stylistic panache: the speech he gives is one of

* Victor Hugo, *La Légende des siècles*, p. 151

self-congratulation (Charlemagne calls it 'un propos hautain') which is subsequently justified by his actions. Hippolyte, on the other hand, is an untamed and timid youth ('J'ai poussé la vertu jusques à la rudesse', l.1110) who fails because he is no orator – because his inner self does not permit him to speak the truth which would cleanse him of all suspicion. The situations and characters are simply not comparable!

It is highly characteristic of French explicators of Racinian texts (Rudler, Roustan) to select passages in which one character outmanoeuvres another with calculated cunning, and not, as would seem to me more to the point, passages such as Phèdre's confession or Esther's prayer. In the 'intrigue scenes' one finds a predominance of those marks of rational rhetoric which are easy to analyse, what Rudler calls the 'mathematics of the soul'. But then the method of *l'explication française*, like all explanations of the poetic, but to an even higher degree than our method, is a rationalisation of the irrational.

It is significant that Péguy, in 'Victor Marie, comte Hugo', underlines the cruelty in Racine (a sign, for Péguy, that Racine, in contrast to Corneille, lived and wrote without a state of grace) and considers the word *cruel(le)* not simply as a remnant of *précieux* language but as a leitmotiv, as 'le mot même de la révélation du cœur'. According to Péguy, cruelty goes to the heart of Racine's characters: 'Tout est adversaire, tout est ennemi aux personnages de Racine; les hommes et les dieux; leur maîtresse, leur amant, leur propre cœur'. By highlighting words he demonstrates in a passage taken to exemplify the 'tenderness' of 'le tendre Racine' the filial savageness of Iphigénie, the cruel daughter of Clytemnestre and Agamemnon:

Mon père
Cessez de vous troubler, vous n'êtes point trahi.
Quand vous commanderez, vous serez *obéi*.
Ma vie est votre bien. Vous voulez le reprendre:
Vos ordres *sans détour* pouvaient se faire entendre.
D'un œil *aussi content*, d'un cœur aussi *soumis*
Que j'acceptais l'époux *que vous m'aviez promis*,
Je saurai, *s'il le faut*, victime *obéïssante*
Tendre au fer de Calchas une tête *innocente*,
Et, respectant le coup *par vous-même ordonné*,
Vous *rendre* tout le sang *que vous m'avez donné*.

Iphigénie IV.iv, 1174–84

(I would also have highlighted *victime*, l.1181 and *une*, l.1182.) Péguy comments:

Il n'y a pas un mot, pas un vers, pas un demi-vers, pas un membre de phrase, pas une conjonction, il n'y a pas un mot qui ne porte pour mettre l'adversaire (le père) dans son tort. Le dialogue racinien est généralement un combat . . . dans le dialogue racinien le partenaire est généralement, constamment un adversaire;

> le propre du personnage racinien est que le personnage racinien parle constamment pour mettre l'adversaire dans son tort, ne se propose que de mettre l'adversaire dans son tort, ce qui est le commencement même, le principe de la cruauté . . . Les victimes de Racine sont . . . plus cruelles que les bourreaux de Corneille. (Péguy, pp. 772–3)

Can it be a coincidence that Grammont lists five pages of examples of 'sifflements' – the harsh sound of scorn, irony, contempt, hatred – in Racine's verse (Grammont, pp. 304–9)? However, I don't think we should ascribe *cruauté* so much to the individual characters of Racine as to the poet's world-view, which was indeed the world-view of a man without the state of grace, in which the human is seen not from the point of view of a suffering fellow-human but observed and objectified from the vantage point of a *rational and objective nature*. In the passage quoted Iphigénie expresses (1) her submission to her father's will, (2) the revolt of the objective against her father's will. She speaks almost literally with two tongues, with the tongue of Iphigénie and with the 'supra-Iphigenial' tongue of objective rationality. Indeed she gives her father 'une réponse terrible . . . d'une sourde cruauté tragique', but only because the gentle tones of Iphigénie sound on the same note as the harsh reproaches of objective reason. It is this 'second voice' that performs the task of putting her 'opponent' in the wrong and which the pro-mystical and anti-political Péguy noticed particularly sharply; it is the voice of Reason, which constantly conducts the argument when applied against another character, and which also affects the spectator as a 'cruel' displacement of felt emotion. All the words and phrases highlighted by Péguy constitute a straightforward accusation of Agamemnon (which could all be summarised by an outraged *vous l'avez voulu, vous*!), but that is precisely the point: less a complaint of an I-subject as an accusation of a you-object; but the accusation must, like an orderly process of law, pay heed to the rules of reason. A character like Phèdre differs from Iphigénie only in that the accused is the accuser herself; the self-mortifying lucidity of Racine's passionate heroine has always been stressed by critics. And the 'double illumination' of which Vossler writes in connection with *Athalie*: is this not the same ability of a Racinian character to see into her human aberration and at the same time to measure it by the standards of reason? (By stressing the sober and reasonable elements in Racine we also get round the difficulties of 'le cas Racine', of the biography of Racine the man, i.e. how did such a cool and calculating man become a great poet, and eventually a pious paterfamilias and opponent of the theatre? In his own lifetime he was very much inclined to double illumination and was himself two-faced.) Racine does not let himself side with or against Athalie: he looks at her case coolly, 'avec des yeux de gentilhomme ordinaire du roi' (Mauriac, with a reminiscence of Nietzsche's 'morality of the master'), and he allows this cool sobriety to flow into Athalie's manner of expression, which does not only alternate between *Cette paix que je cherche et qui me fuit toujours* (II.iii, 438) and *Je jouissais en paix du fruit de ma sagesse* (II.v, 489). In accordance with Racine's custom, Athalie's language often hovers between calm and disturbance, between understanding and instinct, between reflection and lyricism.

We still actually know relatively very little about the genesis of the formal language of the modern Romance literatures. E. Norden has shown that the ornamental style of the baroque–*précieux* of the sixteenth and seventeenth centuries was conditioned by Greek and Latin models. But to my knowledge it has never been shown how these ornamental forms came to be calmed and controlled to produce classical style. I hope the present essay has provided some small preparatory sketch for the huge task that remains. A glance at the *sources* of the individual stylistic devices of Racine's classical *piano* shows in nearly every case a model from classical antiquity (at most one can see in the symbolic system of *Phèdre* something of a Christian–dualistic, Hugolian black/white polarity). This is a remarkable observation, as Racine tends to be presented as a Christian and Jansenist poet. On a stylistic level, however (and not excluding the biblical plays, disregarding the material reference of the comparisons), he is entirely under the spell of the classics as transformed by Petrarch. He modulates the overbaroque and exaggerated traits of the archaising imitators, he spiritualises classical formulae, but his forms of language and his formulaic language are classical. I would therefore disagree with Vossler (e.g. on p. 167 of his *Jean Racine*) and accept the 'learned and humanist character' of Racinian writing. Moreover Vossler concedes the point himself on p. 152: 'Racine's poetry can be described as humanist only in respect of its shaping, not in respect of the experience it communicates'. But how can experience not agree with the shape in which it is put? The 'élégance de l'expression' which Racine aimed for (according to the preface to *Bérénice*) he learnt from the poets of Greece and Rome.

Racine also speaks in the preface to *Bérénice* of 'la violence des passions' as appropriate to the stage, which does not favour Vossler's thesis that Racine is a 'poet of renunciation'. What makes the *piano* of form in Racine comprehensible is precisely that *passion* is the object of representation through such attenuated language. Erich Auerbach has argued in his Marburg lecture and elsewhere against the 'almost invincible prejudice that a perfectly harmonising and faultless *form* must be matched by a psychic *content* of similarly classical harmony'. 'To put it plainly for once: French classicism is not classical in the German sense, it is baroque.' [Cf. also Auerbach, 'Racine', p. 341.] I for my part have come to the same view from a consideration of the baroque outside of France in Racine's period, and of French baroque art which was supposed to stand beside contemporaneous literary classicism. French baroque is a measured, classical-like baroque, 'un romantisme dompté' as Gide says in 'Incidences' (1924), his famous essay on Poussin as a modulated Rubens. Note that even nowadays the movements and diction in a performance of one of the classical dramas at the *Comédie française* can still be called 'baroque'. Hatzfeld has also established on the basis of religious lyric poetry the baroque character of French classicism, which is a special kind of baroque.

Racine's linguistic inventions are delicate, elegant loosenings of classical shapes, subtle variations of ancient forms, rather than bold and daring plunges into the hot springs of language-creation. We are led by this argument to the image, which has unfortunately become so traditional, of the gardens of Versailles, and of the French as a 'nation of gardeners', as Keyserling puts it:

> The French mind has produced truly original things more rarely than any other, and that's a fact. It is certainly inventive, but only on the basis of immutable premises; its ideal mind is that of a finishing school.

But the new saplings in a long-established garden are surely still living, beautiful trees! One might also be reminded here of Hugo von Hofmannsthal's fine words about French writing:

> Within such constant change ambition has been directed not towards escape but towards the fulfilment of traditional requirements. A great observer said that, for the French, rigorous discipline in personal expression was to be preferred to the impact of the unique . . . In this most sociable of nations there has developed also in its literature that predominant feature of sociability of which the basis is a constantly wakeful mutual attentiveness and rivalry . . . This great attentiveness itself ensures victory for decorous beauty, for a single felicitous trait, for elegance. Originality has only a conditional acceptance . . . but relative superiority, a slight overstepping of a lesser degree, is highly prized (Hofmannsthal, 'Schrifttum', p. 12)

In conclusion, I would like to take up this sentence of Marty-Laveaux's, quoted by Gonzague Truc, p. 109:

> La règle la plus ordinaire contre laquelle il importe de se prémunir d'abord quand on veut étudier la langue d'un écrivain, c'est de croire que tout ce qui dans ses œuvres s'éloigne de l'usage actuel doit lui être attribué en propre, caractérise sa manière, sa langue à lui, porte la marque de son tour d'esprit et de son génie.

Marty-Laveaux is writing from the point of view of a historian whose task is to insert a writer's language into the language of the age in which he lived. However, poetic language and its enveloping period-language affect us in a particular way. If Racine is a child of his age, he also carries in him the significant features of his personality: and thus what we notice as special in him we take to be characteristic of him, not merely of his period. This alone is enough to justify the present attempt to analyse Racine's language directly, *with the linguistic sensitivity that we have as we are now in the twentieth century*, and without making a long detour through the evidence of contemporary usage which is in any case contradictory and incomplete. Racine belongs to his own time; but he also belongs to us.

To take a case in point, the philologist Marty-Laveaux informs us (*Préface*, p. xiii) that the expression *Chatouillaient de mon cœur l'orgueilleuse faiblesse* (*Iphigénie*, l.82), usually attributed to Racine, was not of Racine's invention and goes back at least to Ronsard. This last detail is certainly useful knowledge for stylistic historians to have, but it contributes nothing to our understanding of the particular pleasure which Racine's work as such gives us; for in the moment of our enjoyment of Racine we know nothing (indeed, we do not wish to know) of Ronsard. However, whether Racine found it in Ronsard or reinvented it himself, *chatouiller* fits the list of examples showing originally concrete expressions brought to the edge of becoming formulae (⟶ 60, 97; and the line quoted also shows *chatouiller* in interaction with other Racinianisms (preposition of dependent complement, oxymoron, substitution of quality for person), so that the borrowed conceit (let's suppose it is borrowed) appears transformed in a completely and peculiarly Racinian way. Strictly speaking, then, no feature of a poet's language can be isolated and compared to (similarly isolated and decontextualised) parallel features in the language of another poet. The individual traits of a poetic opus are to be compared in the first instance *to each other*, as the members, or elements, or props of a system, stable and entire unto itself. To excise an element from the organ with which it interacts and to put it in relation with elements of other earlier systems does not do justice to the poet: it makes the creator look like a plagiarist.

Marty-Laveaux also teaches us that *détruire* as applied to persons (*Montrer aux nations Mithridate détruit, Mithridate,* l.921) is not a Racinian invention but is attested in Corneille and earlier. But the line in which it occurs also exhibits the characteristic Racinian *montrer* (reference to history as drama) and the Latinate participial construction. Similarly it is not enough to refer to the *précieux* usage of *naissant* = *jeunes* (e.g. 'Les Dames aiment la jeunesse et vous êtes naissant') when commenting on *Enfin Néron naissant / A toute les vertus d'Auguste vieillissant* (*Britannicus* I.i, 29) since we are dealing here not with *naissant* but with *Néron naissant*, a medallion of the gestating monster in opposition to *Auguste vieillissant*, the medallion of ageing virtue. It is known that Racine wished to stress the gestation of a monster in this play ('Mais c'est ici un monstre naissant', *Première Préface* (1670)): he extracts from the *précieux* usage of *naissant* all its force of meaning and emotion – and all its dramatic dynamic.

The *piano* of Racine's language alienates him from the heart of modern Frenchmen too. I venture to suggest that the average educated Frenchman (with a few individual exceptions) does not have in his heart of hearts nearly so many Racinian shrines as official panegyrics, propped up by the education system and public authorities, would have us believe. With all the clarity and straightforwardness one could wish for, the eminent and utterly French linguist Meillet confessed:

> Si conservateur que l'on soit, il faut avouer que Shakespeare et Racine sont des auteurs du passé, pour la langue comme pour le fond.

His adversaries, the classicists, have to concede the fact:

> Le public de la Comédie française qui écoute une tragédie de Racine, aujourd'hui, ne saisit plus d'un tiers du texte . . . je gagerais qu'il n'a même pas la patience d'écouter jusqu'au bout les phrases un peu longues. (Boulenger–Thérive)

For my part I would say: *Racine remains for ever close to us* (to Frenchmen, to the whole literary world) *because he is eternally distant*.

A young Frenchman, hearing that I was engaged in writing the present study of Racine, wrote to me to express a view quite different from the measured conservatism of Meillet, Brunot or Boulenger–Thérive, an attitude full of the forward-striving enthusiasm of the new France:

> Racine est si près de nous que nous avons souvent pour lui cette espèce de lâche affection que l'on porte à un parent très proche, souvent mauvais sujet et même un peu prodigue. Et vous ne sauriez imaginer quel plaisir j'éprouverais, si vous alliez confirmer mes passions par une étude . . .

But is there not even in this voice the sound of a guilty French conscience, treating its allegedly most representative poet as a *prodigal* son?

The distance of Racine's language from our own forbids close and comfortable familiarity. It is quite likely that many modern readers are already irritated by the novels of the Goncourts, despite and because of the familiarity of their language, just as many an impressionist painting can be irritating in its familiarity, whilst a Claude Lorrain or a Poussin remains for ever 'close' to us, i.e. near by the fact of its distance. Veiled images entice the spectator to pierce the veil, whilst unveiled ones do not allow us to come any closer than we are already: it is the former that hold the dynamic imperative. *And distance is itself a poetic element.* A renaissance portrait is foreign to us in the dress it shows and in the setting depicted, but foreignness calls to be conquered.

Distance is increased by the passage of time, which adds a supplementary poetic patina to the writer's poetic creation. To substantiate his views on the 'pastness' of Racine quoted above, Meillet points out the obsolete past historic and the rhyme in *-ée* with an obsolete bisyllabic value in these famous lines:

> Ariane, ma sœur, de quel amour blessée
> Vous mourûtes au bord où vous fûtes laissée. *Phèdre* I.iii, 253–4

But the past historic is all the more poetic for being an archaism, and the *-ée* says something to the educated *reader* at least. And older listeners too can remember enjoying up until about fifteen years ago the sound-value of bisyllabic *-ée*! Besides which, every Frenchman knows song lyrics where a mute *e* has syllabic value. The poetry of mute *e* lies in its latent potential which may be realised in any given instance. To express increased tenderness or intimacy in contemporary French the final vowel on *amie* can be lengthened; alternatively it can be pronounced [amijə], with a particular colouring described by Roger Martin du Gard:

> Vous permettez que j'allume une cigarette, Amie? – Il était incorrigible et délicieux. Il avait une manière à lui de prononcer le mot *Amie,* en laissant l'*e* final mourir au bord des lèvres, comme un baiser. (Martin du Gard I.i, 70)

French is supposed to be a rational language, but in the mute *e* it has acquired a sentimental musical accompaniment that rises and falls, now *piano*, now *mezzoforte*, alongside the principal melodic line.

So in the end I come down to a paradoxical formulation not unlike the title of Thérive's book, *Le Français, langue morte?* As he prizes the 'dead' quality of French literary language because it remains the only living element in the natural and all-destroying flow of linguistic change, so I see in the conscious distance and foreignness of Racine's language a sanctuary from vulgar promiscuity, from the distastefulness of excessive familiarity. To liberate oneself from an all too trivial concept of 'life' as the chaos of lived experience, to oppose 'everything flows' with 'the One remains': these are valid projects. Racine could have said what his admirer Napoleon said of himself, which Nietzsche re-used as the 'Greek formula' (cf. Bertram, p. 214); 'J'ai refermé le gouffre anarchique et débrouillé le chaos. J'ai ennobli les peuples.' But perhaps given Racine's specifically French role one should alter the last sentence to: 'J'ai ennobli *mon* peuple.'*

* An appendix on Schiller's translations of Racine has been omitted.

A Reply to my Critics (1931)*

One reviewer of this essay on Racine urges Frenchmen not to leave the establishment of a lexicon of Racine's language to foreigners (Meillet, 1929); another claims I have not stressed sufficiently the unmodulated aspects of Racine's style alongside the classical *piano* (J. Schmidt). Those aspects are covered in the body of my essay nevertheless, even if they are not indicated by my title, which should be taken to mean 'everything related to the general subject of modulation in Racine'.

The objection has been made that I do not adequately insert Racine's style into the period style to which it belongs (Heiss, 1931). The point here really is that I do not deal with the history of ideas [*Geistesgeschichte*]. Not everyone agrees with my conception of a great literary personality as 'an internally stable cosmos'; but I wish to stress once again the unlimited creative freedom of the individual, and to argue against the fatalism and determinism of the history of ideas, that last-born child of theology. When I see the great writers standing (as they have to stand) 'at definite points in the intellectual-historical development of culture', I am reminded of Dante's seating plan of the Other World in the *Divina Commedia*, where souls take the places allotted to them, as they have to. The difference is that Dante's doctrine is ascribed to God, whilst the points in any scheme of 'intellectual-historical development' come out of the head of the 'intellectual' historian alone!

Another objection made is that 'no aesthetic emotion . . . can be supported by linguistics to this extent' (Kuttner). I still fail to grasp why people who use 'their natural, human and aesthetic sensibility' as a criterion should be debarred from also doing linguistics. Of course the aesthetic analysis of literary art is more subjective than so-called historical grammar; the aesthetic analysis of pictorial art is also dependent on the same sources of judgment and misjudgment. However, it is wrong to think that scientific methodology has the same degree of flexibility and malleability in all fields of intellectual endeavour – if it had, natural scientists could not recognise the existence of the human sciences. I quote Heidegger:

> Mathematical knowledge is no stricter than philosophical or historical knowledge; it possesses the character of *exactness*, which is not coincidental with strictness. To demand exactness from history is to reject the specific strictness of the human sciences. (Heidegger, p. 25)

I have never claimed to provide the 'correct' linguistic–aesthetic interpretation of Racine. I have given only *an* interpretation – my interpretation arising from my feelings and measured against a French and a

* I have summarised only the main points made by Spitzer in his 'Nachtrag' – a traditional appendix to reprinted articles in German scholarship.

German sensibility. It is not so much a matter of defending my own (as it were incidental) interpretation of a particular author or of a particular passage. It is much more important to claim and proclaim the right to interpret (including the right to understand the artistic use of language) as a person *contemplating his own enjoyment of the work of art.*

II

SAINT-SIMON'S PORTRAIT OF LOUIS XIV

1931

This essay attracted very little attention until 1979, when it was translated into French. It is arguably the best, and was certainly the first, of the very few modern studies of Saint-Simon from a literary and stylistic point of view. Erich Auerbach, in *Mimesis*, devotes pp. 414–33 to the *Mémoires* and follows Spitzer in finding in Saint-Simon 'a precursor of modern and ultramodern forms of conceiving and representing life'; Jules Brody also acknowledges Spitzer as the 'inspiration immédiate' of his essays on Saint-Simon republished in A44 (which also contains a bibliography of writing on Saint-Simon since 1959).

Spitzer's essay is partly an offshoot of his major work on Proust (B10), where Saint-Simon is briefly investigated as a model for the long sentences of *A la recherche*. This study of the portrait of the Sun-king can also be seen as an indirect reaction to the political situation in Germany in 1931 – as a scholar's contemplation of another tyrant, of another power-hungry 'small man who wanted to be big', seen through the eyes of a hostile historian conscious of the vanity of all earthly things. The vocabulary of pre-war politics used by Spitzer ('the Maintenon enclave', 'spheres of influence', etc.) creates for us now a 'period' flavour which serves to underline the involvement of the critic in his own historical situation. Thirdly, this essay also develops the concept of the baroque put forward in chapter I and applied more rigidly in chapter V; and it is of some methodological interest in the fourth section, where Spitzer defends not only immanent criticism, but the right of the critic to disregard all previous scholarship in order to 'see with his own eyes'. (This section was omitted from the French translation.)

All quotations from Saint-Simon are given from the Pléiade edition of the *Mémoires*.

DB

De ce tout il résulte qu'on admire et qu'on fuit. (Saint-Simon, on Versailles)

1. Character and History

Saint-Simon's portrait of the *roi-soleil*, 'toute cette longue digression sur le caractère, le règne et la vie journalière de Louis XIV' (Boislisle, p. 1n), is a huge expansion of an already extensive addition that he made to Dangeau's *Journal* under the date of 13 August 1715 (printed in Boislisle, pp. 383–461). A character-portrait of such enormous dimensions (it fills pp. 940–1079 of vol. IV of the *Mémoires*) suggests a very particular conception of *character*. For Saint-Simon, character is the structure which arches over all the facts of history; it is the totality which embraces historical personalities in their full extent and substance. Character is like some Trojan Horse concealing historical acts, events and customs, which can climb out of its belly and yet leave a clearly visible skeleton.

The résumé of the portrait given (in the Pléiade edition) at the head of chapter LI (but originally written in the margin throughout the manuscript) shows how the character of the king was conceived of as an all-embracing structure. It is out of his character that the history of his reign develops, and so history is built in to the character-portrait. The essential traits of the character unfold themselves in historical actions; the historian's art is to reinsert the chronological sequence of actions into the stable, static, sharply delineated contours of the character. Character is here the unmoved mover, the essence or Being from which the Becoming of history springs: individual historical events flow from individual aspects of Being as honey, so to speak, may flow from the separate cells of a single honeycomb. At the head of the résumé stands 'Caractère de Louis XIV'; the character is formed by Mme de la Vallière, but immediately shows itself for what it is. *Le Roi hait les sujets, est petit, dupe, gouverné, en se piquant de tout le contraire*' (p. 940). Now come the facts: '*L'Espagne cède la préséance . . . Guerre de Hollande; paix d'Aix-la-Chapelle; siècle florissant. Conquêtes en Hollande et de la Franche-Comté*', etc. The end-points of the first and second periods of the king's reign are indicated. But before the third period, which takes Louis from the full flowering of his reign to its ultimate decline, Saint-Simon brings out his psychology of the king: *'Vertus de Louis XIV; sa misérable éducation; sa profonde ignorance; il hait la naissance et les dignités; séduit par ses ministres'*. This allows Saint-Simon to incorporate the warmongering of the Louvois ministry and the events of the Spanish War of Succession up to the Peace of Utrecht into the overall structure of the character – as the result of Louis's hatred of true worth and of his vulnerability to ambitious ministers.

Saint-Simon does of course devote the bulk of his portrait to this third period, and he emphasises early on the contrast between a majestic exterior and the inner decay:

> Le troisième âge s'ouvrit par un comble de gloire et de prospérité inouie. Le temps en fut momentané. Il enivra et prépara d'étranges malheurs, dont l'issue a été un espèce de miracle. (p. 949)

At this point he repeats the formulation of the king's character given at the very beginning: 'L'esprit du roi était au-dessous du médiocre, mais très-capable de se former' (p. 950; on p. 941, 'Né avec un esprit au-dessous . . .' etc.; the same formula occurs in the original addition to Dangeau).

The derivation of the historical facts from the psychological disposition of the king is expressed, in grammatical terms, by Saint-Simon's use of psychological qualities as the subjects of his sentences (⟶ 25, for a similar feature in Racine). For example:

> *Ce même orgueil*, que Louvois sut si bien manier, épuisa le royaume par des guerres et par des fortifications innombrables. (p. 958)

> *Ce fut la même jalousie* qui écrasa la marine dans un royaume flanqué des deux mers . . . *Cette même jalousie* de Louvois contre Colbert dégoûta le Roi des négotiations. (p. 959)

> *L'orgueil du roi* voulut étonner l'Europe par la montre de sa puissance, . . . et l'étonna en effet. Telle fut la cause de ce fameux camp de Compiègne. (p. 972)

> *La même politique* continua le mystère de cet amour . . . *Le mystère* le fit durer . . . (p. 1013)

[In the last example, the personifications of *politique* and *mystère* probably derive from the *précieux* jargon of love (⟶ 129, comments on *air*).] When the king's character suffers the blows of fate, Louis XIV is disaggregated into his component psychological parts, but restored almost immediately by an inclusive generalisation to a totality of personality and event:

> Mais bientôt après le Roi fut attaqué par des coups bien plus sensibles: *son cœur*, que lui-même avait comme ignoré jusqu'alors, par la perte de cette

charmante dauphine; *son repos*, par celle de l'incomparable dauphin; *sa tranquillité*, sur la succession à sa couronne, par la mort de l'héritier huit jours après . . .; *tous* ces coups frappés rapidement, *tous* avant la paix, presque *tous* durant les plus terribles périls du royaume. (p. 1063)

Each blow of fate affects here a single psychological feature of the king. This disaggregation of character in decline is a corollary to Saint-Simon's general treatment of events as mere pretexts for the display of psychological properties, as for example on p. 943, '*Bientôt après, la mort du roi d'Espagne fit* saisir à ce jeune prince avide de gloire *une occasion de gloire*'; p. 959, 'Ce fut donc dans cette triste situation intérieure que *la fenêtre de Trianon* fit la guerre de 1688' (Louvois, insulted over a window being constructed under his supervision, declares war to make himself indispensable to Louis XIV).

To conclude these stylistic observations: Saint-Simon gives us history as chronology and development, but he always traps it in the static honeycomb structure of character.

In the third period, Louis is at the height of his power. Saint-Simon's résumé of chapter LIII: '*Bonheur du roi en tout genre. Autorité du Roi sans bornes; sa science de régner; sa politique sur le service, où il asservit tout et rend tout peuple*' (p. 971). This levelling policy, designed to elevate the king above all else, results in extremely diverse acts of government – the introduction of *ancienneté*, '*la cour pour toujours à la campagne*', '*Le Roi veut une grosse cour*', '*Politique du plus grand luxe*', Versailles, Marly (résumé of chapter LIV, p. 994), '*amours du roi*' (chapter LV, p. 1009) – and in the king's love-life, magnified beyond the limits of propriety by a lust for power, Mme de Maintenon establishes her huge enclave in Louis XIV's sphere of influence with historical effects that disturb the entire state. Madame de Maintenon is thus built in to the character-portrait of the king, and many historical actions – e.g. the revocation of the edict of Nantes, the foundation of Saint-Cyr, etc. – are reincorporated into the character of Mme de Maintenon ('goût de direction', 'dévotion', etc.). The picture of Maintenon is constructed by analogy with that of Louis, the *mécanique* of her life is similarly depicted, as is her precise relationship to the great men of her time. Almost one-quarter of Saint-Simon's chapters on Louis XIV deal with the Maintenon enclave, with Maintenon as an excrescence or tumour on the king's character, with the debasement of the king at the hands of this woman, all of which sets in an advantageous light Louis's considerations on morality in the face of death. The death of the king should bring to an end Saint-Simon's representation of his character through the historical working-out of its imprinted forms, but the historian, who traces external actions and events from the inner dimensions of character, possesses an intermediate domain between the inner character and outer action of his subject: namely, the habits and customs that derive from character (they can 'characterise princes', p. 1079) but which have nonetheless the material quality of external events. Saint-Simon calls this 'l'écorce extérieure de la vie de ce monarque' (p. 1079) or, elsewhere, 'la mécanique [des temps et des heures]' (pp. 1024 and 1035), and under this heading he gives us the daily routine that belongs to him and also to the public, which continues to serve after his death, without further historical development, making at the close out of his character once again a static and timeless phenomenon, an unmoving mover.

This reading of chapter LIX of the *Mémoires* involves rejecting the gloss given by Saint-Simon's editors on the phrase 'tout ce qu'on a vu d'intérieur' (p. 1079). It stands in opposition to 'l'écorce extérieure de ce monarque' and refers not to the 'internal life of the court' (note 2, p. 1246) but to the inner life of the king. 'Intérieur' is frequently used by Saint-Simon with reference to Louis:

> Louvois, qui était toujours bien informé de l'intérieur le plus intime, . . . sut les manèges de Mme de Maintenon pour se faire déclarer . . . et que la chose allait éclater. (p. 962)

There are also examples of 'écorce' applied to outer life:

> le mystère de cet amour, qui ne le demeura que de nom, et tout au plus en très fine *écorce* . . . (p. 1013)

> discerner la vérité des apparences, le necessaire de *l'écorce* . . . (p. 1026)

> cet attachement pharisaïque à l'extérieur de la loi et à *l'écorce* de la religion . . . (p. 1076)

[For similar usage in Spanish, see Gracian, *Criticon* I/11.] *Eclater*, on the other hand, means for Saint-Simon (as it does for Racine; ⟶ 21) 'to make known to other people', as in

> Bientôt après, elle [i.e. Maintenon's favour with the king] *éclata* par l'appartement qui lui fut donné à Versailles. (p. 1022)

Saint-Simon's historical portrait is a unique attempt to compress the moving *course* of a life into a static *image* of a life and thus to explain what a man becomes by what a man is. The subject's Being is a non-derivative, composite but rationally graspable given which triumphs over the complexity of history. There is no concession to the formlessness and chaos of the stream of life, but lots of clearly labelled character-traits with their consequences in train, and no trace of impersonal or supraindividual forces. The only secret that remains is the personality, a balloon full to bursting point, producing deeds and habits, but simply standing there in its magnificent pregnancy. It is as if Saint-Simon's king-figure had been stuffed and bloated on the corpse of all those historical forces that go beyond the individual. The theory of history that underlies Saint-Simon's art of the portrait is a mystical belief in the breadth, substantiality and effective power of personality. He states this basis explicitly on p. 979:

> Ce peu d'historique, eu égard à un règne si long et si rempli, est si lié au personnel du Roi qu'il ne se pouvait omettre pour bien représenter ce monarque tel qu'il a véritablement été.

And by implication:

> ce peu qui a été retracé du règne du feu Roi était nécessaire pour mieux faire entendre ce qu'on va dire de sa personne. (p. 949)

Character is the stamped image of personality; it has, like a stamp, clear edges; it is comprehensible and powerfully explicit. In such portraiture there can be nothing left unsaid, vague or shaded. But such a conception of character as a monstrously bloated *thing* also demands a very particular type of composition that traces all the excrescences of the personality.

The claim that Saint-Simon did not compose is simply wrong. He composed his portrait according to the relative importance of the parts for the whole, and this accounts for the huge protuberance of Maintenon next to the single page devoted to the first love, Mme de la Fayette, because the revocation of the edict of Nantes is encapsulated in the Maintenon section.

The organisation of character is significant in Saint-Simon also in the sense that all qualities (and the deeds and events that follow from each quality) are derived from a common denominator, reduced to a single fundamental trait. The virtuosity of the character-drawer consists therefore of unravelling this fundamental trait in areas that seem utterly remote from it: 'Il faut montrer les progrès en tous genres de la même conduite dressé sur le même point de vue' (p. 994). Louis XIV's basic trait is that he was born 'avec un esprit au-dessous du médiocre', and as this situation drives him to 'orgueil', he fears nobility of birth and intellect: 'Il . . . craignait [la noblesse] autant que l'esprit' (p. 951). He requires the flattery of his ministers, generals, mistresses and courtiers, which produce the 'superbe du roi, qui forme le colosse de ses ministres sur la ruine de la noblesse' (p. 940). Further on, Louis's involvement in all sorts of details is derived from his intellectual limitations: 'Son esprit, naturellement porté au petit, se plut en toutes sortes de détails' (p. 952). The delight in minutiae, the grandeur of his ministers, and the king's pleasure in his own greatness produce a series of consequences: the levelling-down of the power of functionaries in the state ('il ne voulait de grandeur que par émanation de la sienne', p. 954), the king's choice of 'gens de rien' for high office, and his inaccessibility except through official channels. The innate, quite clearly, forms the basis of the character from which the details follow. Nonetheless Saint-Simon was not quite clear about the distinction between nature and nurture. For if the king's less-than-average mind *had* been capable of refinement, his education would not have been as neglected as it was. Some qualities are given as acquired, and at the same time inherited:

Ce fut dans cet important et brillant tourbillon où le Roi se jeta d'abord, et où il *prit* cet air de politesse et de galanterie qu'il a toujours *su* conserver . . . On peut dire qu'il était *fait pour elle* . . . (p. 942)

Saint-Simon's reader is thus put in the same position as the spectator of a Racinian tragedy in which the most diverse consequences flow 'naturally' from a character's circumstances like an example illustrating a mathematical rule: he must follow the unwinding of a clockwork machine, an indeflectible and logical sequence of events. But whilst the dramatist may think up a character and its logical derivates in abstract, Saint-Simon sees basic traits and consequences in concrete historical reality. The psychological feat of the historian is to have found in the multiform material of history precisely that basic feature which simplifies a complex picture into a line drawing, which reduces the disparate to a denominator. His function as historian is to make an order from the impenetrable, confused mass of facts – an order which he then buries and almost destroys by inserting his substantial concrete evidence into the cellular structure of his character-portrayal. That is why a superficial reader can easily arrive at a notion of Saint-Simon's description as disorder. Braunschvig's condensation of the whole enormous portrait of Louis XIV into a few pages (in his *Littérature française étudiée dans les textes*) certainly shows the high degree of organisation, composition, unity, order and clarity in Saint-Simon's work – all he lacks is precisely the historical substance, the concrete material, the unclear and the multiform from which Saint-Simon originally constructed his order. Here the whole enterprise of 'littérature française étudiée dans les textes' shows itself to be of questionable utility and reveals its huge ignorance of artistic qualities because, although its approach is based on the 'evidence' of 'texts' alone, it leaves out all that which the text is evidence of, its imbrication in the whole, its value-content and its perspective within the whole . . .

The deductive form of the portrait is the product of Saint-Simon's organisation of the character, of his massing of individual traits and facts around a basic feature. That is why he uses expressions like *de là* together with a deleted verb (*vint*) to indicate the almost automatic nature of the deduction:

De là [i.e. Louis's pride] ce désir de gloire qui l'arrachait par intervalles à l'amour; de là cette facilité à Louvois de l'engager en grandes guerres; . . . De là ce goût de revues . . . (p. 951)

De là les secrétaires d'Etat et les ministres successivement à quitter le manteau, puis le rabat, après l'habit noir . . . (p. 953)*

For transitions to such formulae, consider the following:

De ces sources étrangères et pestilentielles lui vint cet orgueil, que . . .; témoin entre autres ces monuments si outrés . . .; et *de cet orgueil tout le reste*, qui le perdit, dont on vient de voir tant d'effets funestes . . . (all on pp. 957–8)

Other expressions having the same effect using *c'est ce qui*, etc.:

C'est ce qui donna tant d'autorité à ses ministres, par les occasions continuelles qu'ils avaient de l'encenser. (p. 951)

C'est là ce qui le faisait se complaire à faire régner ses ministres sur les plus élevés de ses sujets . . . (p. 955)

Introduction of new information as if it were 'the same':

Ce *même* orgueil, que Louvois sut si bien manier, épuisa le royaume par des guerres et des fortifications innombrables. (p. 958)

Ce fut la *même* jalousie qui écrasa la marine dans un royaume flanqué de deux mers. (p. 959)

These formulae are all intended to work out, release and unfold things that are wrapped up in the basic conception of the character. In Saint-Simon, the character possesses an internal contradiction: Louis XIV is small, but wants to appear big. This produces a baroque dynamic, a pendulum rhythm within the portrait from the smallness that Louis wants to hide to the grandeur which he cannot impose entirely. The parvenu on the royal throne has not in reality 'arrived', he has to fight continually to keep his position. The static quality of the portrait is not as absolute as I claimed to begin with; or, rather, the portrait is static, but the subject of portrayal is not: he is at pains throughout to appear other than what he is, and so the portraitist is obliged for his part to adjust the focus throughout and to uncover what lies behind the mask.

The organisation of character as the logical development of a basic feature would make an altogether too comforting image if Saint-Simon had not allowed his own search for truth to penetrate to the inner secret of Louis's being – if he had excluded his evaluation, or rather, his devaluation of his subject, and not devoted his art to the destruction of an idealised image.

* On *à* + infinitive constructions, see Spitzer (1930) in the List of References.

2. Character-Portrayal and Panegyric

One might expect a character-portrayal as extensive as this to deal with a model that is worthy of the historian's interest and emulation – after all, why take so long to depict a nullity? The opening sentence of chapter LI thus shocks the reader:

> Ce fut un prince à qui on ne peut refuser beaucoup de bien, même de grand, en qui on ne peut méconnaître plus de petit et de mauvais, du quel il n'est pas possible de discerner ce qui était de lui et ce qui était emprunté. (p. 940)

Similarly, two paragraphs later:

> Né avec un esprit au-dessous du médiocre, mais un esprit capable de se former, de se limer, de se raffiner, d'emprunter d'autrui sans imitation et sans gêne, il profitait infiniment d'avoir toute sa vie vécu avec les personnes du monde qui toutes en avaient le plus. (p. 941)

Reflections of this sort occur throughout the portrait, which ends with the following paragraph in the section headed *Le Roi peu regretté*:

> Quel surprenant alliage! De la lumière avec les plus épaisses ténèbres . . . Quelle fin d'un règne si longuement admiré, et jusque dans ses derniers revers si étincelant de grandeur, de générosité, de courage et de force! et quel abîme de faiblesse, de misère, de honte, d'anéantissement, sentie, goûtée, savourée, abhorrée, et toutefois subie dans toute son étendue, et sans en avoir pu élargir ni soulager les liens! O Nabuchodonosor! Qui pourra sonder les jugements de Dieu, et qui osera ne pas s'anéantir en leur présence? (p. 1065)

So it is a portrait of a less than mediocre prince, with more shade than light, who though feared and admired at first was not mourned at his end. The personality that Saint-Simon presents does not measure up to the dimensions of the portrait, appropriate to a panegyric or in any case an apologia. The subject turns out to be neither a hero nor a martyr, but just a little man raised *ad absurdum* by History, naked beneath his imperial garb. Though the drawing could not be fuller, its human subject is – empty; it is a lovingly detailed picture of an intellectual nonentity. And Saint-Simon does not lay bare one level after another to lead us progressively towards the inner emptiness of the man, but warns us from the first line on. We experience the unmasking of a 'great' historical figure without enthusiasm and without false expectation: Louis XIV is taken up to his final *anéantissement* before God at the moment of death, but his character is reduced to nothing from the start. In Saint-Simon, the feeling for the mysterious 'key' to a whole personality is not incompatible with the moral uncovering of the personality's mediocrity. In this pre-Rousseauistic mental world (the chapters on Louis XIV date from 1745), a character does not have to be an original genius to be worthy of a portrait, only the portrait must form 'un tout', a closed entity. Saint-Simon's attitude towards his king is basically the same as Philippe de Commynes's towards his monarch: panegyric accompanied by unmasking, praise of his king's worldly glory alongside his moral nothingness before God. There are some striking parallels:

Ce monarque si altier gémissait dans ses fers, lui qui avait tenu toute l'Europe . . . (p. 1066)

Est-il donc possible de tenir ung roy, pour le garder plus honnestement, en plus estroicte prison que luy mesmes se tenoit? (Commynes, II.323)*

But the dualistic atmosphere of the late Middle Ages in the biography of Louis XI is replaced in the portrait of Louis XIV by the duplicity of the baroque courtier, half pagan and half Christian, convinced both of the power of personality and of its nothingness before God. Saint-Simon, the barometer of court life with aspirations to the status of a latter-day Bossuet, turns the panegyric or funeral oration (the portrait of Louis XIV is entered in the *Mémoires* under the year 1715, and its pretext is the king's death) into the unmasking of a character believed by others to be great. The portrait is not organic, it is not recounted or experienced from the inside of the subject's personality – it is a prejudged, predirected application of moral categories and impersonal criteria to a personality. In the very first sentence we are told: *bon*, *grand*, and *petit*, *mauvais*; and at the end: 'Quel surprenant alliage! De la lumière avec les plus épaisses ténèbres!' The portraitist composes the picture from a set of features each carrying its specific consequences, but the character's features are extrapolations from Saint-Simon's general experience of men and life rather than derived from the individual, lived experience of the character of Louis XIV. The necessary basis for this kind of portraiture is coolness and distance between the painter and his model, of the sort made possible only by observation at short range, which was Saint-Simon's customary method and which he liked to invoke, as in the following:

Après avoir exposé avec la vérité et la fidélité la plus exacte tout ce qui est venu à ma connaissance par moi-même, ou par ceux qui ont vu et manié les choses et les affaires pendant les vingt-deux dernières années de Louis XIV, et l'avoir montré tel qu'il a été, sans aucune passion . . . (p. 1079)

Nothing could be less appropriate to such a style of portraiture than the image of the tree of life (paradoxically, so near to the metaphor of the 'écorce extérieure de la vie de ce monarque') – there is no sense of the sap running through the personality of the king; on the contrary, the 'good' branches and the 'bad' are neatly sawn off in advance. Panegyric and unmasking *alternate* in the portrait, producing abrupt transitions between praise and criticism, even in the chapter résumés:

* Commynes is referring here literally to Louis XI's living accommodation. It is hard to see why Spitzer thought this a 'striking parallel'.

Vertus de Louis XIV; sa misérable éducation; sa profonde ignorance . . . (ch. LI, p. 940)

Politique du plus grand luxe; son mauvais goût. (ch. LIV, p. 994)

Malheurs des dernières années du Roi; le rendent plus dur et non moins dupe. (ch. LVIII, p. 1053)

A particularly remarkable feature is the way praise is rendered hollow, as unmasking follows on the heels of a laudatory phrase – the opening sentence of the portrait quoted above being a good example. It leads up to 'good' and 'great' then falls without transition to 'more that was small and bad' before concluding with the impossibility of distinguishing in Louis XIV what was his own from what was borrowed: not only is the king diminished, but he is deprived of all individuality. Another example:

[A maxim of the king's] ce fut de gouverner par lui-même, qui fut la chose dont il se piqua le plus, dont on le loua et le flatta davantage, et qu'il exécuta le moins. (p. 941)

The sentence leads us to a climax (*dont il se piqua le plus*) which is then taken beyond its plausible limits (people praised the king for his personal government more than he even praised himself) and then plunges directly into a negative superlative (*qu'il exécuta le moins*). A similar trick:

Il voulait régner par lui-même; sa jalousie là-dessus alla sans cesse jusqu'à la faiblesse. Il régna en effet dans le petit; dans le grand il ne put y atteindre et jusque dans le petit il fut gouverné. (p. 942)

By sleight of hand strength is turned to weakness, the strong king is made into a weak and trifling man.

Saint-Simon uses a whole variety of stylistic devices to undermine the character of Louis XIV. Perhaps the most perfidious type of transition from positive to negative is the (frequent) use of *Heurex si* + conditional clause, which raises a possibility only to withdraw it beyond reach, e.g. on p. 942, the king is said to be created for love:

Heureux s'il n'eût eu que des maîtresses semblables à Mme de la Vallière . . .

but of course we know that he had other less reliable mistresses, and the beatification (*Heureux!*) turns into an anathema. (For other examples of the same device, see p. 949, 'heureux s'il n'eût survécu', and p. 1065, 'Heureux si, en adorant la main . . .').

Another type of undermining involves the use of negative exclusive expressions:

Jamais personne ne donna de meilleure grâce et n'augmenta tant par là le prix de ses bienfaits; *jamais personne* ne vendit mieux ses paroles, son souris même, jusqu'à ses regards. (p. 1001)

Louis XIV is unequalled, but in the overpricing of his gifts and favours.

> *Jamais il ne lui échappa* de dire rien de désobligeant à personne, et, s'il avait à reprendre, à réprimander ou à corriger, ce qui était fort rare, c'était toujours avec un air plus ou moins de bonté, presque jamais avec sécheresse, jamais avec colère, si on excepte l'unique aventure de Courtenvaux . . . quoiqu'il ne fût pas exempt de colère, quelquefois avec un air de sévérité . . . (p. 1001)

In this example, the irreproachably impassible and idealised façade of Louis XIV is loosened up by obvious modulators (*presque* jamais, *quelquefois* avec un air . . .), by intensifiers that are actually delimiters (*fort rare*), by sliding scales (*plus ou moins* de bonté), by exceptions (*si on excepte* . . .) and through concessive clauses which destroy what the main clause establishes (*quoiqu'* . . .), letting in through the back what the front door shuts out.

In the next example, Saint-Simon gives the lie to Louis's 'natural' courtesy by stressing the calculated graduation of the king's expressions of politeness:

> Jamais homme si naturellement poli, ni d'une politesse si fort mesurée, si fort par degrés, ni qui distinguât mieux l'âge, le mérite, le rang . . . Ces étages divers se marquaient exactement dans sa manière de saluer et de recevoir les révérences . . . (p. 1001)

Note the colloquial, spoken-language register of this type of *jamais* . . ., which is quite common in Saint-Simon, e.g. 'Ce dernier talent, il le poussa souvent jusqu'à la fausseté, mais avec cela *jamais de mensonge*' (p. 1000).

In the next example, Saint-Simon moves from praise to criticism without transition:

> Il aima en tout la splendeur, la magnificence, la profusion. Ce goût il le tourna en maxime par politique, et l'inspira en tout à sa cour . . . Il y trouvait encore la satisfaction de son orgueil par une cour superbe en tout, et par une plus grande confusion qui anéantissait de plus en plus les distinctions naturelles. C'est une plaie qui, une fois introduite, est devenue le cancer qui ronge tous les particuliers . . . (p. 1004)

The uses of *Il* and *en tout* in this passage call for some remarks. The repetition of anaphoric subject pronouns is sometimes very extensive in Saint-Simon: e.g. in the second paragraph on p. 1004, there are eleven occurrences of *il* referring to Louis in sequence; in the second paragraph on p. 1011, seven occurrences of *elle* referring to Mme de Fontrevault. There is a similar constant repetition of *on*, for example on p. 1027. In La Bruyère pronominal repetition of this sort is used to represent the 'fâcheux', the 'importun', irritatingly cropping up where he is not needed. In Saint-Simon it is more designed to portray the monotonous unity of the character of Louis XIV. As for *tout*, it has here a specific *panegyric* usage, perhaps deriving from religious discourse, depicting a generalised completeness, in contrast to its use as a precise quantifier appropriate to a factual description. Contrast for example

> [une galanterie] toujours majestueuse . . . et jamais devant le monde rien de déplacé, mais jusqu'au moindre geste, son marcher, son port, *toute* sa contenance, *tout* mesuré, *tout* décent, noble, grand, majestueux . . . (p. 1003)

With the material restriction on *toujours* in the following:

> ses réponses en ces occasions étaient *toujours* courtes, justes, pleines, et *très rarement* sans quelque chose d'obligeant, *quelquefois* même de flatteur. (p. 1003)

Saint-Simon's style is no different in the portrait of Mme de Maintenon given on p. 1024. Positive terms alternate, without transitions, with negative ones. She is 'une femme de beaucoup d'esprit', 'que la galanterie avait *achevé* de tourner au plus agréable'. But in the very next sentence she has become 'flatteuse, insinuante, complaisante, cherchant toujours à plaire'. She possesses 'une grâce incomparable à tout', 'un air d'aisance', 'un langage doux, juste, en bons termes', but her principal characteristic is 'la dévotion' with which 'la droiture et la franchise' are said to be incompatible. And so on: each quality is doubled and negated by a fault. There is perhaps no more perfidious style of description possible. An artist (I mean a real painter) presents us with an image that we perceive in a single moment; his picture allows us to see the advantages and drawbacks of a human being in a single sweep. But the writer, working with words that run on in a sequence in time, can parade advantages and drawbacks one after the other in the order that suits him or seems most appropriate – to fool the reader or to take him by surprise. In Saint-Simon, the venom of his character-portrayal creeps up behind the rosy embellishments of his introductory remarks. In the description of Mme de Maintenon we see first the wonderful *salon* lady, the virtuoso of sociability rising to her perfection ('. . . d'abord avait été soufferte . . .' – 'achevé de tourner au plus agréable'), and then her drawbacks – duplicity and intrigue. Her intriguing was sometimes only an appearance, and sometimes she used it to work for other people, but she is nonetheless a schemer through and through, and her accomplishment can provide an aesthetic by-product (words like *les adresses* are charged even in this context with a positive value). Considered from the outside alone, the scheming lady of salon life stands before us as a picture of grace and tact, her low social origins (*sa longue bassesse*) quite imperceptible.

Saint-Simon's editor makes the critical point that 'le précieux et le guindé' in Mme de Maintenon cannot be reconciled with her 'grâce incomparable', her 'langage juste, en bons termes et naturellement éloquent et court' and her 'air d'aisance' (Boislisle, p. 216). Now it is often unclear whether *air* should be understood as 'a touch of' or as 'adopted pose', whether in fact Saint-Simon means a real atmosphere or a hypocritical attitude when he uses this term. But this indecision between truth and fiction belongs essentially to the very *air* and atmosphere of *précieux* society, where the appearance of an atmosphere merges with the atmosphere itself in a social life treated as representation. The contradiction pointed out by Boislisle, though, is but one of several in a portrait built on contradictions, on the continuous countermanding of one character-trait by another. We are made to observe the development of Mme de Maintenon's 'style guindé' and manneredness from something that simply hides her low origins into bigotry, into an assumed second identity which destroys all the rest of her being (*tout le reste y fut sacrifié sans réserve*). The verdict of falseness is mitigated, to be sure – she was perhaps not born false, but had falseness thrust upon her; she was perhaps more frivolous than false – but frivolity is the unmistakable, ineradicable trace of the low-born soul without a tradition to uphold, that has small thoughts and narrow feelings: Mme de Maintenon remains Mme Scarron and that is the import of the attack from which the scornful aristocrat, Saint-Simon *duc* and *pair*, cannot get away. The apparent rise of Mme de Maintenon was mere fiction. In reality she remained *abjecte*, *basse* and therefore *dangereuse*. All the panegyric and superlative expressions (*au plus agréable*, *incomparable*, *merveilleusement*, etc.) wither away at the final unmasking. Once again, Saint-Simon wraps the history of a life in the stillness of a portrait (external rise, internal fall or rather inconstancy of the king's favourite), but he also wraps in his motionless representation the inner dialectic of the character, which falls apart before the reader's eyes and displays its contradictions. The poles of this dialectic – Mme de Maintenon's *bourgeois* nature, and her *savoir-vivre* and position in life – conduct an underground battle in Saint-Simon's portrait, and the writer succeeds in showing in the end the bestially dangerous nature of putting a small personality in a position of greatness, just as he had shown in the ungreatness of Louis 'the great' a disharmony of Being and destiny between which no synthesis could be sought or found. Never before had anyone depicted with such penetrating and profound vision or with such gruesome factuality the *petit-bourgeois* on the throne of power, exercising his majesty with all his *bourgeois* cravings and resentments, with false grandeur and real pettiness. What tragic desperation must have possessed Saint-Simon to make him show his king so hemmed in, so tightly hemmed in by his pettiness without any possibility of escape or transcendence – occupied solely with outer appearances, with the will to the appearance of grandeur in all the smallness of his being – hemmed in by the fate of seeking to be a big man whilst being small!

What is uncanny in these portraits is that Saint-Simon does not proceed in a straight line, so to speak, towards the revelation of his characters, but that he allows his moral destruction and intellectual judgment to break out from under expressions of admiration and praise: an uncanny juxtaposition, an amazing proximity of panegyric and character-revelation. An example from p. 942: 'Il faut donc avouer [in respect of Louis XIV's gifts] que le Roi fut plus à plaindre que blâmable de se livrer à l'amour, et qu'il *mérite louange* d'avoir su s'en arracher par intervalles en faveur de la gloire' – praise for the king because he was able to tear himself away from love 'from time to time'! Saint-Simon's praise is stranger and more uncanny than his blame. We cannot imagine how esteem can pass so abruptly into scorn. Nowadays, and especially for those who consider the mystical unity of the writer and his subject an absolute necessity for the artistic representation of a personality, there is something hardly thinkable about Saint-Simon's attitude. He seems as an observer of men to be quite monstrous, capable of sincere deference whilst gazing into the abyss; his perceptiveness comes from hatred, and yet he always seems to be just.

If one looks more closely at the values which Saint-Simon enters on the credit side of Louis's account, one finds (with the exception of the recognition of the king's religious behaviour on his death-bed) almost uniquely worldly, social values which constitute the personality's façade – and for us, who take purely human values much more seriously, the moral balance dips far deeper into the red than it would have done for the contemporaries of the *roi-soleil* and the age of rococo, more convinced as they were of the positive value of the sociable. Sociability, with its art of living on the edge of an abyss without showing it, with its ability to conceal the most hostile emotions behind a smooth outward surface, can lead to its own kind of gruesome horror, as Péguy discovered in his 'gentle' Racine (⟶ 105). In the portrait of Louis XIV the panegyric passages (*jamais* . . .) generally refer only to the king's outer attitudes – individual traits which in other people we would interpret as movements of the heart are in Louis XIV merely external attitudes taken up, out of calculation and the mentality of a ruler, in order to maintain decorum – like his taste for making gifts, or his love of splendour. The 'vertus de Louis XIV' are public, his failings are private. Versailles represents for Saint-Simon a tyranny over nature: 'la violence qui a été faite partout à la nature repousse et dégoûte malgré soi'; 'de ce tout il résulte qu'on admire et qu'on fuit' (p. 1006). Similarly, he examines Louis's character in terms of its naturalness. The character is aligned between the two poles of art and nature, and beneath the superficial artistry of the façade the truth of nature can be seen only through the few chinks that remain. Saint-Simon's involved manner of expression corresponds to the scant allowance made for a nature that cannot be seen at first glance. The observer is *per*-spic-ax, he 'sees through it', he looks behind the disguises, masks and façades of his figures whose extension reaches down not into depths of feeling but into further concealment. Saint-Simon has a constant sense of the puzzle in personality; even in death the king's personality offers a puzzle: 'Est-ce artifice? Est-ce tromperie? Est-ce dérision jusqu'en mourant? Quelle énigme à expliquer?' (p. 1073). And he solves the enigma. His psychological glance must delve deep into the personality but in a rational and detective manner; Saint-Simon does not want to delve into recreated emotional 'depth', but to show the monarch 'as he really was' – 'représenter ce monarque tel qu'il a véritablement été' (p. 979).

That is how Saint-Simon gets to those climax-like amplifications that occur when a failure is pointed out: the reader sees the surgeon's knife cutting into the wound, as in the portrait of Mme de Maintenon discussed above, pp. 128–9, that embroils us more and more deeply in her duplicity, or in these words on Louis XIV:

> Ses ministres, ses généraux, ses maîtresses, ses courtisans s'aperçurent, bientôt après qu'il fut le maître, de *son faible plutôt que de son goût pour la gloire*. Ils le louèrent à l'envi et le gâtèrent. *Les louanges, disons mieux la flatterie*, lui plaisait à tel point, que *les plus grossières étaient bien reçues, les plus basses encore mieux savourées*. Ce n'était que par là qu'on s'approchait de lui . . . *La souplesse, la bassesse, l'air admirant, dépendant, rampant*, plus que tout l'air de néant sinon par lui, étaient les uniques voies de lui plaire . . . (p. 951)

Listings with climactic effects such as these are very typical of Saint-Simon's style. In the course of writing (or, more to the point, of talking) he gets into his subject, gets more excited and finds better and better descriptive terms. His text is not a finished written object, but we can see it 'writing itself' before our eyes. In the following sentence Saint-Simon's rage at Louvois is aroused by the word *adresse*, which then unleashes the multiple list that follows:

> Tel fut l'aveuglement du Roi, telle fut l'*adresse*, la *hardiesse*, *la formidable autorité* d'un ministre . . . (p. 961)

In the following description of Louis's increasing powerlessness, there is a progressive, step-by-step movement towards the abyss, a drive towards self-destruction, a leap into the dark:

> . . . une conviction entière de son injustice et de son impuissance, témoignée de sa bouche, *c'est trop peu dire*, décochée par ses propos à ses bâtards, et toutefois un abandon à eux et à leur gouvernante, devenue la sienne et celle de l'Etat, et *abandon si entier* qu'il ne lui permit pas de s'écarter d'un seul point de toutes leurs volontés; qui, presque content de s'être défendu en leur faisant sentir ses doutes et ses répugnances, leur immola tout, son Etat, sa famille, son unique rejeton, sa gloire, son honneur, sa raison, enfin sa personne, sa volonté, sa liberté, et *tout cela dans leur totalité entière*, sacrifice digne par son universalité d'être offert à Dieu seul, si par soi-même il n'eût pas été abominable. (p. 1065)

In other places this attraction of *le néant* (revealing itself in this quotation in Louis's policy of levelling out differences of birth) is made apparent and palpable through the rhythm of the sentence structures:

Mais cette dignité, il ne la voulait que pour lui, et que par rapport à lui; et celle-là, *même* relative, il la sapa presque toute pour mieux achever de ruiner toute autre et de la mettre, peu à peu, comme il fit, à l'unisson, en retranchant tant qu'il put toutes les cérémonies et les distinctions, dont il ne retint que l'ombre, et certaines trop marquées pour les détruire, en semant *même* dans celles-là des zizanies. (p. 962)

The two *même* point up stages in the downward movement, just as in the passage on p. 1069 beginning 'Piqué de n'oser égaler la nature . . .' the stages are marked by *enfin*, *après*, *enfin* and reach a kind of inverted climax in *Ce ne fut pas tout* . . ..

Like Proust, Saint-Simon worked over his sentences and made secondary insertions in order to give a more appropriate and concrete form to Louis's 'attraction towards the abyss'. For example:

First draft (from the 'Addition au *Journal* de Dangeau')	Final draft (p. 1005)
Saint-Germain, lieu unique pour rassembler les merveilles de la vue, l'immense plain-pied d'une forêt unique par sa situation et sa beauté, l'avantage et la facilité des eaux, les agréments des hauteurs et des terrasses et les charmes de la Seine, il l'abandonna pour Versailles, le plus ingrat de tous les lieux, sans bois, sans eaux, sans terre (presque tout y est sable mouvant ou marécage), sans air par conséquent, qui n'y peut être bon. Boislisle, p. 416	Saint-Germain, lieu unique pour rassembler les merveilles de la vue, l'immense plain-pied d'une forêt toute joignante, unique encore par la beauté de ses arbres, de son terrain, de sa situation, l'avantage et la facilité des eaux de source sur cette élévation, les agréments admirables des jardins, des hauteurs et des terrasses, qui les unes sur les autres se pouvaient si aisément conduire dans toute l'étendue qu'on aurait voulu, les charmes et les commodités de la Seine, enfin une ville toute faite, et que sa position entretenait par elle-même, il l'abandonna pour Versailles, le plus triste et le plus ingrat de tous les lieux, sans vue, sans bois, sans eau, sans terre, parce que tout y est sable mouvant ou marécage, sans air par conséquent, qui n'y peut être bon.

The move from Saint-Germain to Versailles, symbolic of the decline of France under Louis XIV, is made more drastic in the second draft by insertions which magnify the positive traits of Saint-Germain. Significantly, there is more strengthening of the positive aspects of Saint-

Germain than of the negative ones of Versailles: the fall from the greatest height is adequately described by the depiction of the height itself (*enfin une ville toute faite*). And of course the rhythm of the sentence helps to make this clear. The description of Saint-Germain is ample, harmonious and linear; but Versailles is given in broken, mostly monosyllabic, polemical disorder.

Another point of stylistic interest is Saint-Simon's incorporation into his portraits of the speech and arguments of the subject of the portrait. Mme de Montespan's complaining about Mme de Maintenon is clearly *audible* in the passage on p. 1020 in expressions like 'une rivale abjecte', 'une rivale si au-dessous . . .', 'cette suivante, pour ne pas dire servante' and so forth. The consuming cancer of Mme de Maintenon portrays itself through language and style, and Saint-Simon uses this image of a cancer explicitly to describe the king's love of splendour:

> C'est *une plaie* qui, une fois introduit, est devenue le *cancer* qui ronge tous les particuliers – parce que de la cour il s'est promptement communiqué à Paris et dans les provinces et les armées, où les gens en quelque place ne sont comptés qu'à proportion de leur table et de leur magnificence depuis cette malheureuse introduction – qui *ronge* tous les particuliers, qui force ceux d'un état à pouvoir voler à ne s'y épargner pour la plupart, dans la nécessité de soutenir leur dépense; et que la confusion des états, que l'orgueil, que jusqu'à la bienséance entretiennent, qui par la folie du gros va toujours en augmentant, dont les suites sont infinies, ne vont à rien moins qu'à la ruine et au renversement général (pp. 1004–5).

This long sentence is itself an image of the progression of a cancer. It strides from the *particuliers* to the *général*, sketching in individual conditions (*états*) and temperaments; it is bloated by a parenthesis and bursts into a flood of different currents which swirl around the reader, drawing his glance towards the infinite and leading him finally 'à la ruine et au renversement général'.

It can now be understood how important the great black *background of Nothingness* was for Saint-Simon's type of portrait. The background puts all earthly grandeur beneath God: one simply does not know, at the end of Saint-Simon's work, whether Louis's dying submission to God is hypocrisy or true recognition. The correct unmasking of a man finally brings about only the revelation of God. It is He who crushes the great of this world and takes away the value of all appearances. The crowning of God – of whom no double portrait is possible and who recognises the vanity of pride – cannot in the end be left out of Saint-Simon's natural hierarchy; and it cannot be other than the rejection of a Caesar aspiring to divinity, his relegation to nothingness.

In Saint-Simon, 'nothingness' (*le néant*) is both a social and a metaphysical–religious concept, since low birth is in his view of the world divinely ordained. He likes to scale the ladder from the bottom of the abyss to the summit of glory in a kind of baroque dynamic:

On a vu . . . les divers degrés par lesquels les enfants du roi et de Mme de Montespan ont été successivement tirés du *profond et ténébreux néant* du double adultère, et portés plus qu'au juste et parfait *niveau* des princes du sang, et jusqu'au *sommet* de l'habilité de succéder à la couronne . . . (p. 1066)

[This double illumination of all human life is reminiscent of Racine's *Athalie*, ⟶ 51–2.]

Louis XIV's presumption, vanity and *hubris* that take him near to rivalling God are stressed many times by Saint-Simon. Louis's upbringing is said to be responsible (pp. 957–8) for 'cet *orgueil*, que ce n'est point trop dire que, sans la crainte du Diable . . . il se serait fait adorer . . .'. His *orgueil* led him to become not only a 'distributeur de couronnes, . . . châtieur de nations, . . . conquérant' but also 'cet homme *immortel* pour qui on épuisait le marbre et le bronze, pour qui tout était à bout d'encens' (pp. 978–9). Mme de Maintenon is part of God's design to bring '*au plus superbe des rois* l'humiliation la plus profonde' (p. 1020), and only the miracle of Louis's repentance (the realisation of his own nothingness, p. 1072, 2nd paragraph) saves France from the complete *anéantissement* which the king's pride would have brought (p. 1072, 1st paragraph).

We are released from the Janus-like two-facedness of the portrait of a mortal man by contemplation of the heavenly Singular that wears no mask. Just as Molière's Tartuffe, rising to threaten the social order, requires the king as his counterpart and as the restorer of justice, so Saint-Simon's king, breaking into the realm of God, requires God as a *deus ex machina*. Or perhaps God is for Saint-Simon not *ex machina* but *ex natura*–the natural hierarchy of true values requiring, for him, a divine pinnacle.

3. Picture and Depiction

From what was said in the first part of this essay it should be clear that Saint-Simon could not reproduce through language the flow of history. Again and again the mass of historical events coagulates–so to speak–into clots, clearly cut off from each other and each producing a separate picture. Or to put it another way: Saint-Simon leads us constantly to individual summits, gloriettes and watchtowers which afford a complete panorama. We are constantly reminded by this structure of the gardens of Versailles, ruled by man, by a landscape gardener. Representation in Saint-Simon is constantly rounded off into a medallion–historical representation is resolved into a series of medallions. So we get sections of Louis XIV's life all having precisely the same 'circular' syntactic form. Everywhere in Saint-Simon we find sentences which present us with a totality: the author repeatedly reconstructs the character before our eyes, laying out in all the appositions and qualifications its whole content and extent, and competing in the *sequential* art of writing with the art of *juxtaposition*, the art of painting:

Dans ces derniers temps, abattu sous le poids d'une guerre fatale, soulagé de personne par l'incapacité de ses ministres et de ses généraux, en proie tout entier à un obscur et artificieux domestique, pénétré de douleur, non de ses fautes, qu'il ne connaissait ni ne voulait connaître, mais de son impuissance contre toute l'Europe réunie contre lui, réduit aux plus tristes extrémités pour ses finances et ses frontières, il n'eut de ressources qu'à se reployer sur lui-même, et à appesantir sur sa famille, sur sa cour, sur les consciences, sur tout son malheureux royaume cette dure domination . . . (p. 1061)

The attempt to achieve a total, static, rounded portrait within a single period leads Saint-Simon to use *anacoluthon* to an extent which (according to e.g. Boislisle) is grammatically incorrect. For example, on pp. 1064–5, the sentence beginning 'Déchiré au dedans par les catastrophes . . .' goes on its second 'leg' with 'incapable d'ailleurs . . .' and finally finds its grammatical subject with 'cette constance, cette fermeté d'âme . . . c'est ce dont peu d'hommes auraient été capables'. The following sentence, similarly, begins 'La grandeur d'âme que montra constamment . . .', but *ce roi*, the logical subject of the subordinate clause *que montra*, turns out to be the grammatical subject of the main verb 'se vit enfin abandonné'. In Racine, on the other hand, the complete subjectivisation of moral value-concepts does not allow anacoluthon, because the abstract forces are the real actors. Saint-Simon sees concrete figures, however, and moralises upon them, and this split vision has its grammatical expression in anacoluthon.

In one of the first 'medallions' in the text Saint-Simon's fascination with his subject comes across clearly:

Roi presque en naissant, étouffé par la politique d'une mère qui voulait gouverner, plus encore par le vif intérêt d'un pernicieux ministre, qui hasarda mille fois l'Etat pour son unique grandeur, et asservi sous ce joug tant que vécut ce premier ministre, c'est autant de retranché sur le règne de ce monarque. (p. 940)

It is as if he could not stop looking at this 'almost great' small man 'born to greatness', as if he were in thrall to the phenomenon of Louis XIV, as if the whole enormous portrait of the king owed its composition to Saint-Simon's bewitched resentment of the regal image.

This allows us to understand the *redites*, the repetitions that are so frequent, and frequently excused (*comme on le verra ailleurs – comme on l'a déjà vu*), in Saint-Simon. At every point in the *Mémoires* he wants to conjure up the figure of Louis in his historical totality, and the temporal flow slows and spreads as a river spreads when dammed. The author asks his audience on p. 949 not to take offence 's'il s'y en trouve des redites, nécessaires pour mieux rassembler et former un tout' – an effort towards gathering in the total personality; on p. 1050, he explains the *redites* by his striving to 'expliquer assez en détail des curiosités que nous regrettons dans toutes les Histoires et dans presque tous les Mémoires des divers temps' – the anecdotal in the service of characterisation.

Saint-Simon's sentence structures are, in their breadth, roundedness and powerful self-enclosure, naturally destined to isolate historical medallions out of the flow of time. It is as if such 'medallion-sentences' simply spring from Saint-Simon's pen as he writes: for example, when on p. 942 he talks of Louis's youth and young loves and opines that the king should have counted himself lucky if he had only had mistresses like Mme de Lavallière, a medallion of the lady follows quite automatically, as the grammatical attribute of the name Lavallière:

> Heureux s'il n'eût eu que des maîtresses semblables à Mme de la Vallière, arrachée à elle-même par ses propres yeux, honteuse de l'être, encore plus des fruits de son amour, reconnus et élevés malgré elle, modeste, désinteressée, douce, bonne au dernier point, combattant sans cesse contre elle-même, victorieuse enfin de son désordre par les plus cruels effets de l'amour et de la jalousie, qui furent tout à la fois son tourment et sa ressource, qu'elle sut embrasser assez au milieu de ses douleurs pour s'arracher enfin, et se consacrer à la plus dure et la plus sainte pénitence!

The whole history of this woman's existence, from mistress to repentant sinner, is compressed into a portrait having the dimensions of a medallion.

One constantly comes across sentences which, although spoken about a specific situation, give the picture of the entire personality – as if Saint-Simon did not wish us to lose sight of the whole structure in any individual detail. On Louvois, for example, we get the following expansion:

> Tel fut l'aveuglement du Roi, tel fut l'adresse, la hardiesse, la formidable autorité d'un ministre, le plus éminent pour les projets et pour les exécutions, mais le plus funeste pour diriger en premier; qui, sans être premier ministre, abattit tous les autres, sut mener le Roi où et comme il voulut, et devint en effet le maître. (p. 961)

The closed, atemporal implication of this sort of 'compressed' portrait is in some sense in opposition to the flow of history, and so the next sentences come as a great surprise: 'Il eut la joie de survivre à Colbert et à Seignalay, ses ennemis et longtemps ses rivaux. Elle fut de courte durée' (p. 962). The picture of lasting power is actually destroyed by that last short sentence, the effect of the portrait somehow suspended.

Those then are the unresolved antimonies between picture and depiction in Saint-Simon.

Now we can see that Saint-Simon must constantly reach back to his beginning and use that style of repeated recapitulation so characteristic of Old French epic. A feeling that he has not expressed himself well enough in any single way, an otherwise quite un-French apprehension of stylistic incompleteness, drives him to a curiously repetitive procedure of retouching, of always saying the same thing in different formal variations and multiplications. That is to say, the writer never believes that his text is a finished product and has to stylise it afresh with new devices. Compare the 'tirades' beginning with *jamais* in the depiction of the king's character (quoted above on pp. 126–7) with the *laisse*-like refrains beginning with *telles* . . . that represent Louis's last years:

Telles furent les dernières années de ce long règne de Louis XIV . . . (p. 1061)

Telles furent les longues et cruelles circonstances des plus douloureux malheurs qui éprouvèrent la constance du roi . . . (p. 1064)

Or the triple return introduced by *on*:

On a vu avec quelle adresse elle [Mme de Maintenon] se servit de la princesse des Ursins . . . (p. 1053)

On ne répétera ce qu'on a vu pp. 776 . . . sur Godet, évêque de Chartres . . . (p. 1055)

On a vu que Monsieur de Chartres était passionné sulpicien . . . (p. 1056)

Saint-Simon repeatedly gathers his views into linguistic forms which remain unfinished, provisional and impressionistically unsettled. The *recommencement* is a linguistic 'standing-in-for' that does not advance – Saint-Simon draws little sketches without ever reaching the 'definitive' picture.

Let us now look at an extended example where these various techniques come together.

Prince heureux s'il en fût jamais, en figure unique, en force corporelle, en santé égale et ferme, et presque jamais interrompue, en siècle si fécond et si libéral pour lui en tous genres qu'il a pu en ce sens être comparé au siècle d'Auguste; en sujets adorateurs prodiguant leurs biens, leur sang, leurs talents, la plupart jusqu'à leur réputation, quelques-uns même leur honneur, et beaucoup trop leur conscience et leur religion, pour le servir, souvent même seulement pour lui plaire. Heureux surtout en famille, s'il n'en avait eu que de légitime; en mère contente des respects et d'un certain crédit; en frère dont la vie anéantie par de déplorables goûts, et d'ailleurs futile par elle-même, se noyait dans la bagatelle, se contentait d'argent, se retenait par sa propre crainte et par celle de ses favoris, et n'était guères moins bas courtisan que ceux qui voulaient faire leur fortune; une épouse vertueuse, amoureuse de lui, infatigablement patiente, devenue véritablement française, d'ailleurs absolument incapable; un fils unique toute sa vie à la lisière, qui à cinquante ans ne savait encore que gémir sous le poids de la contrainte et du discrédit, qui environné et éclairé de toutes parts, n'osait que ce que lui était permis, et qui, absorbé dans la matière, ne pouvait causer la plus légère inquiétude; en petit-fils dont l'âge et l'exemple du père . . . rassuraient . . .; un neveu qui . . . tremblait devant lui . . .; descendant plus bas, des princes du sang de même trempe, à commencer par le grand Condé, devenu la frayeur et la bassesse même . . .; Monsieur le Prince son fils, le plus vil et le plus prostitué de tous les courtisans; Monsieur le Duc . . . hors de mesure de pouvoir se faire craindre . . .; des deux princes de Conti . . . l'aîné mort si tôt, l'autre mourant de peur de tout, accablé sous la haine du Roi . . .; les plus grands seigneurs lassés et ruinés . . .; leurs successeurs séparés, désunis, livrés à l'ignorance . . .; des parlements subjugués . . .; nul corps ensemble, et par laps de temps, presque personne qui osât même à part soi avoir aucun dessein . . .; enfin jusqu'à la division des familles les plus proches . . ., l'entière méconnaissance des parents et des parentés . . .; peu à peu tous les devoirs absorbés par un seul que la nécessité fit, qui fut de craindre et de tâcher à plaire. (pp. 980–1)

This cross-section of the entire state of France comes in a chapter headed 'Bonheur du Roi en tout genre'. The 'happiness' or rather pseudo-fortune of the despot consists of the suppression of all forces that might have threatened his own power. I do not need to mention the irony that illuminates and uncovers this 'fortune' of the king in the qualifications and subordinate clauses – 'sujets adorateurs prodiguant . . . leur réputation . . . leur honneur . . . leur conscience et leur religion'; 'une épouse vertueuse . . . d'ailleurs absolument incapable', and so forth. What is of interest here is the gradation of the king's fortune by the echelons of the kingdom's hierarchy. 'Le bonheur du Roi en tout genre' is seen not from the people's or the state's point of view but from the king's, and it flows from the leader at the summit down to each lower level. What looks like Augustan *fortuna* from the top is, seen from below, dissolution of the state, oppression, and slavery. In this France the dominant view is the one from above. The syntactic thread holding the passage together is *Heureux en* . . ., because in this despotic state the decisive factor is the king's good fortune with respect to this, that or the other. Even the construction *heureux en famille . . . en mère . . . en frère* etc. on the same level as *heureux en santé* is rather 'regicentric' (if I may coin the term by analogy with 'egocentric'). The physical good fortune of the king communicates itself to his whole sphere of influence, and his family, his court and his entire state naturally belong to that sphere. Saint-Simon could have found no better way of depicting the debilitation of the body politic by the all-consuming power of tyranny than this little preposition *en* that connects everything – men and things – to the total fortune of the highest-born like items to be added up in a column of figures. It is absolutely clear that Saint-Simon's conception of character as a static entity, of history as the effect of character, together with his belief in a natural order, could not but produce this sort of hierarchically graduated cross-section. What he shows in any case is the undermining of the old order by Louis XIV, burrowing and working through the echelons and divisions created by the old order. The developments brought about by the king's reign are given in passive past participles, as *faits accomplis*: 'les plus grands seigneurs *lassés* . . . leurs successeurs *séparés* . . . des parlements *subjugués* . . .', or in durative imperfects: 'en frère dont la vie . . . se noyait dans la bagatelle . . .; un fils . . . qui à cinquante ans ne savait que gémir . . .'. It is the stasis of an Augustan age, but we had been warned against it in the short, sharp sentence preceding: 'La décadence est arrivée à grands pas' (p. 979).

The picture of 'the king's good fortune' stands as a pendant or balance to the picture of the people's relief at the king's death given at the end of the volume ('*Le Roi peu regretté*') on pp. 1093–6. Here is the main skeleton of the sentence:

Louis ne fut regretté que de ses valets intérieurs, de peu d'autres gens, et des chefs de l'affaire de la Constitution. Son successeur n'en était pas en âge; Madame n'avait pour lui que de la crainte et de la bienséance; Mme la duchesse de Berry ne l'aimait pas, et comptait aller régner; M. le duc d'Orléans n'était pas payé pour le pleurer, et ceux qui l'étaient [= les bâtards] n'en firent pas leur charge. Mme de Maintenon était excédée du Roi depuis la perte de la Dauphine; . . . ainsi quoiqu'elle perdît en perdant le Roi, elle se sentit délivrée, et ne fut capable que de ce sentiment . . . On a vu jusqu'à quelle joie, à quelle barbare indécence le prochain point de vue de la toute puissance jeta le duc du Maine. La tranquillité glacée de son frère ne s'en haussa ni baissa. Madame la Duchesse . . . n'avait plus besoin de l'appui du Roi . . . elle se trouva donc fort à son aise et en liberté . . . Mme la duchesse d'Orléans . . . [cried and spent a few days in bed]. Pour les princes du sang, c'étaient des enfants. La duchesse de Ventadour et le maréchal de Villeroy donnèrent un peu la comédie, pas un autre n'en prit même la peine. Mais quelques vieux et plats courtisans . . . regrettèrent de n'avoir plus à se cuider . . . dans les raisonnements et l'amusement journalier d'une cour qui s'éteignait avec le Roi. Tout ce qui la composait était de deux sortes: les uns, en espérance de figurer, de se mêler, de s'introduire étaient ravis de voir finir un règne sous lequel il n'y avait rien pour eux à attendre; les autres, fatigués d'un joug pesant, toujours accablant . . . étaient charmés de se trouver au large; tous, en général, d'être délivrés d'une gêne continuelle, et amoureux des nouveautés. Paris, las d'une dépendance qui avait tout assujetti, respira dans l'espoir de quelque liberté, et dans la joie de voir finir l'autorité, de tant de gens qui en abusaient. Les provinces, au désespoir de leur ruine et de leur anéantissement, respirèrent et tressaillirent de joie, et les parlements et toute espèce de judicature anéantie par les édits et les évocations, . . . se flatta, les premiers de figurer, les autres de se trouver affranchis. Le peuple, ruiné, accablé, désespéré, rendit grâces à Dieu, avec un éclat scandaleux, d'une délivrance dont ses plus ardents désirs ne doutaient plus. Les étrangers, ravis d'être enfin . . . défaits d'un monarque qui leur avait si longuement imposé la loi . . ., se continrent avec plus de bienséance que les Français . . . Pour nos ministres et les intendants des provinces, les financiers, et ce qu'on peut appeler la canaille, ceux-là sentirent toute l'étendue de leur perte.

That is truly a picture of the afterlife of a man who ruled over so many that it can be summed up in the phrase *omnis moriar*. It is a negative picture of fame, the inverse of a Renaissance *gloria*, graduated just as in some large historical group portrait with all the individual figures and forces in adoration of the Sun-king – but here they are doing something different from adoring! They approach with empty hands and without bending the knee. As in a large historical painting the individual figures are subtly distinguished from each other and it is Saint-Simon's virtuosity to indicate the specific attitude – and in this case of obligatory mourning, the specific pose – of each one, and finally to bring together a whole range of psychological attitudes into a single collective stance, that of 'little regret'. We saw earlier how the separate traits of the monarch's character composed a unity; here, in the same sense, the individual attitudes of the men destined to carry the king's 'glory' further, compose a collective stance of rejection. Frozen as in the manner of a historical painting, this *historical* moment is grasped as a *static* one in which the pressure of the situation (or, rather, the removal of pressure on the king's underlings after his death) calls forth the true, underlying attitude and stance of the subject. It is an unmasking scene on a grand scale. Though Saint-Simon imposed the question of authenticity and falseness on his material elsewhere, here history itself offers him the opportunity to report in these terms the truth about the mood of the whole country. The dynamic which Saint-Simon had to work into an otherwise static portrait is in this instance something that was quite perceptible in history. Therefore Saint-Simon is fond of depicting such 'revealing events' or moments of truth in all their multiple effects, and likes these snapshots of a whole historical moment (another example is the death of the Dauphin). And he surely enjoys the firm order in which the entire people of France in its social ranks expresses its opinion. Rather like some medieval dramatist, whose figures are restricted to their *mansions* on stage, and speak from their indicated places only, so the latter-day champion of medieval social ranks has the court, the *états* and the people take up a stance on Louis XIV's death 'from their indicated places'; and the towering importance of Louis in his own lifetime, out of all proportion to his merits, is utterly flattened by his death, for his passing is regretted only by *la canaille*!

The conception of national attitude as a single block, cut like a stone into multiple facets of different kinds in the hierarchically ordered individual figures of history, is the psychological principle of order which Saint-Simon shares with Molière and Racine – the difference being of course that the historical portrait possesses the concrete fullness and breadth of frame that the playwrights neither have nor wish to have. That means that what destroys the king is finally the *people's judgment*, the judgment of the people that can only be hinted at as latent forces behind or beside the stage in classical drama. So Saint-Simon, champion of the medieval orders, is more modern than he knew; amazingly, for such a deep-dyed aristocrat, the spirit of what is spoken from the separate *mansions* of his stage is an egalitarian one. Freed from surveillance and fetters, France can now contemplate its past dispassionately, but also with a degree of cruelty towards itself, and formulate a bleak and cutting judgment. First, the view of the cold and calculating court: 'Madame n'avait pour lui que de la crainte et de la bienséance; Mme la duchesse de Berry ne l'aimait pas et comptait aller régner.' The further we descend towards the social depths, the more genuine, passionate, pathetic and insubordinate is the tone: the courtiers are merely 'fatigués d'un joug pesant' or 'amoureux des nouveautés', but Paris is 'las d'une dépendance . . .', the provinces are 'au désespoir', the courts of justice feel 'anéantie' and the people are 'ruiné, accablé, désespéré'. In each *mansion* of the stage set there is a specific and particular shade of feeling; each of the represented personalities displays its 'emotional' attitude, so to speak. An order rules over the complete insubordination of all concerned with the levelling and destruction of Louis XIV, for which they finally thank God 'avec un éclat scandaleux'. This is some kind of panopticon of frozen, upright figures, a 'Last Judgment' taking place in this world and with rigid social ranks unchanged!

With his way of seeing and transforming the becoming of history into a set-piece stage and a gallery of medallion-portraits, Saint-Simon is a long way from the historical thought of the eighteenth century and remains much closer to the stable and hierarchical seventeenth century. Saint-Simon corresponds to the baroque counter-reformation of seventeenth-century Spain, whose literature sang of decay, defilement, disappointment and vanity in the most splendid formal beauty. Like the great Spanish portrayers of *desengaño* (disillusionment) he depicts life not as a mixed reality having both its ugliness and its beauty, but rather in an antithetical–polemical way, life as magnificent in its very nothingness. Thus he introduces a movement into the immobility of his edifice – the movement of inner subsidence, the worm in the apple. The impact of his writings is undecidable and ambiguous, but in any case an intrinsically dynamic one: admiration and aversion together, as I tried to suggest in the epigraph of this essay. One recalls that Boileau saw Corneille's response to the precepts of Aristotle's poetics in the arousal not only of fear and pity but of admiration also (Boileau, *Lettre à Perrault*, p. 119). Saint-Simon is the antidote to Corneille: his admiration leads without transition to disenchantment.

4. On the Method of the Present Essay

I have discussed above only the portrait of Louis as a kind of overgrown medallion, although I could have demonstrated the same features in Saint-Simon's other portraits. For a work as gigantic as the *Mémoires* a 'sample test' recommended itself, in my view, rather more than the collocation of significant passages throughout the work as a whole. I am of the opinion that careful, basic reading of an important and relatively closed section of a larger work must bring better results than jumping about from one high point to another in different parts. The harmony and relevance of details to the whole, the living organism of the work, can be made apparent only through absorption in a whole of manageable proportions – and in any case, the same stylistic blood flows through all of the *Mémoires* so that a sample must produce the same result wherever it is taken. To a quite special extent Saint-Simon is a man of repetition in a higher sense: not just in terms of content, but in his way of moulding his material, as we established in our study of the portrait of Louis XIV. He obeys – of course! – his own biological rhythm, which compels him only ever to reconstruct the same thing, the total picture of an ample personality grasped in its antinomies and external effects. His larger complete portraits show the same special features: for example, the portrait of Fénelon (1711) is built up from the single proposition that 'sa passion était de plaire', and d'Autin's formula is 'le plus habile et le plus raffiné courtisan de son temps'. In both cases an opposition between the external effect and the inner nature of the respective subjects has to be produced – in the one case, in the 'unmasking' of Fénelon, in the other, in a consideration of what the duc d'Autin had made of his 'brutal', 'shamelessly Gascon' temperament. With such externally projected characters, their relationship to their environment can be determined with almost mathematical precision. Fénelon's courtliness, like Louis XIV's, is 'toujours mesurée et proportionnée, en sorte qu'il semblait à chacun qu'elle n'était que pour lui, avec cette précision dans laquelle il excellait'. The natural and the ceremonial are so intertwined that Saint-Simon can speak of the 'grâces naturelles et qui *coulaient de source* . . . dont *il tenait*, pour ainsi dire, le *robinet* . . .'. Here too that amazing transition from praise to blame, from panegyric to invective, occurs – but frequently also the reverse, from blame to praise. The duchess of Burgundy is first presented as 'properly ugly' with pendulous cheeks, an insignificant nose, biting lips, etc.; but she is eventually stylised into a 'déesse sur les nuées' at whose feet 'les grâces naissaient d'elles-mêmes'. The duke of Burgundy, with his conflicting spiritual and physical impulses, is made into the *vas electionis* of God: 'Mais Dieu, qui est le maître des cœurs, et dont le divin esprit souffle où il veut, fit de ce prince un ouvrage de sa droite.' Here the *anéantissement* of men before God, the only true power, is once again presented. The duke of Burgundy dies, like Louis XIV, in the arms of his faith (and is compared to 'une imitation de Jésus-Christ sur la croix'), and Saint-Simon's tone rises to the power and theatricality of Bossuet. And in all of these portraits the flow of history is dammed and forms a lake, a mirror, a static picture.

It will have been noticed that I have departed from my earlier practice and subordinated stylistic observation to literary commentary. Linguistic and stylistic remarks appear in this essay in their rightful and modest place as the necessary but as it were secondary expressions of the writer's temperament. Not only is the linguistic not represented independently: it was not even observed for its own sake but always with a view to, and subordinate to, the literary particularity of the writer as a whole. In this way I avoid the tiresome double repetition of the observational method which requires first a study of the literary features of the work (frequently based on the work of other scholars) and then a second specialist linguistic study. The danger of mistaking the meaning and of forcing the interpretation is not easily avoided in such a double procedure where the literary and linguistic are treated as two almost separate research activities – and anyway, a writer's work is not something that is first literary then linguistic (or vice versa) but something unified that all sorts of different readers can study. It is a thoroughly egocentric procedure to smuggle one's own specialist point of view into the heart of the work itself. If this makes questions of pure style drown and dissolve into literary criticism, then that is intentional: style studies can only ever be a preparatory step in the proper study of literature. I have been described as a man seeking a 'belle alliance' of grammar and criticism (Ludwig), but nowadays I would rather talk of a 'belle victoire' of literature over grammar. Stylistics is nothing more than a special procedure of literary study, from which it can never be independent. I hereby declare my opposition to any claims to magisterial chairs or regal thrones, to all dreams of autonomy or hegemony, that may be made by stylistics, word-science, call it what you will: *ne ultra crepidam*!

To preserve the unity of literary and linguistic study the student must remain in a single mind, and so, breaking with usual practice, I have ignored the bibliography on Saint-Simon. Of course I cannot pretend that my earlier reading of books about Saint-Simon, or hearing lectures in my youth or writing lectures later on, or especially the preparation of my comparison between Saint-Simon and Proust have had no influence at all on my present views – but I can go so far as to assert that for this essay on Saint-Simon I neither read nor reread anything about the *Mémoires*, not even Adam's book on the language of Saint-Simon, nor E. Schwarz's thesis or the one by A. Franz on French portraiture. I believe that sometimes in our learned treatises we should dare to put, under the heading 'Works consulted', simply 'None'. Let us read the primary texts more than the secondary 'literature' – then our secondary creations will be more living, nearer to the primary and more directly influenced by it. I wanted to approach Saint-Simon 'unprepared', as a *tabula rasa*, as a simple reader seeking to enjoy. Maybe I have overlooked much of substance or repeated things that have been better said by others before me, but I would like to claim only that I have tried to *see things for myself*. A good precept for beginners would be: Pretend that nothing has ever been written on your subject – and write away! And in the end of course artists too must always 'begin anew', 'see with new eyes'. Everything has already been seen, but we have to try to see it in new ways. Whether we succeed is not for us to judge.

III

CORNEILLE'S *POLYEUCTE* AND THE *VIE DE SAINT ALEXIS*

1932

This 'explanation' of *Polyeucte* by the means of the medieval legend of Saint Alexis, like the chapter on Saint-Simon, seems to have been forgotten by almost all subsequent critics and scholars – with the exception of R. A. Sayce, who lists it in the bibliography to his excellent edition of the play, used for all quotations here. Spitzer's essay is a polemical piece, written in anger (somewhat muted by translation), in which aggression directed against other critics is balanced and complemented, as it were, by an *a priori* submission to the necessary perfection of Corneille's text. Curiously, however, the primary target of aggression cannot be found (see the note on p. 147 below); and I have come across no replies or rejoinders to this spirited defence of Corneille's 'christian tragedy'.

DB

Soyez chrétien pour l'engager à l'être! (Julie to Saint-Preux, on M. de Wolmar, in Rousseau's *La Nouvelle Héloïse*, p. 742)

It is a terrible task to imitate the inimitable. I well perceive, my dear friend, that there can be genius in anything, even in martyrdom.
(Goethe, *Elective Affinities*, p. 299)

Julius Schmidt states that 'interpretation . . . must be the central concern of the philologist' and that the scholar's labour of linguistic, cultural and artistic cognition should be directed towards the discovery of the artist's underlying personality. Because I agree with this view entirely and believe, like Schmidt, that texts are worth 'reading, seeing and hearing' properly, I must declare that, owing to Schmidt's personal bias, unjustified evaluation has supplanted objective comprehension in his study of *Polyeucte* IV.iii, where Corneille is put (as usual) in the shadow of Racine, where relative judgments are rigidified into precipitate and sweeping generalisations about cultural history, and where the actual meaning of the text is thoroughly obfuscated. By way of introduction to his study of Act IV sc.iii, Schmidt gives his general view of Corneille and compares the characters of Polyeucte and Pauline. Corneille, he says, has no 'physical feeling'; his works are 'rational constructions' in which a 'powerful, legalistic rhetoric' allows 'established' ideals to confront each other – ideals established in a period ruled by 'unnatural [feelings] of preciosity' and the 'exaggerated concept of honour of a decadent nobility'. Pauline is 'Corneille's finest female figure' and goes through an inner development, according to Schmidt.

Pauline is genuine in her soul, not simply a foil for the rigid Polyeucte. She fails to understand his position (and no wonder, given his stilted, *précieux* attitude and his abstaining from any action that might make his thoughts easier to understand!), but remains open to new insight . . . Instead of speaking for an audience, Pauline really talks to Polyeucte. She opens herself up, and seeks to grasp the problem in human terms. Thus her language is simpler and more urgent, and antithetical rhetoric relaxes its grip somewhat on the lines she speaks. Unfortunately the same cannot be said of Polyeucte: despite a few tears he is the unfeeling trumpet of his own dogma, which is entirely foreign to the true sense of Christianity.*

* Spitzer's reference to the location of Schmidt's article (*Neuphilologische Monatsschrift* 3.148ff) and his subsequent quotations from it have to be taken on trust. The title itself is not listed in Dietrich–*IBZ*, but Professor Harri Meier informs me that a journal of this name was published by Quelle und Meyer in Leipzig from 1930 to 1943. However, vol. 3

Consequently Polyeucte's language is external, formal and hard, and gives in IV.iii no real expression of his true self, according to Schmidt; with no word of feeling for the fate of his unhappy wife, the fastidious Cornelian hero places himself beyond all 'homely' feelings, and evades conflicts instead of overcoming them; he is a 'player, *torero* or champion (or whatever you want to call it)', and instead of being 'the carrier of a conflict in which we could participate, he is the advocate of an established doctrine; we do not identify with him and thus the label *tragedy* loses its justification'.

This apparently 'modern' interpretation is not methodologically sound in so far as it does not use the internal structural principle of the individual scene as a basis for describing the structure of the *whole* play and of Corneille's theatre in its entirety; instead, an overall interpretation of Corneille is laid down in advance and used to make individual points on a particular scene. The armature of the scene is not brought out, and therefore the armature of the interpretation also remains in the dark. What Schmidt is in fact doing is to revive the old prejudice against Corneille the rational legalist and precious rhetorician, a view which really only had a historical justification in Lessing. Schmidt denies that *Polyeucte* is a tragedy but only because he thinks tragedies are works in which we can participate with the protagonist because he is shown in human terms that are moving and comprehensible. Pauline is humanly moving and comprehensible and so she is 'Corneille's finest female figure'. '*Unfortunately*' the same cannot be said of Polyeucte – he is 'stiltedly *précieux*', 'a fastidious virtuoso', 'a *torero* or champion' and in the last analysis unchristian.

It would be strange indeed if Corneille had written a *tragédie chrétienne* which was foreign to the true sense of Christianity. That was, however, Lessing's view of *Polyeucte* in 1767:

> Is such a play (in which only the christian is of interest) at all possible in fact? Is not the character of the true christian somehow quite untheatrical? Is there not a contradiction between the calm composure and unalterable gentleness which are the principal features of a true christian, and the whole business of tragedy which seeks to purify the passions through passion? (Lessing, pp. 11–12)

But the house of christianity has many mansions. What Lessing had in mind when he wrote of a 'christian as christian' was an evangelical-cum-pietistic christianity of inwardness and withdrawal, not the active

is not to be found in Konstanz, in Bonn, or in Cologne university libraries – nor, indeed, would it seem, in any library belonging to the interlibrary loan system in W. Germany (though a few other volumes of the journal have been located, if not actually seen). Furthermore, there is no reference to an article on *Polyeucte* by the (very real) Julius Schmidt in the 1927/35 bibliography of the *Zeitschrift für romanische Philologie*, nor even and perhaps more significantly in Schmidt's own list of publications in his entry in Kirschner's *Gelehrten-Lexikon*. I must thank Harri Meier for his efforts on my behalf, and admit myself defeated.

christianity of the *ecclesia militans* in search of heavenly glory. Also, Lessing sees christian content as incompatible with the frame of classical tragedy; he does not seek to extend that frame towards christianity.

Lessing's view was foreshadowed in France by Saint-Evremond, in *De la tragédie ancienne et moderne* (1692):

> L'esprit de nôtre Religion est directement opposé à celui de la Tragédie. L'humilité et la patience de nos Saints sont trop contraires aux vertus des Héros que demande le théâtre . . . Polieucte a plus envie de mourir pour Dieu, que les autres hommes n'en ont de vivre pour eux. Neantmoins ce qui eût fait un beau Sermon, faisoit une misérable Tragédie . . . (Saint-Evremond, pp. 173–4)

Jules Lemaître rejected such an attitude, expressed by phrases like 'Quelle dureté de cœur, quelle inhumanité chez ce saint!' etc. (Lemaître, I.27), but a recent German critic comes back to the same idea that Polyeucte is not a dramatic figure, whilst Pauline is one of Corneille's most human heroines, and that the 'tragedy of martyrdom' is inherently impossible (Klemperer, *Corneille*, p. 248). If only modern literary historians, who do not have on their side the same grounds as the social critic Saint-Evremond or the writer Lessing, would stop *deeming* 'impossible' whatever from their limited standpoint *seems* impossible!

On the other hand, the Middle Ages spoke of Christ as *tragicus noster*. Boileau attacks *Polyeucte* in the *Art poétique*:

> De la foi d'un chrétien les mystères terribles
> D'ornements égayés ne sont pas susceptibles (III.199–200)

but mentions at the same time that *tremendum* is characteristic of christianity. Before he adopts an opinion denying the christianness of *tragédie chrétienne*, the critic would be well advised to first reconsider his own opinion of the meaning of christianity. One could moreover ask whether the differing conceptions of the two principal characters in IV.iii (Polyeucte as the trumpet of dogma, Pauline as the woman of sensitive human feeling) are not justified precisely by the word *chrétien* which Corneille thoughtfully added to the title *tragédie*. With his characteristic clear-sightedness, Corneille states the following in the *Examen de 'Polyeucte'*:

> Ceux qui veulent arrêter nos héros dans une médiocre bonté, où quelques interprètes d'Aristote bornent leur vertu, ne trouveront pas ici leur compte, puisque *celle de Polyeucte va jusqu'à la sainteté, et n'a aucun mélange de faiblesse* . . . Je reviens à Polyeucte, dont le succès a été très-heureux. Le style n'en est pas si fort ni si majestueux que celui de *Cinna* et de *Pompée*, mais il a quelque chose de plus touchant, et *les tendresses de l'amour humain y font un si agréable mélange avec la fermeté du divin*, que sa représentation a satisfait tout ensemble les dévots et les gens du monde. (*Examen*, p. 7, lines 20–2; p. 8, lines 68–74)

So: Corneille felt that the special property of his *tragédie chrétienne*, by contrast with classical (Aristotelian) tragedy, was the unalloyed saintliness and love of God of the christian martyr untouched by earthly things, which together with the earthly love of a woman produces an 'agreeable mixture' for the stage. Polyeucte's character is unmixed (*fermeté de l'amour divin*) – two voices mix on stage in a duet of love human and divine. The earthly can make no impact on the divine armour, but the two forces nonetheless come together on one stage. The worldly theatre of the renaissance had moved the public away from the liturgical drama of the Middle Ages; Corneille wished to make a christian legend fit for the stage in a period in which the devices of the medieval theatre, with their religious origins, had been forgotten. It would have taken another renaissance of christian theatre to make all the old Passion material usable on the stage again, a renaissance that did not take place and which even Claudel and Péguy in the twentieth century have failed to achieve. Corneille was confronted with a submerged religious theatre, and a lively classical one, dealing only allusively with christian themes: religious people went to church, and worldly men to the 'comédie'. Corneille cannot allow himself to upset either his christian or his theatrical public with his religious play; both the *dévots* and the *gens du monde* must be catered for – and it is touching to see the theatrical technician and the christian that Corneille was, at work mixing elements and ingredients from both spheres. The *dévots* want *sainteté*, not *médiocre bonté* – whilst the *gens du monde* do not want to be torn from the realm of theatrical conventions, they require *le vraisemblable* and *l'agréable*. Corneille justifies himself on the first point: 'A mon gré, je n'ai point fait de pièce où l'ordre du théâtre soit plus beau et l'enchaînement des scènes mieux ménagé' (*Examen*, pp. 8–9, l.74–6). Theatricality, *l'ordre du théâtre*, is ensured primarily though not uniquely through respect of the three unities, which were seen in the period as equivalent to the dictates of *vraisemblance*. (Thus Corneille actually describes the sacrifice which occurs immediately after Sévère's arrival, to maintain the unity of time, as *invraisemblable*, but subordinates it to the higher verisimilitude of which the three unities are a token: 'cette précipitation sortira du vraisemblable par la nécessité d'obéir à la règle' (*Examen*, p. 9, l.84–5). That is to say, *precisely because* the christian tragedy goes beyond the bounds of the purely human, the conventions of the theatre must be observed all the more rigorously.

I am not sure that Mornet is on the right track when he makes the assumption that Corneille preferred 'les combinaisons plus savantes' of his other plays to the limited plot of *Polyeucte* (Mornet, II.62). What Corneille says is:

J'ai fait *Pompée* pour satisfaire à ceux qui ne trouvaient pas les vers de *Polyeucte* si puissants que ceux de *Cinna* et leur montrer que je saurais bien en retrouver la pompe quand le sujet le pourrait souffrir. (Quoted by Mornet, II.63)

This clearly means that Corneille voluntarily did without *pompe* when dealing with a christian subject. Belief, when put on stage, had to appear untheatrical. Legend is bad theatre: it seeks to edify everyman.

G. Müller has shown that legend – unlike short fiction – always has the same theme, the 'contact of heaven and earth' through a *miracle*. The central, edifying content of legend lies less in its manner of telling than in what it tells, and so literary and aesthetic shaping has no sovereignty over legend as it does over the short story which can deal with 'any direction of the human weather-vane' (Müller, p. 459). What matters in legend is solely the transparency of its edifying meaning. Evidently, Corneille knew what legend was.

To integrate into the framework of his theatre an action which explodes its conventions is something of a virtuoso turn for the classical craftsman Corneille, as if to prove that 'impossible n'est pas français'. In any case, if miracles are to find a way into christian tragedy, the concept of verisimilitude has to be expanded. It has to become a '*vraisemblance* in the context of legend', a legendary *vraisemblance*, instead of the conventionally rational kind of verisimilitude. As Corneille says of the miraculous conversion of Pauline and her father Félix:

Ces deux conversions, quoique miraculeuses, sont si ordinaires dans les martyres, quelles ne sortent point de la vraisemblance, parce qu'elles ne sont pas de ces événements rares et singuliers qu'on ne peut tirer en exemple. (*Examen*, p. 11, l.163–7)

Miraculous conversions belong to the stage props of legend, are themselves a convention like the conventions of the stage and can therefore be added to them in a legendary tragedy.

I was obliged to discuss first how Corneille fitted the legend of martyrdom into the general frame of his theatre, with its constraint of verisimilitude, in order to show that he took equal pains to balance it with the 'agréable' which the audience has a right to expect. In the *Abrégé du martyre de Saint Polyeucte* Corneille recognises the right of the *dévots* to respect for the holy, and the right of the theatregoer to entertainment by the agreeable; he also narrates here the source from which he took the legend of *Polyeucte*:

Comme il a été à propos d'*en rendre la représentation agréable*, afin que *le plaisir* pût insinuer plus *doucement* l'utilité, et lui servir comme de véhicule pour la porter dans l'âme du peuple, il est juste aussi de lui donner cette lumière pour démêler la vérité d'avec ses ornements, et lui faire reconnaitre ce qui *lui doit imprimer du respect comme saint*, et *ce qui lui doit seulement divertir comme industrieux*. (*Abrégé*, p. 5, l.34–41)

In the *Abrégé*, Corneille carefully lists as 'inventions et embellissements de théâtre' (p. 6, l.111) his own additions to the traditional legend (e.g. Pauline's dream, the love of Sévère, etc.), but he leaves out the opposition of the inhuman Polyeucte and the human Pauline – simply because this 'agréable mélange' is already contained in the source material, where Félix is said to send Pauline to Polyeucte 'afin de voir si ses larmes n'auraient point plus de pouvoir sur l'esprit d'un mari que n'auraient eu ses artifices et ses rigueurs' (*Abrégé*, l.96–8).

Therefore to see Polyeucte as an unfeeling angel blowing a trumpet for the world to hear, or as a champion sportsman playing for the crowd, and Pauline as a well-formed human being, is to fail to recognise Corneille's intention. *The opposition of the two characters is not an opposition of failed and successful artistic achievement but a necessary contrast in the artistic linking of a divinely unyielding man and of an earthly, yielding woman.* Of course it would be more 'modern' to have a more human and romantically pliant hero vacillating between God and his wife, but it is an ancient tradition of legend that the christian hero, the martyr, is open to God alone and that all human love passes him by: the warm spring of human loves breaks against the rock of faith whose hardness is its true love, and has the power to awaken the spring of faith in the unbelieving (the reversal of Pauline's love through Polyeucte). It is one of the genuinely christian paradoxes that the gentle faith can use stony hardness in its own defence (Peter is *petra*, 'stone'), just as Christ spoke harshly of his disciples. The true christian, following his divine model, and in order to live the good christian life, takes all the curses upon himself, and allows a *torrent d'injures* to flow over him:

> Ce n'est plus cet époux si charmant à vos yeux:
> C'est l'ennemi commun de l'Etat et des dieux,
> Un méchant, un infâme, un rebelle, un perfide,
> Un traitre, un scélérat, un lâche, un parricide,
> Une peste exécrable à tous les gens de bien,
> Un sacrilège impie, en un mot, un chrétien.
>
> *Polyeucte* III.ii, 779–784

Voltaire attacked this scene for 'le ridicule produit par cet entassement d'injures' (Voltaire, 'Remarques sur *Polyeucte*', p. 396): he was unable to understand the paradox of the christian hero whose faith is at its purest in the moment of his deepest abasement. Note that Polyeucte is in III.ii an iconoclast, a breaker of pagan deities, and that is what makes him christian – and that by reversing the point of view to that of a christian, it is *he* who makes the accusation of immorality (against the pagans). A passage parallel to the one quoted above occurs in V.iii where Polyeucte is speaking to the heathen Félix:

> Voyez l'aveugle erreur que vous osez défendre:

Des crimes les plus noirs vous souillez tous vos dieux;
Vous n'en punissez point qui n'ait son maître aux cieux.
La prostitution, l'adultère, l'inceste,
Le vol, l'assassinat, et tout ce qu'on déteste,
C'est l'exemple qu'à suivre offrent vos immortels.
J'ai profané leur temple et brisé leurs autels;
Je le ferais encor, si j'avais à le faire . . .

Polyeucte v.iii, 1664–71

In exactly the same way Polyeucte, who in struggling against his wife fails to see the struggle *within* her, comes to reproach other people for their callousness – whilst he remains, in God's eyes, saintly. The christian paradox of 'having as if one did not have', of being in the world as if one were in the beyond, is incarnated in this play in the opposition of the characters who embody having and not-having respectively. There's no question of Polyeucte being 'preciously stilted' – he is a hero of christian legend and nothing else. It is much more likely that his baroque tears (cf. Malherbe, 'Les Larmes de Saint Pierre') are a concession to the *précieux* view of the world which perhaps valued the chivalry of love more highly than Polyeucte's chivalry of faith. As Lanson said: 'L'on sait que ce n'est pas la religion qui a sauvé *Polyeucte*' (Lanson, *Etudes*, p. 69).

I must now prove that this martyr's hardness is really christian. One of the oldest and best-known French texts comes immediately to mind: *La Vie de Saint Alexis*, against which, significantly, the same reproach of unchristianity has been raised. Winkler, for example, writes in his otherwise perceptive study:

The *Vie de Saint Alexis* is poor in philosophical and moral values. The attitude and the profundity of the poem have been remarkably exaggerated. The piety of the *Alexis* . . . is external, like a church procession. Even its asceticism is ritual or liturgical, and not really internal; it gains no reward, whilst powerful acts of the will and the mortifying conquest of earthly temptation open the realm of heaven. Without any inner effort Alexis on earth stands already in the hereafter . . . In order to *evade feebly** a scarcely noticed conflict between obedience to his father and his ascetic inclination, Alexis even sins *against the church.** He makes his marriage – a bond which the church nonetheless considers sacred – unseriously and halfheartedly, almost with internal reservations:

Quant vint al fare, dunc le funt gentement.
Danz Alexis l'espuset belament,
Mais ço'st tel plait dunt ne volsist nient:
De tut an tut ad a Deu sun talent. (*Alexis*, 47–50)

(When it came to doing it [i.e. getting married] they did it nobly / My lord Alexis marries her with a good grace / But it was a suit he didn't want at all: / his mind was altogether given to God.) (Winkler, *Alexius*, p. 588)

* Spitzer's italics.

Actually Alexis does not sin 'against the church': he is his father's obedient and christian son. Marriage is arranged by the parents, and Alexis is dutifully obedient, although, as l.59 makes clear, he doesn't want the marriage himself. His father commands him to sleep with his bride (l.52–3), and Alexis has no wish to anger him – 'Ne volt li emfes sum pedre corocier', l.54. Only when he is faced with the matrimonial bed and with his bride, which remind him of original sin (*cum fort pecet m'apresset*! 'What a heavy sin bears down upon me'), does his orientation towards the divine become activated. His dialogue with God, in which his decision matures, precedes his lecture to the maiden and his indication of a celestial bridegroom. The sight of the bed and of the beauty of earthly woman releases the spiritual energy of the divine seeker; only now can he be free of paternal authority.

Winkler also thinks that Alexis's posthumous destination of his 'Charte' to the Pope and not to his father is 'a humanly alien, hieratic feature, typical of the ascetic spirit'. Certainly this feature is 'humanly alien' but it is not alien to humanity. One should remember that the reified virtue of a saint has to be established by an *objective* procedure (even, since the seventeenth century, in the procedure of canonisation). The exercise of active virtue during the saint's life is not enough, nor even are posthumous miracles – saintliness has to have hard evidence, and the best evidence is that written down ceremoniously by the saint himself, as a kind of legal document. [See Spitzer's remarks in A20, vol. I, p. 27, on the degree to which writing was itself a ceremonial act in the Middle Ages.] The document must reach the right hands, which are not those of Alexis's parents, mere private individuals, but those of the judge recognised as competent by the temporal powers, that is to say of the Pope who is alone empowered to canonise as he has the highest powers over men's souls (cf. *Alexis* l.366), in contrast to the temporal grace given by God to the Emperor. All that is of course hieratic – note that the Pope does not read the document himself, but has it read to him by his chancellor – but it is also legally sound as a procedural guarantee of security. Similarly, Corneille's 'legalism' does not contradict his christianity. Winkler goes on:

> Alexis hardly bothers to exhort his bride to christianity or to share with her a part of his own illumination. What a self-centred asceticism! . . . Alexis fails to take any part in the pain of his dependent . . . From the first moment on, Alexis is as removed from any sympathetic *human* involvement on our part as any christian relic in its cloud of incense and glass showcase . . . The *Vie de Saint Alexis* is the poem of his death and sainthood, not of his life. (Winkler, p. 597)

So we have here an identical criticism to Schmidt's attack on *Polyeucte*, and to the judgments quoted by Lemaître ('quelle gloutonnerie mystique', etc.): the saint is too saintly to be human or to allow us poor mortals, who cannot attain sainthood quite so easily, any human participation. That is certainly a very modern way of thinking, based on the modern concept of the common humanity of all men, but it misses entirely the essence of legend. Legend does not offer sympathetic or common humanity, but the superhuman and exemplary by which the grace of God distinguishes a few individuals as *imitable*, presented as models for weak mortals to emulate.

> What does the saint signify to the community? . . . Saints . . . are persons in whom the Good is reified in a particular way.
>
> That is why the community does not ask how the saint feels when he is pious, when he acts, when he suffers. For the community, the saint is not human like other human beings, but a means by which a virtue may be seen as an object, exponentially raised to the highest and heavenly power. (André Jolles, p. 35)

The saint must suffer, but his suffering is not the passion of the redeemer in which we participate. Christ removes the space for a martyr's passion, for in his passion he suffered for us once and for all; subsequent torment must be silent before the pain of the man from Galilee; the sufferings of a martyr must be seen *objectively* in the wake of Christ, *subjectively* they must be muted, as an accessory. Legendary saints are types, never individuals, more or less incidental recipients of grace given from on high. Illumined by efficient grace, the saint already partakes of a heavenly atmosphere, and rational interpretation does an injustice to the properly legendary element of a legend. Psychological readings of legend can quickly descend into the absurd, e.g. Francisque Sarcey's witty interpretation of Polyeucte as a man 'pris d'une sorte de colère douloureuse, de cette colère que nous avons tous éprouvée quelques jours. Voyons! elle est pourtant charmante et bonne, elle devrait comprendre. Mais non! je lui semble fou! Ah! petite tête obstinée!' (reported in Lemaître III.73).

Saints are to be emulated by true believers as emulators of Christ; believers are scarcely likely to equal the saints by their emulation (they would then be saints themselves) just as the saints do not suffer the martyrdom of Christ. The imitation of Christ on earth (which can never reach its goal) is a paradox, just as being in the world as if one were not in the world constitutes a christian paradox. The irruption of the divine into the things of this world cannot be the occasion of human participation, but only of awe and emulation. The less human a martyr is, the more he is a hero of legend. And how better can one substantiate his non-humanity than through 'inhumanity'? How could his envelopment in the divine be more clearly and calmly demonstrated than through his lack of concern for human impulses? Alexis is the 'fullest illustration of Matthew 10.37–8 and Luke 14.26–7' (L. Olschki, p. 15). Compare:

Plus aime Deu que trestot son linage *Alexis*, line 250

('He loves God more than all his lineage')

with *Si quis venit ad me, et non odit patrem suum, et matrem, et uxorem, et filium, et fratres et sorores, ad huc autem et animam suam, non potest meus esse discipulus* ('And if any man come to me, and hate not his father, and mother, and wife, and children, and brethren, and sisters, yea, and his own life also, he cannot be my disciple': Matthew 10.26, Latin Vulgate and Authorised Version). The hardheartedness of the martyr is an *imitatio* of Christ's hardness in whose mouth we find the word *hate*, and applied moreover to a man's nearest and dearest. By the arguments of Schmidt and Winkler, Christ would not be a christian! An integral part of the *imitatio* is that the individual 'imitators' detach themselves from their former, lower rank and from each other and relate only to the higher level. As Jolles says, 'the holy man is a figure in whom the immediate and the wider group experience *imitatio* . . . Jesus . . . is the holy of holies whose emulators are the other saints. And conversely the events of the life of Jesus can also be understood in terms of imitation, if one takes them as the fulfilment of an earlier life' (i.e. as the repetition of the sacrifice of Isaac). The *imitatio Christi* is thus itself represented as *imitabile*: the whole of humanity is carried upwards towards the heavenly leader on a chain of imitation – Christ imitates the Old Testament to some extent, the martyrs imitate Christ, the faithful emulate the martyrs, unbelievers follow the faithful – a round dance, if I may borrow the title of Arthur Schnitzler's ominous play *Der Reigen* (1900) – going from earth to God. Of course the medieval farandole of divine love is not in any other way comparable to Schnitzler's vision, and the chain-plot is to be found in many other places, e.g. Racine's *Bérénice*, where A loves B, B loves C, and so forth. In legend, it is the love of God which allows one man to raise the next on the ladder. A Polyeucte or an Alexis cannot concern themselves 'directly' with their followers but must exercise their chastening influence by the indirect means of showing the example to follow. The rise of the saint in itself raises his followers: the miracle of conversion would not be miraculous if the saint entered into direct dealings with the mind of the not-yet-faithful, or swayed them in the manner of a *directeur de conscience* or a psychoanalyst. Sainthood is active virtue made into an object which exercises power: the Old French noun *vertu* meaning 'virtue' also meant 'mighty strength'. Miracles, the favourite children of faith, are confirmation of the saint's power of grace: conversion *miracles* go together with the saint's insulation from human contact. The martyr's exemplarity distances him in earthly terms as it brings him closer in heavenly terms. Alexis's abandoned bride imitates her husband in the service of God: *Deu servirei, le rei ki tot guvernet*, 'I shall serve God, the king who governs all', she says (l.494), echoing l.85 where it is said of Alexis, *de Deu servir ne cesset*, 'he does not cease serving God'. Distance on earth brings them closer in heaven:

Sainz Alexis est el ciel senz dutance,
Ensembl'ot Deu e la compaignie as angeles,
Od la pulcela dunt se fist si estranges;
Or l'at od sei, ansemble sunt lur anames. *Alexis*, 606–9

(Saint Alexis is in heaven without doubt / together with God and in company with the angels, / with the maiden to whom he had behaved so unnaturally; / Now he has her with him, their souls are together.)

The intention of the author of this legend–poem must have been to stress that disunion on this earth makes heavenly union possible. The christian paradox is at its harshest and sharpest where it tears asunder the closest of bonds between men and women. That is why the exclusion of cohabitation within the family is accompanied, in the legend, with the physical proximity of the saint to his family. Alexis under the staircase in his father's house is a visible representation of the world/other-world contrast, of the paradoxical proximity/distance of the saint to his family (and thus it was in fact frequently represented pictorially). Anthologies of medieval French poetry always select the stanzas where Alexis's relatives bemoan their plight in humanly moving terms – stanzas partly of the poet's own invention, i.e. not taken from the Latin *Vita* – but these complaints must be taken together with, first, the indeflectibility of Alexis in his brief passage through this world:

Soventes feiz lur veit grant duel mener
E de lur oilz mult tendrement plurer,
E tut pur lui, unces nïent pur eil.
Danz Alexis le met el consirrer;
Ne l'en est rien, si'st a Deu aturnét. *Alexis*, 241–5

(Many times he sees them giving vent to great grief / and crying tears most tenderly, / and all for him, not a bit for themselves. / Lord Alexis meditates upon it; / It is nothing to him, so firmly is his mind fixed on God.)

(The *aturnét* in l.245 seems to me a *visible* image of absorption in God.) These 'human' stanzas must also be seen, in the second place, in the context of Alexis's joy in his preparedness for heaven:

Suz le degrét ou il gist e converset,
Iloc deduit ledement sa poverte. *Alexis*, 261–2

(Beneath the stair where he lies and dwells, / he there experiences his poverty joyously.)

Furthermore, his adoration by the Pope, the Emperor and the people, the Pope's reference to joy in having a spokesman in heaven (l.503–4, *Chi chi se doilet, a nostr'os est il goie, Quar par cestui avrum boen adjutorie*, 'Whoever might grieve, it is a matter for joy for our part, for by this man [Alexis] we shall have great assistance'), and the joy of souls in heaven contrasted with the sorrow of earthly joys, all counterbalance the lyrical stanzas.

> Ne vus sai dirre cum lur ledece est grande 610

('I cannot tell you how great their joy is' [of Alexis and his bride in heaven]).

> Cesta lethece revert a grant tristur 70

('This joy ends up in great sadness' [said by Alexis to his bride of love in this world]).

The three lamentations on Alexis's death are certainly given very fine psychological nuances: the father laments the loss of an heir for his worldly wealth and of a continuer of the family tradition of chivalry (l.392–420); the mother bemoans the loss of her *porteure*, 'offspring' (l.442), of the son she carried in her body; the bride bewails the loss of the husband to whom she was bound in body and soul (l.468–95). Such psychological subtlety does not occur in the depiction of the purposeful, God-oriented saint who strives to reach his object in an almost rationalistic manner. (We are allowed to observe his conversations with God, l.59–60, 201–10, and we are privy to his intentions, e.g. l.249, *Co ne volt il que sa mere le sacet*, 'He did not want his mother to know him': we do not in fact ever experience a conflict within him.)

In any case the martyr is less unconcerned about the *spiritual salvation* of his relatives than about their being related to him. Alexis does exhort his wife to godliness before fleeing from his father's house; and he does justify his request for accommodation in the same house by referring to love for the lost son:

> Eufemien, bel sire, riches hom
> Quar me heberges pur Deu an ta maison;
> Suz tien degre me fai un grabatum
> Empur tun filz dunt tu as tel dolur;
> Tot soi amferm, sim pais pur sue amur *Alexis*, 216–20

('Euphemien, good sir, and man of power / Lodge me in your house for the sake of God; / make me a pallet under your stair, / for the sake of your son who gave you so much grief; / I am utterly infirm, feed me for love of him.')

These lines allude to the godliness of sheltering the poor and the sick, which means Euphemien is doing something for his own soul and not for Alexis by taking him in; but Alexis's subsequent appeal to the earthly feelings of the father underlines the paradox of the ascetic's rejection of family feelings. The father should do good by a stranger for the sake of a lost son – but the stranger *is* the lost son. Pain can bring joy, and men do not know the full resonance of their own actions; what is near is far, and what is distant, close. Alexis has thus acted cunningly but despite appearances for the salvation of his family: not 'selfishly' but by giving up his whole self to the will of God. The divine absorption of the saint is itself psychologically inexplicable, unquestionable, enclosed, but inside of it Alexis can calculate with cunning and with psychological insight, whilst his poor relations, blind and earth-bound, struggle with a higher and incomprehensible destiny. Psychology cannot explain the miracles either. *Les vertus si apertes*, 'the revealed powers' (l.562) of the saint are the healing of the sick, and the turning of people away from material goods in emulation of Alexis:

> De lur tresors prenent l'or e l'argent
> Sil funt jeter devant la povre gent . . .
> A cel saint hume trestut est lur talent. 526–30

(They take gold and silver from their treasure / and throw it before the poor people . . . They are completely given up to this saintly man [mind and wealth].)

Psychology must cease where miracle and revelation begin.

Let us now return to *Polyeucte.* Act IV sc.iii shows Corneille's martyr at the stage in which Alexis is from before the start of the medieval French poem. Polyeucte's character is quite evidently subject to a development, and only in the fourth act does he reach the thoroughly explicit attitude of asceticism that Alexis has towards his wife. He can now give Pauline his teaching, as Alexis does in the first scene in the older poem. Corneille's tragedy begins with Néarque's exclamation:

> Quoi? vous vous arrêtez aux songes d'une femme!

to which Polyeucte replies:

> Mais vous ne savez pas ce que c'est qu'une femme:
> Vous ignorez quels droits elle a sur toute l'âme . . .
> *Polyeucte* I.i, 9–10

and further on

> Ces pleurs, que je regarde avec un œil d'époux
> Me laissent dans le cœur aussi chrétien que vous . . . I.i, 43–4

However, concern for Pauline makes him put off his baptism for one day. Néarque describes such thoughts as the seductions of the devil.

> POLYEUCTE: Pour se donner à lui faut-il n'aimer personne?
> NÉARQUE: . . . Il faut ne rien aimer qu'après lui, qu'en lui-même,
> Négliger, pour lui plaire, et femme, et biens, et rang,
> Exposer pour sa gloire et verser tout son sang.
> I.i, 69–76

That is, of course, as in *Alexis*, a reformulation of the biblical injunction in Matthew 10.26, and it is repeated by Polyeucte like a leitmotiv at the end of Act II after he has shown himself to be still an admiring and loving husband to Pauline. In Act III Pauline contrasts Félix's national-patriotic attitude with the attitude of the christians:

> Ils cherchent de la gloire à mépriser nos dieux;
> Aveugles pour la terre, ils aspirent aux cieux . . . III.iii, 947–8

In Act IV Polyeucte comes clean with himself in his monologue in lyrical stanzas:

> Honteux attachements de la chair et du monde
> Que ne me quittez-vous, quand je vous ai quittés? VI.ii, 1108–9

> Et je ne regarde Pauline
> Que comme un obstacle à mon bien . . . 1143–4

> Je la vois; mais mon cœur d'un saint zèle enflammé,
> N'en goûte plus l'appas dont il était charmé. 1157–8

In the following scene, IV.iii, Polyeucte is then completely armour-plated against the devil who also speaks through the voice of the astounded Pauline. As Lanson pointed out, there is a significant symmetry between Polyeucte's statements in Acts I and IV:

> Je vous aime,
> Le ciel m'en soit témoin, cent fois plus que moi-même . . .
> I.ii, 113–14

> Je vous aime
> Beaucoup moins que mon Dieu, mais bien plus que moi-même.
> IV.iii, 1279–80

In Act V, Polyeucte finally says to Pauline:

> Je ne vous connais plus, si vous n'êtes chrétienne V.iii, 1612

and she is baptised in her dying husband's blood, and converts. Corneille's notion of drama was of a final crisis, in the renaissance tradition, and so he has transformed the staying-power or stamina of the hero of legend into a development, disciplined by the unities, and concluding with the 'heureux trépas'. Polyeucte is allowed to die within the prescribed Aristotelian twenty-four-hour day by the grace of God: 'Et sortant du baptême, il m'envoie à la mort' (IV.iii, 1290). (Cf. similar virtuosity and speed in *Le Cid*: 'Rodrigue a pris haleine en vous la racontant' [la bataille] (IV.V, 1458).) Polyeucte's death effects a miracle by its exemplarity: through it Pauline, who is always one rung lower, whose first link with him is a personal one, accedes to truth:

> Je chéris sa personne et je hais son erreur. III.ii, 800

> Je vois, je sais, je crois, je suis désabusée . . . V.V, 1727

Her father follows, then Sévère, all of them rising upwards as in the *Vie de Saint Alexis*, imitatively drawn upwards by the martyr:

> Son amour épandu sur toute la famille
> Tire après lui le père aussi bien que la fille . . .
> C'est ainsi qu'un chrétien se venge et se courrouce.
> Heureuse cruauté, dont la suite est si douce! v.vi, 1775–80

As Faguet puts it in his excellent remarks on *Polyeucte*:

> Polyeucte par l'amour qu'il inspire à Pauline conduit Pauline au sacrifice et par elle Sévère à la magnanimité et par Sévère Félix au repentir tardif; *il tire tout le drame à lui** . . . (Faguet, *En lisant Corneille*, p. 141)

Parallel structures can be found in many other places, most notably perhaps in the Old French version of the Holy Grail legend (*La Queste del Saint Graal*) where Sir Galahad, the image of Christ, is similarly depicted as an 'entraineur d'âmes' (Gilson, *Les Idées et les lettres*, p. 73). Even Rousseau's *La Nouvelle Héloïse* still follows the basic structure of legend: Julie d'Etanges, like the feminine counterpart of a legendary saint, draws all on in her train. She dies a saintly death after she has convinced her lover and her husband; and one imagines her in the hereafter looking down upon the men who loved her 'à les voir *imiter ses vertus*' (p. 745). But before her death she does of course participate in the emotions of her lovers since she is not a saint but, as Faguet says, 'une mourante philosophe'. Yet Julie's sentence 'La vertu qui nous sépare sur la terre nous unira dans le séjour éternel' (p. 743) sounds as if it came out of the *Alexis*, like the quotation used as one of the epigraphs to this article. Goethe, on the other hand, quite intentionally endowed Ottilie, his heroine of renunciation in *Elective Affinities*, with the death of a legendary martyr together with the obligatory posthumous miracle. In his tragedy *Iphigenie auf Tauris*, the heroine – as it were a Greek saint – has an effect not *on* but *in* all the other characters of the play: she, or rather her character, 'is the common destiny of all', as Gundolf put it. And, finally, we can see in Rodin's monumental group *The Burghers of Calais* (1884) a non-transcendental depiction of a similar collective movement of a chain of characters.

All this makes it nonsense to talk of an opposition of 'established' ideals in the drama of Polyeucte. What we see on the stage are men in whom ideals themselves struggle and finally emerge triumphant. It is likewise nonsense to describe the christian hero as an 'unfeeling trumpet of dogma': the subject of Corneille's dramatic poem is the 'gentle harshness', *l'heureuse cruauté* of heroic christianity – designated in Augustine by the oxymoron *felix culpa*. The expression belongs to the classical–christian tradition and remains alive throughout the whole of French classical tragedy, down to Racine's *Athalie*, where it gives the

* Spitzer's italics.

automatic 'double illumination' of the earthly and the divine (⟶ 51–2). For Alexis, the joys of this world end in sadness, but death brings the greatest joy; and Polyeucte dies in an *heureux trépas* (v.v, 1733).

The point to make now is that such *harshness in the service of the gentle faith is entirely compatible with Corneille's heroism of the will*; furthermore the conversion miracles in Polyeucte fit in well with the miraculous deeds of other Cornelian heroes. The typical Cornelian hero reaches a 'closed' personality by worldly–chivalric means, as it were. Just as *Polyeucte* unites within itself medieval religious drama and the worldly drama of the renaissance, so the character of Polyeucte is a synthesis of cartesian self-assertion and religious devotion. Polyeucte is a christian *parce qu'il l'a voulu*: and his character is perhaps more enlightening than that of other Cornelian heroes because of the transcendence of the self contained in his religious stance. The otherwise virtuoso-like self-glorification of the hero conquering all through the power of his will is suspended and overshadowed here by the grandeur of the lord whom he serves. When Polyeucte says: *Je vous aime, / Beaucoup moins que mon Dieu, mais bien plus que moi-même*, he situates himself in between God and Pauline, and as the go-between – what he takes from her he gives to Him; and in any case religious devotion is a more giving gift than the social *dévouement* of other Cornelian heroes, who can only increase their moral perfection by first heightening their personal worth.

Corneille's presentation of the martyr is not nearly as oriented towards the conventional social expectations of the seventeenth century as some critics have made out. Polyeucte's smashing of the idols *angered* many contemporaries, who criticised the dramatist for showing a hero contravening the law and order of the state (according to Voltaire, p. 394).

It is significant that Corneille's christian martyr appears *harsh*, as harsh as Horace or le Cid, and that he speaks lines that could belong to either of the other two heroes:

> Je ne hais point la vie, et j'en aime l'usage,
> Mais sans attachement qui sente l'esclavage,
> Toujours prêt à la rendre au Dieu dont je la tiens . . .
>
> v.ii, 1515–17

This attitude of stoical detachment towards life – living as if one did not have to live – is very similar to that of Alidor in the early comedy *La Place Royale* (1635):

> Je veux la liberté dans le milieu des fers.
> Il ne faut point servir d'objet qui nous possède;
> Il ne faut point nourrir d'amour qui ne nous cède:
> Je le hais, s'il me force . . . I.iv, 204–7

Similarly, Polyeucte's insistence on smashing pagan idols – *Je le ferais encor, si j'avais à le faire* (v.iii, 1671) – is the same voluntary pride, expressed in the same words, as that of Rodrigue in *Le Cid*. I really do not understand why Schmidt wants to reduce the import of *Polyeucte* by claiming that the hero 'does not do what internal deliberations dictate but only what public opinion requires'. The ethical values of the community also have power within the individual; Polyeucte is the incarnation of general human conflicts.

In fact Corneille knows how to go into the conflicts of duty which result from a *single* but passionately held obligation. The service of God conflicts with service to a (God-given) family. Polyeucte overcomes the diabolical dialectic of God's conflicting interests:

> Pour opposer à Dieu l'intérêt de Dieu même
> Vous vous joignez ensemble! v.iii, 1652–3

Here, the christian dualism of God and Devil merges with a cartesian hierarchy of values.

In Polyeucte, whose inhumanity serves the highest Being, the inhuman side of the Cornelian hero is at its most acceptable. Schmidt should not have derided *raison d'état* in Corneille as a 'mere theatrical prop', for state and country are values guaranteed by the higher authority of God. Corneille turns the classical patriotic virtue of *dulce est pro patria mori* ('it is sweet to die for one's country') into a cartesian acceptance of the supreme Being in lines such as these:

> Si mourir pour son prince est un illustre sort,
> Quand on meurt pour son Dieu, quelle sera la mort?
> IV.iii, 1213–14

It is a distortion of Corneille's concept of will to forget that the higher value emerges from a struggle against a lesser value. The lesser is not a mere 'prop' but a *repoussoir* or a negative pole (if we must use technical terms) of spiritual current. Values are clearly set out in almost tabular form in Corneille, the plus-values set against the minus-values, and the outcome is the result of the hero's struggle, of his passion: in *Le Serment des Horaces* (1784) the painter David could translate the value-table into architectural and dimensional relationships.

The reasonable language used by Corneille's characters is thus an expression of controlled intensity, a formal envelope, and not, as Schmidt thinks, 'distasteful bragadoccio' (in any case Corneille voluntarily toned down Polyeucte's language) or merely 'heroic self-exposition'. Polyeucte's language is a means of pulling himself together and of elucidating his highest obligation:

> J'ai de l'ambition, mais plus noble et plus belle . . . IV.iii, 1191

It is the higher ambition, not the 'I', which here carries the stress. Of course this line is also rhetorical and presupposes some self-knowledge, in contrast to the spontaneous effect of divine grace upon the one who receives it. Corneille managed to combine a fixed hierarchical system of values with a religious hierarchy of spirits: just as love of God stands on a higher rung than love of country or love of family, so Pauline (who *is* love of family) stands on a lower rung of illumination than Polyeucte. Her speaking 'from the heart', which Schmidt finds so touching, does not yet have the higher rationality of the state of grace (influenced by divine illumination). It is Polyeucte who says quite clearly *Je vous aime, / Beaucoup moins que mon Dieu, mais bien plus que moi-même*, for he knows the rarity of divine grace and the hopelessness of those without it. Polyeucte's 'stoniness' shows one thing only: clear, grace-given understanding of the ladder of values and the hierarchy of souls:

> Mais que sert de parler de ces trésors cachés
> A des esprits que Dieu n'a pas encor touchés? IV.iii, 1231–2
>
> Ce Dieu touche les cœurs lorsque moins on y pense.
> Ce bienheureux moment n'est pas encor venu;
> Il viendra, mais le temps ne m'en est pas connu . . . IV.iii, 1276–8
>
> Mais ces secrets pour vous sont fâcheux à comprendre:
> Ce n'est qu'à ses élus que Dieu les fait entendre. V.ii, 1539–40

Now critics like Schmidt, who are looking for a modern, 'experiential' scene between husband and wife, naturally find Polyeucte's 'cold scorn' for Pauline in IV.iii 'particularly unfriendly'. Schmidt sees that Polyeucte makes no attempt to win Pauline over to his side, but fails to grasp why; whereas her outburst beginning *Cruel, car il est temps que ma douleur éclate* (l.1235) is prized as a 'magnificent passage full of power and real feeling'. But as we have shown, Polyeucte cannot be 'friendly' and soothe his wife with sympathetic words: for he knows she is not yet free enough to understand him. Her liberation will come by a miracle. The wife's passionate outburst is as necessary as the value-determined 'cruelty' of the husband. Polyeucte is highly concerned about Pauline's *spiritual salvation*, for she is in her propriety entirely deserving of grace; his sighs and tears make his human involvement perfectly clear, but also his inability to prophesy the future. He would even be ready to add his blood to his tears for her, to undergo martyrdom for her sake: with *Ce que de tout mon sang je voudrais acheter* (IV.iii, 1274) he takes on himself a substitute for Christ's cross for the sake of another being, and that is what in the end succeeds; as Pauline says:

> De ce bienheureux sang tu me vois baptisée . . . V.v, 1728

It must be understood that the christian Polyeucte has rejected Eve's seduction (spiritually sublimated in Corneille's play) in that he seeks to release her from Satan's grasp (*des enfers esclave infortunée . . .*, IV.iii, 1271).

If Polyeucte is *cruel, cœur insensible* in Pauline's eyes, she is a *cœur trop endurci* in his eyes; Polyeucte sees *aveuglement* in Pauline, and she sees *étrange aveuglement* in him. Pauline tries to 'seduce' Polyeucte but talks of him 'seducing' her. If Polyeucte is from a worldly point of view poor and blind, Pauline is just as poor and blind from the point of view of God: christian bifrontality! Thus in the final duet of the two characters every word has a different meaning for each of them. One could represent it thus.

Au nom de cet amour { ne m'abandonnez pas — PAULINE
{ daignez suivre mes pas — POLYEUCTE
C'est peu de me quitter { tu veux donc me séduire?
{ je veux y vous conduire

{ Tu préfères la mort à l'amour de Pauline!
{ Vous préférez le monde à la bonté divine! — IV.iii, 1281–8

Even the rhyming words unite and disunite at one and the same time: *séduire/conduire, Pauline/divine*. The use of stichomythia in this scene is not 'word-play . . . like that in a comedy', as Schmidt claims; just because the same technical device also occurs in comedy it does not have to have exactly the same *function* in tragedy. Nor does the pointed repetition of the other speaker's words (e.g. *ennemie/ennemis* in l.1166, 1167; *bontés/bontés* in l.1124, 1125) constitute 'the tone of tragi-comedy' – critics should steer clear of categorising the functions of stylistic devices so definitively! – but the cut and thrust (*riposte* is also a term of fencing) of a complementary dialectical division. The possessives, admittedly, spring from the characters' partiality of vision: the device is posited from the start of the play with *Votre Dieu* (I.i, 91) and destined to soften in the loving union of Pauline's final *mon époux* (V.v, 1724); in IV.iii it remains pointed in *vos chrétiens* (l.1199) and *vos Césars* (l.1190). These are polemical possessives which delimit the theme of a speech as if it were an undesirable and undesired possession – or in other words, they are the necessary shibboleths of disunion, 'separation words' in the discussion. There are balanced correspondences even in the 'emotional' part of IV.iii, e.g. when Pauline's exclamation *Te peut-elle arracher une larme, un soupir*? (l.1246) is actually followed by Polyeucte crying and sighing.

It is as unjustifiable to 'take sides' with the style of either one or the other of the two main characters (or of individual passages and parts of the dialogue) of *Polyeucte* as it is to take the side of one or the other of the two principles of the content of the play which is comprehensible only as the connection of two poles. In the 'dissertation antithétique' (Mornet) of Cornelian drama, the two members or partners of the antithesis have equal importance. Act IV sc.iii is conceived in a cartesian manner as a *dialogue of two values* which can only be contrasted in terms of rationality, and it is also conceived as a *dialogue of two beings* in the form of an emotional argument which leads the first to separation, the second to union, and both reaching a climax in a 'dialectical duet' (cf. *Le Cid*, though there both sides recognise the same values) which formally and musically binds the separation of thought into a union of feeling. The scene can be divided into three parts:

1. Rational dialogue of values; family *vs* God
2. Emotional dialogue of man and woman; Pauline's reproaches, Polyeucte's prayer
3. Musical duet of the humanly related but morally divergent couple (*Au nom de cet amour . . .*)

Schmidt failed to mention or to see that every line in the scene is in its right place, that the construction of the scene is conditioned by the architectonics and dialectic of the particular values that are in conflict here. (Note how the theme-word *sang* runs through all three parts and holds them together, for it carries in it the life-and-death motif, the motif of parental lineage and of the martyr's determination to die:

> Daignez considérer le sang dont vous sortez
> Mais, pour en disposer, ce sang est-il à vous?
> Ce que de tout mon sang je voudrais acheter.

There are similar linkages forged by the repetition of *amour, aimer.*) There is an eternal beauty in this scene where the struggle of antinomic values is transformed into the ordered architecture and the passionate music of union in disunion. Onto the impossibility of communication between the heathen and christian worlds, between joy in living and the longing for death, between feeling and reason, between sacrifice and self-preservation, paired antithetical connections of thought, of verse and rhyme construct the connectedness and reciprocal involvement of all these polarities:

> PAULINE: Va, cruel, va mourir; tu ne m'aimas jamais.
> POLYEUCTE: Vivez heureuse au monde, et me laissez en paix.

Such pairing and coupling is not in contradiction with the figure of the hierarchical leader striving upwards alone: in the struggle of values the higher value is the victor – as he is in Act IV sc.iii, as the supreme peacefulness of Polyeucte's closing line shows.

I trust I have not given the impression that Corneille's legendary tragedy can *only* be explained by medieval legend. I set out to prove just one thing, that Corneille himself knew what medieval legend was, and thus to read him properly we too must know what it is. Corneille, moreover, held his knowledge from *reflection*, not naively or simply by habit of thought as would have been proper to a medieval poet. The legendary hero of the Middle Ages had no *will* like Corneille's hero but went on his calm and obvious way towards God. The medieval hero was not torn between God and wife, nor did he lay bare his inner self in monologues or dialogues: his becoming was a self-enclosed given that was merely revealed in the resistance he had to overcome (the sufferings of his family, martyrdom, etc.). It would not have occurred to medieval man that smashing pagan idols could be frowned upon as a politically dangerous act, nor that heathens could heap insults upon a christian man, as happens in *Polyeucte.* Above all, Corneille's play on two dramatic platforms, the religious and the worldly, would have been quite alien to the Middle Ages, and especially his notion of a *convention* of legend, where for the believer it is simply a matter of the eternally recurring contact of the divine and the human. There are no good grounds for assessing the conscious and pondered achievement of the dramatist Corneille, separated from the Middle Ages only by the renaissance, in his attempted recreation of what had disappeared for ever, by any criterion other than that of this conscious intention, which his own declarations leave in no doubt at all. It is immaterial whether he really did recreate the original concept of legend. Corneille is knowledge, will and reflection – granted! But that should not allow modern readers to accuse him of artistic failure in what was, in his mind, the real problem of composing a christian tragedy.

IV

THE ART OF TRANSITION IN LA FONTAINE

1938

This important and charming piece, written shortly after Spitzer's arrival in America at the age of 49, is dedicated to the Italian aesthetician Benedetto Croce (1866–1952). Although Croce's view of the work of art as the 'soul' of the artist is not dissimilar to Spitzer's own position, particularly in his earlier essays of the 1920s, the Italian was totally opposed to the assimilation of technical linguistics and literary criticism in the Spitzerian manner. Much surprise was thus expressed that an article containing an implicit, but very clear, attack on Croce's views should be offered in honour of the latter's seventieth birthday. Spitzer's answer (given in A32, p. 205) was that his intention had been to distance himself from the views of the masters he otherwise held in great esteem, Croce and the German idealist Karl Vossler: 'La Fontaine, it seems to me, cannot be grasped properly by Croce's or by Vossler's categories.'

Spitzer later retracted one part of his interpretation of 'Les Deux Pigeons' in a note published in Italian (B53, and in A32, pp. 205–8); I have indicated the sense of Spitzer's retraction in a paragraph inserted on pp. 195–6 below.

A more recent and wider-ranging treatment of La Fontaine's style (though clearly indebted to Spitzer) is J. D. Biard, *The Style of La Fontaine's Fables* (Oxford: Blackwell, 1966).

All quotations from La Fontaine are given from the Classiques Garnier edition of the *Fables*, ed. G. Couton.

DB

For Benedetto Croce on his seventieth birthday.

Ce La Fontaine qu'on donne à lire aux enfants ne se goûte jamais si bien qu'après la quarantaine . . . (Sainte-Beuve)

. . . ce style
Tant oublié, qui fut jadis si doux
Et qu'aujourd'hui l'on croit facile. (Musset, *Sylvia*)

In a splendid article Ulrich Knoche has demonstrated the art of 'hidden transitions' in the Satires of Horace, which implement the poet's recommendation that 'it is not enough that poems should have beauty; if they are to carry the audience with them, they must have charm as well' (*Non satis est pulchra esse poemata; dulcia sunto / et quocumque volent animum auditoris agunto: On the Art of Poetry*, II.99–100, transl. T. S. Dorsch). To take an example given by Knoche, in Satire II.6 Horace describes the importunate petitioners who besiege him on the Mons Esquilinus and gives three examples of the petitions made. All three are formally similar – in direct speech, using the vocative case and so forth – but the third request ('Get Maecenas's signature on these papers') has hidden within it a special feature or function. It contains the key-word *Maecenas* which secretly prepares the reader for the ensuing narration of Horace's relationship with Maecenas, which itself leads on through more hidden transitions to other matters. Knoche concludes with the observation that it was precisely Horace's art of flowing transitions which was appreciated by his contemporaries. This stylistic quality of *suavitas*, considered characteristic of the 'middle style' (*genus medium*) appropriate to disputation, dialogue and satire, was defined by Cicero in terms of its 'fluidity': 'he . . . speaks flowingly, in an even tenor (as one says), and [his words] bring only fluency and a smooth calm' (*is . . . uno tenore, ut aiunt, in dicendo fluit nihil afferens praeter facilitatem et aequabilitatem: Orator*, 6.21).

La Fontaine's *Fables* are of course reminiscent of Horace's *Sermones* both in their conversational form and in their satirical content. The expression *faire passer*, used once in the *Fables* (but with reference, admittedly, to the moral of the tale), suggests *suavitas* quite directly. But not all of La Fontaine is like Horace. Let us look for example at the opening of I/14, 'Simonide préservé par les dieux':

On ne peut trop louer trois sortes de personnes
Les Dieux, sa maîtresse et son roi.

Malherbe le disait; j'y souscris, quant à moi:
 Ce sont maximes toujours bonnes.
La louange chatouille et gagne les esprits:
Les faveurs d'une belle en sont souvent le prix
Voyons comme les Dieux l'ont quelquefois payé.

La Fontaine, I/14, 1–7

These rambling, conversational lines – Saint-Marc Girardin called this passage a 'causerie' and a 'digression charmante' – set up an obviously humorous triad, and the gods of the last quoted line do indeed play a role in the following fable. But since all three members of the triad are present in the first two lines, there is no effect of surprise when we return to the gods after the digression of lines 3–6. (I leave out of consideration here the ending of the fable, introduced by the sentence 'Je reviens à mon texte', which gives a threefold moral that is quite unrelated to the opening triad; it does not matter that the admonition to praise 'Les Dieux et leurs pareils' is intended humorously to include mistresses and kings among the peers of the gods.)

The opening of Book V of the *Fables* is on the other hand much more like Horace. Fable V/1 begins with an *ars poetica* bearing La Fontaine's own personal stamp, and then moves on to tell the story of 'Le Bûcheron et Mercure'. The fable proper is clearly intended to embody the artistic principles laid out in the first part. Briefly, the principles are: first, that the poet should avoid 'soin trop curieux, / . . . des vains ornements l'effort ambitieux'; second, that the poet should delight and instruct, *plaire et instruire*; third, that balanced oppositions (*vice–vertu, sottise–bon sens*) should give an image of a universal poesy embracing all levels and forms of life in the world. In critical terminology one might rephrase the first precept as a refusal of baroque preciosity but not of stylistic refinement, a precept that characterises the classical age after about 1600. In a line like III/1, 7, 'Je t'en veux dire un trait assez bien inventé', it is not necessarily a baroque 'invention' of style that is meant; the line could well refer to the invention of content in the general sense of VI/1, 3–5:

Une morale nue apporte de l'ennui
Le conte fait passer le précepte avec lui
En ces sortes de feinte il faut instruire et plaire.

That line does of course repeat the second precept of the 'theory' laid out in V/1. *Plaire et instruire* (= *ridendo dicere verum*), set in contrast to 'Herculean force' (l.16), suggests intellectual and witty satire in which pathos has no place as an expressive device but from which moralistic intentions are not excluded. The fable of 'Le Bûcheron et Mercure' thus exhibits features of concentration and refinement, a lack of pathos, and a balanced opposition between self-restraint and covetousness – the reasonable woodcutter is content with a wooden heft to his axe, the unreasonable clamour for the god to give them golden ones. Just as the fable deals with modesty and truthfulness in its content, so is it cast in a modest and truthful form, illustrating an artistic theory that can be summed up in the words 'ne point mentir, être content du sien' (l.66).

Some aspects of La Fontaine's art – particularly his concentration, refinement and refusal of pathos – come out most clearly in a comparison with Rabelais, who gave a version of the same myth of Jupiter and the woodcutter in *Le Quart Livre* (pp. 14–18). The point has been made before by Hippolyte Taine, who says that the imagination of Rabelais 'déborde et noie *l'esprit*', whilst La Fontaine found 'le milieu entre la sécheresse et l'abondance, entre la rareté et l'entassement des détails' (Taine, p. 253). Taine's mistake, however, was to allow himself to be diverted into a normative revaluation of the later writer instead of grasping the objective, historical differences between the artistic purposes of two different centuries and between two different artistic temperaments. Rabelais's Jupiter is overworked and involves himself in the dispute only to get some peace and quiet. The affairs of men are seen from the point of view of the gods as petty and irrelevant so that Rabelais's gods become both renaissance heroes and caricatures of deities. Jupiter gives Mercury the task of making 'Couillatris' choose between three different axes. All that occurs is thus controlled by a capricious deity. In the cosmic vision of Rabelais, the tension derives from wondering: what will the mortal do? In the down-to-earth view of La Fontaine, the question is: what will the gods decide?

It has perhaps not yet been brought out clearly enough how La Fontaine's 'ample *comédie* à cent actes divers / Et dont la scene est l'Univers' (v/1, 27–8) articulates the transition between the *dramatic* world-view of the medieval mystery play and Balzac's nineteenth-century *human* comedy, which has nothing dramatic about it apart from its title. La Fontaine maintains a cosmic reference to his art or, rather, introduces a pantheistic intuition of the world; at the same time he paves the way for the theory and practice of seventeenth- and eighteenth-century fiction which fragments the universe into a set of miniatures, a 'slide show' of life as one critic has said.

It should be clear, in any case, that La Fontaine cannot effect a transition from the theoretical part of v/1 to its practical realisation by simply stating 'That was the programme – now for an example': such a procedure would be self-indulgent, over-deliberate and out of key. He is thus obliged to conceal the real connection between the two parts beneath a fictitious one of a quite different nature. Instead of following the main line from 'programme' to 'realisation' the reader is gently shunted from the first part to the second along an apparently fortuitous branch. This is where La Fontaine reaches something like the fluid *suavitas* of 'le bon Horace': he always shows opposites in his fables, he says:

> . . . faisant de cet ouvrage
> Une ample comédie à cent actes divers
> Et dont la scène est l'Univers.
> *Hommes, dieux, animaux*, tout y fait quelque rôle,
> *Jupiter comme un autre. Introduisons celui*
> *Qui porte de sa part aux Belles la parole:*
> Ce n'est pas de cela qu'il s'agit aujourd'hui. v/I, 26–32

In the passage from Horace the key-word *Maecenas* arose quite casually as one of many examples of men inconvenienced by importunate petitioners, but then was transformed into the theme 'Maecenas'. Similarly in this passage from La Fontaine Jupiter first appears simply as an example, an addition to a democratic list implying the equal participation of all beings. Jupiter is brought down to the same democratic level as everyone else and, because he ought to be raised out of the indistinct mass and figure with the rank of first and best, he seems here to be carelessly disregarded: there is no hierarchical order in *hommes*, *dieux*, *animaux*, *tout . . . Jupiter*. [Note La Fontaine's fondness for enumerations of this sort which correspond to his picture of the disorder and capricious irregularity of the world; e.g. in VII/14 there is a fortune-teller

> à qui toute la ville
> Femmes, filles, valets, gros Messieurs, tout enfin
> Allait comme autrefois demander son destin.]

But Jupiter is here essentially an auxiliary device and disappears once his purpose is served: stylistically, he is the herald or lead-in to the title-role of Mercury, defined in an archaistic periphrasis as Jupiter's amorous messenger to mortal beauties. However, this definition clearly falls outside of the scope of this fable, in which Mercury is only the envoy of the gods and the executor of Jupiter's will. The gratuitousness of the reference to Mercury's role as an amorous go-between is actually stressed by the poet in such a way as to play on his artistic liberty and to take the wind out of the objecting reader's sails: 'Introduisons celui qui . . . / Ce n'est pas de cela qu'il s'agit aujourd'hui'. But of course the reference is not really gratuitous. When La Fontaine seems to reproach himself for digressing and for *à peu près* ('Ce n'est pas de cela'), he is on the right track, and talking very much *à propos*. The introduction of Jupiter was not superfluous. The king of the gods remains in the background from now on, but the shadow he casts over Mercury remains palpable (a power such as his can never play a secondary role). When the woodcutter loses his axe and calls out 'Jupiter! rends-la-moi', Jupiter does not actually appear. 'Sa plainte de l'Olympe fut entendue' –

note the *passive* construction – 'Mercure vient' – his command is obeyed but not voiced. He does become more clearly visible after the clamour of the covetous woodcutters:

> Le roi des Dieux ne sait auquel entendre
> Son fils Mercure aux criards vient encor. l.59–60

The word *fils* indicates the relationship between Mercury and Jupiter, and the *encor* presupposes a long habit in the giving and execution of tasks of this kind; together these words move the reader towards the indirect involvement of the father of the gods through his envoy and prepare for the final emergence of Jupiter in the closing moral as the real opponent of mortal folly: 'Que sert cela? Jupiter n'est pas dupe' (l.69). So it turns out that Jupiter, largely suppressed in La Fontaine's *ample comédie*, plays the foremost role in this fable, and it becomes clear that the movement into the story of 'le bûcheron et Jupiter' did not lead from Jupiter to Mercury, but from Jupiter to Jupiter. Looked at from the point of view of the final effect, it is Mercury, not Jupiter, who is gratuitously 'introduced' and whose function is that of an auxiliary. All this cunning game of poetic deceit, all this artful *suavitas* which switches foreground into background and vice-versa with dummies and illusions, and makes the mind a little dizzy, serves really only to soften the sharp and difficult transition from the didactic to the narrative part of the poem.

In the following case, where the principal character of the playlet represented in the fable is named in advance, in the setting-up of the time and place, the transition device is less clever:

> Les Alouettes font leur nid
> Dans les blés, quand ils sont en herbe,
> C'est-à-dire environ le temps
> Que tout aime et que tout pullule dans le monde,
> *Monstres marins* au fond de l'onde
> *Tigres* dans les Forêts, *Alouettes* aux champs.
> Une pourtant de ces dernières . . . IV/22, 4–10

The clumsiness lies in the fact that the selection of *one* lark from *all* animals is effected at the price of a tautology, i.e. 'Les alouettes font leur nid . . . environ le temps, que les alouettes aux champs aiment et pullulent'. All the same this serves as another example of La Fontaine's fidelity to the enumeration device, after the classical pattern, in which the special object of the poem arises quite casually; one could cite also IX/1, where the poet enumerates all the types of character dealt with in his fables:

> Je mets aussi sur la Scène
> Des trompeurs, des scélérats,

Des tyrans et des ingrats,
Mainte imprudente pécore,
Force sots, force flatteurs;
Je pourrais y joindre encore
Des légions de menteurs. I.13–19

The key-word is of course *menteurs*, and the ensuing fable of 'Le dépositaire infidèle' deals precisely with that object, lying. Here too a prologue to a book of fables is welded into the book's first fable. A natural element of the prologue is the stressing of the fictitiousness of all poetry and this theme is also related to the lie-motif; La Fontaine takes his cue from the words of the psalm, 'Tout homme ment' ('All men are liars': Psalm CXVI, 11). The lower classes have in their poor material circumstances reason for lying, but the upper classes do not always lie:

Et même qui mentirait
Comme Esope et comme Homère,
Un vrai menteur ne serait.
Le doux charme de maint songe
Par leur bel art inventé,
Sous les habits du mensonge
Nous offre la vérité . . .
Comme eux ne ment pas qui veut.
Mais mentir comme sut faire
Un certain dépositaire . . .
Est d'un méchant et d'un sot . . . IX/1, 29–42

Chamfort took exception to this juxtaposition of lying and poetic fiction: 'Quel rapport y a-t-il, dit Bacon, entre les mensonges des poètes et ceux des marchands?' (quoted in Régnier, II.354). According to Régnier, the fault lies in the transition 'Et même', which fails to make an adequate separation between falsehood and fiction; but this 'veil of poetry from the hand of truth'* is in no sense a gratuitous ornament or an artistic mistake. In a manner appropriate to his 'connecting' vision of the world La Fontaine points up what is common to two opposites. Line 39, 'Comme eux ne ment pas qui veut', emphasises quite adequately the essential difference between the poet and the ordinary liar, and is in its function reminiscent of 'Ce n'est pas de cela qu'il s'agit aujourd'hui' in the prologue to Book V mentioned already. La Fontaine insists on demonstrating his detachment from his material and his freedom to shape it as he will. He could go on here to speak of poets (as in V/1 he could have continued with Jupiter's amorous adventures) – but that is not what he chooses to do. [For another example of the introduction of the hero of a fable in an enumeration, see XI/7, 'Le Paysan du Danube', where, to strengthen the sentence 'appearances deceive', Socrates, Aesop and the Danubian peasant are listed as illustrations.]

* Goethe's phrase, from his poem *Zueignung (Dedication)*, §12.

In the *Discours à Madame de la Sablière* (IX) we find the same 'laudable' trinity as in I/14 discussed above. The subject is the taste for flattery:

> Elle est commune *aux Dieux, aux Monarques, aux belles*
> Ce breuvage vanté par le peuple rimeur,
> Le Nectar que l'on sert au *maître du Tonnerre,*
> Et dont nous enivrons tous *les Dieux de la terre*,
> C'est la louange, Iris. Vous ne la goûtez point;
> D'autres propos chez vous récompensent ce point . . . l.7–12

The grouping of *Dieux – Monarques – belles* (in I/14 it is *Dieux – maîtresse – roi*, with the first member (*Dieux*) relayed) prepares the connection on the last member, *belles*, out of which the transfer to the conversational themes liked by Iris (= Mme de la Sablière) is created. La Fontaine then uses an apparently very sophisticated technique of multiple listing to smuggle in a truth which would have seemed too daring if expressed on its own:

> Propos, agréables *commerces*,
> Où le hasard fournit cent matières diverses,
> Jusque-là qu'en votre entretien
> *La bagatelle* à part: le monde n'en croit rien.
> Laissons le monde et sa croyance:
> *La bagatelle, la science*,
> Les chimères, le rien, tout est bon. Je soutiens
> Qu'il faut de tout aux entretiens. l.13–20

Régnier remarks that La Fontaine's tempered view of the 'femme savante' puts only one word, *science*, on the serious side where it is almost lost among *bagatelle*, *chimères*, *rien* and collective words like *tout*, *de tout* (Régnier II.460). The fable goes on:

> Ce fondement posé, ne trouvez pas mauvais
> Qu'en ces Fables aussi j'entremêle des traits
> De certaine Philosophie
> Subtile, engageante, et hardie. l.24–7

As La Fontaine will mix *de tout* in the *entretiens* (= *sermons*, *discours*), so will he also mix philosophy with fable. But the *certaine* prepares and introduces *subtile*, *engageante*, etc.; so we have a kind of chain running forward on a sprocket in the following manner:

Louange aux Dieux – Monarques – Belles
Vous ne la goûtez point; plutôt bagatelle, science, chimères
J'entremêle des traits de certaine philosophie
Subtile, engageante, et hardie

Like the *introduisons* of V/1, 30 discussed above, *ce fondement posé* is a waggish finger pointing at the *suavitas* that has been achieved, a kind of self-denunciation of the poet. La Fontaine has the conversational audacity to draw our attention to his own wilfulness: *introduisons* (Mercury), *ce fondement posé* – anything can be brought in to cover what is really being introduced (Jupiter, philosophy). It reminds you of those *entremeses* (farces played as interludes between the acts of Spanish Golden Age drama), where an opponent is smuggled in behind a curtain held up in front of him – but the difference in La Fontaine is that you cannot tell, in the moment of illusion, whether Jupiter masks Mercury or Mercury Jupiter. Horace's fluidity has become a conjuring trick: the reader is not only led by La Fontaine – he is led by the nose.

We find similar subterfuges in the first fable of Book III. La Fontaine begins (l.1–6) by speaking of the 'finds' that modern poets (*nos Auteurs*) can make in the field of the genres invented by the ancients, including the fable; up to this point III/1 could be a literary-historical introduction to the possibilities of innovation by the moderns in these fields, in the style of the *querelle des anciens et des modernes* giving victory to the *anciens* as inventors of the genres. [Note that the word *feinte* in l.5 means simply 'imaginative literature': see VI/1, 5.] La Fontaine continues, addressing the dedicatee, M. de Maucroix:

> Je t'en veux dire un trait assez bien inventé
> Autrefois à Racan Malherbe l'a conté.
> Ces deux rivaux d'Horace, héritiers de sa Lyre,
> Disciples d'Apollon, nos Maîtres pour mieux dire . . . l.7–10

It sounds as though the merits of these modern poets who can rival the ancients are now going to be trumpeted, and samples of their poetry provided – but not a bit.

> Se rencontrant un jour tout seuls et sans témoins
> (Comme ils se confiaient leurs pensers et leurs soins),
> Racan commence ainsi . . . l.11–13

Racan asks Malherbe as the elder and more experienced for a piece of advice as to what station in life he should choose, and Malherbe then tells the well-known fable of 'Le Meunier, son fils et l'âne', but not as his own invention – it is something he had 'read somewhere' (l.27) 'si j'ai bonne mémoire' (l.29). The 'trait assez bien inventé' is not to the credit of the two French disciples of Apollo and masters of their successors, but belongs to some anonymous poet. Racan and Malherbe provide no example of modern poetry equalling the ancient; one of them adopts an old fable, the other finds himself in a position where he can apply its lesson. And so the poetic performance, the harvest of all the fields, is to the credit of La Fontaine alone, the modest artist of imitation, the *dernier venu*. Instead of saying '*I* will tell an old fable in a new form', La

Fontaine brings in, to deceive us, a framing story with Racan and Malherbe as its heroes which takes up and makes vivid the fable of the miller, his son and the ass.

Sometimes La Fontaine makes a point of deluding his reader into believing he has led him by the shortest, smoothest path to a given point – which he never dreamt of reaching, and the reader, once there, looks in consternation at the detour he has made. The finest example of this is certainly I/11, 'L'Homme et son image', a fable dedicated to La Rochefoucauld. A latterday Narcissus in love with himself decides to avoid mirrors which return a distorted image. Like another Alceste, he goes off to the wilderness but finds there too a truth-giving mirror in the form of a clear pool of water which he also wants to avoid but whose beauty attracts him.

> On voit bien où je veux venir
> Je parle à *tous*: et cette erreur extrême
> Est un mal que *chacun* se plait d'entretenir.
> *Notre* âme, c'est cet homme amoureux de lui-même;
> Tant de miroirs, ce sont les sottises d'autrui,
> Miroirs, de nos défauts les peintres légitimes;
> Et quant au canal, c'est celui
> Que chacun sait, le livre des *Maximes*. I/11, 21–8

The words I have highlighted are there to mislead: La Fontaine is playing with the allegorical explanation of his fable and apparently resorts only to those interpretations that are already clear and well known to the reader. It seems as though, in accordance with classical practice, he had allowed only a single particular case to appear for his obligatory generalisation: *Je parle à tous . . . chacun . . . Notre âme . . .* The reinterpretation of abstractions by abstractions of a higher order (e.g. self-love as an allegory of the human soul) hints at a dense and intricate conceptual interplay behind which unspoken moral *sententiae* are hidden (mirrors are *les sottises d'autrui*, but these are in turn *de nos défauts les peintres légitimes*, i.e. we can only recognise our own faults in those of our neighbours – a conceptual play of a second order!). After the man in love with himself and after the mirrors, the canal has to receive its transferred meaning – there is no way of escaping the logic of the allegorical system here; but here there is a *coup de théâtre*: a reference (given, I repeat, as something that goes without saying) to something quite concrete, namely a particular book by a contemporary moralist. The reader can recover from this violent expulsion from the world of ideas by reflecting, as the poet allows us to, that the *Maximes* resemble a canal in the beauty of their surface which strikes even the reader who is repulsed by the ugliness of the images he sees in them; La Fontaine himself admits in X/14 that he learnt from La Rochefoucauld the formula 'il faut laisser / Dans les plus beaux sujets quelque chose à penser' (l.55–6). And we realise that the allegory has turned without our noticing into a pointed homage, a disguised piece of literary criticism. Looking back over the route we have followed, we feel confused – in the first place by the plethora of mirrors that we have looked into. The word *miroir(s)* occurs six times in the first part and twice in the second part of the fable. Mirrors not only bewitch the physical eye that cannot but look into them; they also evoke a dizziness in the mind's eye – Narcissus reflects himself, our soul reflects Narcissus's faults, La Rochefoucauld reflects the soul – a frightening, shimmering world of represented and reflected derivative meanings. However, the artful *suavitas* of the transition is combined in this fable with a closing line which, like the endings of the *Maximes* themselves, effects a reversal like some poetic jack-in-the-box. The surprising turn taken at the close is nonetheless fully and logically justified; subsequent reflection does not jib at the poem's mirror-logic. The eye may be sore from the sight of evil in a thousand mirrors, but it can rest at the end on the liquid clarity of simple beauty. The art of La Rochefoucauld – the control of truth through beauty – has generated a work of La Fontaine which not only defines but reproduces, mirrors the dynamics of La Rochefoucauld. *Suavitas*, the flow of La Fontaine's handling of his reader, leads us from confusion to the gentle movement of a *canal si beau*.

[La Fontaine's shaping of the Narcissus motif is reminiscent of Nietzsche's, quoted in a recent psychoanalytical paper on the 'Narcissus concept' (Pfandl, p. 286):

Einsam mit dir	Lonely with thee
Zweisam im eignen Wissen	Double in my mind
Zwischen hundert Spiegeln	Between a hundred mirrors
Vor dir selber falsch . . .	Standing false before thyself . . .
Selbstkenner!	Self-knower!*

In La Fontaine there is a premonition of the relationship between Narcissism and reflection, the general reflective aspect of the mind. It's not surprising that mirrors appear in material and linguistic forms of modish preciosity, e.g.

Les Conseillers muets dont se servent nos Dames . . .
    Miroirs aux poches des galands
    Miroirs aux ceintures des femmes. l.7–10

The work of the moralist La Rochefoucauld, on the contrary, is compared to a natural object (or, rather, to a human product possessing natural beauty – a canal). Appearance and truth are contrasted through fashionable ephemera and the clarity of nature.]

The mirror-theme in La Fontaine goes far beyond this single fable, of

* Friedrich Nietzsche, *Werke* (Leipzig: Naumann, 1899), vol. 8, p. 414 (my translation).

course; it should be understood as including the numerous mirrorings of the morals in the narratives of fables and vice-versa, the pendulum effect of paired fables, echo-fables like 'Le Coq et la perle' (echo is an acoustic mirroring, and thus Echo and Narcissus are frequently connected in myth and legend). La Fontaine takes pleasure in *reflection*, in both senses of the word; his essence and inclination are reflective. As he says in the *art poétique* discussed above:

> J'oppose quelquefois, par *une double image*
> Le vice à la vertu, la sottise au bon sens,
> Les Agneaux aux Loups ravissants
> La Mouche à la Fourmi . . . v/1, 23–6

Antithetical images give mutual illumination, and in La Fontaine, long before Victor Hugo, antithesis (or polarity) is already a profoundly French way of representing the world.

In this fable it is interesting to note that the mirror, which had served the baroque as a means of moral teaching, as an image of inwardness and withdrawal from the world, acquires autonomous value for La Fontaine as a *beautiful* mirror; that is to say, that the moral aspect is here supported by the aesthetic. However, La Fontaine does not generally put aesthetic values in the service of moral aims; it is rather the reverse, that moral teaching is made to serve his aesthetic purpose. It is to be assumed that he shares La Rochefoucauld's ideal of the beauty of a mirror of morals. Many critics have already pointed out that La Fontaine's explicit assurance of the opposite point of view (in vi/1: 'Une morale nue apporte de l'ennui / Le conte fait passer le précepte avec lui . . .') is not to be taken too seriously.

Let us now turn to vii/9, 'La Laitière et le pot au lait', where the kind of gentle control of the reader noted in i/11 is used to create an oneiric effect. The moral of the fable begins:

> Quel esprit ne bat la campagne?
> Qui ne fait châteaux en Espagne?
> Picrochole, Pyrrhus, la laitière, enfin tous,
> Autant les sages que les fous.
> Chacun songe en veillant; et n'est rien de plus doux:
> Une flatteuse erreur emporte alors nos âmes:
> Tout le bien du monde est à nous,
> Tous les honneurs, toutes les femmes.
> Quand je suis seul, je fais au plus brave un défi;
> Je m'écarte, je vais détrôner le Sophi . . . l.30–9

The democratic enumeration of all kinds of (day)dreamers harks back stylistically to the opening of 'Le Bûcheron et Mercure' (the milkmaid is here included indiscriminately with a list of kings). The device is varied in numerous different expressions – *quel . . . ne* (l.30), *tous* (32), *autant . . . que* (l.33), *chacun* (l.34); then in l.35–6, the sociative *nous* (*nos*) gently drifts us away from the daydream. *Tout* belongs to *nous* and thus also to *moi* (*je*, l.38). The first person plural is dissolved by an exemplifying singular, which however suddenly becomes a 'real' *I*, that is to say, the poetic *I* of the first-person hero who rises to a personal apotheosis (although this sort of wild dream hardly fits La Fontaine's discretion and modesty; perhaps it is only the exemplifying *I* that speaks here, but the poet wishes to leave the matter ambiguous).

> On m'élit roi, mon peuple m'aime;
> Les diadèmes vont sur ma tête pleuvant – l.40–1

But there follows a rude awakening from this dream-life:

> Quelque accident fait-il que je rentre en moi-même;
> Je suis gros Jean comme devant. l.42–3

Obviously, the gentle transition from waking to daydreaming achieved by the *Dulcia sunto* device (*il n'est rien de plus doux*, l.34) is necessary to make the reawakening strike the reader all the more sharply; similarly, the second part of the fable, the pendant so to speak, contains daydreams of such boldness (a kingdom!) as to set off the down-to-earth, logical and limited nature of the milkmaid's musings (on wealth!). Thus in the first part we have the expected sequence of tenses in narration (*Quand je l'eus*, l.17), in the second we have a merging of persons. The lines beginning *quel esprit* (l.30) constitute an artfully discreet transition from the first to the second collapse of fantasy. The last line, 'gros Jean comme devant', returns the fable to the rustic theme which opens and closes its first part with the repetition of the words *pot au lait* (l.29). What La Fontaine means here is that everyone, even I, Jean La Fontaine, is a bit of a rustic, a bit of a peasant, a dreamer of clumsy calculations; and daydreams cross over with accounts; La Fontaine sees 'transitions' between distant phenomena.

According to Chamfort (quoted by Régnier, I.149), this fable is 'charming' up to l.23, 'Adieu, veau, vache . . .', but becomes 'cold' in the following lines:

> En grand danger d'être battue.
> Le récit en farce fut fait. l.27–8

Against this view one must point out first that the danger of violence represents the reality of awakening from the daydream; secondly, the mention of the farce version is necessary to allow the repetition of *pot au lait* as the title; and it serves as a premonition of other literary treatments of the same type of personality, Picrochole and Pyrrhus, to be introduced a few lines later.

We saw in I/14 a case of *suavitas* serving to modulate the surprise-effect of a transition; we turn now to consider a fable where the artistic intention itself is masked by a soft and subtle connection. In VII/4, 'Le Héron – La Fille' (a double fable printed in some editions as two separate pieces), the moral applying equally to both parts is placed in the middle.

> Ne soyons pas si difficiles:
> Les plus accommodants ce sont les plus habiles:
> On hasarde de perdre en voulant trop gagner.
> Gardez-vous de rien dédaigner;
> Surtout quand vous avez à peu près votre compte.
> Bien des gens y sont pris. Ce n'est pas aux Hérons
> Que je parle; écoutez, humains, un autre conte;
> Vous verrez que chez vous j'ai puisé ces leçons. l.27–34

Lines 27–31 present a range of personal pronouns which are manifestly all variants of the gnomic pronoun. But it is more than coincidence that makes the initial first person plural (*soyons*) refer inclusively to the poet and his reader. The reader is retrospectively involved in the preceding narrative by this plural; impersonal constructions in l.28–9 then give general truths which lead on to an equally impersonal *vous* in l.30 (*gardez-vous* = *one* should take care) which in l.33–4 is craftily transformed into a quite different kind of second person plural – the preaching, distancing, pathetic form of vocative address: 'écoutez, humains . . . Vous verrez'. Particularly sly is the little sentence 'Bien des gens y sont pris', which combined with the preceding 'Gardez-vous' warns us of 'getting caught' as others have been caught – the emphasis seems to lie on *pris*, but the covert introduction of *gens* opens the way to *humains* in l.33. In itself, the short sentence 'Ce n'est pas aux Hérons que je parle' is superfluous – no reader really thinks La Fontaine intended to give a sermon on fishing to the herons addressed by the vocative *vous*. The poet gives a playful sign of his complete artistry that has led us to the point he wanted, and he takes pleasure in his cunning victory: 'I'm not talking to the herons; you've noticed already, haven't you, that *de vobis fabula narratur* (the tale concerns you)!' But what is the point of such wanton, arrogant *suavitas*? What is the purpose of the subtle transition? Line 34, 'Vous verrez que chez vous j'ai puisé ces leçons', lets the mask fall and announces the poetic intention. La Fontaine hasn't written the double fable of 'Le Héron – La Fille' just to put two parallel cases next to each other; in reality, of course, he wanted to write about the excessive fastidiousness of the *précieuses* towards their suitors, and to present them with a ridiculous image of themselves in the shape of a heron with comically large eating organs but an awkward taste, rejecting any catch that was easily had. (It is indicative of La Fontaine's practice that the heron is used here; the bird's passive behaviour in taking its prey was observed by Buffon.) So the *fille* casts an ironic retrospective light upon the humanised heron, and conversely the stupid behaviour of the *précieuse* is condemned in advance by the fate of the *héron*. Line 34 reveals the logical priority of *la fille* over *le héron* but its expression has to be somewhat indirect from the reader's point of view so as to avoid a too clearly didactic, paraenetic tone in the fable: the sharp point of the poem's attack on its readers is unsheathed very gradually to begin with. The *fille*-fable is then no mere repetition of the *héron*-fable; it serves to make more explicit the psychology of the *précieuses* who have the same instincts as everyone else but want to appear more discriminating, and whose arrogance is humbled only by the ravages of advancing years. Such human stupidity is figured by the image of the elongated, supercilious beak of the heron, waiting in vain for better and waiting still. Animal caricature and human stereotype merge into an inseparable unity. The artistry of the transition masks this process of merging.

Note that the long-necked, long-legged, long-beaked beast is presented as thoughtless and aimless in spatial terms (going 'je ne sais où', l.1) whilst the *précieuse* ignores the temporal law: 'ses soins ne purent faire / Qu'elle échappât au temps . . .' l.66–7. The time-sequence is pointed up with considerable detail in l.26–36, lines which stress the gradual decline of physical beauty; in the preceding lines, the many refusals of suitors correspond to the two refusals made by the heron in the first part. The opening 'Je ne sais où' sets the tone of story-telling but, for the reader who allows the entire fable to make its impact on him, it becomes a symbolic image of quixotic pointlessness (*Don Quixote* opens with: 'At some place out in La Mancha whose name I do not wish to remember . . .').

The two fables of 'Le Héron – La Fille' are also tied together by a number of repetitions of motifs, which are in reality reduplications of a unitary vision: the direct speech of the heron and the girl are identically structured, *tout heureux et tout aise* (l.25, heron) matches *tout aise et tout heureuse* (l.76, girl), *de rencontrer un limaçon* (l.26, heron) matches the closing line of the whole fable, *de rencontrer un malotru* (l.76), etc. Elsewhere in La Fontaine the fable is a form combining an animal-story with a moral that applies to men: here, in VII/4, the narrative of animal life has been turned back into its own real source, and the parable is transformed into the vision which was its origin and point of departure. The mirror-principle inherent in all fables is made explicit. La Fontaine's technique of transition can be made to fit the structure of every individual fable; each one is an *organism* possessing a solid internal foundation, and numerous reciprocal relations between its parts which reveal themselves only slowly; the classical requirement, that the details in a work of art should connect 'as the parts of a body' (Knoche, p. 373), is thus met by La Fontaine.

Many critics have failed to see how tightly controlled every element is in La Fontaine's fables, ruled down to the smallest detail by the technique of transition and organic connection. For example, l.15–16 of 'Le Chêne et le Roseau' (I/22):

> Mais vous naissez le plus souvent
> Sur les humides bords des royaumes du vent.

are seen by Emile Faguet as inappropriately lyrical in the mouth of 'un homme robuste' like the oak-tree (Faguet, *Dix-septième Siècle*, p. 319). Now the infinite expansion of the horizon suggested by these lines is certainly atmospheric; but nothing in La Fontaine is mere lyrical expansion: everything is constructive, calculated and psychologically consequent. Here, the oak pretends to despair of finding protection for a plant so distant from the *oak's own* horizon. Such rhetorical despair, taking its tone from the deepest lyricism, is actually comic, because the reed grows in a poetic environment which the oak can only see as an 'injustice of nature'. The lyrical expression of l.16 is a transition to l.17, 'La nature envers vous me semble bien injuste'. Similarly, Rudler (*L'Explication*, p. 75) fails to see the irony in 'Le Chat, la Belette et le petit Lapin' (VII/15), l.5–7:

> Elle porta chez lui ses pénates un jour
> Qu'il était allé faire à l'Aurore sa cour,
> Parmi le thym et la rosée.

A lyrical landscape, certainly, which sounds as clear as the morning dew, but its real function is to prepare and justify the next line, 'Après qu'il eût brouté, trotté, fait tous ses tours', and to present the ironic self-confidence of the rabbit whose abode is being taken over in the meantime by the weasel. Another example of a line that can read poetically but which was certainly intended sarcastically occurs in 'L'Astrologue qui se laisse tomber dans un puits' (II/13). Who can pretend to know the mysteries of the future, the poet asks, apart from God?

> Qui les sait, que lui seul? Comment lire en son sein?
> Aurait-il imprimé sur le front des étoiles
> Ce que la nuit des temps enferme dans ses voiles?
> A quelle utilité? . . . l.20–3

These lines were certainly intended ironically, but we can read them today quite differently in the light of the 'infinite extensions' of romantic and post-romantic poetry; compare the fate of Racine's 'Dans l'Orient désert quel devint mon ennui!' (*Bérénice*, 1.234). Note at the same time how 'voiles' is connected to God's 'sein', and the contrast between the associations night – breast – veil and starlight – forehead – unveiling.

In 'Le Héron – La Fille', l.3–6 are often quoted as an example of La Fontaine's landscape description:

> Il cotôyait une rivière
> L'onde était transparente ainsi qu'aux plus beaux jours;
> Ma commère la carpe y faisait mille tours
> Avec le brochet son compère. VII/4, 3–6

However, the glance at the joyful, bustling movement of the natural world is no more important than the rigorous, close, intellectual connectedness of these lines: the *rivière* is a transparent *onde*, therefore the play of the fish can be seen in it (*y*). The phonetically and atmospherically beautiful l.4 is at the same time one of those sly transition lines. It does no dishonour to La Fontaine as a poet – on the contrary! – to see intellectual acuity beneath the setting of the lyrical tone, and producing a brilliant combined effect. And *Ma commère la carpe* followed by *le brochet son compère* is also a psychological device, in the sense of a device to lead the reader: first the animal world is brought into touch with the human reader (the writer), and only then do the animals relate to each other independently. The first eight lines of the second part are shaped in parallel:

> Certaine fille . . .
> Prétendait trouver un mari . . .
> Point froid et point jaloux: notez ces deux points-ci.
> Cette fille voulait aussi
> Qu'il eût du bien, de la naissance,
> De l'esprit, enfin tout. Mais qui peut tout avoir?
> Le destin se montra soigneux de la pourvoir. l.35–42

The quoted sections of lines 35–40 serve as an introduction of the young lady to the reader, but with *enfin tout* in l.41 the text takes us into her speech and is now to be understood as coming from her point of view. Eventually we hear the *précieuse* say of her suitors in indirect speech (following direct speech, on the model of the heron part of the fable):

> L'un n'avait en l'esprit nulle délicatesse;
> L'autre avait le nez fait de cette façon-là;
> C'était ceci, c'était cela
> C'était tout . . . l.48–51

These lines mimic the very sound of aimless female chatter – *c'était ceci, c'était cela . . . et patati et patata.* But the poet plunges back into objective narration. *C'était tout* is certainly more plausible as authorial comment than as indirect speech, as the generalising and sententious follow-on shows: 'car les précieuses / Font dessus tous les dédaigneuses'. The first *c'était* (l.50) is the conversion point from narration to speech, the last (l.51) marks the reconversion from speech to narration.

In La Fontaine the speech and thought of characters is sometimes not represented in the same technical manner as in Flaubert and Zola, where introductory signals of speech are simply omitted (the 'free indirect'). La Fontaine creates subtle transitions from narration to represented speech and back again, allowing the character's voice to be heard fleetingly, like an echo: in *c'était ceci*, *c'était cela* a real ambiguity remains – is it subjective or objective language? Instances of this type must be the starting point for any explanation of this stylistic device (see Spitzer (1928), p. 327). The syntax of the following passage in 'La Mort et le bûcheron' (I/16) has made it famous among linguists:

> Il met bas son fagot, il songe à son malheur.
> Quel plaisir a-t-il eu depuis qu'il est au monde?
> En est-il un plus pauvre en la machine ronde?
> Point de pain quelquefois, et jamais de repos.
> Sa femme, ses enfants, les soldats, les impôts,
>   Le créancier, et la corvée
> Lui font d'un malheureux la peinture achevée. l.6–12

Here the represented speech must logically end with *corvée* (l.11) but it flows into objective narration with the greatest *suavitas*. In examples of this kind the poet's empathy with his characters is traditionally pointed out (e.g. by Taine), but attention should also be paid to his discreet transition from the authorial voice to that of a character, which demonstrates a stylistic intention quite different from that of the moderns who *give themselves up* to their characters. La Fontaine *lends himself* to his characters, and takes himself back again. Compare the following passage from 'Les Animaux malades de la peste' (VII/1, 56–9):

> Un Loup quelque peu clerc prouva par sa harangue
> Qu'il fallait dévouer ce maudit animal,
> Ce pelé, ce galeux, d'où venait tout leur mal.
> Sa peccadille fut jugée un cas pendable.

Line 58 lets us hear the wolf's voice; it has the ranting, insulting tone of some barrack-room lawyer's case for the prosecution of the poor ass – but *d'où venait tout leur mal* spreads a semblance of objectivity over his speech, and with *Sa peccadille* in l.59 we return to fully objective narration, the wolf's voice no longer to be heard (see Lips).

I presume that H. Gmelin is thinking of 'Le Héron – La Fille' when he writes of 'the personal inclination of La Fontaine the nature-lover, who would dream up his fables beside a babbling brook and liked to cast them back into the world of nature'. So he would see in our fable 'a good example of a humorous animal portrait with a moral appendix'; in the first eleven lines he discovers 'the eye resting with pleasure on the heron strutting by the sunny stream, the poet clearly and flawlessly reflected in its mirror-like surface'. No, the moral of the fable is *not* an appendix; it enters in the very first line. The heron does not 'strut': La Fontaine sees nothing majestic in the bird but presents it as a caricature, as a comic figure; he criticises it first in l.7, then again in l.9, l.11 and so on. And in the 'babbling brook' (actually it is not so much babbling as transparent) the heron could have had a reasonable catch, but does not – so that the stream is the mirror only of the bird's stupidity. No one knows whether La Fontaine dreamt up his fable by the banks of a river or at his desk – the opposition is a false one in any case. You can dream at your desk and you can calculate by the waterside. Finally, Gmelin's sentence 'The degree of humour in the form can almost do as a measure of the childishness of the fable' is a reminiscence of the myth only too current in Germany that La Fontaine is a children's writer. No, La Fontaine is a subtle poet who by means of his art achieves the impression of a (second-level) naturalness that is *child-like*. That is simply beyond the understanding of critics who take the product of such artistry for a mere love of 'nature'.

The art of transition can also serve to cover up a point of rupture or a division running through a whole fable. Vossler maintains that in 'Les Membres et l'estomac' (III/2) La Fontaine has 'broadened' the idea of a kingdom to that of an 'imperial principle' and thus denied or undermined the idea of a personal monarch, and moreover turned it into some kind of notion of 'social solidarity': instead of giving a glorification of French absolutism, says Vossler, La Fontaine puts 'one foot into the socialist camp'. He continues, 'That's what happens when an unpolitical mind starts talking politics. He gives himself away and without noticing, like the innocent child of nature that he is, he stumbles into a doctrine that is treasonable and prejudicial to the state' (Vossler, *La Fontaine*, p. 144). Now this idea of La Fontaine as an 'innocent child of nature' is one of those distortions caused by Vossler's historical situation – his book, based on lectures given to a broad public, was conceived during and just after the First World War and took for its subject one of the 'few men in France' to whom even 'the most Germanic of Germans' could relate without feeling hemmed in by 'political and other kinds of tendentiousness'. Consequently Vossler crudely turns La Fontaine into a German soul and even brings in the old German woodcuts of the Nuremberg miniaturist Virgil Solis to assist in the process; the woodcuts certainly have, as Vossler says, 'a quality of liveliness, of homely loveliness', but they are found only in Nevelet, La Fontaine's model, and could never have appeared in any of his own collections which they do not suit at all. La Fontaine is not an innocent child of nature, and least of all is he one who 'gives himself away'. In III/2 he did of course *consciously* put the monarchy of his own country and time in the place of the classical city-state, which he was perfectly entitled to do and which we do not consider to be 'prejudicial' in any sense. (We are after all accustomed to accept the symbolic meaning of the king in classical theatre – and to see the God of christianity behind the Greek and Roman deities.) Of course La Fontaine understood nonetheless the historical hiatus between the Roman republic and the French monarchy. The two principles converge on a single point, on the conception of the state as an organism which protects society. I cannot see why it should be treasonable to compare any state, an absolute monarchy like any other, to a physical organism: and I would guess that it would never have occurred to anyone in the France of Louis XIV to reproach La Fontaine for representing monarchy as an impersonal principle. That is what it is in any case, and even the unhistorical claim 'L'Etat, c'est moi' contains within it the reverse meaning that at least a part of 'moi', the monarch(y), is the state. Moreover, to see La Fontaine's alleged 'socialism' as 'prejudicial' Vossler must see some relationship between 'socialism' and 'danger', as perhaps in Kaiser Wilhelm II's relationship with the German socialists – but that would involve a quite unfounded extension of the meaning of the unambiguous term 'socialism'. Alternatively, if by 'socialism' he means to say that the state has social functions, which no one in a thousand years has ever denied, then it cannot be described as even remotely 'dangerous chatter'.

In fact La Fontaine's technique of transition allows him to overcome whatever relativism may be implied in the recognition of varying forms of the state. From the start of 'Les Membres et l'estomac', he expresses in a kind of surprise tactic his daring and disrespectful comparison:

> Je devais par la Royauté
> Avoir commencé mon Ouvrage:
> A la voir d'un certain côté,
> Messer Gaster en est l'image . . . l.1–4

The first two lines, imitating the *Ab Jove initium*, are a general assurance of loyalty; the comparison follows, humorously modulated by an 'as it were'. 'Messer Gaster' is not quite as direct as would be the use of 'estomac' in l.4, and bathes the whole point in an atmosphere of Rabelaisian humour. Now comes the mirroring procedure: just as in VII/4 the heron is displaced by 'la fille', so here in III/2 the members of the body are taken over by the members of the state, of the body politic: 'Chacun d'eux résolut de vivre *en gentilhomme* / Sans rien faire . . . Bientôt *les pauvres gens* tombèrent en langueur . . . *les mutins*'. If the comparison of a monarchy with an idle, passive stomach could seem disrespectful at first sight, the conclusion of this part of the narrative gives an unambiguous teaching: 'Que celui qu'ils croyaient oisif et paresseux, / A l'intérêt commun contribuait plus qu'eux' (l.22–3). From l.24 on, royal power climbs to ever greater heights. 'La Grandeur royale' is painted in broad strokes in lines full of majesty and *gravitas*, in a crescendo culminating in l.31: 'Distribue en cent lieux ses grâces souveraines' – note the divine attributes of ubiquity, benevolence and omnipotence – which goes on to the short line 'Entretient toute seule l'Etat' (l.32), giving the king the divine attribute of Unity and proclaims the *hen kai monon* of absolute monarchy. This line equates kingdom and state. But the word *état* is the hinge-word. *Suavitas* rises here to the level of genius as the poet makes the short line 'Ménénius le sut bien dire' follow directly on from the key-word *état*, itself introduced quite naturally as the culmination of the preceding panegyric of monarchy: Menenius undeniably represented the concept of the *state*. The reader, his eye caught by *seule*, has not noticed the smuggled introduction of the Roman concept of the state. Nor does he notice the artfulness of the *le* in 'Ménénius le sut bien dire'. Looked at grammatically it must seem that Menenius also said that 'la grandeur royale' nourishes all and 'distribue en cent lieux ses grâces souveraines' (l.31) – but in reality he said what is given later in l.41–3 of La Fontaine's fable, which corresponds precisely to Livy's report in Book II, xxxii: 'This fable of the revolt of the bodies' members Menenius applied to the political situation, pointing out its resemblance to the anger of the populace against the governing class; and so successful was his story that their resentment was mollified' (*Comparando hinc, quam intestina corporis seditio similis esset irae plebis in patres, flexisse mentes hominum*: transl. Aubrey de Selincourt). Of this, of course, the reader knows nothing yet, and by the time he has got to the point ten lines later he will have long forgotten that unremarkable and deceitful *le*. The mention of Menenius and the state now allows the poet to turn suddenly to the struggle between *commune* and *sénat*, l.34 (the *seditio plebis* of Livy), that is to say a revolt against the power of the state, without the ominous word 'republic' or any of its seventeenth-century synonyms occurring. Whilst only the peaceful social benevolence and ideal balance of the monarchy were represented in l.25–32, the complaints of the people against the upper classes of Rome in Menenius Agrippa's day can be laid out as broadly as the providence of the caring monarchy had previously been expounded: the Revolution is played out at a certain distance from the peaceful monarchical meadows. Finally, l.31 and l.41–4 give a frame to the uprising which shuts it out of the state of Louis XIV: 'Ménénius le sut bien dire', 'Quand Ménénius leur fit voir / Qu'ils étaient aux membres semblables, / Et par cet apologue, insigne entre les Fables / Les ramena dans leur devoir . . .' It should be noted that it is by this framing device that the idealised picture of the monarchy comes to stand quietly, majestically and magnificently in the centre of the poem, framed by two revolts – that of the body's members and that of the Roman plebs – so that it is ensconced at the centre of the fable like the stomach in the body's centre (in l.19 *cœur* is ambiguous between 'stomach' and 'heart'), or like the Senate in the centre of Rome (whilst the plebs 'hors des murs était déjà posté', l.39). The two acts of pacifying fanatics and bringing them back into the social circle provide two pendants (one a historical event, the other a parable) in which revolt is put down to the central, unmoving power of monarchy: this is classical symmetry and modulation. The first line, beginning the fable with the king ('Je devais par la Royauté / Avoir commencé . . .'), is like an entrance-sign illuminating this monument to the monarchy, made of materials which, though brought from afar, do not appear to have suffered in transit because a wise craftsman has carefully hidden all the cracks. There is not a trace here of the 'high treason' of a 'child of nature' – but there is the supreme artistry of a shaper well versed in the dangers of transferred material. The creator of the fable 'Les Animaux malades de la peste' (VII/1), which openly demonstrates the hypocrisy of a personal monarch, of king Lion (and can do so because no self-respecting king takes responsibility for the actions of a bad monarch), did not need to 'chatter away' when he spoke of monarchy. Vossler, who criticised Taine's political and anachronistic reading of the poetry of the *Fables*, is himself somehow still subject to a political obsession.

Let us now look at another skilful technique of transition in La Fontaine – the speeches put in the mouths of the hypocritical characters in the fables, which take off imperceptibly from the introductory narrative main clause to reveal the character's own opinions. Of particular interest are those 'circular' speeches that lead back into the narrative main clause, leaving the inadmissible thoughts in the centre of the frame; for example, in I/22 the speech of the oak is introduced thus:

> Le Chêne un jour dit au Roseau:
> 'Vous avez bien sujet d'accuser la Nature . . .

and ends:

> La nature envers vous me semble bien injuste'.

Or in VII/1, the lion begins:

> Que le plus coupable de nous
> Se sacrifie aux traits du céleste courroux . . . l.18–19

and ends:

> . . . mais je pense
> Qu'il est bon que chacun s'accuse ainsi que moi . . .
> Que le plus coupable périsse. l.30–3

In the first example, the 'comparative thought' (Vossler's phrase) leads to self-aggrandisement and the attitude of a protector on the oak's part, and eventually to a kind of mild feigned despair at the unfavourable conditions in which the reed has to grow – 'Sur les humides bords des royaumes du vent' – with the result that the recapitulation at the end of the speech sounds like a sad shaking of the head and an insistence on the starting position: 'La nature envers vous me semble bien injuste'. (No doubt in modern prose one would put *décidément* at the head of that sentence.) In the second example, the Lion similarly uses a procedure of comparison (who is more guilty than the others?) and moves from the general to the particular (to his own case) only in order to leave open the question whether he is the guiltiest one. He controls the notion of sacrificing one for the good of all by starting the attempt to identify the most appropriate victim (l.15–19) with his own case. So the repetition of his demand in l.30–3 has the effect of a parody of its first expression in l.15–19, where it could still almost be taken sincerely. The question arises as to whether La Fontaine is using a technique of reversal or surprise in cases like this, rather than a technique of transition. My own impression is that reversals are in general so well prepared in La Fontaine that they have no shock-effect at all. For example, in 'Le Héron – La Fille' (VII/4) the heron's words 'J'ouvrirais pour si peu le bec! aux Dieux ne plaise!' (l.22) seem abruptly reversed by the following line, 'Il l'ouvrit pour bien moins . . .'. But the third-person report in l.23 is not only contrasted with but tightly linked to the hubris of the preceding speech by the repetition of the verb *ouvrir*. The voice of the speaker rising to the invocation of the gods falls away only after *bien moins*, so greatly is this disappointment linked with the earlier expression of hubris. A comparable case occurs in 'La Grenouille qui se veut faire aussi grosse que le bœuf' (I/3):

> . . . Regardez bien, ma sœur;
> Est-ce assez? dites-moi; n'y suis-je point encore?
> – Nenni. – M'y voici donc? – Point du tout. – M'y voilà?
> – Vous n'en approchez point. La chétive pécore
> S'enfla si bien qu'elle creva.

The bursting is indeed ironical (introduced by *si bien*) but so consequential upon the stages of (literal) inflation that it can hardly surprise the reader. Even where appearances are unmasked, the disillusionment is prepared and made to be expected – as for example in the 'Un Animal dans la lune' (VII/17) where deception and truth seem to collide within a pair of lines:

> Le monstre dans la lune à son tour lui parut
> C'était une souris cachée entre les verres. l.51–2

But the preceding treatise on the equal roles of *sens* and *raison* in perception has prepared the reader fully for the observational mistakes that can derive from faulty equipment.

A further question arises as to whether La Fontaine changed, or refined, or lost interest in his technique of transition *in the course of his poetic development*, in other words whether there is in this respect a 'revolution' between the first collection of fables of 1668 and the second of 1678/9. I have the impression that the art of transition was even more conscious in the second collection and that it was exercised under much more difficult constraints. For example, La Motte's criticism of 'Les Deux Pigeons', accepted with reservations by Chamfort, is well known: the main idea of this fable, he says, is quite unclear.

> . . . on ne sait quelle est l'idée qui domine dans cet apologue, ou des dangers du voyage, ou de l'inquiétude de l'amitié, ou du plaisir du retour après l'absence. (Quoted in Régnier, II.359)

Régnier reacted sharply to this, calling La Motte's use of the 'règle d'unité' ridiculously narrow. 'Tout ne tend-il point parfaitement à ce large but . . . qui est de montrer combien, à tous égards, pour deux vrais amis, il fait bon être ensemble?' The same critic nonetheless points out that the narrative part of the fable deals with friendship (as between brothers: *frère*, l.6, 16, 24) but that the epilogue moves the subject to love (*Amants, heureux amants* . . ., l.65). Emile Faguet even thinks that the poet forgot his subject: 'La Fontaine oublie qu'il a parlé de frères et s'adresse aux amants . . .' (Faguet, *Dix-septième Siècle*, p. 314). But we know that La Fontaine doesn't 'forget' anything: his creation is conscious, and so we must make the effort to understand his technique of transition. The first obvious point is that l.1 of the fable speaks of 'tender love' – 'Deux pigeons s'aimaient d'amour tendre' – which can (but does not have to be) taken conventionally to refer to mating; and the second striking point is that what La Motte calls the 'inquiétude de l'amitié' is attached to the pigeon which suffered the most as the result of his 'désir de voir' and 'humeur inquiète' (l.20). When the unhappy wanderer returns home, 'demi-morte et demi-boiteuse' (l.59),

> Voilà nos gens rejoints; et je laisse à juger
> De combien de plaisirs ils payèrent leur peines. l.63–4

Faguet is right to underline *gens* in l.63, as it is often used by La Fontaine to refer to animals: but what the critic has in mind is the zoological disguise of man in the fables – 'Plus de pigeons, nos héros sont des hommes' (quoted in Régnier, II.271 and III.81). Just as important as the disguise, however, is the intentional, subtle transition to the subsequent song of love. *Nos gens* is both a familiar humanisation of animal heroes *and* a preparation for *amants* (l.65). *Plaisirs* (l.64) similarly leads on to the same end, since it can be interpreted both as pleasures in general or the pleasures of love in particular. (Note the same ambiguity in l.18, 'Bon soupé, bon gîte, et le reste' – 'quelle finesse sous-entendue!' wrote Chamfort; and the reminiscences of Virgil's Dido, woven into the speech of the pigeon that stayed at home, which refer to sexual love.) Even the apostrophe of the happy lovers who have no need of travel because they are for each other 'un monde toujours beau, / Toujours divers, toujours nouveau' is really only a transition to the theme of the ageing poet's nostalgia for love. 'J'ai quelquefois aimé' in l.70 seems at first simply an example of true love – giving up the whole world for the loved one – but slowly the example from the past is transformed into a present-time, personal and *unreciprocated* love. Line 77, on the 'shepherdess' whom 'Je servis, engagé par mes premiers serments' produces the mood of a particular moment:

> Hélas! quand reviendront de semblables moments?
> Faut-il que tant d'objets si doux et si charmants
> Me laissent vivre au gré de mon âme inquiète? . . .
> Ne sentirai-je plus de charme qui m'arrête?
> Ai-je passé le temps d'aimer? l.78–83

The theme of reciprocated love as in the story of the pigeons is lost; we are dealing here with one being (any of many) who may stop you in your tracks. The connection with the pigeon-story is made through the two rhyme-words *inquiète* and *arrête*. La Fontaine has seen the connection between a desire for travel, usually felt to be characteristic of youth, and a feeling of instability or unfulfilment, which he feels to be a sign of age: in this context the differences between love and friendship, between a desire for travel and a feeling of dissatisfaction, become quite small. Now we can understand why the ambiguous term *amour tendre* is put at the apex: the poet is aware of being empty of love. So a didactic fable on *inquiétude* has really become a personal, *lyrical* poem. La Fontaine has performed a feat of magic in tying together two moods of such contradictory kinds. It is a peculiarly tender and at the same time a sad poem, as the contemplation of the pigeons' idyll of recovered happiness leads on surprisingly but convincingly to the melancholy awareness of the poet's own ageing, of his inability to love and of his instability in life; an exeedingly well-organised narrative ends with a disconcerting question, and in anguish. This fable vibrates with the same melancholy wisdom and repressed tragedy that we find in Voltaire; and perhaps also with the regret for not having loved enough in youth. Without his technique of transition which maintains the intellectual motif of *inquiétude* but drops the motif of reciprocated love, La Fontaine would not have been able to allow himself this personal outburst. Perhaps this is the place to mention Gide's remarks on the *Fables*, which he took with him on his journey to the Congo:

Je ne vois trop de quelle qualité l'on pourrait dire qu'il ne fasse pas preuve. Celui qui sait bien voir peut y trouver trace de tout; mais il faut un œil averti, tant la touche, souvent, est légère. (Gide, *Congo*, p. 88)

The pigeon-story in IX/2 is a mask for the pain of advancing age. The seventeenth-century poet was obliged to take such a mask if he spoke of himself: he could no longer freely sing like Ronsard *Carpe diem et carpe rosam:* 'Cueillez dès aujourd'hui les roses de la vie'.

[In a later note, Spitzer retracted a part of his interpretation of 'Les Deux Pigeons' (Bibliography, B53 and A32, pp. 205–9): I am no longer convinced that the fable deals with two *friends* represented as pigeons [he wrote.] Every critic is exposed to what the Germans call *Systemzwang*, the drawing power of his own system of explanation. In this case, it was the idea of 'transition' which led me to throw to the winds the whole of human experience which should have told me that *friendship* is not *love* and that the subtle psychologist La Fontaine would have been the last man to confuse two sentiments of such fundamental difference . . . Today I have no doubt that this fable deals only with love and thus that there is no *transition* from the 'amitié' of the fable to the 'amour' of the epilogue, but an *identity* of subject (*amour–amants*). Not only should *amour* in l.1 be taken in the sole sense of physical love and *plaisirs* in l.64 in the sense of physical pleasure, but also the reference to Virgil's Dido in l.7–11 cannot be explained unless La Fontaine saw the pigeon who stayed at home *as a woman*. Line 17 reinforces our impression: the pigeon who stays at home asks 'Mon frère a-t-il tout ce qu'il veut, / Bon souper, bon gîte, et le reste?' Chamfort was right to exclaim 'quelle finesse sous-entendue'; we should understand 'et le reste' as 'erotic satisfactions' . . . But how can we explain the three uses of *mon frère*, if the fable deals with love? Note first that only the pigeons, not the narrator, use this term. Now in Old French lovers addressed each other conventionally as *doux frère*, *douce suer*. . . Thus saying 'brother' does not exclude sexual love: on the contrary, 'le reste' is naturally included. But there is another, deeper, reason for these uses of *frère*: what is being referred to is not the love of the senses alone, but the love that cares for the other, for the 'fraternal' partner. And it is precisely this aspect of reciprocated love . . . to which the epilogue of the fable returns . . . *Mon frère*, *votre frère* correspond to the 'l'un à l'autre' of the moral . . . The interchangeability of the partners within the matrimonial nest is also the reason why La Fontaine uses only *frère* and not *mon frère*, *ma sœur* as in Old French . . . Thus one can read the fable without needing to assume any puns or artificial transitions within it . . . The scheme of the real transitions in the epilogue is:

1. Lovers should be the whole world to each other and should not be unrequited.

2. I, in love once upon a time, saw my *young* mistress as a world and was not unrequited on the *first* declaration of love (the motif of reciprocated love is now abandoned; the words in italics are the hinges of the transition).
3. Such moments do not return in old age; I am unrequited because I can no longer love.

In other words, Spitzer maintains all of his reading of the Epilogue of 'Les Deux Pigeons'.]

The transitions in La Fontaine's second collection of fables are all the more refined as the subjects move away from behaviour towards ideas. In 'Un Animal dans la lune' (VII/17) two intellectually quite distant notions are dealt with in sequence, namely (a) the parts played by the physical senses and by the mind in perception, and (b) the desire for peace so that the arts and sciences may flourish (a theme much closer to La Fontaine's heart than the first). Some mediation between the two parts is needed: indeed, the interweaving of the two themes in a single poem absolutely requires a justification. The transitional section includes l.42–55:

> Naguère l'Angleterre y vit chose pareille,
> La lunette placée, un animal nouveau
>   Parut dans cet astre si beau;
>   Et chacun de crier merveille:
> Il était arrivé là-haut un changement
> Qui présageait sans doute un grand événement.
> Savait-on si la guerre entre tant de puissances
> N'en était point l'effet? Le Monarque accourut:
> Il favorise en Roi ces hautes connaissances.
> Le Monstre dans la Lune à son tour lui parut.
> C'était une Souris cachée entre les verres:
> Dans la lunette était la source de ces guerres.
> On en rit. Peuple heureux, quand pourront les François
> Se donner, comme vous, entiers à ces emplois?

Lines 48–9 use the (erroneous) sighting of an elephant on the moon as a pretext for discussing the possible influence of the event on earthly destinies (wars), and that is the first mention of the war motif. Since protection against war is one of the responsibilities of the head of state, the entrance of the King of England is justified and, since he is an Englishman, his interest in astronomy is quite natural – he runs to the scene (*accourut*, l.50) and does not use his carriage of state, so great is his excitement about this scientific event, and underlines thereby the motif of peaceful concern with the Muses. [The telescope is an early-seventeenth-century invention; crude microscopes were first used by the Royal Society in London in 1662.] But neither of the motifs of protection against war or the service of the Muses is sufficiently developed to be able to carry the transition to the second part of the fable. First the optical error must be explained by an examination of the telescope – 'Dans la lunette était la source de ces guerres'. A technical fault in the apparatus is responsible for the misleading image. Since the latter was viewed as a miraculous apparition in the moon and seen as the cause of wars, La Fontaine can say paradoxically that the telescope gave rise to 'these wars' – or, more accurately, to the erroneous opinion about the wars' causes. By this device he puts within our grasp the notion that other wars can arise from mistakes of vision and from error. The line 'Dans la lunette était la source de ces guerres' is the most solid of joints between the two parts of the poem. What a beautiful and significant thought: wars are perhaps optical errors! What a thoughtful kind of pacifism, born of an overall view of appearances and their connections, and a discovery of Ariadne's thread in the labyrinth of the world! La Fontaine's technique of transition becomes, when used to weld ideas together, an expression of his vision of the connectedness of all things – it really is wrong to say La Fontaine had no head for philosophy! The mistake is now clarified: 'On en rit. Peuple heureux, quand pourront les François . . .' Laughter and happiness. The English are fortunate to be able to pursue astronomical studies: why shouldn't the French do so also? This idea, artfully introduced and expanded through the motif of the favour shown to the Muses by King Charles of England, results in the closing refrain:

> O peuple trop heureux, quand la paix viendra-t-elle
> Nous rendre comme vous tout entiers aux beaux-arts? 1.71–2

To blur the impression that he wanted to lecture his own king, Louis XIV, with the panegyric of the English monarch, La Fontaine invented an extremely subtle transition. He puts out the idea that victory (la victoire, / Amante de Louis', 1.58–9) is always on the French side.

> Ses lauriers nous rendront célèbres dans l'histoire.
> Même les filles de Mémoire
> Ne nous ont point quittés: nous goûtons des plaisirs:
> La paix fait nos souhaits et non point nos soupirs.
> Charles en sait jouir . . . 1.60–4

History is made from tradition and *memory* – and this is what allows the Muses to be referred to as the 'daughters of Mnemosyne', although *all* the Muses are meant (of science as of the arts: cf. *ces emplois* (1.58) referring to astronomy, and *beaux-arts* (1.72)). Line 62 asserts an unusual state of affairs: inter arma *non* silent Musae (in war the muses are *not* silent); 1.63 mentions only a wish for peace, not the suffering of war (though in reality the opposite would have applied). In the little sentence *Charles en sait jouir*, where *en* connects innocently with the thought of peace, Charles is invoked as a *channel* of peace, not as an opponent of Louis XIV. Only in a probing afterthought does the reader grasp that the pacifier of the world, Augustus, is placed higher than the conquering Caesar, and serves as the model for the English king; the warlike Louis XIV ranks only as a Caesar. Both in the connecting of two widely separated themes and in the diplomatic and courtly opposition of a warmongering French king and a peace-loving foreign monarch the poet has overcome intellectual and political points of rupture through his mature art of *suavitas*. A philosophical essay finally turns into an ode of supplication for peace.

Chamfort reproaches 'Le Paysan du Danube' (XI/7) for the 'mediocre' moral which forms the fable's first line: 'Il ne faut point juger des gens sur l'apparence'; the upright nature of the barbarian should have led to a different moral from the one which La Fontaine has, as he says in l.3–4, already given in 'Le Cochet, le Chat et le Souriceau' (VI/5). Régnier remarks that this casual moral is only put in to temper artificially the high eloquence of the piece (quoted in Régnier, III.143). But the technique of transition in the introductory passage must be pointed out:

> Jadis l'erreur du souriceau
> Me servit à prouver le discours que j'avance.
> J'ai, pour le fonder à présent
> Le bon Socrate, Esope, et certain Paysan
> Des rives du Danube . . . l.2–6

This contains of course an example of La Fontaine's now-familiar democratic and egalitarian technique of smuggling in a humble protagonist in a list of illustrious names (see also e.g. VII/9, 32, where the milkmaid comes in a list of ambitious kings). In l.8 La Fontaine insists again that the individual fable is a little piece of the mosaic that makes up his *ample comédie*:

> On connait les premiers: quant à l'autre, voici
> Le personnage en raccourci.

Basically the introductory 'moral' of l.1 is the object of La Fontaine's irony. Even the Senators of Rome agree, after they have heard the Danubian peasant's speech, that good qualities may be hidden beneath a rough appearance – but they listen to his speech only as a speech and are not prepared to make any material changes. La Fontaine's irony points up the incompatibility of honest, moral convictions with a form-ridden routine which uses aesthetics to devalue ethics. In fact the world of rhetoric collapses in the end – that is how I read the last lines, on which commentators have wasted remarkably few words – no less than the false judgments such as the introductory moral. The fable leads us along a lengthy path from worldly casualness to the (hidden) verdict of history.

In the last book of fables as well, divergent motifs are united through *suavitas*. 'L'Amour et la Folie' (XII/14) contains a prologue in which La Fontaine announces, as is his custom, his detachment from the subject and his neutrality in the dispute about love. The actual narrative, in which the gods condemn 'la Folie' to serve evermore as guide to 'Amour' blinded by its fault, also fails to give a reasonable decision. Folie's sentence is a formal one: in reality it makes the blindness of love eternal, and thus signifies a real victory of madness over love. There is just as little real judgment given here as in the prologue, where no decision is reached either.

> Tout est mystère dans l'Amour
> Ses Flèches, son Carquois, son Flambeau, son Enfance.
> Ce n'est pas l'ouvrage d'un jour
> Que d'en épuiser cette Science.
> Je ne prétends donc point tout expliquer ici.
> Mon but est seulement de dire, à ma manière,
> Comment l'Aveugle que voici
> (C'est un Dieu), comment, dis-je, il perdit la lumière;
> Quelle suite eut ce mal, qui peut-être est un bien;
> J'en fais juge un Amant, et ne décide rien. l.1–10

The poem stands under the vault of *mystère* (l.1). The inexhaustibility of love is asserted in terms of some medieval *ars amandi* (*science–expliquer*). This *material* incompleteness of a science of love leads to the paradoxical nature of love: it is a god, but a blind god; it is a misfortune, but also a blessing. The poet leaves the verdict to the lover, i.e. to him who is riven by these opposites and who like all gods, Jupiter, Nemesis and those of the underworld, is unable to pass sentence. Love remains a 'blind god'.

All my remarks on La Fontaine's art of elegant transitions are confirmations of the insights of Paul Valéry. It is not surprising that the champion of 'pure poetry' should have a special sense for La Fontaine, who also raised the prosaic to the level of *chant* and also knew how to 'poeticise' philosophical discussion. Valéry's essay on La Fontaine appeared in 1924 (*Au sujet d'Adonis*, in *Variété I*) but still doesn't seem to have had any impact on literary scholarship, because there are such thick institutional barriers between the criticism of practising poets and the work of scholars (cf. Pourtalès, p. 72).

> Prenons garde que la nonchalance, ici, est savante; la mollesse, étudiée; la facilité, le comble de l'art. Quant à la naïveté, elle est nécessairement hors de cause: l'art et la pureté si soutenus excluent à mon regard toute paresse et toute bonhomie . . . La véritable condition d'un véritable poète est ce qu'il y a de plus distinct de l'état de rêve. Je n'y vois que recherches volontaires, assouplissement

des pensées, consentement de l'âme à des gênes exquises, et le triomphe perpétuel du sacrifice . . . Même un fabuliste est loin de ressembler à ce distrait, que nous formions distraitement naguère. *Phèdre* est tout élégances; le La Fontaine des *Fables* est plein d'artifices. Il ne leur suffit pas, sous un arbre, d'avoir ouï la pie dans son babil, ni les rires ténébreux du corbeau, pour les faire parler si heureusement: c'est qu'il y a un étrange abîme entre les discours que nous tiennent les oiseaux, les feuillages, les idées, et celui que nous leur prêtons: un intervalle inconcevable. (Valéry, *Adonis*, pp. 56–8)

La Fontaine's technique of transition has been shown to be a classical inheritance, whether consciously learnt from the Roman poets or simply present in the poet's bones. It is also somewhat different from the manner of Horace, in that La Fontaine frequently points to his own *suavitas*, taking a perverse pleasure in demonstrating and proving his art of seduction, making fun of his own virtuosity. He is a conversational story-teller who mischievously lets the reader feel his power at precisely the moment that he has subtly seduced him. And this technique is finally the expression of a world-view that perceives transitions, convergences and correspondences between all things.

Techniques of transition were clearly not a trivial matter in the practice of the art of satire in the French classical period. Boileau wrote to Racine on 7 October 1692, on the subject of *Satire X*:

C'est un ouvrage qui me tue par la multitude des transitions, qui sont, à mon sens, le plus difficile chef-d'œuvre de la poésie. (Boileau, *Œuvres*, IV.139)

Lanson on the other hand took Boileau to task for the artificiality of his transitions:

Les transitions n'ont jamais tourmenté un orateur, ni un homme qui écrit de passion. Elles ne gênent que ceux à qui le détail fait prendre la plume, et qui fabriquent leur ouvrage de pièces patiemment rapportées. Ainsi sont faites les *Epîtres* et les *Satires*, où les coutures sont vraiment trop nombreuses et trop apparentes. (Lanson, *Boileau*, p. 66)

In the introduction to his edition of Boileau's *Satires*, Charles Boudhors gives an example of what he calls their 'symphonic' thematics from the fifth *Réfléxion*. From the start, he says, the underlying harmony of 'Zoilos = Perrault' is postulated:

Par de longs détours, le 'motif' Zoïle se dévoile, s'enchaîne à Perrault (mais Claude! et non pas encore Charles), se dégage; des modulations délicates (*savant*, *lettré*, *pédant*) accueillent et suggèrent par allusion l'autre 'motif' qui enfin émerge, déborde, s'étale dans un 'finale' écrasant Perrault (Charles). (Boileau, *Satires*, p. xlix)

So there is a certain analogy between the composition of Boileau's preface and La Fontaine's verbal transitions: Zoilos – (Claude) Perrault – (Charles) Perrault. In the original this is somewhat obscured by the manner of reference: 'M.P. . . .', 'M.P. le médecin', 'Monsieur son frère le médecin', 'M.P. . . .'. La Fontaine is actually far wittier when he has occasion to use ambiguous naming devices. In 'Le Chat, la Belette et le petit Lapin' (VII/15) Dame Belette and Janot Lapin quarrel about the dwelling stolen by one from the other in the following terms:

(D.B.) Et quand ce serait un Royaume,
Je voudrais bien savoir, dit-elle, quelle loi
En a pour toujours fait l'octroi
A Jean fils ou neveu de Pierre ou de Guillaume,
Plutôt qu'à Paul, plutôt qu'à moi. l.20–4

(J.L.) Ce sont, dit-il, leurs lois qui m'ont de ce logis
Rendu maître et seigneur, et qui de père en fils,
L'ont de Pierre à Simon, puis à moi Jean, transmis. l.26–8

Rudler points out only that these are 'noms de vilains' in a 'langage d'apparence proverbiale' (Rudler, p. 83). But it would be more to the point to note that these are not simply peasant names, but the usual fictitious names used in legal language for juridical persons (as in Italian Tizio, Gaio, Sempronio, etc., in German A, B, C). In the *foreground* therefore is a legal debate on the grounds of ownership conducted according to the habits of language of the law. Dame Belette acts first as if she meant by *Jean* not the Jean Lapin before her but some Tom, Dick or notional Harry; and the sense of the sentence as well as the condescending *fils ou neveu* underlines the random nature of the names *Jean* and *Paul* (cf. Italian *un tizio* = 'somebody or other'). After this list of legal fictions the *moi* at the end of the line comes up as a sudden and unconcealed surprise: the legalisms turn out to have been only a cover for egoism, a subtle transition playing on the double sense of the name *Jean*. The claimant alone can allow herself these linguistic ambiguities; the defendant takes the names in one sense only – *Pierre*, *Simon*, *moi Jean* trace a simple and graspable genealogy and show the rabbit *maître et seigneur* to have a sense of identity naively based on consanguinity. Boileau's manner is really quite different: it has no *hidden* threads and, unlike Boudhors, I cannot see any 'symphonic' variations in, for example, *Satire IV*. It is much more a set of separate pieces each in its own key, laid next to each other without any of those transitions or bridge-passages which every music-teacher inculcates in his pupils. The theme of *Satire IV*, 'the most foolish thinks he is wise', is dealt with by a sequence of particular examples: *Un Pédant . . . D'autre part un galant . . . Un libertin d'ailleurs . . .* Then representation is abandoned and the reader's attention is directed towards the poet's own conclusions, without La Fontaine's light and conversational touch:

Et pour rimer ici ma pensée en deux mots: . . .

En ce monde il n'est point de parfaite sagesse.
Tous les hommes sont fous . . . 1.36–9

What we have here, then, is summary and exemplification. The *Satire* goes on to claim that all fools are lenient towards their own faults and therefore fortunate, and again cases in point are given – *Un Avare* . . . (1.60), then 'cet autre fou' (1.67) the big spender, then the gambler. 'Mais laissons-le . . .' (1.85), 'Il est d'autres erreurs' (1.87): namely, Chapelain the self-satisfied rhymester, . . . Bigot the visionary, and finally the theme is laid out: 'que le plus fou est souvent le plus satisfait'. The indirect biographical allusion to the father of Le Vayer (to whom the satire is dedicated) does not appear explicitly in the text. There is no trace here of symphonic structure, but just a tidy piece of joinery.

Satire VIII is a similar case. Boudhors's opinion is that Boileau makes a fluid transition to the couplet referring to Louis XIV's ultimatum to the King of Spain:

Un Aigle, sur un champ prétendant droit d'aubaine
Ne fait point appeler un aigle à la huitaine 1.139–40

The wolves, bears, tigers, vultures in the preceding lines are, says Boudhors, so many theatrical props supporting the introduction of the principal character; Boileau gets to his point by 'les feintes et les détours, les transitions et les avances' (Boileau, *Satires*, p. xlix). But I take all these animal examples simply as illustrations of the general sentence:

L'homme seul, l'homme seul en sa fureur extrême
Met un brutal honneur à s'égorger soi-même 1.151–2

The Lion and the Eagle are also not protagonists in any sense. They simply introduce the examples to show that fox does not fight fox, the hind does not fight the stag.

The satire on woman (*Satire X*, which was the cause of the sigh of pain quoted above from Boileau's letter to Racine) is also, as the poet himself says, constructed out of a series of little scenes:

Nouveau prédicateur aujourd'hui, je l'avoue,
Ecolier ou plutôt singe de Bourdaloue,
Je me plais à remplir mes sermons de portraits.
En voilà déjà trois peints d'assez heureux traits,
La femme sans honneur, la Coquette et l'Avare.
Il faut y joindre encore la revêche Bizarre . . . 1.345–50

An *additive* procedure! And we also have here that characteristic opposition and pairing of two extremes, of which the common denominator has to be something as abstract as 'excess' (between the pathetic Fury and *la douce Ménade*, the hypochondriac; or, as quoted above, between the miser and the big spender). No gradual transition here, but clear distinction, and emphasis on the poet's own role:

> Mais quoi? Je chausse ici le cothurne tragique
> Reprenons au plus tôt le brodequin comique 1.389–90

Further on, the *Satire* uses the form of the parade, inherited from Petrarch's *Triumphs* (*Trionfi*):

> Mais à quels vains discours est-ce que je m'amuse?
> Il faut sur des sujets plus grands, plus curieux
> Attacher de ce pas ton esprit et tes yeux.
> *Qui s'offrira d'abord*? *Bon*, c'est cette Sçavante . . . 1.422–5
>
> *Mais qui vient sur ses pas*? C'est une précieuse . . . 1.438
>
> *Sçais-tu bien cependant* sous cette humilité
> L'orgueil que quelquefois nous cache une Bigotte? 1.508–9
>
> Il te faut de ce pas en tracer quelques traits . . . 1.511

In fact Boileau, like Quevedo in his *Sueños*, continues the medieval satire of estates with its roots in the Dantesque architectonics of sin and punishment in the Other World. The particular coldness of this kind of satire, which subordinates types to a *genus proximum*, lies in its use of this classification system but without any animating force of metaphysical conviction. The transitions are purely local, mere juxtapositions; they are the predetermined result of translating analogies into local contiguities. So what do the transitions which gave Boileau by his own admission so much trouble consist of? Obviously, they consist of the variations in the form of the juxtapositions which are effected purely logically, by the elimination of the *differentia specifica*. For example, Boileau moves on from the jealous wife to the hypochondriac (*Satire X*, 373–98) by the introduction of the following detail:

> Souvent de ta maison gardant les avenues
> Les cheveux hérissés, t'attendre au coin des rues . . . 1.381–2

This allows not the 'calm Fury' of the opera *Isis*, but 'la vraie Alecto peinte dans l'Enéide' to be introduced: the precise opposite of Alecto, *la douce Ménade* who is constantly on the point of fainting, is thus predicated. So: the jealous wife = 'not the calm but the raging Fury'; 'soft Maenad' = the hypochondriac – a transition reminiscent of the one discussed above from Zoilos to Claude Perrault to Charles Perrault. Both are logical operations, not manipulations of the reader's mind. Where appropriate, and in accordance with the customary layout of triumphal avenues and cemeteries, a smaller statue is placed to one side of the principal monument. The poet has to transform the proximate into the sequent, e.g. associate the Tartuffe with the spiritual leader.

Boileau takes us by surprise, rather than leading us to the secondary figure:

> C'est ce qu'en vain le Ciel voudrait exiger d'elle
> Et peut-il, dira-t-elle, en effet l'exiger?
> Elle a son Directeur, c'est à lui d'en juger.
> Il faut, sans différer, sçavoir ce qu'il en pense.
> *Bon! vers nous à propos je le vois qui s'avance.*
> Qu'il parait bien nourri! Quel vermillon! Quel teint! 1.554–9

That is to say, Boileau stages an ironical consultation of the oracle, and the 'Directeur de conscience' does him the special favour of stepping up on cue, without such an *esprit d'à propos* being given any justification. Reading the ensuing and extremely lively portrait of a Tartuffe, we realise how in Boileau all the tableaux are actually frozen, and in La Fontaine how liquid and carried along by a common movement they are. As has often been said, Boileau's strength is his (essentially unspiritual) vision, his recognition of particular 'petites choses' and his ability to translate that vision exactly into words (for example, Louis XIV's establishment of lace-making schools in France (*Epître I*, 1.140–2), or an arithmetical calculation: 'Cinq et quatre font neuf, ôtez deux, reste sept' (*Satire VIII*, 210). 'Le moins intelligent des grands classiques' (Brémond, p. 18), 'l'homme nature' (Thibaudet, 'Boileau', p. 150), Boileau does not have La Fontaine's connecting vision of the world which reveals relations and correspondences between quite different things. Boileau, the hearty satirist who is good at depicting the exaggerated, could only order his different scenes on the threads of excess and abnormality, whilst in La Fontaine the thread itself is the object of poetic discovery which can lead us, Ariadne-like, through the labyrinth of earthly appearances.

The fluidity of La Fontaine expresses a view of man's action in the world as from a tower of artistic irony, and can lead us where it will; Boileau's moralising, rhetorical and argumentative manner, on the other hand, is less philosophical in its restricted point of view than La Fontaine's creation of relations and transitions between all and everything, and his sermonising attitude must in the end break down and crush the reader. Boileau undertakes an *artistic perambulation* through a picture gallery; La Fontaine effects an *artistic transformation* which dissolves the images. Boileau is a poet of examples, La Fontaine a poet of metamorphoses. The author of the *Fables*, like the French sculptor of the bas-reliefs on the Marmorbad* in Kassel, knows how to represent Daphne *in the moment of her metamorphosis* into a laurel tree.

To what extent the art of transition is a common property of the

* The 'Marble Bath' at the Orangerie at Kassel (Hessen), built in 1722–9, was decorated with eight bas-reliefs by P. E. Monnot depicting scenes from Ovid's *Metamorphoses*.

classical period is a question that has yet to be studied (the techniques are not absent from Bossuet's sermons, for example). It is certain that even today the tradition remains alive in the language of the Académie française. Pierre Benoit, for example, in his *discours de réception* for Claude Farrère had to move from his first theme – a eulogy of Farrère's deceased predecessor, Barthou – to his second – a eulogy of the new member, Farrère. He did this by listing all the government posts held by Louis Barthou over a career of forty-five years, in which 'il n'a pas trouvé le moyen d'être, une seule fois, ministre de la marine. C'est dommage. Sa présence à la tête de notre flotte, maintenant que c'est de vous, monsieur, qu'il me faut parler, m'aurait fourni une transition dont je me serais fort bien arrangé' (as reported in *Le Temps*, 24 March 1936). This foregrounding of the *absence* of a transitional theme is of course in itself an amusing exercise in the traditional art of transition.

For Giraudoux, the art of transition became a nightmare. In America, thinking of France, the writer begins to dream:

> Je rêvais que la soirée continuait. Je rêvais que le roi des transitions prononçait son discours. Il décrivait sa ville natale, Worcester, mais l'on sentait qu'il voulait maintenant parler de Paris; il faisait en vain mille efforts, s'aidant des premiers mots venus pour quitter Worcester, y renonçant, désolé, prêt à rendre son titre; quand soudain, il trouvait enfin, et, passant de sa ville à ma ville par des avenues les plus larges, il disait: Worcester, c'est la beauté; la beaute, c'est l'amitié; l'amitié, c'est Paris . . . (Giraudoux, *Amica America*, p. 140)

To return to La Fontaine: at the beginning of his article on Horace, which was quoted at the start of this essay, Ulrich Knoche recalls the 'organic' requirement put upon art in the classical period: every individual part of the work was supposed to connect with the whole as 'a limb to a body', so as to produce variation without dissipation, concentration on the principal end throughout digressions, and of course the 'flowing manner'. In works of art conceived as organisms, you cannot have, in Horace's words, 'a beautiful woman . . . ending in a black fish's tail' (*Ut turpiter atrem / desinat in piscem mulier formosa superne: Ars Poetica*, 4). Although he extended the laconic genre of the fable into a *causerie*, La Fontaine also saw each line of his poems as an organic whole of limited dimensions, subject to both general laws and to its own particular rules. One such general law is the technique of transition, which we have sought to substantiate here; another is the antinomy between the laconic and the digressive; and a third, the law of variation. As even Cordemann admits: 'It is impossible to say how La Fontaine *generally* relates the moral to the fable, because he proceeds differently in each case' (Cordemann, p. 37).*

* I have omitted a number of footnotes attacking this 'distasteful', 'mediocre', 'schoolgirlish' thesis.

Alongside these general rules, each fable is also a self-enclosed whole with an individual construction, its own specific proportions and its own set of internal correspondences. It is therefore obligatory to avoid the approach of, for example, Mario Roustan (although his interpretations are in individual cases successful): that is to say, one must not excise *one part* only of the *Fables* or, as is so frequent in writing on La Fontaine, look at only fragmentary excerpts in order to demonstrate the poet's 'observation of animal life' or his 'philosophy' or his 'moral views'. It is much truer to say that the economy of the whole indicates quite specific internal functions to the sentimental, observational, philosophical or moral elements within it. In La Fontaine, nature-poetry or philosophy or moralising is never there for its own sake; these elements exist only in functionalised form. La Fontaine is probably the first poet in world literature (there are at the most only a couple of renaissance sonnets worth mentioning as forerunners) to have applied the organic model, or concept of the monad, to a short literary genre, the first poet to sense the breath of the entire *theatrum mundi* in the modest *actes divers* of ordinary life, to have an intimation of the laws of creation within the artificial limits of the miniature. The humility of the medieval view of creation, modelled on a concept of man as a microcosm in a macrocosm, had to combine with the pride of the renaissance poet, seen as an accomplice of the divine in the invention of a world, in order to decipher the proudly modest miniature work of art which models the universe in earthly terms. What then can be the sense of making La Fontaine into a mere player of rococo games, an artist practising solely for the sake of play, in the way that Klemperer, for example, drones on with the same old story about the ludic character of La Fontaine's art? For there is *one* thing the poet did not play about with: the subordination of artistic form to the intuitive rule of the work of art.

It will no doubt be apparent that I have endeavoured in this essay as in many of my other studies to grasp a whole artistic practice by starting from an element of detail. The single fully exploited feature thus tends to stand out to an excessive, almost caricatural extent. From this, many of my critics, who take the specialised titles of my articles too seriously, deduce that I have *only* seen the single element in the whole *œuvre*, to the exclusion of other contradictory or converging traits. (That has unfortunately been the fate of my essay on Racine, and of the one on Proust.) In reality I only foreground the element I have picked out because it is one that seems to me to have been neglected previously and left in the background. Better-known features are mentioned, but less fully developed – in the hope of some future synthesis by other scholars who will get the proportions right. I am concerned above all with providing *new observational material* for further research. I know I shall not find it easy to present a personality 'in the round': I tend to be struck more by prominent features, salient edges, protrusions – and what strikes the eye guides the mind. I don't believe, however, that my seeing the uneven places and working out the previously unnoticed is connected only with my personal and polemical cast of mind: it's not easy for anyone to describe a perfect orb or the surface of still water. You can only make a ball of wool by first pulling at a single thread and winding it on and on. You have to start somewhere on the initially ungraspable whole; perhaps it doesn't even matter *where*, since the complementary features will eventually be noticed by the attentive observer. Every critical study derives from a specific initial insight (a particular rapprochement, a particular analogy) which cannot be hidden from the reader simply because its revelation would allow him (if he thinks it ill-chosen or ill-conceived) to bring down the whole construction. For myself, the image of La Fontaine that I had held within me for many years and the wealth of observations that can be made on his style only crystallised at the moment of reading Ulrich Knoche's fine study of Horace. Not only the gratitude one feels in such an instance, but, even more, the refreshing pleasure of that experience of 'meeting' is what one would like to transmit to one's reader.

V

THE 'RÉCIT DE THÉRAMÈNE' IN RACINE'S *PHÈDRE*

1948

This essay was written in English by Spitzer, and I have made no editorial changes apart from integrating footnotes into the main text and adjusting references, quotations, spelling conventions and punctuation.

It is in effect a long *explication de texte*, drawing substantially on Spitzer's earlier work on Racine but stressing more clearly here a particular notion of French classical style as 'baroque'. Auerbach, although he supported the 'baroque thesis' in the 1920s (see above, p. 107), was not convinced by this presentation of it, and also doubted – as seems reasonable – whether Thésée should really be considered the central character of Racine's *Phèdre* (see D2).

Despite these reservations and others that could be made, I have included this article to complete Spitzer's presentation of the seventeenth century, and also to show at least something of the Germanic style, which comes through much more clearly in Spitzer's English than in mine. If it is less good than chapter 1, it also complements it and brings out more clearly the underlying period-concepts of 'classical' and 'baroque'; and it shows that Spitzer's 'immanent criticism', however narrow its focus may appear to be, always in fact relies upon and enriches a historical understanding of literature.

All quotations are given from the current Nouveaux Classiques Larousse edition of *Phèdre*.

DB

THÉSÉE: Théramène, est-ce toi? Qu'as-tu fait de mon fils?
Je te l'ai confié dès l'âge le plus tendre.
Mais d'où naissent les pleurs que je te vois répandre?
Que fait mon fils?
THÉRAMÈNE: O soins tardifs et superflus!
Inutile tendresse! Hippolyte n'est plus.
THÉSÉE: Dieux!
THÉRAMÈNE: J'ai vu des mortels périr le plus aimable,
Et j'ose dire encor, Seigneur, le moins coupable.
THÉSÉE: Mon fils n'est plus? Hé quoi? quand je lui tends les bras,
Les Dieux impatients ont hâté son trépas?
Quel coup me l'a ravi? quelle foudre soudaine?
THÉRAMÈNE: A peine nous sortions des portes de Trézène,
Il était sur son char; ses gardes affligés
Imitaient son silence, autour de lui rangés.
Il suivait tout pensif le chemin de Mycènes;
Sa main sur ses chevaux laissait flotter les rênes.
Ses superbes coursiers, qu'on voyait autrefois
Pleins d'une ardeur si noble obéir à sa voix,
L'œil morne maintenant et la tête baissée,
Semblaient se conformer à sa triste pensée.
Un effroyable cri, sorti du fond des flots,
Des airs en ce moment a troublé le repos;
Et du sein de la terre une voix formidable
Répond en gémissant à ce cri redoutable.
Jusqu'au fond de nos cœurs notre sang s'est glacé.
Des coursiers attentifs le crin s'est hérissé.
Cependant sur le dos de la plaine liquide
S'élève à gros bouillons une montagne humide.
L'onde approche, se brise, et vomit à nos yeux,
Parmi des flots d'écume, un monstre furieux.
Son front large est armé de cornes menaçantes;
Tout son corps est couvert d'écailles jaunissantes;
Indomptable taureau, dragon impétueux,

Sa croupe se recourbe en replis tortueux.
Ses longs mugissements font trembler le rivage.
Le ciel avec horreur voit ce monstre sauvage;
La terre s'en émeut, l'air en est infecté;
Le flot, qui l'apporta, recule épouvanté.
Tout fuit; et, sans s'armer d'un courage inutile,
Dans le temple voisin chacun cherche un asile.
Hippolyte lui seul, digne fils d'un héros,
Arrête ses coursiers, saisit ses javelots,
Pousse au monstre, et d'un dard lancé d'une main sûre
Il lui fait dans le flanc une large blessure.
De rage et de douleur le monstre bondissant
Vient aux pieds des chevaux tomber en mugissant,
Se roule, et leur présente une gueule enflammée,
Qui les couvre de feu, de sang et de fumée.
La frayeur les emporte; et sourds à cette fois,
Ils ne connaissent plus ni le frein ni la voix.
En efforts impuissants leur maître se consume.
Ils rougissent le mors d'une sanglante écume.
On dit qu'on a vu même, en ce désordre affreux,
Un Dieu qui d'aiguillons pressait leur flanc poudreux.
A travers les rochers la peur les précipite;
L'essieu crie et se rompt. L'intrépide Hippolyte
Voit voler en éclats tout son char fracassé;
Dans les rênes lui-même il tombe embarrassé.
Excusez ma douleur. Cette image cruelle
Sera pour moi de pleurs une source éternelle.
J'ai vu, Seigneur, j'ai vu votre malheureux fils
Traîné par les chevaux que sa main a nourris.
Il veut les rappeler, et sa voix les effraie.
Ils courent. Tout son corps n'est bientôt qu'une plaie.
De nos cris douloureux la plaine retentit.
Leur fougue impétueuse enfin se ralentit:
Ils s'arrêtent, non loin de ces tombeaux antiques
Où des rois ses aïeux sont les froides reliques.
J'y cours en soupirant, et sa garde me suit.
De son généreux sang la trace nous conduit:
Les rochers en sont teints; les ronces dégouttantes
Portent de ses cheveux les dépouilles sanglantes.
J'arrive, je l'appelle; et me tendant la main,
Il ouvre un œil mourant, qu'il referme soudain.
'Le ciel, dit-il, m'arrache une innocente vie.
'Prends soin après ma mort de la triste Aricie.
'Cher ami, si mon père un jour désabusé
'Plaint le malheur d'un fils faussement accusé,
'Pour apaiser mon sang et mon ombre plaintive,
'Dis-lui qu'avec douceur il traite sa captive;

'Qu'il lui rende . . .' A ce mot, ce héros expiré
N'a laissé dans mes bras qu'un corps défiguré,
Triste objet, où des Dieux triomphe la colère,
Et que méconnaîtrait l'œil même de son père.
THÉSÉE: O mon fils! cher espoir que je me suis ravi!
Inexorables Dieux, qui m'avez trop servi!
A quels mortels regrets ma vie est réservée!
THÉRAMÈNE: La timide Aricie est alors arrivée:
Elle venait, Seigneur, fuyant votre courroux,
A la face des Dieux l'accepter pour époux.
Elle approche: elle voit l'herbe rouge et fumante;
Elle voit (quel objet pour les yeux d'une amante!)
Hippolyte étendu, sans forme et sans couleur.
Elle veut quelque temps douter de son malheur;
Et ne connaissant plus ce héros qu'elle adore,
Elle voit Hippolyte, et le demande encore.
Mais trop sûre à la fin qu'il est devant ses yeux,
Par un triste regard elle accuse les Dieux;
Et froide, gémissante, et presque inanimée,
Aux pieds de son amant elle tombe pâmée.
Ismène est auprès d'elle; Ismène, toute en pleurs
La rappelle à la vie, ou plutôt aux douleurs.
Et moi, je suis venu, détestant la lumière,
Vous dire d'un héros la volonté dernière,
Et m'acquitter, Seigneur, du malheureux emploi
Dont son cœur expirant s'est reposé sur moi . . .

This time I shall not, according to my usual procedure, start from a detail (of style) but shall first seek to establish the meaning of the whole (the tragedy) before coming to the *récit* itself, and to the linguistic details therein. Since, in this case, we are dealing with a division of a work of art, rather than with the work of art as a whole, it is obvious that this division must first be placed rightly within the whole before any treatment of linguistic detail can be considered. In some cases (compare my essay on Claudel),* it is possible to state this relationship in a single sentence, and then proceed to the linguistic detail. But in the present case, the relation of the 'récit de Théramène' to *Phèdre* as a whole – and, indeed, the purpose of the play itself – have not, I feel, been clearly recognised in previous scholarship, so that the necessity of a 'prestudy' seems to impose itself.

When we consider the play as a whole it will be seen that the terrible events in *Phèdre* are meant for the disillusionment of the only one of the main characters who survives: Thésée; it is on him that Phèdre's guilt and the death of the innocent Hippolyte produce their cumulative effect, by revealing to him the tragic truth that the gods persecute those

* B36 and A27.

they seem to protect. *Phèdre* is then a baroque tragedy of *desengaño*, disillusionment. The 'récit de Théramène' in the fifth act, parallel to the 'récit de Phèdre' in the second, but intended for the king himself, has the function of driving home at last the truth of divine perfidy and human helplessness.

In the properly linguistic part of the article I take up three stylistic features of the récit which I show to be characteristic of Racine's style in general: the frequency of the sense-word *voir*, with its intellectual connotation ('to see' = 'to witness, to understand'), the 'Klassische Dämpfung' ('classical *piano*', see chapter I above) by which the emotional stream of narrative is interrupted by intellectual evaluations (e.g. *digne fils d'un héros*, l.1527), and the paradoxical mode of expression by which Racine is wont to formulate the unnatural in nature (e.g. *Le flot, qui l'apporta, recule épouvanté*, l.1524). These three traits belong to the baroque background of Racine, in whose imagination antagonistic polar forces play: senses and intellect, emotion and intellect, anarchy and order. In other words: Racine's vision of a world in which the gods counteract their own doings, repudiate their own creation, makes itself felt in a linguistic form which, although hovering precariously on the verge of anarchy, manages always to maintain its poise.

[The two most recent contributions to criticism of the 'récit de Théramène' are to be found in an article of Mr Carlos Lynes Jr, 'A Defense of the "Récit de Théramène"', and a note of Professor Lancaster appended to this article. Mr Lynes takes exception to the previous statement of Professor Lancaster's (in *A History of French Dramatic Literature in the Seventeenth Century*, IV.199) that the lengthiness and ornateness of the *récit* is to be explained by Racine's overzealous admiration of the ancients. Mr Lynes believes that these characteristics were intended to invite 'aesthetic repose' on the part of the audience. Professor Lancaster, in his answer, seems to concede the effect of 'aesthetic repose', but contends that this very repose rather enhances the poignant appeal of the poetry than gives emotional relief. The debate (which is taken up again in *Modern Language Notes* 59 (1944) 584–6, each of the two opponents blaming the other for having shifted his attitude in the course of the discussion) seems, to this somewhat puzzled *tertius gaudens*, somewhat tangential.]

Since the time of Racine himself, critics have discussed the great length and ornate style of the 'recit de Théramène' in Act V of *Phèdre*, and generations of French schoolboys have had to struggle with the problems which this passage presents. If I feel impelled to offer my own contribution to the famous scene, it is because two American critics have recently attempted explanations which seem to me to lead in wrong directions: on the one hand they have not been 'microscopical', on the other they have not been 'macroscopical' enough; it is the correct combination and dosage of both approaches which, alone, can yield an insight into Racine's artistic endeavours. To posit 'correctness' as a criterion may seem like begging the question; and yet any method that is able to explain more of the features extant in a work of art must be held more correct.

I shall divide this study, which will, evidently, be determined by the 'Zirkelschluss',* into two parts. In the first, we will proceed from the macroscopic to the microscopic, in an attempt to answer the questions: what is the design of the whole play, and how does the 'récit de Théramène' fit into this whole? In the second, the procedure will be the reverse, from the microscopic to the macroscopic; we shall ask: what stylistic features characterise the *récit*, and are these features also characteristic of the whole tragedy – and, possibly, of the art of Racine in general? In this way, I hope to be able to point out, incidentally, the reason for the ornateness and lengthiness of the 'récit de Théramène'.

What is the design of the play? Let us begin by considering the elementary fact that, of the six characters (which does not include Ismène and Panope) in *Phèdre*, three die and three survive. All who die are guilty: Phèdre, whose guilt is evident from the beginning; Œnone, the nurse, the accomplice in her mistress's crime; and Hippolyte, whose guilt is slight but, according to Racine himself, is none the less a guilt (it is against his father's will that he loves Aricie). Of those who survive, Théramène and Aricie are blameless, while Thésée, never a figure of virtue (divided as he has always been between the labours of a hero and his less glorious erotic adventures), commits the crime, though out of blindness, of sacrificing virtue in the person of his son Hippolyte, whom he curses and sends into exile. Why, then, it may be asked, is the criminal Thésée allowed to escape unscathed? He, too, however, is crushed in the double role of victim and perpetrator of a crime which has destroyed his whole family and which he is forced to acknowledge. My interpretation is that he is spared death in order to comprehend and to acknowledge – not only his own crime and its consequences but also the perversity of the world-order. The king, to whom Théramène's *récit* is addressed, is on the stage before us, a bewildered spectator of what can befall a royal family; he is involved in the action only by his one act of blindness; for the most part he stays in his 'private loge on the stage', witnessing a drama that unfolds before him. While his son Hippolyte is destroyed by the action of the play without understanding (no god appears to explain to him the reason for his death, as in the play of Euripides, who has Hippolytus brought back before his death to be enlightened and encouraged by Artemis), and while Phèdre is destroyed with the full understanding, from the beginning, that she and her family,

* See the introduction, p. xxviii above.

especially the female branch, are persecuted by Venus, Thésée must witness the destruction of his son and his wife before he is brought to see the shape of his doom. He emerges from the play as the most important character, who will, grimly, knowingly, survive his torture, and will be the living example of the lesson he has learned 'dramatically'. What is this lesson? Perhaps, 'timeo deos et dona ferentes': the gods crush those whom they favour most. He, the protégé of the god Neptune, has been made the instrument of doom; the denouement of the action elicits his final understanding that, when he thought himself to be protected by a loving god, he was, in reality, his victim. Two gods are responsible for the devastation wrought on the family of Thésée (the destruction of the family has not been sufficiently emphasised by critics – who were misled, no doubt, by the title of the play and by Racine's failure to mention Thésée in his *Préface*). Unlike Euripides, who allows the vengeance of Aphrodite to be counteracted by the ever-loyal Artemis, Racine presents his two gods, though working separately and by different procedures, as contributing jointly to the destruction of the family: the one by direct persecution (Venus ⟶ Phèdre), the other by 'loving protection' (Neptune ⟶ Thésée) – and both together by warring against each other in the breast of Hippolyte. [This crisscross design of divine influences is the invention of Racine: with Euripides, the chaste Hippolyte had, as his patron, the chaste Diana. Since, in Racine's version, he was not 'entirely chaste', he had to be a worshipper of the patron god of his father, Neptune – and, to some extent, of Venus.]

Faced by such a conjunction of forces there is no possibility that the characters may escape; the whole tragedy, as the most crushing, the most tragic of tragedies, amounts to an accusation of the world-order, and invites man's revolt against the gods.

After the unprovoked wrath of the gods has been sated, there is left to Thésée only the one gesture which his dying son had asked of him: to be kind to the guiltless Aricie. The calm of the last lines spoken by Thésée is one of conscious desperation. He has finally become a *désabusé*, as Hippolyte had predicted in his dying words; he has tasted that *desengaño* which all the Spanish moralists of Racine's time knew so well.

Since Thésée is the one for whose benefit the disillusioning events of the play are staged, we must feel him present during the whole play (the first part of the drama is full of his name, and from the beginning we look forward with suspense to his entrance in Act III), and we must seek to observe the process of his disillusionment – which begins the moment he enters the stage. Those critics who have taken exception to his 'undramatic' character have not pondered the drama of enlightenment which goes on within him; it starts, as we have said, when he crosses his threshold, once again victorious through Neptune, eager to greet his wife and son – and sees first one, then the other, withdraw from him on some pretext. His suspicions are aroused, are given a focus by Œnone, and finally vent themselves when he banishes his son. At this point, though disillusioned about human relationships, he still thinks Neptune to be his ally; moreover, his grief over his son is still endurable, because coupled with anger. The report of Théramène will give him his second, his greatest, shock: he will learn that Neptune has listened only too well to his impulsive prayer for revenge, and boundless desperation will overwhelm him. The final blow will come when, in the last scene, he learns from Phèdre's lips that his son was blameless, and had to perish as an innocent victim of his father's commerce with the gods. [Blameless, of course, only in so far as concerns the pure nature of his love for Aricie (for the *fact* of this love is presented as a flaw). On the other hand, every precaution is taken by Racine to indicate that Hippolyte's listless mood, which may have caused his waning attention to the horses that he had trained, is due to this love; cf. l.551–2, where Hippolyte complains that his love-longing has interfered with his once favourite sport of horse-taming, and which anticipate somewhat l.1535–6 of the 'récit de Théramène': '. . . et sourds à cette fois, / Ils ne connaissent plus ni le frein ni la voix'.] Now the utter chaos and perversity of the world-order stand revealed. The 'récit de Théramène', as the second step in this development, is intended exclusively for the enlightenment of the king as to man's relationship to the gods, and must be studied in this light.

The picture of Hippolyte's death, 'cette image cruelle' (unforgettable to Théramène: l.1545), becomes for Thésée a picture of universal destruction. In the scene which follows our *récit*, Thésée, who has had time to digest its awful import, succeeds in formulating the lesson he has learned: the dubious character of divine protection, and the perversity of the cosmic scheme:

> Confus, persécuté d'un mortel souvenir,
> De l'univers entier je voudrais me bannir.
> Tout semble s'élever contre mon injustice.
> L'éclat de mon nom même augmente mon supplice.
> Moins connu des mortels, je me cacherais mieux.
> Je hais jusques aux soins dont m'honorent les Dieux:
> Et je m'en vais pleurer leurs faveurs meurtrières,
> Sans plus les fatiguer d'inutiles prières.
> Quoi qu'ils fissent pour moi, leur funeste bonté
> Ne me saurait payer de ce qu'ils m'ont ôté. v.vii, 1607–16

Since the allusions to the persecution of Phèdre and her kin by Venus ('C'est Vénus toute entière à sa proie attachée', l.306) seem to have been better understood by critics than have those to the (equally destructive) protection of Thésée by Neptune, we must study the latter more closely. It will be seen how, throughout the play, the Neptune motif combines with the Venus motif; and how the 'récit de Théramène' takes up the first, while the second is dealt with in other scenes. And, as we watch the interplay of these two motifs, we will see how carefully Racine has plotted the course of the 'wrath of the gods' in this tragedy of a Greek royal family.

As the play opens, Hippolyte, in the course of his conversation with Théramène, distinguishes two modes of behaviour observable in his father's career, corresponding to the works of Neptune and those of Venus: on the one hand, the slaying of monsters by the 'héros intrépide', on the other, his less glorious love affairs, for which Théramène excuses him, saying: 'Quels courages Vénus n'a-t-elle pas domptés?'. We learn that Hippolyte has not, to his regret, equalled his father in his feats of monster-slaying; he does, however, give involuntary signs of having fallen in love – that is, of having given himself up to the power of that Venus who shares with Neptune the ascendancy over his father and who exclusively dominates Phèdre – and, through her, the whole family. Théramène, reminding Hippolyte of his earlier prowess in the service of Neptune, indicates the shift in his allegiance which has taken place:

> Avouez-le, tout change; et depuis quelques jours
> On vous voit moins souvent, orgueilleux et sauvage,
> Tantôt faire voler un char sur le rivage,
> Tantôt, *savant dans l'art par Neptune inventé,*
> *Rendre docile au frein un coursier indompté* . . .
> Chargés d'un feu secret, vos yeux s'appesantissent.
> Il n'en faut point douter: vous aimez, vous brûlez.
>
> I.i, 128–35

(We may compare l.991: 'Quel funeste poison / L'amour a répandu sur toute sa maison!'). Hippolyte, then, has inherited his father's double nature – if on a lesser scale. When we come to the 'récit de Théramène', the reader will find a parallel to the verses highlighted above in the lines:

> J'ai vu, Seigneur, j'ai vu votre malheureux fils
> Traîné par les chevaux que sa main a nourris.
> Il veut les rappeler, et sa voix les effraie. 1547–9

Hippolyte, once the worshipper of Neptune, will at the end of the tragedy be punished for his allegiance to Venus by the god of horse-taming (there is no doubt that, in l.1538: 'On dit qu'on a vu même, en ce désordre affreux, / Un Dieu qui d'aiguillons pressait leur flanc poudreux', this Racine-invented god, to whom some critics take exception, is Neptune), and will no longer be able to 'faire voler un char sur le rivage', or to 'rendre docile au frein un coursier indompté'. To these examples for the 'chariot' motif there may be added l.176–8 in Act I, when Phèdre depicts her tortured state of mind to Œnone (before giving her any explanation of her condition) by means of two images of the peace which is denied her; one of these contains precisely the motif of the chariot:

> Dieux! que ne suis-je assise à l'ombre des forêts!
> Quand pourrai-je, au travers d'une noble poussière,
> Suivre de l'œil un char fuyant dans la carrière?

No sooner has she made this admission than she realises that she is no longer mistress of her spirits:

> Insensée, où suis-je? et qu'ai-je dit?
> Où laissé-je égarer mes vœux et mon esprit?
> Je l'ai perdu: les Dieux m'en ont ravi l'usage.
> Œnone, la rougeur me couvre le visage. 179–82

Here we can discover the delicate working of Racine's psychology of love, of that love which restricts the field of vision and turns everything therein into a means of torture. Euripides had offered a list of possibilities which would refresh Phaedra's soul: a spring, poplars on a meadow, mountains, horseback-riding – a variety of pleasures in which to find recreation. These distractions Racine limits to one – toward which the tortured soul of Phèdre turns: she craves to be outside of turmoil, a spectator of life; she wants not to ride herself but to watch from the shadow the 'noble dust' from a speeding chariot. Then, immediately, this very picture of peace is turned into poison: if she sees a race she must think of the youthful and gallant chariot-driver Hippolyte.

Here, we have been given an insight into the awakening of Phèdre's self-poisoning imagination. Racine has used restriction in the choice of the possibilities, but has intensified the efficacy of one element.

[In a lecture given at the Johns Hopkins University by Dr Richmond Lattimore of Bryn Mawr College, the speaker pointed out that the young, Amazonlike Phaedra of Euripides is presented throughout as an Outlander, il-acclimated to Troezen: horseback-riding was not a 'lady-like' activity in the eyes of Euripides's public. In Phaedra, according to Dr Lattimore, Euripides has created one of his numerous characters who are ill at ease and dissatisfied with the environment in which they must live. Thus, while in Euripides, Phaedra's desire for change and recreation shows mainly her nostalgia for the activities of her native climate, in Racine, Phèdre's same desire for equestrian feats – in which Hippolyte, not she, should figure – only serves to bind her the more to her passion.]

Thus the *récit* is anticipated by the opening scene, with its reference to Neptune as the inspiration of Hippolyte's (former) accomplishments – a motif reiterated in identical terms in II.ii, 549–52, when Hippolyte himself laments:

Mon arc, mes javelots, mon char, tout m'importune;
Je ne me souviens plus des leçons de Neptune;
Mes seuls gémissements font retentir les bois,
Et mes coursiers oisifs ont oublié ma voix.

As for the protection accorded by Neptune to Thésée (at least, to the 'hero' Thésée), this is alluded to throughout the play. When, in Act II, we learn of rumours to the effect that Thésée is dead and has perished in the sea, in the element of Neptune ('Les flots ont englouti cet époux infidèle', l.381), Hippolyte maintains stoutly: 'Neptune le protège, et ce Dieu tutélaire / Ne sera pas en vain imploré par mon père', l.621–2; in the last words, tinged with filial pride, we can sense a tragic irony – since, later, Thésée's success with Neptune will be scored at the expense of Hippolyte's life:

Et toi, Neptune, et toi, si jadis mon courage
D'infâmes assassins nettoya ton rivage . . .
Je t'implore aujourd'hui. Venge un malheureux père.
J'abandonne ce traître à toute ta colère. IV.ii, 1065–6, 1074–5

Here, it is on his prowess as a slayer of monsters that Thésée relies in his appeal to Neptune – an appeal which he is confident will be granted: 'Neptune . . . / M'a donné sa parole, et va l'exécuter', l.1158–9; 'Neptune me la doit, et vous serez vengée', l.1178; 'Espérons de Neptune une prompte justice. / Je vais moi-même encore au pied de ses autels / Le presser d'accomplir ses serments immortels', l.1190–2. But this mood of confidence fed by desperation is shaken by the news of Œnone's suicide (I find it significant that it is in the element of Neptune that she meets her death: 'Et les flots pour jamais l'ont ravie à nos yeux', l.1467), an event which seems to the messenger an inscrutable mystery ('On ne sait point d'où part ce dessein furieux', l.1466). Has Neptune a 'dessein furieux' against Thésée's household? Immediately afterwards, the king learns of Phèdre's collapse and of her desire for death, and his wrathful certitude of Hippolyte's guilt begins to crumble. With a new despair he revokes his prayer to Neptune: 'Ne précipite point tes funestes bienfaits, / Neptune; j'aime mieux n'être exaucé jamais', l.1483–4. The paradoxical phrase 'funestes bienfaits' is echoed later by 'faveurs meurtrières', l.1613, and 'funeste bonté', l.1615, while the motif 'j'aime mieux n'être exaucé jamais' will be strengthened at the close of the play by l.1650 in which Thésée resolves to 'expier la fureur d'un vœu que je déteste'. In the very moment when Thésée, wavering in his judgment of Hippolyte's guilt, and sensing the imminence of death which threatens his household, seeks to hold back Neptune's intervention, Théramène enters. The sight of Hippolyte's governor can only sharpen the anxiety of the father: 'Théramène, est-ce toi? Qu'as-tu fait de mon fils? / Je te l'ai confié dès l'âge le plus tendre', l.1488–9 – a marvellous Racinian sentence, with its example of the 'short-cut' which betrays the progress of the father's anguish and self-torture; he speaks as though he knows already what Théramène has come to tell him, and must blame the messenger for the sad news he brings. And Théramène's words confirm his darkest apprehensions: 'O soins tardifs et superflus! / Inutile tendresse! Hippolyte n'est plus', l.1491–2. Once more, *ce dieu tutélaire* has answered the prayer of his protégé. Thus we see how the Neptune motif fits into the development by which the scales are made to fall at last from Thésée's eyes.

There is a corollary motif which must be considered here, for this, also, leads up to and expands within the 'récit de Théramène': the monster motif. The traditional Greek hero (a Theseus, a Heracles), aware of his divine extraction, distinguishes himself by 'labours', by superhuman exploits which rid the world of monsters, that is from the infra-human bestiality which infests it and which is liable to imperil the triumph of human reason and civilisation. The motif of 'monster-slaying', which indeed permeates our whole play, is to be seen in connection with that of 'the hero agreeable to Neptune'. In Thésée the two are perfectly reflected, and the same might have been expected of the hero's son: this implication is not lost upon Hippolyte, when he comes to ask permission of his father to embark upon heroic enterprises: 'Souffrez, si quelque monstre a pu vous échapper, / Que j'apporte à vos pieds sa dépouille honorable', l.948–9. And it is in just this light that Hippolyte is seen by Phèdre when she first falls in love with him – according to her own words; Racine, with a marvellous grasp of the psychology of love, anticipating modern experience, has Phèdre pretend to see in Hippolyte a younger Thésée (thus she remains faithful to the type represented by her husband, so true is it that love is 'typologically monogamic' and that matrimonial infidelity, after the passage of years, can be a form of faithfulness to the original lover!) – not, of course, the impudent lover Thésée who sacrifices to a cheap Venus, but the hero who slew *le monstre de la Crète*:

> Tel qu'on dépeint nos Dieux, ou tel que je vous voi.
> Il avait votre port, vos yeux, votre langage,
> Cette noble pudeur colorait son visage,
> Lorsque de notre Crète il traversa les flots . . . II.V, 640–43

– 'flots', the element of Neptune. But irony demanded that Hippolyte should not conform entirely to type: as we know, and as Phèdre was later to learn to her hurt, he has ceased to give sole allegiance to Neptune. But at the moment the mirage is complete – as Phèdre betrays her illusion by the 'short-cut' of the outburst: '. . . ou tel que je vous voi' (in which the fallacy rests in the 'ou'). It is another irony that later, all hope and pretence abandoned, she must ask Hippolyte to resemble his father, the monster-slayer, by slaying the monster that *she* has become: 'Délivre l'univers d'un monstre qui t'irrite . . . / Crois-moi, ce monstre affreux ne doit point t'échapper', l.701, 703. This use of 'monstre' in reference to evil human beings whose destruction is urged as a heroic deed is most significant in our play, where it frequently recurs: Aricie herself applies the term to Phèdre, whom she implores Thésée to exterminate:

> Vos invincibles mains
> Ont de monstres sans nombre affranchi les humains;
> Mais tout n'est pas détruit, et vous en laissez vivre
> Un . . . v.v, 1443–5

(note the powerful *enjambement*, reminiscent of the famous 'Moi!' of Corneille's *Médée*). To Thésée, whose soul is poisoned by Œnone's slander, the innocent Hippolyte appears as a 'Monstre, qu'a trop longtemps épargné le tonnerre, / Reste impur des brigands dont j'ai purgé la terre', l.1045–6 – as he had, earlier, to the tortured mind of Phèdre. The idea of the human monster is also implicit in Thésée's reference to his most recent conquest: 'D'un perfide ennemi j'ai purgé la nature; / A ses monstres lui-même a servi de pâture', III.v, 969–70. And into this network of motifs fits the death scene of Hippolyte. So far as I know, no critic has noted the new significance, in Racine's play, of the sea-monster as the instrument of death. In Euripides's drama this instrument was a bull emerging from the sea to avenge Venus; Racine's sea-monster has a closer relationship to Neptune, it has been created, by an unjust god, as a tool of senseless *contrappasso* against the family of monster-slayers.

If, then, we consider Thésée primarily as the hero, the monster-slayer agreeable to Neptune, we are better able to understand what his reactions must be when he listens to Théramène's recital. As he grasps the import of the words, we are allowed to guess the course of his thoughts by the occasional outbursts which interrupt the tragic tale, and which betray not so much regret for the son he has lost as consternation over the trickery of the gods: 'Dieux!', l.1493; 'Les Dieux impatients ont hâté son trépas?', l.1496; 'Inexorables Dieux, qui m'avez trop servi!', l.1572. It seems to me that the criticism of Mr Lynes is far too much concerned with the probable reactions of the public to Théramène's report; it is Thésée's reaction which is all-important here – and the public watches *this*! From the general conclusion of Théramène, 'des Dieux triomphe la colère', l.1569, Thésée can only draw the specific implication: the 'un dieu' of Théramène is Neptune to Thésée. Later, Phèdre will enter the stage and, as the king hears her confess her guilt and Hippolyte's innocence, he will realise that her doom, too, has been willed by a god ('Le ciel mit dans mon sein une flamme funeste', l.1625), that, in fact, all the sufferings endured by his family have their origin in the gods. The *récit*, far from being a negligible part of the tragedy, is highly important; it is a high plateau which invites us to a contemplative repose before the full vista of the doomedness of man. This contemplation of the condition of man as that of a 'triste objet, où des Dieux triomphe la colère' can be called lacking in dramatic value only if drama be considered exclusively as outward action – a conception which is evidently much too narrow if one remembers the choral parts of the Greek drama, especially such hymns as *Eros anikate makhan*. The gradual dawning upon man of his own tragic condition is, in reality, the greatest drama imaginable.

[Batteux has excellently realised that, in Racine's fifth act, the interest shifts from Phèdre to Thésée:

> Phèdre, après la scène de la rivalité, n'intéresse plus; Thésée est le seul qui reste, ou du moins qui domine sur la scène. Cette translation de l'intérêt ne se trouve pas dans la pièce grecque. Hippolyte, donné pour point de vue dès la première scène, intéresse continuement et d'une façon dominante jusqu'à son dernier soupir. (Quoted in Mesnard, III.280–1)

But the reason for this shift is not given by Batteux: that with Racine we see an almighty and heroic king blindly and desperately groping (like another King Lear, since he is close to madness) to find where truth lies, groping with the problem of the world-order. Phèdre at the end of the tragedy is less important than is the king, before whom the whole picture must be unrolled.]

Thus, those critics are quite right who relate the ornateness and lengthiness of our *récit* to its contemplativity; what, perhaps, they have failed to grasp is the extent of the picture we are called upon to contemplate: the condition of man under the inexorable and unjust rule of the gods. From the crudest possible vision of reality, of blood, disorder and debris, Racine extracts, as by a kind of supreme wager, the most intellectual and poetic formulation, a transposition into the language of a compassionate and detached philosopher. Théramène belongs to that ancient theatre, of which Racine says, in a passage of his *Préface* (where commentators are wont to see only the compromise made by an artist with the moralising Jansenists, but which may well contain the true ethical direction ascribed to dramatic poetry by Racine and, after him, by Schiller): 'Leur théâtre était une école où la vertu n'était pas moins bien enseignée que dans les écoles des philosophes'. Théramène is a scholar in philosophy on the stage; he is, in fact, the voice of Racine. And what Sainte-Beuve once said of Racine could be said of Hippolyte's tutor: 'Il y a le calme de l'âme supérieure et divine même au travers et au-dessus de tous les pleurs et de toutes les tendresses' (*Port-Royal*, p. 600). The whole of this tragedy consists of transposition and indirect rendition of reality; the 'récit de Théramène' is a most concentrated precipitate in the dramatic alembic of Racine. Mr Lynes was quite close to that truth when he wrote: 'As a classical dramatist Racine does not wish actual tears at all, but only intense aesthetic contemplation.' But he went astray, in my opinion, when, instead of seeing in the 'récit de Théramène' a reduction *in nuce* of the general aesthetics of Racine, he attributes to the poet an intention to temper our indignation against Phèdre, whereas the truth seems to me to be that Racine's *main* purpose was to show us the collapse of the world-order as revealed to Thésée. [When Mauriac, in his *Vie de Jean Racine*, says of Phèdre: 'Le soleil pour elle seule, contre elle seule. Les autres humains n'existent pas. Hippolyte même n'apparaît que dans la fulguration du désir de Phèdre', he is right in so far as he means only to characterise Phèdre's monomania. This certainly is not true of the architecture of the play from an objective point of view.] For Hippolyte's death is not, as Mr Lynes would have it, to be explained in terms of human responsibility: granted that Phèdre was responsible for Thésée's curse, it was Neptune who fulfilled it by sending his monster out of the blue ocean that lapped the shores of 'aimable Trézène'.

[There is, in *Phèdre*, a particular motif of doom attached to a location (a motif not unknown to the ancients) – especially to Trézène. The anger of the gods brings about the situations in which the family will be destroyed by making them go to that ill-omened Trézène which, on the surface, presents itself as the 'aimable Trézène': when Hippolyte says, near the beginning of the play, 'Et je fuirai ces lieux que je n'ose plus voir', and Théramène answers, 'Hé! depuis quand, Seigneur, craignez-vous la présence / De ces paisibles lieux, si chers à votre enfance?', l.28–30, Hippolyte counters: 'Tout a changé de face, / Depuis que sur ces bords les Dieux ont envoyé / La fille de Minos et de Pasiphaë', l.34–6. Schlegel has indicted the expression *la présence de ces lieux* ('Have you ever heard that places have a presence?').* *Pace* Schlegel, it might be stated that in this tragedy places do have a presence: we must accept the clear indication of this artistic intention by Racine. The critic, instead of indicting a striking expression, should take therefrom the clue to his understanding: a striking expression in a masterpiece cannot be due to chance – it is rather a pass-key! Consider, for example, some of the allusions to the doom by which Trézène is weighed down: 'Voyage infortuné! Rivage malheureux, / Fallait-il approcher de tes bords dangereux?' Œnone, I.iii, 267–8; 'Vaines précautions! Cruelle destinée! / Par mon époux lui-même à Trézène amenée, / J'ai revu l'ennemi que j'avais éloigné' Phèdre, I.iii, 301–3; 'Je ne la cherchais pas: / C'est vous qui sur ces bords conduisîtes ses pas. / Vous daignâtes,

* See footnote to p. 15 above.

Seigneur, aux rives de Trézène . . .' Hippolyte, III.v, 927–9; 'Que vois-je? Quelle horreur dans ces lieux répandue / Fait fuir devant mes yeux ma famille éperdue?' Thésée, III.v, 953–4. The temple of faith and purity, where the wedding of Hippolyte and Aricie should have taken place, is 'aux portes de Trézène' near the ancient tombs of noble ancestors (l.1392). But it is precisely there ('nous sortions des portes de Trézène' says Théramène, l.1498 – and he repeats the words of Hippolyte, '. . . ces tombeaux / Des princes de ma race antiques sépultures', in a minor key: 'ces tombeaux antiques, / Où des rois ses aïeux sont les froides reliques', l.1553–4) that Hippolyte is destroyed; and there, consequently, Aricie will voice her accusation of the gods. Little wonder that Thésée will, at the end, flee 'loin de ce rivage, / De mon fils déchiré fuir la sanglante image', l.1605–6. His is a cursed race on a cursed soil.]

And why did Hippolyte's horses, a moment before so sensitive to their master's mood that they were sharing his taciturn sadness, refuse, at the critical moment, to obey the familiar hand of their master? The guilt of Hippolyte's death rests entirely on the gods, and the *récit* is not intended so much to lessen our anger against Phèdre as to lift us to that higher serenity in which the bitter lesson for humanity can be received. The dying Hippolyte himself, whose closing eyes are open to abiding truth, formulates most clearly this same bitter lesson: '*Le ciel* . . . m'arrache une innocente vie . . . / Cher ami, si mon père un jour désabusé / Plaint le malheur d'un fils faussement accusé . . .', l.1561–4. The victim places the responsibility for the calamity on the Heaven that permitted the calamity to happen.

Nor is the 'récit de Théramène' the only passage that offers us an opportunity to contemplate the sorry condition of man: the other is what might be called the 'récit de Phèdre' in I.iii, which seems to have escaped the censure of the critics because of its lesser length (though it is equally 'ornate') and because, in this passage, it is the principal character who is exposing her own doomed situation, so that this can be no mere 'hors-d'œuvre'. In this *récit* we are shown the devastation wrought by Venus upon her victim, which, evidently, offers a parallel to Théramène's account of Neptune's vengeance; we witness the physical dying, more painful than death, of a beautiful body ('Un reste de chaleur tout prêt à s'exhaler', l.316), which is no less moving a spectacle of human decay than that depicted by Théramène ('Tout son corps n'est bientôt qu'une plaie', l.1550). Phèdre has to divulge no sudden disastrous blow but a sequence of sufferings; Neptune strikes swiftly, Venus works insidiously in the blood. Théramène is a messenger describing a sudden, violent incident, Phèdre is an autobiographer recounting years of suffering; she begins this biography with the words: 'Mon mal vient de plus loin', l.269 – and, in fact, the malady whose course she traces had darkened the history of her family for generations. The *récit* of Phèdre, coming from a passionate woman who is at the same time a conscious witness of her own doomedness, excites us more; that of Théramène, who is a wise and ultimately dispassionate observer, is the more objective, making the effect of a final chorus which dismisses the audience with the truth for which they had been waiting. The two messages have converged in us. But we, the audience, must linger awhile longer, until our own understanding is echoed and corroborated by that of Thésée. When he first learns of Hippolyte's death, he may think Neptune's vengeance too violent, but not illegitimate; only in the following scene does he learn, from Phèdre, that Hippolyte was blameless. But we, whose suspicions of the gods had been aroused by Phèdre from the beginning, and who knew throughout of Hippolyte's innocence, are able to understand Théramène's reference to the accusing eyes of Aricie ('Par un triste regard elle accuse les Dieux', l.1584) before it is given to Thésée to grasp the full import of her accusation.

For, though we have called Phèdre's explanations to Œnone the 'récit de Phèdre', she has stayed silent toward Thésée throughout the play; and this 'éternel silence', which is emphasised in several passages, has served, by the intervention of the more active Œnone, to involve Hippolyte in his father's suspicions. In the paradoxical dramatic world of Racine, where the best intentions of man are hopelessly twisted by the gods, the fatal silence had its origin in the noblest side of Phèdre's nature: it is the main instrument of the self-imposed tortures by which Racine has sought to redeem this character (we read in the *Préface*: 'Elle fait tous ses efforts pour surmonter la passion. Elle aime mieux se laisser mourir que de la déclarer à personne'). The outcome is, as we know, that her pledge of silence is twice broken (Œnone, Hippolyte), with dire results in each case – while the silence she maintains with Thésée until the final moment has equally dire results.

[Racine is careful not to allow Phèdre to act directly: he makes her guilty in her thought (it is, as R. A. Schröder has pointed out, the thought, not only the deed, which makes a christian soul guilty): just as no overt action is involved in Phèdre's love for Hippolyte, Phèdre being criminal only in her amorous thoughts, so she commits no act herself to bring about Hippolyte's death. But her evil thought ratifies Œnone's evil action.

Racine has squared the circle by making his unfortunate queen 'act without acting' in the scene where she decides against her earlier impulse to reveal Hippolyte's innocence to Thésée – stung to jealousy by the king's reference to Aricie. By this act of decision she espouses, by her sin of omission, the evil adviser's sin of commission; this is the maximum of action granted her before she takes poison (her death, itself, being extremely undramatic, and the exact *contrappasso* to that insidious poison of love to which we have seen her subjected). The baroque princess, reduced to a suffering body and soul, a figure gagged and bound, as it were, must submit throughout the play to the fatality of guilt which has elected her as victim. Œnone is the evil thought of Phèdre become action; Phèdre is not allowed the outlet of direct evil action.]

Thus, as we listen to Théramène give his passionate–dispassionate revelation of the doom weighing on man, we wonder how much longer Phèdre will be able to maintain the rule of silence toward Thésée. And when, after Théramène's recital, she finally cries out: 'Non, Thésée, il faut rompre un injuste silence,', l.1617, we feel a vast relief to hear at last the long-repressed confession of a woman eaten up by worms of passion – a confession which testifies to the same unjust world-order as that revealed by Théramène. The play can come to an end only when all the evidence of the workings of the gods piles up before Thésée; it is Racine's procedure, motivated so skilfully, of retarding this confession that has made possible the gradual unfolding of the picture.

Before we close the chapter on the dramatic connections between the 'récit de Théramène' and the play as a whole, let us stop to consider for a moment the relationship between this *récit* and Théramène himself; we will see that Théràmene's role, in Act v, as well as the particular quality of his report, is dramatically prepared from the beginning. And, in this connection, I must question the procedure of my predecessors in criticism who are not enough 'at home' in the play they discuss, who have not spent enough effort in visualising the data and the relationships which Racine has placed at their disposal. The critic should be so familiar with the play he is studying as to be able to reconstitute the interplay between all the characters and situations, to release all the springs which the author has built into the structure of his play. To be at home in a play of Racine does not entail living in many mansions, for Racine is not Shakespeare; nevertheless, in his one-mansion edifices we must focus on many cross-relationships existing between the different characters and situations. For example, in the case of Théramène and Œnone, both are mentors, both teach their royal pupils to yield to love; but Œnone encourages a criminal, Théramène a healthy love – consequently, she must die while he is allowed to survive. Although Théramène and Œnone never meet on the stage they have been conceived in obvious parallelistic antagonism. Racine has very few characters on the stage, but he exhausts all the possibilities of relationship between them; he restricts the field of vision, but he has filled it with manifold parallelograms of forces. The Théramène whom we hear speak in Act v is no mere 'messenger' in the Euripidean sense; we have seen him, in the opening scene of our play, as the philosophical tutor of Hippolyte, who had the task of instructing him in the accomplishments of a ruler (among them, history with its noble or evil examples) and, at the same time, as the appointed historian of Thésée's family. We learn from Hippolyte himself how Théramène was wont to acquaint him with the events of the family history; the prince describes the eagerness with which he would listen as his tutor depicted the heroic exploits of Thésée:

> Attaché près de moi par un zèle sincère,
> Tu me contais alors l'histoire de mon père.
> Tu sais combien mon âme, attentive à ta voix,
> S'échauffait aux récits de ses nobles exploits,
> Quand tu me dépeignais ce héros intrépide . . . I.i, 73–7

– but also the regret and impatience aroused in him by the account of less glorious episodes: 'Tu sais comme à regret écoutant ce discours, / Je te pressais souvent d'en abréger le cours', l.91–2. Here we have obvious analogies with the 'récit de Théramène': in both, Théramène is the 'family chronicler' and, in both, his picture of nobility is clouded by painful truths that the listener shrinks from hearing. In the *récit* he must tell the most tragic of truths: however much we might prefer to dwell on the beauty and heroism of the young prince, we must be made to face the wrath of the gods, and we must allow the long and ornate threnody, which has no equal on the French stage, to sink in. This is, perhaps, what Racine might have answered his critics who (in his own words) 'le pressaient d'abréger le cours du récit de Théramène'. It is as if Racine had anticipated, in the first scene, the criticism which his *récit* was to arouse. This careful preparation for an action which will develop only in the fifth act reminds us of the parallel case in which the death of Œnone is foreshadowed in her words in Act I:

> Quoiqu'il vous reste à peine une faible lumière,
> Mon âme chez les morts descendra la première.
> Mille chemins ouverts y conduisent toujours,
> Et ma juste douleur choisira les plus courts. 229–32

The commentary of the *Grands écrivains* edition (Mesnard), with its predilection for information concerning things extraneous to the play, gives the ancient source for the third of these lines, but fails to explain the functional value of the lines within the play: to sound the note of tragic irony. The dramatist has conceived both scenes in relationship to each other, in relationship both to the character of Théramène and to the nature of his teaching. Théramène, like Racine himself, is a humanistic historiographer who can teach only in a lengthy and ornate fashion, because history is a solemn and sad spectacle which can be unveiled only by a sage who steps beyond it and speaks of it from a higher, 'transposed' plane. Consequently, the question 'why did Racine make the "récit de Théramène" so lengthy and ornate?' is asked from a point of view outside the tragedy: from the aprioristic prejudice that a play should not (evidently for the sake of *vraisemblance*) contain lengthy and ornate *récits*. (And, of course, the answer of Professor Lancaster, '. . . because Racine came to indulge more and more in descriptive writing from the period of *Iphigénie* on', has a slightly tautological flavour.)

We must be more modest when facing the great works of art; we must forget our critical attitudes which are, so often, only aesthetic prejudices abstracted from a routine reading which does not consider the meaning of the individual work of art. We would understand better a great masterpiece like *Phèdre* by affirming the adage of which Professor Lancaster declares himself sceptical: 'tout est au mieux dans la meilleure des tragédies'. Why should we not, a priori, engage in a *critique des beautés*, believing, as a working hypothesis, and until the contrary is proved, that a great masterpiece *is* perfect in all its parts? Indeed, any *explication de texte*, any philological study, must start with a *critique des beautés*, with the assumption on our part of the perfection of the work to be studied and with an entire willingness to sympathy; it must be an apologia, a theodicy in a nutshell. In fact, philology has its origin in the *apologia* – of the Bible or of the classics. For philology is born from biblical criticism and humanistic endeavours, both of them attempts to justify the *So-sein*, the 'being so and not otherwise' of exemplary texts. A criticism which insists on faults is justifiable only after the purpose of the author has been thoroughly understood and followed up in detail. The glibness with which critics, especially great German critics (Lessing, Schiller, and Schlegel), have slandered French classical drama is only to be explained on the basis of premature judgments drawn from a quite extraneous comparison with Shakespeare.

Professor Lancaster's partial acknowledgement of the 'beauty' of *Phèdre* may remind us of the similar statement of Menéndez y Pelayo (XXXIII.182) on Lope's masterpiece, *Fuente Ovejuna*: 'There is much to praise in this play, or to put it better, almost everything in it is excellent' – a statement which has elicited the protest of a scholar of the new generation, Joaquin Casalduero, who, quoting Proust's allusion to 'les œuvres d'art achevées où il n'y a pas une seule touche qui soit isolée, où chaque partie tour à tour reçoit des autres sa raison d'être comme elle leur impose la sienne' (i.e. to the 'circular' quality of works of art), opposes the relativism of his predecessor in violent terms:

> In his own time what Menéndez said was a discovery; today it is a commonplace which, apart from being more or less meaningless, reveals in whoever uses it excessive mental inertia and rigidity. No: Lope wrote perfect works . . . *Fuente Ovejuna* belongs to the class of works in which everything is excellent.

The time is past when a critic could read a masterpiece at his ease, feeling no obligation to relate parts to whole, here approving, there disapproving, as his eudaemonistic sensibility happened to be impressed. How can the average literary critic, who is so seldom a poet–critic (like Diderot or Hugo), justify his temerity in assuming as his working hypothesis: 'tout n'est pas au mieux dans la meilleure des tragédies'? Does it give him comfort that he can find flaws in the masters? If, at least, these flaws were real – and not, rather, the critic's own flaws of aesthetic understanding projected back into the work he studies! To leave it to the taste of the individual reader to decide whether or not Racine was justified in inserting such a *récit* reveals an attitude of critical agnosticism which is at variance with the readiness to admit flaws, and which amounts to a renouncement of aesthetic canons: if there *are* flaws we must condemn them on aesthetic grounds; if the lengthy, ornate *récit* is out of place, it is no longer a matter of 'taste' to find it so. The critic who goes so far as to raise up before us the possibility of a Racinian error should not stop before dealing the lethal blow. If Racine has erred, we must prove it; if we cannot prove it, let us rather not suggest the possibility of error.

After having proceeded from the whole of the play to the part, to the 'récit de Théramène', which we found to reflect microcosmically the whole and to have a definite place therein, we will now reverse the procedure, asking ourselves what stylistic traits are offered by this fragment that are necessarily characteristic of the whole of the play.

1. Let us begin by considering Racine's preoccupation with the act of 'seeing', which cannot fail to strike any observer of Racinian style. Twice in the *récit*, Théramène stresses the visual apperception of the event he has experienced: once when he mentions his own reaction to the horrid spectacle:

> Excusez ma douleur. Cette image cruelle
> Sera pour moi de pleurs une source éternelle.
> *J'ai vu, Seigneur, j'ai vu* votre malheureux fils
> Traîné par les chevaux que sa main a nourris . . . 1545–8

and again when he presents to us Aricie's grief on discovering the dead body of Hippolyte:

> . . . *elle voit* l'herbe rouge et fumante;
> *Elle voit* (quel objet pour les yeux d'une amante!)
> Hippolyte étendu, sans forme et sans couleur . . .
> Et, ne connaissant plus ce héros qu'elle adore,
> *Elle voit* Hippolyte, et le demande encore.
> Mais trop sûre à la fin qu'il est devant ses yeux,
> Par un triste regard elle accuse les Dieux . . . 1577–84

To Théramène the dead youth has already become a picture ('cette image cruelle') and this crystallised image is transmitted to Thésée who, though he has not seen the 'sad object' with the physical eye (and, as he is told, would have been unable to recognise it: 'Triste objet . . . que méconnaîtrait l'œil même de son père', l.1569–70), will be haunted evermore by what he has seen with the eyes of the soul ('De mon fils déchiré fuir la sanglante image', l.1606). This insistence on the act of seeing, whether physical or 'transposed', which is not isolated in Racine, cannot fail to impress us with the importance of 'sight' for Racine's *Weltanschauung* (in the literal sense of the German word, 'view of the world'): we cannot brush aside as 'poetic formulae' such phrases as *L'œil d'un père = un père*, or the repetition of *voir* (although this is an imitation of the 'anaphora' of the ancients, it must, like the many other ancient formulae borrowed by Racine, be granted a new meaning in Racine's poetic system). In the poetic world of Racine, all 'things seen', all events in their matter-of-fact brutality, are, for the most part, excluded: they appear only indirectly, as things spoken of. From the visible world an intellectual vision is extracted which is revealed to the public only through words: by conversation all the light of the intellect is cast upon brutal reality, so that its essence shines out before us. To present this vision, Racine must often introduce intermediate persons who lend us their eyes. In the 'récit de Théramène' we are allowed to see things through the medium of a reporter who tells us 'J'ai vu, j'ai vu . . .', and who even goes so far as to impose upon us a secondary visualisation: his seeing of what Aricie saw: here we have an extreme case of Racine's care in preventing the bloody scene itself from striking our senses too abruptly. Moreover, in addition to the 'refraction' achieved by the use of such human intermediaries, Racine interposes still another element between us and crude reality, which is his particularly poetic and intellectual language (thus, in the case of Aricie we have two intermediary persons plus a tertiary medium: a multiplication of planes which may remind us of the baroque 'mirror' technique of Velásquez).

If, now, we try to reconstruct the scene actually seen by Aricie, we will first notice that Racine, contrary to the practice of a modern naturalist, does not depict directly the bloody corpse of the young hero. [Incidentally, it may be added that the intellectual nature of Aricie's perception in this scene is not at all 'unrealistic': in moments when the most terrible sights strike our vision, there comes about a crystalline lucidity in which we are most clearly aware of our mental operations: if Aricie had been the one to report on her exact impressions at the moment, she would, perhaps, have been most true to reality in saying: 'Je m'approche; je vois l'herbe . . ., je vois (quel objet . . .)' etc.] Even blood is not directly mentioned, only implied by the reference to the vestiges recognisable on the grass ('herbe rouge et fumante'). Physical blood, warm, human blood, is absent – not only from the stage but from the picture in words. (Later, it is true, Thésée speaks of the 'sanglante image', but the very word-order shows that he has sensed not a 'bloody picture' but a picture of carnage: the preposed* adjective does not describe physical facts but draws moral implications from the bloodshed, implying and transcending 'blood'.) [It is true that, in the words of the dying Hippolyte as reported by Théramène, we find the line 'pour apaiser mon *sang* et mon ombre plaintive'. Here, however, 'blood' refers not only to physical blood: it is also a metonymical periphrase for 'death' – with the biblical implication that the blood of the murdered cries out for revenge. But this suggestion of a cry of vengeance immediately gives way to an appeased sigh of a softly plaintive Virgilian, or Dantean, shadow-soul.]

In *Andromaque*, also, we are offered (as Miss Hatcher will point out in her forthcoming article) a picture of a bloody corpse: i.e. when the captive heroine describes the scene *her eyes* beheld the night of Troy's destruction:

> Seigneur, voyez l'état où vous me reduisez.
> J'ai vu mon père mort, et nos murs embrasés;
> J'ai vu trancher les jours de ma famille entière,
> Et mon époux sanglant traîne sur la poussière,
> Son fils seul avec moi, réservé pour les fers . . . 927–31

But this reference to a bleeding form dragged in the dust does not offer a photographic reproduction of a mutilated body to our physical vision: we are not invited to visualise physiological details. It is the husband of Andromaque (*mon époux*) who has perished, it is the last of the Trojan heroes. And this figure is shown us against the background of the burning city; the framework of the whole is the destruction of Troy, the destruction of a civilisation. Moreover, the description of Hector follows upon *trancher les jours* . . .; this portentous reference to the death of a dynasty ennobles the blood-grimed figure in the dust – in the symbolic dust of defeat. For, in this passage describing Aricie's discovery, Racine focusses our attention not on the sad object of physical vision, but on the act of seeing itself – which represents an attempt to recognise, to identify. [With Racine, the words for 'seeing' are always fraught with connotations of intellectual clarification and cognisance, as Miss Hatcher will prove; in my previous study of Racine (i.e. chapter I above) I had ventured some rather tentative remarks in this connection. The preferential place given to 'sight' in comparison with the other senses, as we find it in Racine, is the continuation of an Augustinian and medieval trend of thought: cognisance, love, sin all come through the sense of senses, the eye.] And this process of identification is presented in slow-motion: Racine prolongs for five lines Aricie's hesitancy about

* Spitzer's original term 'post-positional' is, I take it, a slip of the pen.

the identity of Hippolyte. She comes to realise that 'this Hippolyte' is defined by the absence of the traits ('sans forme et sans couleur') which make him Hippolyte, 'ce héros qu'elle adore'. We could also point out that, to the picture offered to Aricie ('Elle voit . . . / Hippolyte étendu, sans forme et sans couleur'), a conceptual analysis has been added: since form and colour are the elements of the (Thomistic) ideal definition of beauty, this sentence must mean that Aricie saw before her a Hippolyte bereft of beauty – and, consequently, was unable to recognise him ('et ne connaissant plus ce héros qu'elle adore'). The cultured listener is no doubt supposed to know this definition of beauty in order to be able to understand the meaning of these lines.

[Just how much this insistence on 'intellectual seeing', which seeks to identify the object seen, is in line with what I shall call later the 'baroque' disillusionment (*desengaño*) can be shown by a German baroque play written earlier than *Phèdre*: Gryphius's *Cardenio und Celinde.* In a passage quoted by Ernst Feise, p. 188, the protagonist tells of a vision in which he saw his daemonic beloved:

> Da sah ich / und erstarrt' in ungeheurem Schrecken
> Da sah ich / und erblast! da sah ich keine Zir!
> Da sah ich / und verging / Olympen nicht vor mir!
> Ich sah ein Totenbild! / ohn Aug / ohn Lipp und Wangen
> Ohn Ader / Haut und Fleisch / gehärt mit grünen Schlangen.

('Then I saw (and grew numb in awful fear) / Then I saw (and went pale) then I saw nothing beautiful! / Then I saw (and my senses reeled) no Olympia before me! / I saw a skeleton, without eyes, without lips and cheeks / Without veins, skin and flesh, with green snakes as its hair.') (transl. T. Harper)

The traits we observe in the passage on Aricie are also found here: not only the attempt to identify the dire sight, but also the hesitancy of the 'seeing' person, who dreads to acknowledge the awful reality – as well as the total *desengaño* to which this seeing leads. There is surely no relationship of dependence between Racine and Gryphius: both write within the same climate; and both have studied Seneca and have adapted his anaphoric style to their baroque purposes.]

The continuity of her lover's being, which she would represent by 'he', has become problematic: is this body 'he'? ('Elle voit Hippolyte, et le demande encore'). The outer and the inner continuity are not congruous. When Aricie is finally forced to recognise that what she sees 'is Hippolyte', she has cognised the destructive world-order responsible for this discrepancy. And all this is to be read in her look accusing the gods. That Aricie does not reappear on the stage at the moment of the denouement (we hear of her in the *récit* and in the final lines of the play) may be motivated by the dramatic reason that the bodily presence of such a figure of light as was Aricie would have distracted attention from the main victims of the gods. She will always be to us 'la triste Aricie' who indicts divinity. Later, when the philosophical Théramène, at the close of his speech, declares that he has come to Thésée 'détestant la lumière' (an expression which would, as we shall see, be appropriate also for Phèdre), we realise that his rejection of daylight is equal in tragic weight to Aricie's accusing glance toward heaven. Compare Hippolyte's statement, 'Le jour n'est pas plus pur que le fond de mon cœur', l.1112, and the following passage:

> ŒNONE: Vous vouliez vous montrer et revoir la lumière.
> Vous la voyez, Madame; et prête à vous cacher,
> Vous haïssez le jour que vous veniez chercher?
> PHÈDRE: Noble et brillant auteur d'une triste famille . . .
> Qui peut-être rougis du trouble où tu me vois,
> Soleil, je te viens voir pour la dernière fois . . .
> I.iii, 166–72

for the relationship between 'daylight' and 'purity'.

The 'récit de Phèdre' is no less 'transposed' than is that of Théramène, since here Phèdre speaks of her bodily and psychological reactions, not only as a woman, but as a woman with the intellect and poetry of a Racine, capable of sifting and stylising her emotions (incidentally, this blend with Racine is an inheritance from Seneca, whose emotional–philosophical Medea is Medea + Seneca: Medea + a philosophical poet). When Phèdre has 'seen', there is involved a seeing of herself, a seeing sharpened by her critical self-judgment:

> Mon repos, mon bonheur semblait être affermi;
> Athènes me montra mon superbe ennemi.
> *Je le vis*, je rougis, je pâlis à sa vue;
> Un trouble s'éleva dans mon âme éperdue;
> *Mes yeux ne voyaient plus*, je ne pouvais parler;
> Je sentis tout mon corps et transir et brûler.
> *Je reconnus* Vénus et ses feux redoutables . . .
> J'adorais Hippolyte; et le voyant sans cesse . . .
> Je l'évitais partout. O comble de misère!
> *Mes yeux le retrouvaient* dans les traits de son père . . .
> *J'ai revu* l'ennemi que j'avais éloigné:
> Ma blessure trop vive aussitôt a saigné.
> Ce n'est plus une ardeur dans mes veines cachée:
> C'est Vénus toute entière à sa proie attachée. I.iii, 271–306

Here, however, we are confronted with new implications of the act of seeing. In Phèdre's case, the 'seeing' is, in a double sense, the tragic mainspring of her being: her sin is to have 'seen' Hippolyte, to have experienced love for him, and her torture is to see (to cognise) that her sin is 'having seen'. Phèdre's *voir* is stained with sin and knowledge of sin. The fire of sin came through the eye (the covetous sense par excellence, according to Saint Augustine); it is for this reason that Phèdre wishes henceforth to shun the light of day ('ne plus voir le jour': note the ambiguity of *jour* = 'life' and 'light of day', an ambiguity of classical origin: 'to see the light' means 'to live' in the *Iliad* (18, 442)), and flees into the darkness of death. In her final words she applies to herself the law of retaliation: 'Déjà je ne vois plus qu'à travers un nuage / Et le ciel et l'époux que ma présence outrage; / Et la mort, à mes yeux dérobant la clarté, / Rend au jour, qu'ils souillaient, toute sa pureté', l.1641–4. Phèdre is the incarnation of god-willed self-destruction that comes through the eye: the eye that cognises; Théramène, the spectator of tragedy, suffers only sympathetically the god-willed destruction in the objective world.

2. In the preceding paragraphs we have had occasion to speak of the reality-sifting quality inherent in Racine's 'intellectual and poetic' language. The reader may have wondered whether the two terms are not mutually exclusive: is not Racine, moreover, the poet of pure emotion, untrammelled by fetters of the intellect? Is he not, better than any other poet of his time, able to let pure feeling breathe through words of incomparable evocatory power – 'Que ces vains ornements, que ces voiles me pèsent', and 'Ariane, ma sœur, de quel amour blessée / Vous mourûtes aux bords où vous fûtes laissée'? But such lines, with their great appeal to our emotional and acoustic imagination, have generally been isolated from the context by modern literary critics who have gone to school to the Romantics; when replaced in their original context, they appear neutralised by more intellectual expressions. For example, the first verse quoted is followed by l.159–60: 'Quelle importune main, en formant tous ces nœuds, / A pris soin sur mon front d'assembler mes cheveux?' Here the epithet *importune* implies an intellectual judgment, at variance with the rest, while the sad flute music of Phèdre's utterances is followed by the cool remark of Œnone: 'Que faites-vous, Madame? et quel mortel ennui / Contre tout votre sang vous anime aujourd'hui?' (l.255–6) where *mortel ennui* represents an evaluation, a diagnosis. But even when these two famous 'emotional utterances' are considered in themselves, it is possible to see how the impact is softened by the expression of an intellectual judgment: in 'ces vains ornements' *vains* is fraught with moral connotations (the biblical 'vanitas vanitatum'); the passage about Ariane contains a full-fledged logical demonstration underscored by repetition of the same syntactical pattern: it had been preceded by Phèdre's ejaculation: 'O haine de Vénus! O fatale colère! / Dans quels égarements l'amour jeta ma mère!', l.249–50, corresponding to 'de quel amour blessée . . .', and ends with the conclusion 'Puisque Vénus le veut, de ce sang déplorable / Je péris la dernière et la plus misérable', l.256–7. Here, underlying the exclamations, we find the logical pattern of a syllogism:

1. dans quels égarements . . . (Pasiphaë was persecuted by Venus)

2. de quel amour blessée . . . (Ariane was persecuted by Venus)

3. *Consequently* (this is implied by the *puisque*), Venus persecutes all the women of the family: I am only a link in the chain.

This passage, in which the lyrical outburst is mitigated by ratiocination, is one example of what I have called, in an earlier article (chapter 1 above), 'klassische Dämpfung', 'classical *piano*': a continuous repression of the emotional by the intellectual. Indeed, it could be said that the alternation between these two conflicting tendencies is the most distinctive characteristic of Racine's style. As such it can be found in the speech of all his characters: Racine has taught them all to speak with his voice.

[The serenely intellectual atmosphere that permeates the last words of Hippolyte is remarkable; we have stressed above, in the text, his clear formulation of the meaning of his death, a formulation which admits of only a slight admixture of 'poetry' ('mon ombre plaintive'). It is as though Hippolyte applied 'classical restraint' to his last words, and to the last moments of his existence. Even when his words are interrupted by the agony of death ('qu'il lui rende . . .') this fits into the classical pattern of 'aposiopesis': there is lacking, for example, the 'naturalistic' effect, depending on the truncation of a single word, as we find it in Ariosto's *Orlando furioso*, 42.14: 'ne menti raccomando la mia *Fiordi* / Ma dir non pote *ligi*, e qui finio' ('May I commend to you my Fiordi. . . / But he could not say . . .*ligi*, and ended there'). Moreover, in the unfinished words of Hippolyte, what is interrupted is not the evocation of a name that embodies the personal happiness of the lover, but the expression of an altruistic thought concerning the welfare of the other being that should live on after her lover's death.]

Classical *piano* is, understandably enough, especially frequent in the language of Phèdre, being a trait thoroughly consonant with her nature: in her, boundless passion and severe analysis coincide to a remarkable degree. In Théramène's character, too, there is a comparable blend of the objective and intellectual (as historian and philosopher) with the subjective (as a compassionate friend of the god-stricken family) – though, with him, as we have said, objectivity must prevail.

Diderot, in his *Paradoxe sur le comédien*, has written immortal lines which seem almost to be meant to apply to the 'récit de Théramène':

Avez-vous jamais réfléchi à la différence des larmes excitées *par un événement* tragique et des larmes excitées par un récit pathétique? On entend raconter une belle chose: peu à peu la tête s'embarrasse, les entrailles s'émeuvent, et les larmes coulent. Au contraire, à l'aspect d'un accident tragique, la sensation et l'effet se touchent; en un instant les entrailles s'émeuvent, on pousse un cri, la tête se perd, et les larmes coulent; celles-ci viennent subitement; les autres sont amenées. Voilà l'avantage d'un coup de théâtre naturel et vrai sur une scène éloquente, il opère brusquement ce que la scène fait attendre; mais l'illusion en est beaucoup plus difficile à produire; un incident faux, mal rendu, la détruit. Les accents s'imitent mieux que les mouvements, mais les mouvements frappent plus violemment. . . . C'est lorsque la grande douleur est passée, quand l'extrême sensibilité est amortie, que l'âme est calme, qu'on se rappelle son bonheur éclipsé qu'on est capable d'apprécier la perte qu'on a faite, que la mémoire se réunit à l'imagination, l'une pour retracer, l'autre pour exagérer la douceur d'un temps passé; qu'on se possède et qu'on parle bien. (Diderot, *Paradoxe*, pp. 370–1)

Théramène is self-controlled and speaks well. Thus it will not be difficult to find in the 'récit de Théramène' the same general tendency of tempering as that noted in the 'récit de Phèdre'. When, for example, he describes how he and his companions followed the bloody path that led them to the body of Hippolyte, he offers vivid, concrete details appealing to our imagination:

> De son généreux sang la trace nous conduit:
> Les rochers en sont teints; les ronces dégouttantes
> Portent de ses cheveux les dépouilles sanglantes. 1556–8

And yet the emotional effect is tempered by moral interpretations: the bloody hair, stuck to the thornbushes wet with blood, become 'les dépouilles'. The ghastly picture is ennobled: we are asked to contemplate the remains of a hero dead in battle. Still more characteristic is 'son généreux sang': the actual blood, as in similar cases pointed out above, is sublimated, transposed by the epithet *généreux* into the moral sphere. Again, in the passage:

> A ce mot, ce héros expiré
> N'a laissé dans mes bras qu'un corps défiguré,
> Triste objet, où des Dieux triomphe la colère,
> Et que méconnaîtrait l'œil même de son père. 1567–70

the expression 'ce héros expiré', in which the defining phrase *héros expiré* is preceded by the demonstrative, has an oratorical ring, with Ciceronian overtones. It appeals to the emotion, if you will, but to the emotion of an intellectual person. One who was still under the impact of an affecting situation would not be so able to 'define' and, instead of the demonstrative, would use, perhaps, the definite article which, by referring to something as already known, allows us to remain within the situation. The 'distantiating demonstrative' (as I have called it), to the contrary, suggests a point of view from outside the situation; when we say, for example, *dans ce pays*, 'in this country', instead of *dans notre pays*, 'in our country', there is effected, at least for a split second, a disinterested comparison with other countries. Similarly, the *ce* of our passage is the expression of a dispassionate historian who feels the necessity of assuring his readers that he is still dealing with the same person.

Moreover, in this same phrase *ce héros expiré* there is another trait of style to be observed, one which had been particularly favoured by Roman historians and by the Roman playwrights who dealt with historical subjects (Seneca, for example) and which has existed in French since the time of the renaissance (cf. Lerch's treatment of this construction under the title 'C'est son rêve accompli'). *Ce héros expiré* stands for *l'expiration, la mort de ce héros* – or rather, we should say that *ce heros expiré / N'a laissé dans mes bras qu'un corps défiguré* is ambiguous by intent: is it the person of the hero (who happened to be dead), or his death, which left the sad vestiges? This type of expression, which ascribes to the agent what really belongs to the resulting action, and which remains on the borderline between the abstract and the concrete, gives an intellectual, sophisticated flavour ('can a dead hero act?') to a passage which otherwise speaks so directly to the heart. Finally, the personality of Hippolyte, of that 'object', is further reduced by the use of the relative adverb *où*, which seems to refer not to a person but to a locality: the object has become a 'place where' the gods have sated their anger. This *où*, of which modern symbolistic poets might have been proud, immediately renders visualisation impossible: we are in No Man's Land somewhere between an object and a place, between the visible and the abstract, the emotional and the intellectual, between a picture and a definition.

In the following passage, which contains a parenthetical remark, the tendency of 'Dämpfung' (attenuation) has found another congruous form, and one which represents a characteristic and oft-repeated pattern in Racine's verse:

> Elle voit (quel objet pour les yeux d'une amante!)
> Hippolyte étendu, sans forme et sans couleur. 1578–9

Here we are ready to identify ourselves with the sorrowing Aricie, to see with her eyes – and Théramène–Racine decides to postpone the picture we are eager to see, perhaps in order to prepare us for the horrifying sight: that is, in order to temper our emotions. Now this parenthesis is, in its syntactical form, an exclamation, an emotional outburst (like Phèdre's 'de *quelle amour* blessée . . .!'), but its contents offer a rational appraisal of the object of vision. There is in the phrase *objet pour les yeux* something definitional and intellectual; the dead youth appears as a 'visual unit', framed as it were, ready to be cognised by a scrutinising eye. The effect is obviously to place us outside the range of Aricie's feelings – since these are defined. We feel for her but not with her; we have the attitude of a sympathetic but dispassionate witness – the attitude of Théramène–Racine. In addition, the presence of the indefinite article ('les yeux d'*une* amante') introduces a comparison of her plight with the normal lot of lovers in general; this projection of the particular case against a framework, this invocation of a general law, is a philosophical and intellectual device, particularly characteristic of Racine (which, with him, may take on a variety of nuances: entreaty, (self-)pity, self-assertion, protestation; the latter is found in Hippolyte's last words: 'plaint le malheur d'*un* fils faussement accusé', l.1564).

We have to do again with an interpolation, if not with a parenthesis, in the following example:

> On dit qu'on a vu même, en ce désordre affreux,
> Un Dieu qui d'aiguillons pressait leur flanc poudreux. 1539–40

Here, all is 'poetic' and 'seen' – and yet, in the interpolated *en ce désordre affreux*, the events narrated are judged, a rational diagnosis is given: by means of the term 'extreme' the canon of normality is brought into play. And, simply by the act of calling something 'extreme', we liberate ourselves from its impact; the impression of disorder or disharmony is not allowed to dominate the scene; on the contrary, the scene is gauged and defined for us. Here, too, however, the approach is not wholly rational: in the epithet *affreux* there is condensed, as it were, an emotional exclamation which sums up the whole scene: 'c'était affreux!' – but, at the same time, this epithet is neutralised by the 'diagnostic' noun *désordre*.

The classical *piano* of Racine may have been learned from Virgil, cf. e.g. *Aeneid*, VI.274–81, describing the vestibule of Hell:

> Luctus et ultrices posuere cubilia Curae;
> pallentesque habitant Morbi tristisque Senectus,
> et Metus et malesuada Fames ac turpis Egestas,
> *terribiles visu formae*, Letumque Labosque;
> tum consanguineus Leti Sopor et mala mentis
> Gaudia, mortiferumque adverso in limine Bellum,
> ferreique Eumenidum thalami et Discordia demens
> Vipereum crinem vittis innexa cruentis.

'Shapes terrible of aspect have their dwelling there, pallid Diseases, Old Age forlorn, Fear, Hunger, the Counsellor of Evil, *ugly Poverty*, Death and Pain. Next there is Sleep who is close kin to Death, and Joy of Sinning and, by the threshold in front, Death's Harbinger, War. And the iron chambers of the Furies are there, and Strife the insane, with a bloody ribbon binding her snaky hair' (transl. Jackson Knight)

The enumeration of the two groups of monsters is, as E. Norden has pointed out in his commentary on the Sixth Book, separated by l.277 with the interpolation *terribiles visu formae* ('ugly, terrible to behold') 'which forms a certain point of repose . . . This all attests thoughtful artistry.' It must be added to these words of Norden that, by this very interpolation, the frightening description of the monsters gives way, for a moment, to a quiet *judgment* in regard to the manner in which they must appear to the eye of the spectator – and this is in line with Racine's habits. That a whole poetic attitude (not only certain devices which are derivative thereof) has been adopted from the ancients (and, necessarily, transformed) by this French classical poet is not an isolated fact: La Fontaine has learned from Horace what I have called his *suavitas* (see chapter IV above).

Again, we may consider the following passage, in which the description of factual events is interrupted by a moral judgment ('digne fils d'un héros'):

> Hippolyte lui seul, digne fils d'un héros,
> Arrête ses coursiers, saisit ses javelots,
> Pousse au monstre, et d'un dard lancé d'une main sûre,
> Il lui fait dans le flanc une large blessure. 1527–30

The eye of the observer is also a moral eye: it moralises while it observes. Not only is the heroism of Hippolyte shown by a description of his exploits: it is also verbally defined.

Such interpolations, which generally fill out the second hemistich of the first line of a couplet, are generally called 'chevilles' (paddings) as if to suggest that the classical poets of the seventeenth century were in the habit of composing, in the original draft, the first hemistich of the first line, together with the whole second line, later to fill out the missing second hemistich of the first line. (According to this suggestion, Molière would have first written in his *Misanthrope*, I.i, 129–30: 'On sait que ce pied plat . . . Par de sales emplois s'est poussé dans le monde', later to add 'digne qu'on le confonde'.) If this analysis, which assumes a 'two-instalment procedure' in poetic composition, were correct, this would mean that the intellectual element must represent an extraneous addition to the emotional (of course, the question as to why such a prosaic phrase was added on second thought would be only the more perplexing) whereas I contend that the rationalistic interpolation was conceived *along with* the emotionally flowing sentence, and is inseparable therefrom (it would evidently be impossible to separate the two elements in the insertion itself: *quel objet pour les yeux d'une amante*!). It is highly significant that, in the interpolations of attenuation, the classical poets put references to that stable world of moral values toward which they most insistently strove. These reminders of a moral and rational realm, in the midst of emotional turmoil, exert a steadying influence; over the waves of passion there shine forth, from these 'lighthouses', the tranquil beams of reason and calm.

3. Now we are ready to consider an aspect of Racine's art, the failure to recognise which has led to misunderstanding on the part of many

critics, from the seventeenth century to our own time. Students of Racine are familiar with the debate between Houdar de la Motte and Boileau, in which the former attacked, the latter defended, l.1524 of our *récit* in which Théramène describes the reaction of Nature to the appearance of the sea-monster: 'Le flot, qui l'apporta, recule épouvanté'.

According to Houdar de la Motte, 'Ce vers . . . est excessif dans la bouche de Théramène. On est choqué de voir un homme accablé de douleur, si recherché dans ses termes et si attentif à sa description' (La Motte, I.27). To this Boileau answers: 'Pouvait-il [Racine] employer la hardiesse de sa métaphore dans une circonstance plus considérable et plus sublime que dans l'effroyable arrivée de ce monstre, ni au milieu d'une passion plus vive que celle qu'il donne à cet infortuné gouverneur d'Hippolyte?' (Boileau, 'Réflexions critiques sur quelques passages de Longin' (1710), in *Dialogues*, p. 182). In other words, Houdar de la Motte bases his attack on the principle of *vraisemblance*, while Boileau (the translator of Longinus!) invokes 'sublimity' in his defence of the passage. What the one refers to as 'excessif' and the other as 'hardiesse de sa métaphore' is, more specifically, the interpretation of the physical fact of a wave's ebb and flow in a sophisticated and clever manner, whereby this natural process is ascribed to the ocean's fear. Since a *précieux* expression is usually defined as 'une métaphore suivie jusqu'au bout' (the classical example being Théophile de Viau's 'il en rougit, le traistre!' in *Pyrame et Thisbée*, V.iii, 1228), or an over-extended intellectual interpretation of a physical fact, we may say that the 'excess' to which the critic Houdar de la Motte objected was the preciosity of the metaphor.

In another passage of the *récit*, we find intellectual criticism expressed by a play on words:

> Ismène, toute en pleurs,
> La rappelle à la vie, ou plutôt aux douleurs. 1587–8

The last hemistich, which indicates a paradoxically pessimistic equation 'life = sorrows', is clearly an extension on the trivial phrase *rappeler à la vie* – which becomes, thereby, didactically ('plutôt') transformed into something like 'call back to the sorrows (in which life consists)': this is life judged from without, not lived from within. The very self-correction which Théramène purports to impose on himself is an intellectual procedure likely to be used by an observer calm enough to pay attention to his choice of words. But to this attitude we should not, like La Motte, attach blame.

But now let us place the incriminated l.1524 in its context (as the classical critics failed to do), and examine the dominant idea of the passage as a whole:

Un effroyable cri, sorti du fond des flots,
Des airs en ce moment a troublé le repos;
Et du sein de la terre une voix formidable
Répond en gémissant à ce cri redoutable.
Jusqu'au fond de nos cœurs notre sang s'est glacé.
Des coursiers attentifs le crin s'est hérissé.
Cependant sur le dos de la plaine liquide
S'élève à gros bouillons une montagne humide.
L'onde approche, se brise, et vomit à nos yeux,
Parmi des flots d'écume, un monstre furieux.
Son front large est armé de cornes menaçantes;
Tout son corps est couvert d'écailles jaunissantes;
Indomptable taureau, dragon impétueux,
Sa croupe se recourbe en replis tortueux.
Ses longs mugissements font trembler le rivage.
Le ciel avec horreur voit ce monstre sauvage;
La terre s'en émeut, l'air en est infecté;
Le flot, qui l'apporta, recule épouvanté.
Tout fuit; et sans s'armer d'un courage inutile,
Dans le temple voisin chacun cherche un asile. 1507–26

Here we are faced with the fact that Nature shrinks back from what she has given birth to, that the monster, though a part of Nature, is repudiated by the whole of Nature. As is well known, the classical procedure for evoking the whole of Nature is that of enumerating the four elements (note, in l.1133, the evocation of Nature, when Hippolyte swears: 'Que la terre, le ciel, que toute la nature . . .': here, Racine has added to the two elements mentioned by Euripides the phrase 'toute la nature'); in our passage the four elements (the sky, the seat of light, replaces the element of fire) respond with fright to the frightful product of Nature – the greatest fear being felt by the sea which gave birth to the sea-monster. Now, if we turn to the 'récit de Phèdre', we find another example of Racinian baroque: Phèdre's address to the 'soleil . . . qui . . . rougis' – and, indeed, of the same pattern of thought: the paradoxical fact of an ancestor who must blush at his own progeny is of the same sort as that of Nature rejecting what she has brought forth. This is, in fact, the situation which obtains for Phèdre also: she, too, is a monster who has been given her monstrous nature (her incestuous love) by Nature (= Venus), but is rejected by her. Where Houdar de la Motte saw only a witty conceit, out of place in a tragedy, and unconvincing because of its excessive *invraisemblance*, there is a deeply felt expression of what was sensed as paradox in Nature. One could ask why La Motte did not equally object to this metaphor used by Phèdre:

Noble et brillant auteur d'une triste famille,
Toi, dont ma mère osait se vanter d'être fille,

Qui peut-être rougis du trouble où tu me vois,
Soleil, je te viens voir pour la dernière fois. 169–72

It could be said that the concept of a 'sun that blushes' is as daring a *précieux* deviation from the normal 'the sun shines', as daring an intellectual interpretation of a physical fact, as is Théophile de Viau's conception of a dagger, red with blood, blushing over its treachery.

On the other hand, the 'sun' in question is also a god, and an ancestor: if Phèdre were thinking of him exclusively in that guise, the reaction of blushing from shame would be wholly congruous. Perhaps we have here a deliberate ambiguity (symbolised by the epithet *brillant*); Phèdre sees the sun both as a shining orb and as a divine being.

In the cases where Racine allows himself to lend human emotions to Nature, this has a functional value for the play. Indeed, the play itself is based on the comparable paradox that the gods repudiate their creatures; they send man into the world endowed with gifts which prove to be Danaic, and abandon him to his doom. We may remember the lines of Goethe, addressed to the gods:

Ihr führt ins Leben uns hinein
Ihr lasst den Armen schuldig werden,
Dann überlasst ihr ihn der Pein,
Denn alle Schuld rächt sich auf Erden.

('You bring us into life and let poor mortal man become guilty; then you leave him to his suffering, for all guilt is avenged on earth.') (*Wilhelm Meisters Lehrjahre*, II.13, p. 136)

Racine's sensitivity to such a paradox as that of 'creation and repudiation' reveals a *Weltanschauung* (world-view) which is essentially baroque.

That the baroque element in Racine's art was not recognised (as such) by his contemporaries is hardly surprising. During this period, the classical ideal of reason and simplicity was accepted so implicitly in France (where it was followed so much more faithfully than was the case in Spain, Italy, England, Germany) that any tendencies which appeared to be in opposition to pure classicism were considered, by the critics, as so many flaws: aberrations from the norm. They were unable to sense in their lifetime the positive nature of such tendencies, whenever these did appear, to see them as manifestations of another artistic ideal which were integral to the work of art; instead, they were viewed only as excesses, as excrescences which could and should be pruned off. Or, if they were condoned, this was apt to be due more to an inconsistent attitude than to critical understanding. (Boileau, for example, defends the line of Racine mentioned above but stoutly condemns the 'clinquant du Tasse'.) But, while such confusion is understandable in the classical critics, who did not have at their disposal the conception of the 'baroque' which modern historians of art and literature have developed, the same excuse will not hold for those of our modern historians of French seventeenth-century literature, to whom this conception has not yet penetrated and who, even after the investigations into the baroque carried on by Wölfflin, Weisbach, Walzel, et al., insist on remaining faithful to the confusion which had its *raison d'être* in circumstances of the seventeenth century.

The literary historians of today, in France and elsewhere, are too prone to repeat seventeenth-century French criticism on seventeenth-century French literature. Their confidence in this criticism is due to the illusion of a homogeneous 'siècle de Louis XIV', brilliant in all fields; whereas the truth is that in that epoch literature alone, not literary criticism, was outstanding. I associate myself with J. Hadamard who writes in his article 'Science et monde moderne', p. 550: 'Le XVIIe siècle a été, et particulièrement en France, un âge de décadence . . . Il semble même que le progrès des sciences positives ait, à ce moment-là, nui aux études historiques en en détournant les esprits que, d'autre part, l'éclat de la production littéraire à la même époque éblouissait. La critique littéraire elle-même, comme le note Renan (*L'Avenir de la science*, p. 144), témoigne de la même faiblesse.'

Brunetière, for example, sees such tendencies as 'la préciosité, le boursouflé, le grotesque' only as flaws contrary to the classical ideal (*Histoire de la littérature française classique*, II.99–106, etc.). And he also makes the mistake of assuming too easily that, with the triumph of classicism in seventeenth-century literature, these unfortunate tendencies were vanquished. But who can overlook the *précieux* vein in Molière, that critic of the *précieuses*? And this preciosity, of course (as well as 'le boursouflé, le grotesque') is a manifestation of the baroque.

The baroque phenomenon in seventeenth-century art and literature must be considered in contradistinction to the (purely) classical art which preceded it: while this follows the path of the golden mean between two extremes, in an atmosphere of calm and of an equipoise easily and inevitably reached, baroque art reveals the conflict of polarities which is so acute that the final equilibrium is achieved only by a violent effort and at the expense of our tranquillity. Even when balance is attained, the vestiges of the struggle remain indelible in the work of art, so that asymmetry prevails. The conflicting forces may be worldliness and religion, sensuousness and a disillusioning recognition of the vanity of the world, passion and intellect, anarchy and authority, but in every case the victory of the second force is hard won. In such a tense atmosphere, the three 'stylistic diseases' mentioned by Brunetière – each of them a distinct trend in itself – can easily flourish. In Italy, Ariosto and Tasso, in Spain, Garcilaso and Góngora represent classic and baroque poetry respectively; among the artists, Raphael represents renaissance art as opposed to the baroque of the later Michelangelo. In France, the baroque factor, whether in art or in literature, was much less conspicuous: what a tame variant of it is offered by the preciosity and the grotesque of Théophile de Viau! Nevertheless, there are baroque elements in Corneille and Racine as well as in Molière – and most of all, in Pascal and Bossuet (the same is true of Poussin, who appears to Gide as a mitigated Rubens).

To return to our play, it is evident that *Phèdre* is the ideal type of a baroque tragedy, not only by its style, but by its basic conception (though this the historians of French literature generally do not say): we need only consider the heroine given over to a burning passion and, at the same time, to an intellectual awareness of it which multiplies her sufferings; Thésée, the heroic monster-slayer and happy lover, powerless against those gods who seem to protect him; kingly beings, enjoying a position far above common mankind, grope in the dark of their passion or their intellectual blindness. Here we have the typically baroque theme of the great of the earth who are creatures with all the frailty, the *Kreatürlichkeit* of such (cf. Shakespeare, *Henry V*, Act IV, sc.i: 'I think the King is but a man, as I am . . . all his senses have but human conditions. His ceremonies laid by, in his nakedness he appears but a man') – together with the motif of the 'dream of life', whose mystery man cannot unravel. Again and again, throughout the play, the characters are involved in a struggle between conflicting forces one of which will be allowed with great difficulty to subdue the other; a resolution is always achieved (by 'classical *piano*'), but one feels the revolt of the senses and of the emotions. The overall impression remains that of a Pyrrhic victory.

In this connection, it is illuminating to consider the alterations which Racine introduced in the characters inherited from Euripides. Of Phèdre he says in his *Préface*:

> Phèdre n'est ni tout à fait coupable, ni tout à fait innocente. Elle est engagée, par sa destinée et par la colère des dieux, dans une passion illégitime, dont elle a horreur toute la première . . . Lorsqu'elle est forcée de la découvrir, elle en parle avec une confusion qui fait bien voir que son crime est plutôt une punition des dieux qu'un mouvement de sa volonté.
>
> J'ai même pris soin de la rendre un peu moins odieuse qu'elle n'est dans les tragédies des anciens, où elle se résout d'elle-même à accuser Hippolyte. J'ai cru que la calomnie avait quelque chose de trop bas et de trop noir pour la mettre dans la bouche d'une princesse qui a d'ailleurs des sentiments si nobles et si vertueux. Cette bassesse m'a paru plus convenable à une nourrice, qui pouvait avoir des inclinations plus serviles.

This means to imply, when interpreted in terms of modern criticism, that Racine has made the character of Phèdre more baroque: the natural nobility of a great queen is in violent contrast with her debasing passion; the play consists of the *mise en jour* (to use Racine's own expression) of the all-too-human baseness of an exalted being. This basic structure of the character of Phèdre is intended to show us how love, a gift of the gods to mankind, can become poison and debasement; by love the mighty are cast down – indeed, dehumanised. To lead us toward the heights only to precipitate us into the abyss, this is the scheme of the gods, and the baroque poet does his utmost to preserve the sharp contrast of the two extremes – as he exposes the shame of the exalted to the eyes of the world. Only death, which has been hovering over the five acts of the drama, brings a resolution of the conflict. No such thought of exposing the frailty of the mighty was uppermost in the mind of Euripides, whose Hippolytus was pure, an innocent victim of the anger of the gods. And the reason for Racine's shift of emphasis from Hippolyte to Phèdre, a shift which has been pointed out by so enlightened a critic as Batteux, must have been that, by making Phèdre the protagonist, Racine was given the possibility of showing a princely being at its most frail ('frailty, thy name is woman' said the one who was the baroque hero par excellence): a woman in conflict between moral nobility and earthly passion.

And once the torn character of Phèdre had become the centre of the play, once its theme had been changed from that of purity persecuted by the inexplicable cruelty of the gods to the baroque inner *Zerrissenheit* ('state of being torn asunder') of a character within whom the god-sent monster rages, then the character of Hippolyte had to be transformed: he, too, must share in the baroque *Kreatürlichkeit* (human frailty) of Phèdre by assuming the role of a lover who loves against the will of his father – endowed, that is, with a flaw, however slight, in conformity with the law of the baroque stage where the limelight is cast not on ideality but on human frailty. Of Racine's innovations in this regard, Batteux writes:

> Phèdre criminelle, et Hippolyte vertueux, tous deux malheureux, sont mieux placés dans Euripide que dans Racine, parce qu'il est dans la nature et dans l'ordre que quand la vertu malheureuse se trouve en concurrence avec le crime malheureux, l'intérêt dominant et l'affection principale soient pour la vertu, qui n'a pas mérité son malheur, plutôt que pour le crime, qui a mérité le sien. L'objet naturel de la pitié, dit Aristote, est le malheur non mérité: d'où il suit qu'il est possible qu'Euripide ait mieux pris son sujet, relativement à l'effet de la tragédie, en subordonnant Phèdre à Hippolyte . . . Phèdre est l'héroïne de la pièce de Racine; et c'est pour rendre son rôle plus beau et plus touchant qu'Hippolyte a été en quelque sorte dégradé. Euripide savait que les héros qu'on veut offrir à la pitié doivent être bons d'une bonté morale; Racine le savait aussi, puisqu'il donne partout l'amour de Phèdre comme l'effet de la colère de Vénus, pour la rendre moins odieuse; mais Euripide n'a eu qu'à suivre son plan simplement et sans aucun effort; Racine a eu besoin de beaucoup d'art pour suivre le sien . . . Ne pouvant diminuer le malheur d'Hippolyte, il a fallu

en diminuer la vertu, sans quoi il eût éclipsé Phèdre et emporté tout l'intérêt. (quoted in Mesnard, III.280–1)

Still another character had to be changed in consequence of Racine's baroque approach: the nurse Œnone. Schlegel, who on moral grounds condemned Phèdre for putting the burden of guilt on Œnone, has not understood what is brought out excellently by Walter Benjamin: that the baroque drama, which shows the rulers and princes in all their earthly glory but also in their congenital depravity as human beings, must give a preponderant part to the evil counsellors who exploit the earthly power of their masters, and thereby precipitate them into the abyss of their human depravity. The kingly character of a baroque drama is sometimes extremely weak (e.g. a Herod), a pawn in the hands of his advisers, 'out-Heroded' by them. Phèdre says to Œnone, who has served her not wisely but too well:

Va-t'en, monstre exécrable . . .
Et puisse ton supplice à jamais effrayer
Tous ceux qui, comme toi, par de lâches adresses,
Des princes malheureux nourrissent les faiblesses,
Les poussent au penchant où leur cœur est enclin,
Et leur osent du crime aplanir le chemin,
Détestables flatteurs, présent le plus funeste
Que puisse faire aux rois la colère céleste! 1317–26

The same has also been expressed by Shakespeare, when he has his King John berate those 'slaves' who serve royal failings:

It is the curse of Kings to be attended
By slaves that take their humour for a warrant
To break within the bloody house of life,
And on the winking of authority
To understand a law, to know the meaning
Of dangerous majesty, when perchance it frowns
More upon humour than advised respect.
King John, IV.ii, 208–14

Œnone works at the behest of that blind predestination which persecutes in the great of the earth their frail humanity, their *Kreatürlichkeit* (that the kingly being is held to be noble by nature, that the adviser could more easily have 'des inclinations serviles' is due not to any contempt of Racine for the lower classes but to his belief in the theocratic order of the state – an order according to which the most exalted person in the state is a 'Sun-king', and consequently should be ideal). On the other hand, classical drama has also furnished famous examples of good counsellors; whatever the moral quality of the counsellor's advice, his role is always a crucial element of baroque drama.

Batteux has seen beautifully the dependence of Hippolyte's transformation on that of Phèdre, but, imbued as he had to be with Aristotelian normative aesthetics, he could not recognise in that change the definite artistic will of Racine, so different from that of Euripides; the baroque poet who had conceived one character according to the pattern of conflict could not but shape the other accordingly. It was not apprehension lest an entirely virtuous Hippolyte eclipse Phèdre (an idea which seems to have left its imprint in Mr Lynes's statements) which led Racine to depict Hippolyte as slightly less perfect: it was because, according to his baroque vision of the prince who is at the same time a human being, it was necessary that all the royal characters be shaken by ontologically conditioned conflicts. Phèdre 'moins odieuse', Hippolyte less perfect: each represents a vision of man as a basically torn being; each of them is as baroque a creation as was Pascal's *roseau pensant*. The criticism of Racine's Hippolyte made by Fénelon (*Lettre*, p. 91) and Arnauld (quoted in Mesnard, III.273–4) is quite beside the mark: they have failed to see the anthropological view underlying Racine's dramatic system. The lover's role assigned to Hippolyte represented no compromise with contemporary society (as has been suggested by the dubious anecdote of Racine's apology: 'Qu'auraient dit nos petits-maîtres?'). In fact, Hippolyte is undermined by his pure passion for Aricie just as truly as is Phèdre by her impure passion. The gradual weakening of Hippolyte's power over his horses (which was to lead to his undoing) is parallel to the undermining of Phèdre's will-power by her consuming love. Hippolyte's love is Phèdre's passion on a minor scale; Racine presents his pessimistic judgment of love in a pure and an impure version: a total criticism which Proust will repeat.

Finally, the de-idealisation of Hippolyte had to entail the creation of the ideal Aricie: this pure princess inherits the original role of Hippolytus in Euripides; and she inherits also his protecting deity, Diana. The character of Aricie was conceived not only in order to motivate the flaw in Hippolyte's character, a 'super' on whom Racine could hang the label 'loved by Hippolyte': it was also necessary that purity be represented in the drama. And Aricie, who stands beyond the reach of the curse which lies on the family of Thésée, is unstained by sin, unshadowed by doom.

We have begun this section by the consideration of a stylistic feature (*préciosité*) which revealed itself as a reflection of a characteristically baroque conception, and we have seen how the fabric of the play itself was shot through with baroque themes, involving the clash of polarities. Now, returning to stylistic questions, we will find not only the feature of preciosity, which is one of the forms of the baroque in French literature, but a device which embodies the basic baroque pattern of contrasted polarities. When, for example, Phèdre's passion is described as a *flamme noire*, we are offered a paradoxical expression of the type to which the ancients gave the name *oxymoron*; such a phrase presents the impossible as possible. The flame that should bring light and life in the being called Phaedra, 'the shining one', in reality brings darkness and death (Phèdre is the daughter not only of Pasiphaë, the 'all-shining', but also of Minos, the god of hell, to whom, unable longer to bear the light of day, she will descend; thus she is herself an oxymoron incarnate). The fire that warms ends in the cold of death. No wonder that the poisoned love that Phèdre bears cannot warm the heart: 'Je *goûtais en tremblant* ce *funeste plaisir*', IV.vi, 1248 – two oxymora are found in one sentence. And we may also remember the expression 'funestes bienfaits' by which Thésée, filled with a presentiment of Hippolyte's death, characterises the Danaic gifts of the Gods. A less obvious type of oxymoron is to be seen in the line (which antagonised the unpoetic critics of Racine's time) from our *récit*: 'Traîné par les chevaux que sa main a nourris', l.1548.

The topos of the 'horse tamed with great effort' as we have it in the line: 'Rendre docile au frein un coursier indompté', l.132, is another typical theme of baroque art (one immediately remembers its frequency with Velasquez). The role given to the horses in *Phèdre* is exceptional among seventeenth-century plays (especially tragedy), if we are to believe Professor Lancaster's erudite study 'The Horse in French Plays', p. 106. However, Professor Lancaster has failed to inquire into the reason for the infrequency of such references in seventeenth-century French tragedy (as opposed to its frequency in Spanish drama) – which reason is precisely the anti-baroque tendency of French classical tragedy. As a matter of principle, studies of this type should, in my opinion, be subordinated to categories derived from the history of art and history of ideas; we should no longer follow the positivistic manner of 'catalogues', inaugurated by the German dissertation of the Stengel school: *Das Ross in den altfranzösischen Artus- und Abenteuerromanen*, 1888.

This oxymoron underscores beautifully the paradox, the *Widersinn* of life: the heroic horse-tamer is trampled by his horses. Here, just as with *flamme noire* and *funestes bienfaits*, there is the suggestion of an intolerable world-order subject to the clash of polarities. And yet, by virtue of having been defined, the disharmonious is overcome: disharmony is conquered by the harmony of form.

As a final manifestation of baroque art in *Phèdre*, let us turn again to the description of the monster which is central to the *récit*. The motif itself was, evidently, given. What Racine has brought out most conspicuously is the element of vital force. In the ancient world, the monster had its legitimate place, accepted as one of the forces of nature: in the world of Christian values, the monstrous must appear as a threat to the cosmos, sent by *natura parens* to inflict death. And this threat is felt in

Racine's description, where nature, in its hideous beauty, is presented in a variety of novel forms worthy of a Baudelaire or a Flaubert:

> Cependant sur le dos de la plaine liquide
> S'élève à gros bouillons une montagne humide.
> L'onde approche, se brise, et vomit à nos yeux,
> Parmi des flots d'écume, un monstre furieux.
> Son front large est armé de cornes menaçantes;
> Tout son corps est couvert d'écailles jaunissantes:
> Indomptable taureau, dragon impétueux,
> Sa croupe se recourbe en replis tortueux. 1513–20

All in these lines is movement and action; in a momentary metamorphosis where the animate takes on the inanimate (*montagne humide*), and the reverse (*dos de la plaine*), strange shapes emerge as if painted by a Rubens or a Bosch. Those critics who have spoken of the 'descriptive style' in the 'récit de Théramène' should, more specifically, have spoken of the 'baroque descriptive style', of the 'description of the hideous and the demoniac'. It is surely significant that this passage, which has always been recognised as one of the most highly descriptive to be found in Racine, is focussed on the demoniac, the monstrous, the gruesome. For, what is a monster unless seen? A monster in the abstract! Since monster it had to be (because of the ancient model), it could be only a baroque monster: a monster presented in all its horrid sensuous reality.

But this anarchy of shapes and movement will be curbed by Racinian verse; the monster will be transposed into the realm of poetry. Since the matter of Théramène's story was the ugly and the destructive, the manner had to be ornate and weighty: the more exciting the events witnessed by Théramène, the more poised must be his description of it – the more of intellectual detachment, of aesthetic repose, of plastic beauty open to contemplation must we be offered. Firmly architectured alexandrines impose their measure on the ghastly vision; rhetorical patterns mould and purify crude reality. By the intellectual act of distinguishing these patterns, the emotions of the listener are held in check; while he is invited to visualise strangeness and horror, he is constantly reminded of the familiar and the traditional – for the devices used by Racine are, for the most part, highly conventional. Let us note just a few of these quite conventional features: the traditionally poetic vocabulary (*onde* for *mer*, which involves the conventional device of synecdoche), chiasmus (*indomptable taureau – dragon impétueux*), anaphoric prefixes (*se recourbe en replis*), onomatopoeia (*l'essieu crie et se rompt*), and finally (e.g. *monstre furieux*) the classical use of 'colourless' adjectives, so obnoxious to a modern critic who is apt to share the opinion of Jules Renard that ' "Ciel" dit plus que "ciel bleu"; l'épithète tombe d'elle-même, comme une feuille morte.' But the 'dead' quality of such epithets is precisely what serves to establish calm and serenity. The ultimate effect of these devices is that the chaotic vital forces on the verge of explosion are stemmed, subjected to rule and form, to 'klassische Dämpfung'. For Racine, the baroque poet, is a French poet; he is not tempted, as a Quevedo might be, to overthrow all boundaries of form, but understands how to subject the baroque flow of vital forces to classical measure. It is true that the 'récit de Théramène' is a 'most baroque' piece of poetry, and its critics have been troubled by its close approach to the anarchic and the chaotic. None the less, the *récit* succeeds in taming the monster by style.

My three divisions devoted to the style of the 'récit de Théramène' were intended to show how reality is sifted by the intellect, how the expression of emotion is attended with 'klassische Dämpfung', how life is seen as a conflict between polar forces. We have also tried to show that former critics have failed to let themselves be guided by the words toward its inner economy and coherence, preferring rather to establish relationships between certain unrelated details of the play and aprioristic criteria extraneous to the play. Since we have chosen to remain within the play, our procedure has been to penetrate from the periphery of the words toward the inner core. For the words of the poet are shafts leading to the innermost part of the mine, while extraneous rapprochements are dead alleys. Criticism must remain immanent to the work of art, and draw its categories therefrom.

VI

THE *LETTRES PORTUGAISES*

1954

This brilliant essay was written in French, and it demonstrated for the first time what has been perfectly obvious ever since: that the anonymous *Lettres portugaises* of 1669 form an exquisite, miniature work of art that could only have been produced by a writer of great classical taste and skill. All modern scholarly work on the *Lettres* flows from this pioneering article and has resulted in definitive proof that the author was indeed Guilleragues, as guessed by Spitzer. Deloffre and Rougeot, in their edition of Guilleragues (Paris: Droz, 1972), from which all quotations are made, give a very full picture of the work carried out since Spitzer; this can be complemented by the various articles in the journal *Œuvres et critiques*, I.I, 'De Jodelle à Guilleragues'.

DB

F. C. Green's question 'Who was the author of the *Lettres portugaises*?' has prompted me to do some research leading naturally to an intrinsically much more important question, namely: 'What is the meaning of the *Lettres portugaises*?' Common sense should have stopped literary historians from tackling the problem of a text's attribution before they had elucidated its meaning: for it is only the correctly established meaning of a text which can allow us to infer the causative force which gave rise to the work. As long as the work itself remains ill-defined, its causative force (the author's personality) must be for ever obscure. Until now it is this latter state of affairs that has prevailed in discussions of the 'authenticity' of these five letters, originally published in Paris by Barbin in 1669 and purporting to be the despairing lamentations of a Portuguese nun, seduced and then abandoned by a French officer. Scholars of the nineteenth and early twentieth centuries sought only to answer the allegedly 'historical' question as to whether the *Lettres portugaises* were the authentic writings of a certain Marianna Alcoforado, a nun of the convent of Beja and mistress of the man who was to become the maréchal de Chamilly. This attribution, which goes back to the Portuguese scholar Cordeiro, has been triumphantly refuted by Professor Green, whose case is almost entirely conducted along 'positivist' lines, i.e. is based on external historical arguments. (He also gives considerable weight to the suggestion that the author of the *Portugaises* was a certain 'Guilleraques' mentioned in the *Registre des Privilèges* for 1668, and who may or may not be Guilleragues, a *bel esprit* known as a friend of Boileau and Racine.)* At the end of his article, Green gives a short paragraph where artistic reasons drawn from the work itself are adduced in favour of his attribution of the text to a 'writerly' author. Although we must applaud Green's argument, I can only say that it does not go nearly far enough towards explaining the *raison d'être* of the five letters as a work of art, which is much more than a single cry of the heart. I am

* The attribution is now definitive; see the note on p. 254.

quite certain that no one would have espoused the view that these letters were 'authentic' epistles written in Portuguese and somehow rescued – in translation – from the archives of history, if critics had recognised from the start the *artistic value* of the text. If we can demonstrate the unity of conception and execution of the five letters in their French form, then we will have ruled out all possibility of a 'naturalist' or 'evolutionary' theory of the concretion of Portuguese originals.

It is in fact the evolutionary prejudice of nineteenth-century criticism which is to blame for insensitivity towards the *artistic intention* which can only emanate from an individual and conscious mind – an insensitivity which the late Bédier brought out into the open in his research into the premeditated unity of the *Chanson de Roland*, a work his predecessors had treated as a fortuitous assembly of weakly integrated 'cantilenas'. Similarly, in the case of the *Lettres portugaises* evolutionary theory has us suppose a lost set of originals brought together by chance in an alleged translation – without explaining how a work of great beauty and of incomparable artistic unity could have been produced by such unintentional processes.

Now I shall have to demonstrate that unity. And first of all I shall formulate the sense of the work by saying that the five letters mark the five stages in the course of an internal evolution of a passionate love (*amour-passion* in Stendhal's phrase) abandoned to itself, left almost without nourishment by the object of the passion, dying so to speak from sentimental malnutrition. The five letters are like five condensed acts of a drama respecting the classical unities, with little variation in the situation, without external events determining the internal movement, consisting entirely of interior monologue or (since all monologues are in theory dialogues) of conversations with the image of the inconstant lover; the conversations are always on the same subject, re-elaborating much the same intellectual material in a bitter dialectic which puts now one, now another aspect in the foreground but always comes back on itself in a fateful circular movement, and ending in the exhaustion of the sentiment which gave birth to the ideas, the fruits of passion.

The gratuitous work of the intellect, its wheels turning but engaging with nothing, in an unhappy passion: that is in effect the slim but vigorously delimited subject of the *Lettres portugaises*. Who, then, can fail to see that this *qualitative* concentration (nothing but passion, external life having virtually no role at all) and this *quantitative* concentration (five acts, whereas the passion must have lasted years – five letters only, whereas an authentic 'Marianne' would have written maybe hundreds) – who can fail to see that this concentration is a triumph of the 'real' author's *classical* taste? (In fact the authentic letters of Mademoiselle de Lespinasse, to which Rainer Maria Rilke compared the *Lettres portugaises*, fill a volume of 536 pages which seemed 'long, too long' to the poet and translator. See Rilke, *Briefe*, p. 270.) It is for the reader to fill the silent spaces between the five letters, or acts, or cross-sections of the heroine's psychological evolution, just as the audience of a classical tragedy supplies the continuous psychological current which ties the five acts of *Bérénice* together.

I must express my absolute certainty that the order of the letters as they have come down to us is correct, and that their rearrangement by Maurice Paléologue, taken up by A. van Bever and by Rilke in their editions, and partly approved by F. C. Green, is wrong. Here is Paléologue's outline:

Letter 4 should come first: 'L'amant de la religieuse vient de quitter le Portugal; à peine en mer, une tempête l'a jeté sur la côte de l'Algarve. C'est par un de ses lieutenants, demeuré à Beja, que la nouvelle de cet accident arrive jusqu'à sa maîtresse. Comment, lui écrit-elle, n'a-t-il pris peine de l'informer directement?'

Letter 2 stays where it is: 'Elle est presque datée du mois de mai 1668, par l'allusion à "la paix de France" qui vient d'être conclue. Depuis six mois, pas un mot de souvenir n'est parvenu à la religieuse.'

Letter 1 becomes 3: 'Enfin, après une attente désespérée, une lettre arrive de France, et la pauvre créature se reprend à croire aux vagues promesses du retour de son amant.'

Letter 3 becomes 4: 'Mais les illusions dont l'infortunée se flattait encore se dissipent bientôt . . .'

Letter 5 stays where it is: 'elle nous fait assister à la crise suprême de cette âme en détresse. Une froide et banale épître, reçue de son amant, l'a pour toujours désabusée.'

This sketch shows that Paléologue tried to coordinate the few external events mentioned in the letters. (These raw chronological data given by the texts are: according to letter 4, one year has passed since the consummation of the love (p. 167), 'five or six months' since a 'fâcheuse confidence' (in writing?) (p. 166); in letter 2, a period of six months' silence on the part of the lover is mentioned (p. 151).) But how can one fail to recognise here a *proton pseudos*? Since only the internal drama is of any importance in the letters, external events are treated distantly, as corroborations of internal changes rather than as instigators of them. It is only to appease Paléologue's geographical conscience that letter 4, with its mention of an incident in the Algarve, has to precede the others where the Frenchman's return to France is indicated: in reality, the author needed a storm and a risk of death unmentioned by a tepid lover who does not associate his mistress with his own life – and the site is probably Cape St Vincent, the most south-easterly point of Europe, only because that is where storms are most dangerous, and not at all because the French officer leaving Beja by boat would go by the Algarve before reaching France. (In any case, why did he not take the land route across Spain? – Surely because the author needed a barely escaped shipwreck!) Moreover, when Marianne displays her hurt at having been less well informed than the lieutenant, her words 'pourquoi ne m'avez-vous point écrit' (p. 160) should not be taken literally since there is later a question of letters (in the plural) which she has received but which show 'une profonde indifférence', which are 'froides, pleines de redites, la moitié du papier n'est pas remplie', in which 'on sent que vous mourez d'envie de les avoir achevées' (p. 164); and in the inordinately long ending to this letter, Marianne writes without hesitation, 'Vous ne m'écrivez point, je n'ai pu m'empêcher de vous dire cela' (p. 168). Did Marianne get any letters, or did she not? Yes and no; she got what are called, but what she would not call, letters, that is to say letters reflecting her own sentiments, and for her it is as if she had received none at all. She is at liberty therefore to contradict herself by saying that she has and has not received any. Are we going to base a rearrangement of Marianne's five letters on the non-arrival of some letter on the Algarve incident?

Paléologue also pays too much heed to the arrival of a letter from the lover after six months' silence, and that is all that puts letter 1 (which becomes letter 3 in his system) after letter 2: but letter 1 also mentions one or several letters – 'votre dernière lettre le reduisit en un étrange état' (p. 148), 'ne remplissez pas vos lettres de choses inutiles, et ne m'écrivez plus de me souvenir de vous' (p. 149). One letter, several letters, a sentence of a letter, what does it matter?

One might well wonder why an officer with the irresponsible character Marianne attributes to him should put himself out to write after he has left (even after a temporary pause of six months). I think this detail is part of the author's clever construction. As we shall see later on, Marianne could only suffer the dreadful shock of the reality she had abandoned on the departure of her lover by comparing her own letters vibrating with passion with the drily indifferent and polite reaction they produce in the man they are addressed to. The officer's earlier letters, mere signs of courtesy without emotional warmth, were at least not *direct* reactions to the nun's letters: they serve only to establish the continuity of the correspondence and to prepare the final disillusionment. Moreover it is in the character of a polite and amiable French officer to show his gratitude to Marianne by writing courteous letters to her.

Marianne is carried away by her turbulent passion and retains only a fleeting impression of the officer's letters: as leaves may lie for a moment on a horse-rider passing through a line of trees, and be blown off again at the next moment. Fundamentally, for Marianne 'letterlessness' is the basic situation; it is not changed to any great extent by the arrival of letters. Even her three-hour faint after reading one of them becomes in retrospect one of her past 'moments agréables' which now serve only 'à tyranniser [son] cœur' – and she takes pride in feeling that she is 'dying of love'. What she wants in the first place is a *Liebestod* (death from love); the letter she received by chance is only its pretext. In letter 3 Marianne does indeed write: 'j'espérais que vous m'écririez de tous les endroits où vous passeriez et que vos lettres seraient fort longues; que vous soutiendriez ma passion' (p. 155), but these words follow the passionate opening sentence, 'Qu'est-ce que je deviendrai, et qu'est-ce que vous voulez que je fasse?' (p. 155). The characteristic order of her thoughts is *first* existential doubt, *secondly* the detail of the absence of letters to corroborate it. And so in letters 1–4 the lover's letters are not in the foreground, and, since they would be incapable of initiating any internal development, they cannot be used to rearrange the order of the letters written by Marianne – whose attitude to the fairly unreal letters of her lover is not very different to her distance from the things and people around her, which are real only in so far as they are connected to her passion or monomania. Marianne is closed to the outside world; she is without reality beyond her passion:

> Je suis sans cesse persécutée avec un extrême désagrément par la haine et par le dégoût que j'ai pour toutes choses; ma famille, mes amis et ce couvent me sont insupportables; tout ce que je suis obligée de voir, et tout ce qu'il faut que je fasse de toute nécessité, m'est odieux; je suis si jalouse de ma passion, qu'il me semble que toutes mes actions, et tous mes devoirs vous regardent. (4, p. 163)

Even her mother has no reality ('je ne sais ce que je lui ai répondu: il me semble que je lui ai tout avoué' (p. 163)); the nuns are a little less unreal, but only in so far as they identify with her passion. Since the only reality in letters 1–4 is that of the lover, it is he who is called upon to reveal the true reality of himself: only in letter 5 does an outside event, viz. the arrival of further letters from the lover, play a decisive role. In 5, Marianne decides with difficulty to send him back his letters and the souvenirs he left, because reading his 'impertinentes protestations d'amitié' and his 'civilités ridicules' (pp. 170–1) that are direct reactions to Marianne's letters 1–4 (*qu'il a donc reçues et lues*) has given her the courage to break off her relationship with him. She will keep only the last two letters, of especial banality, because rereading them will make permanent separation easier for her. The author took pains to indicate that, whilst the missives of the inconstant lover mentioned in 1–4 are quite unreal for a despairing and abandoned human being, the lover's direct reaction to her own letters 1–4 is of capital importance. In letters 1–4 Marianne's imagination turns in a void, but in 5 she has discovered reality, shattering reality: the lover's personality emerges entire, unmasked and dethroned, as a nullity.

But the main argument against Paléologue's reordering is that letter 1 must be left in its place for psychological and artistic reasons. First, the name *Marianne*, of great importance to the reader who must fix his attention on a well-defined heroine, figures in 1 (cleverly slipped into the discourse of Fate), but not in 4. Secondly, it is only at the beginning of 1 that Marianne addresses the lover as *tu* and calls him 'mon amour'; she changes in the same letter (at the point where she is thinking of her lover's voluntary 'distancing' of himself) to the *vous* form, which is kept for the rest of the correspondence. It is this abrupt opening, 'Considère, mon amour . . .', plunging us *medias in res*, which produces an extraordinarily poignant impression upon the reader. It is as if the initial *tu* linked the first letter, written (so it might seem) the day after the lover's departure, to the intimacy of physical presence enjoyed by the couple before the fatal departure, whilst the *vous* is appropriate to the painful ceremoniousness of 'distance'. Subsequently, Marianne does not alternate *tu* and *vous* in a single passage, as do heroines of classical tragedy like Roxane and Hermione (⟶ 95–6): directly 'spoken' passion is no longer given to her – we hear but a distant echo of it in letter 1.

Another point: only in 1 do we find *précieux* language (metaphors followed through to the end), considered at that period to be proper in love-letters, with its underlying tone of banter and even good humour, before the tragic tone becomes the only one to be heard:

> . . . j'envoie mille fois mes soupirs vers vous, *ils vous cherchent* en tous lieux, et *ils ne me rapportent* pour toute récompense . . . (p. 147)

> Votre dernière lettre (le) reduisit [mon cœur] en un étrange état: il eut des mouvements si sensibles qu'*il fit*, ce semble, *des efforts pour se séparer de moi et pour aller vous trouver* . . . (p. 148)

> . . . je ne puis quitter ce papier, il tombera dans vos mains, *je voudrais avoir le même bonheur* [= 'de tomber dans vos bras'] . . . (p. 150)

A further detail: in 1, there is a three-hour faint and various physical indispositions; in 2 Marianne is a little better at least physically, since she is 'busy' acting as door-keeper; in 3, she speaks of her efforts to recover from her pains, and of 'la crainte de ruiner entièrement le reste de [sa] santé par tant de veilles et tant d'inquiétudes' – there is no question now at least of acute physical illness. Finally, a detail of the greatest importance: only in 1 does the heroine imagine herself *united* with her lover in a common fate and in common feelings. He is presented as equally unhappy and equally in love – his passion caused him 'un mortel désespoir', Fate 'ne saurait séparer *nos cœurs*' (p. 150). Only here does Marianne ask for news of 'l'état de son cœur'; later on she will know only too well what to think of it! In 1, she can still appreciate the joy of writing to him, and of being 'déchirée par la douleur'; dying of love is still a pleasure. Tragic notes are already present, but they are not pronounced yet by Marianne herself: these anxious apprehensions are whispered by Fate, whom she invokes and makes to speak in a prosopopoeia which is also unique to letter 1:

> Cesse, cesse, Marianne infortunée, de te consumer vainement, et de chercher un amant que tu ne verras jamais; qui a passé les mers pour te fuir, qui est en France *au milieu des plaisirs*, qui ne pense *un seul moment* à tes douleurs, et qui te *dispense* de tous ces transports, desquels il ne te sait aucun gré. (p. 148)

Marianne seems here still to be protecting herself against sentiments which are supposed to be not her own: 'Mais, non, je ne puis me résoudre à juger si injurieusement de vous' (p. 148).

This whole passage is obviously very close to high tragedy. The reduplication of *cesse*, the introduction of the speaking subject in the third person, the five relative clauses leading up to a climax – everything is stylised and literary. See my examples from Racine: reduplications ⟶ 71–2; third person⟶ 17–20; relative clauses⟶ 90–1.

Quite obviously, letter 1, with its relative optimism, must open the correspondence. Suffering is still accepted as a good emanating from the loved one: as is shown by this paradoxical exclamation of a heart allowing itself the delights of torture, in the troubadour manner: 'Adieu, aimez-moi toujours; et *faites-moi souffrir encore plus de maux*' (p. 150).

Proceeding now to the analysis of Marianne's feelings in the subsequent letters, we note that in 2 tender feelings have already given way to bitterness, as one of the very first sentences indicates:

> . . . Je ne puis m'empêcher de vous dire, bien moins vivement que je ne le sens, que vous ne devriez pas me maltraiter comme vous faites, par un oubli qui me met au désespoir, *et qui est même honteux pour vous* . . . (p. 151)

Adverbial *même* marks Marianne's decision *en ce moment* to pronounce a word she would have rejected immediately afterwards. The reproaches are more clearly formulated: the lover should have had 'un procédé de meilleure foi'; he has an annoying tendency to 'betray' her; he only wanted from her 'quelques plaisirs', and she imagines him enjoying 'des plaisirs que vous donnent vos maîtresses de France', whilst in letter 1 she saw him only 'au milieu des plaisirs' of France. 'Je n'envie point votre indifférence, et vous me faites pitié'; she wishes to 'pardon all his faults'. In 1, reproaches insinuated themselves into the reverie; in 2, it is rather that reverie insinuates itself into the reproaches, and (a very subtle observation by the author) the lengthening separation brings back erotic memories with increasing insistence: 'je regarde sans cesse votre portrait', 'je ne vous verrai jamais en ma chambre avec toute l'ardeur, et tout l'emportement que vous me faisiez voir', 'je suis bien aise que vous m'ayez *séduite*' (p. 153) – the word itself! Consequently the affirmation of love in the midst of pain is more explicit and more desperate: 'J'aime mieux souffrir encore davantage que vous oublier'; 'je ne mets plus mon honneur et ma religion qu'à vous aimer éperdument toute ma vie, puisque j'ai commencé à vous aimer' (p. 153); 'mon amour ne dépend plus de la manière dont vous me traiterez', a sublime phrase which touched Rilke deeply. Passion detaches itself from its object and becomes 'autarchic'. It borders on paroxysm and loss of consciousness: 'Je suis au désespoir, votre pauvre Marianne n'en peut plus, elle s'évanouit en finissant cette lettre . . .' (p. 154). Fainting is not reported as in 1: it takes place as it were before the eyes of the lover (and before ours) whose pity she asks for ('Adieu, adieu, ayez pitié de moi'). This is the last time she will bring her *name* into a letter – as if to suggest to her lover the feelings which he *should* hold for his beloved.

Let us now contrast the end of letter 2 with the ending of 3 so as to grasp the development that takes place between them: 'Adieu, ma passion augmente à tout moment. Ah! que j'ai de choses à vous dire!' (p. 159). Marianne now refuses the lover's 'pity' and realises the futility of her 'over-long' letters. It is she alone who has so much to say; her self-feeding passion is making progress. Letter 3 is the apogee of passion living off itself: 'j'aime bien mieux être malheureuse en vous aimant, que de ne vous avoir jamais vu' (p. 158); 'je vous remercie dans le fond de mon cœur du désespoir que vous me causez' (p. 159). However, Marianne feels herself superior to her lover (because she 'loves violently' whilst he only allows himself to be loved) but alone: 'Hélas! que je suis à plaindre . . . d'être toute seule malheureuse: cette pensée me tue . . .' (p. 155). To get out of her isolation, Marianne must either wish her lover not to share her misery, or envy 'tout ce qui vous donne de la joie, et qui touche votre cœur et votre goût en France' (p. 157), or imagine gratuitous sacrifices for her unfaithful lover: 'je vis, infidèle [!] que je suis, et je fais autant de choses pour conserver ma vie que pour la perdre' (p. 157). It is now that suicide first appears as an idea (it will last until the end of the correspondence) as a means to make an impression upon the truly unfaithful one; it would thus be a 'demonstration' suicide: 'Adieu! promettez-moi de me regretter tendrement si je meurs de douleur' (p. 158). But it is also a means of making certain that her feelings are in no way literary. 'Ah! j'en meurs de honte: mon désespoir n'est donc que dans mes lettres?' (p. 157) is her first doubt and already a critique of letter-writing as a substitute for real life: Marianne feels she is alive *through* her letters – has she gained a second, literary, existence which dispenses her from living for her love? Suicide would decide that question.

Letter 4 is the longest, and it serves to establish more clearly in Marianne's eyes the gratuitousness of her one-sided correspondence:

'j'écris *plus pour moi* que pour vous: je ne cherche qu'à me soulager' (p. 168). This painful realisation will lead her to recognise later in letter 5 that her passion is independent of the loved one. And the exceptional length of letter 4, which many times comes to an ending but carries on again nonetheless, does indeed portray psychological 'perseveration' in an activity that has become valued in and for itself, irrespective of the person to whom it was originally directed: 'la longueur de ma lettre vous fera peur, vous ne la lirez point' (p. 168). Marianne writes for the sake of writing and she prolongs her letter even when her feelings tell her she should long since have ended it: 'Il y a longtemps qu'un officier attend votre lettre . . . elle est trop extravagante, il faut la finir. Hélas! il n'est pas en mon pouvoir de m'y résoudre . . .' (p. 167); 'L'officier qui doit vous porter cette lettre me mande pour la quatrième fois qu'il veut partir' (p. 167); 'je vais recommencer, et l'officier partira: qu'importe . . .' (p. 168). Marianne realises that she is no longer writing *to* anyone, she is happy just to write, to write (to) herself. At the same time the bond that held Marianne to her lover is loosened: she no longer demands forlornly to be loved ('je n'ose plus vous prier de m'aimer', p. 168) though she abandons herself all the more blindly and wildly to her passion and grows fiercer in her reproaches: her lover, she says, could have found a more beautiful mistress in Portugal, 'avec laquelle vous eussiez eu autant de plaisirs, puisque *vous n'en cherchiez que des grossiers*' (p. 162). Note also the remark – a brilliant touch on the author's part – about the French officer hurrying Marianne to finish her letter: 'il abandonne sans doute quelque malheureuse en ce pays' (p. 167). The epigram falls with all its weight on the lover who is the cause of this kind of bitter generalisation. In this fourth letter also, Marianne is more able to recall to mind the beginnings of her love without hope, as the landscape of Mértola seen from the balcony reminds her of the lover's first appearance, and her first feelings of love; and she can conceive more fully her own capacity for sacrifice, as she asks now for the portrait and some of the letters of the French lady her lover no doubt now loves; like some new Griselda, she promises that she would have 'assez de soumission pour servir celle que vous aimez' (p. 166). Nonetheless one can feel, in letter 4, that the climate has changed: the critical spirit has come further forward, even if psychological 'perseveration' along inveterate lines of behaviour pushes the letter-writer to even greater extremities.

Letter 5 is the letter of farewell, though without the word *adieu* actually occurring, as it would be too tender for the occasion. Marianne loves no more and wishes her lover to know it. She has decided, though she continues to struggle against her decision, to return his souvenirs and letters to the inconstant lover whom she judges henceforth with complete coldness after his last banal letter: 'vous m'avez enfin persuadée que vous ne m'aimiez plus, et qu'ainsi je ne dois plus vous aimer' (p. 169); 'Sachez que je m'aperçois que vous êtes indigne de tous mes sentiments et que je connais toutes vos méchantes qualités' (p. 171); 'Il faut avouer que je suis obligée à vous haïr mortellement . . . si quelque hasard vous ramenait en ce pays, je vous déclare que je vous livrerais à la vengeance de mes parents' (p. 175). But the vindictive tone soon gives way to one of lassitude: 'je n'ai plus, hélas! la passion qui m'empêchait d'en connaître l'énormité [des crimes]' (p. 175). In her new lucidity of mind, she realises that fact which destroys love, 'que vous m'étiez moins cher que ma passion. (p. 170) – she now knows the egotistical side of her own feelings, whereas before she had been aware only of her lover's egoism. This analysis of a passion for another which turns out to be a passion 'for itself', without reciprocity, frees Marianne from the 'movement out from the self – movement towards him' and leaves her alone with herself. She can now see herself, for a moment, as the mistress of someone other than her lover, even see herself in principle as the ideal mistress (a nun living outside society is more likely to remain faithful, p. 173) and an objective and loving glance, unusual in a monomaniac, is cast even upon her own formerly rejected family: 'ma famille, qui m'est fort chère, *depuis que je ne vous aime plus*' (p. 174) – another brilliant authorial touch. The world that she had excluded from her passionate existence makes its return. Some contradictions remain in a being that is returning slowly to new life: after declaring at the opening of 5 that this is her last letter, Marianne nonetheless promises her lover another one which is supposed to show him her 'nouvel état paisible'. She is still rather forced and rigid in her renunciation: 'je connais bien que je suis encore un peu trop occupée de mes reproches et de votre infidélité' – *un peu trop* is really an understatement, and a two-member expression of the type 'mes reproches et votre infidélité' is still too reminiscent of a permanent model in the *Lettres portugaises*, the model of '*vous et moi* conjugués dans une étreinte désespérée' (⟶ 279). Even the very last sentence of 5 still contains a trace of stifled affection: 'il faut vous quitter et ne plus penser à vous; je crois *même* que je ne vous écrirai plus . . .' (p. 177). The *même*, which presents the decision not to write as a matter of this moment, is heart-rending. It suggests that despite the final decision contrary impulses are at work within Marianne. However, despite a last-minute threat of suicide, which serves only to emphasise the lover's despicable indifference, we can see the final cure emerging and life returning to its normal course.

As my friend Georges Poulet reminds me, Madame de la Fayette's 'C'est assez que de vivre'* is not too distant from the *smorzando* of the

* The sentence 'C'est assez que d'*être*' is quoted by Georges Poulet in his *Etudes sur le temps humain* (1949), Paris, Plon, 1950, p. 132, and attributed to Madame de la Fayette in the volume *Segraisiana* (1723), I.86.

last letter. The Italian scholar Mario Pelaez has a quite different impression (in his article *Alcoforado* in the *Enciclopedia italiana*): for him, Marianne's love remains full and admiring to the last, and letter 5, he believes, only reveals this love to be 'invincible.' Of course I don't deny the sentimental contradictions and fluctuations that occur in Marianne up to the end, but I think that one can nonetheless make out behind the zigzags a clear linear development of growing disaffection.

The 'epistolary drama' of the *Lettres portugaises* thus ends on a note of exhaustion. Such a closure would have been impossible in a real stage tragedy which would have contained in its last scene a dimly glimpsed grave of the victims of Fate. What dies at the end of the letters is not a human life, but a passion that filled a life.

I hope this sketch has shown satisfactorily that the five letters form a cleverly composed artistic whole in which everything holds together and of which all the parts relate to each other. Almost all the motifs that are touched upon in one letter recur in the other letters, with the particular colouring specific to that letter. The remembrance of the happiness of the onset of amorous feelings or of the erotic pleasures that followed, the disillusionment caused by the lover's departure, the torments of absence; the bitter judgments of the lover's character, the imagining of more fortunate rivals, relations with relatives and the other nuns in the convent, and the fact of writing itself – all these elements recur in almost every letter, and are connected either by the principle of parallelism or by contrast, in such a way that the psychological development of the heroine can be glimpsed through the particular mix of the same motifs at each of the five stages represented by the five letters. The waters of the heart do not change, but their flow alters.

In the seventeenth century, at a time when La Fontaine was elaborating quite admirable miniature forms of literary art in which internal structure and the texture of leitmotivs are all-important, critics were quite unable to appreciate the subtle small-scale art of the *Lettres portugaises*:

> Et en vérité n'est-ce pas une grande misère quand il faut lire un livre pour si peu de choses? D'ailleurs il n'y a pas même de style; la plupart des périodes y sont sans mesure, et ce que j'y trouve de plus ennuyeux, ce sont de continuelles répétitions de ce qui méritait à peine d'être dit une seule fois. (Gabriel Guéret, quoted in Larat, p. 627)

The non-literary question of the 'authenticity' of the letters was already the dominant one and simply removed any possibility of aesthetic appreciation. Even Paléologue, in the twentieth century, objected to the numerous 'repetitions' and *redites*, and found the letters 'monotonous': these critics really ought to have had more musical sensitivity, to hear the delicately varied orchestral ornamentations over the great *arioso continuo* theme of the violin – Marianne's passion. And surely the monotony of the psychology of love is harder to bear in a marathon work like Rousseau's *La Nouvelle Héloïse* than in our elegant worklet which observes the classical unities to the point of showing one single actor and one single sphere of action, and is devoted to a profound investigation of one of the great subjects which have always fascinated men and women.

Clearly, the stages are more obviously marked in the 'outer' letters 1 and 5 (Marianne imagines her love continuing – Marianne turns away from her love) than in 2–4, where the fluctuations of feeling are more intricate. Nonetheless we can recognise the apogee in letter 3 and in 4 the decline of the paroxysm of love. Letters 1 and 5 are also radically opposite to each other in their style: relatively speaking, 1 is *précieux*, 5 is realist. The author himself underlines the markedly different quality of the style of 5: 'j'espère vous faire connaître par *la différence des termes, et de la manière de cette lettre*, que vous m'aviez enfin persuadée que vous ne m'aimiez plus . . .' (p. 169). How have critics failed up to now to recognise in this remark attributed to the heroine the masterful signature of an author conscious of his style?

To digress for a moment, I must say that the comte de Guilleragues seems to me to have a serious claim to the authorship of the *Lettres portugaises*, to judge by his letter to Racine (1684) published by Lanson.* The following points should be noted:

1. Guilleragues praises the tragedies of Racine thus:

> La vraisemblance y est merveilleusement observée, avec une profonde connaissance du cœur dans les différentes crises des passions.

The same could be said of the author of *Les Lettres portugaises*.

2. Whilst the ancients imaginatively exaggerated their descriptions of concrete places in Greece, Racine, according to Guilleragues, was not intent on 'saying what is', but 'followed, sustained and almost always enriched' the great ideas of the ancient Greeks who left 'de grands exemples de vertu comme de style'. Basically, he says, it does not matter what country heroes come from: a poetic consecration could be given to the town of Senlis or the rue de la Huchette in Paris – so why not the convent of Beja, which the author of the *Lettres portugaises* treats as cavalierly as Racine treats the real Greece?

3. There is a parallel between the compliment given to Louis XIV in letter 4 and this sentence in Guilleragues's letter to Racine:

> Vous savez cent fois mieux que moi tout ce qu'ont écrit les poètes et les historiens, plus abandonnés à leurs charmantes imaginations qu'exacts observateurs de la vérité, qui vous fournit une matière abondante, mais qui, pouvant

* Guilleragues's works and correspondence have now been published in full: see under Guilleragues in the List of references, below.

aussi vous accabler et paraître peu croyable à la posterité, me laisse à douter si vous et monsieur Despréaux, historiens du plus grand roi du monde, êtes ou plus heureux, ou plus malheureux que les anciens. (Guilleragues, *Correspondance*, II.995–6)

The flattery of Louis XIV, incidentally, only acquires its full meaning in the *Lettres portugaises* if it was deliberately put by a French author into the mouth of a foreigner as 'objective' evidence of the great monarch's power and chivalry – if Marianne Alcoforado were really the author, the compliment would lose much of its flavour if not all of its point.

It is interesting, also, to consider the possible parallels between the *Lettres portugaises* and the letters of Abelard and Heloise. Schmeidler has suggested that the latter were in fact composed by Abelard alone, though perhaps drawing on authentic letters written by both. In this interpretation, Abelard invented a basic motif of which the function was to justify the start and the continuation of the correspondence: viz. Heloise cloistered in the convent of Paraclete, separated and without news of the lover to whom she still belongs in body and soul, communicates with him by the only means available, that is *by letter*, and is led by Abelard's replies to true devotion and to divine love surpassing all earthly loves.

I must say I am not convinced by Gilson when he argues for the authenticity of Heloise's letters. The unity of style in the letters of the two correspondents, the ideas and quotations common to the two sets of letters seem to me to go far beyond what might be explicable by some osmosis between master and disciple. The role which Gilson attributes to Heloise – taking the veil and living forty years of her life in a convent as an act of sheer obedience to Abelard without any real adherence to the ideal of christian charity (which Gilson calls 'le mystère d'Héloïse' and which seems to me an attitude of promethean defiance of Jesus) – is in my view *humanly* impossible. However, the attitude expressed in Heloise's acts of submission to her master and lover without any explicit statement of her attachment to monastic life is explicable in a *literary* construction.*

Against Gilson, Friedrich Heer sees, as Schmeidler does, the correspondence of the two lovers as a monument constructed by Abelard alone to the spirit of individualism, as a *renaissance* of this reformer of the monasteries. Abelard based his institutional reform on the belief that women were weaker than men and thus more open to divine grace (Eve – Mary – Mary Magdalen). Thus Heloise is shown in the correspondence, according to Heer, developing from the wife of Abelard to the wife of Christ. The letters attributed to her would thus be no more of

* Spitzer's suspicion of the authenticity of the letters of Abelard and Heloise is shared by Charlotte Charrier (1933) and by John F. Benton (see Radice, p. 48), but by few other medieval scholars. Radice's introduction gives a good account of the issues involved.

a 'falsification' than the pious legends of the saints or the apocryphal acts of donation of the medieval monasteries.

I also believe – and I don't think this has been said before – that letters 2 and 4 of the twelfth-century correspondence of Abelard and Heloise played an important part in the composition of the *Lettres portugaises*. In Bussy-Rabutin's French translation of the Latin originals* we find in letter 2: 'nous vous conjurons de nous apprendre, par de fréquentes lettres, quels sont les *naufrages* au milieu desquels vous êtes encore ballottée'; and 'vous avez écrit à votre ami une longue lettre où, pour le consoler de ses adversités, vous lui racontez les vôtres. Dans ce récit trop fidèle, la consolation que vous lui offrez a mis le comble à notre désolation, et lorsque vous espériez fermer ses blessures, vous en avez ouvert de nouvelles dans notre douleur.' [The corresponding passages in the English translation are: 'we beseech you to write as often as you think fit to us who are his handmaids and yours, with news of the perils in which you are still storm-tossed', Radice, p. 110; and 'You wrote your friend a long letter of consolation, prompted no doubt by his misfortunes but really telling of your own. The detailed account you gave of these may have been intended for his comfort, but it also greatly increased our own feeling of desolation; in your desire to heal his wounds, you have dealt us fresh wounds of grief as well as reopening the old', Radice, pp. 110–11.] These passages must have inspired the opening of letter 4 of the *Portugaises* where Marianne complains that her lover's lieutenant is better informed than she is of the storm off the Algarve. Furthermore, the idea of the loving couple violating the sanctity of the convent of Beja by their lovers' tryst obviously comes from the episode related by Abelard in his fifth letter (letter 4 in Radice) on his visit to the convent of Argenteuil and the scene of 'uncontrollable desire' which took place in 'a corner of the refectory, since we had nowhere else to go' (Radice, p. 146). This 'literary' source would explain the presence of an implausible motif in the *Portugaises* which so shocked its contemporary critics. Finally, the relative length of letters 4 and 5 of the *Portugaises* seems modelled on the length of the last two letters (6 and 7 (Radice)) of the correspondence of Abelard and Heloise, though their tone is admittedly quite different.

If Marianne is then a Heloise *rediviva*, it in no way diminishes our admiration for the originality of the French author of the *Lettres*

* As E. M. Dronke pointed out, Bussy-Rabutin's translation did not appear until 1687, eighteen years after the *Lettres portugaises*. I have consequently omitted a long passage of Spitzer's here, where individual sentences of the two works are compared. However, there were other seventeenth-century translations of Abelard and Heloise, and the Latin text had appeared in two separate editions in 1616. I have thus retained and recast Spitzer's comparison of motifs which are not invalidated by chronology and remain suggestive. On this complicated question, see Deloffre and Rougeot on p. 106 of Guilleragues, *Portugaises*.

portugaises. In a manner characteristic of the classical period, he has pruned back the tangle of his twelfth-century predecessor (the 'novel of the self in letters' in Schmeidler's description of the supposed correspondence of Abelard and Heloise). The epistolary 'novel' composed by Abelard clearly had the didactic aim (which the modern reader finds hard to assimilate) of showing the design of providence in the story of his love: Heloise the bitter sinner, the woman who had been pure carnal passion, who had preferred to be Abelard's mistress, even his prostitute, rather than his wife, who even when she was a nun was ready to sin, who consented to make love in the refectory and could not stop herself from carnal imaginings even during mass, is led gradually by the wise advice of Abelard, a man who has accepted his fate, to true monastic purity by the fulfilment of her duty, namely the organisation of an ideal convent; and Abelard spends the two long final letters defining this objective task. Thus Abelard has subordinated Heloise's development to his own. In his first letter addressed to a friend he had given a long *historia mearum calamitatum* ('story of my disasters') – and it is this letter which falls into the hands of Heloise and thus instigates the correspondence. In this letter he keeps to his initial plan and justifies his adversities by the design of providence. The display of amorous sensuality (of 'fornication'), which modern readers find a little shocking, in his own youth and that of Heloise, is made necessary by the Augustinian model of public confession. The lowliness of the lovers had to be shown in the strongest colours in order to show also their ascension and purification by the transcendent task. The more Abelard blackens the past, the more he glorifies the triumph of religion. Where the modern reader sees only the author's personal vanity (eager to tell how much he had been loved!) the medieval writer wanted to castigate the *vanitas vanitatum* of all earthly love. Where modern readers are embarrassed by the sacrifice of psychological verisimilitude to a didactic intention, the medieval author was concerned only with achieving his pious intention, the edification of his audience.

The French author of the *Lettres portugaises* thus eliminated the entire spiritual and didactic superstructure of the medieval text and restricted himself to the confessions of the forsaken woman, of which the psychological truth was beyond doubt. He was also able to show the decay of passion *coming from within the passion itself*, not commanded from on high, that is to say the 'pure' drama of passionate love in its underlying unity.

There are of course many modern cases of pseudo-correspondence in literary works. Kressmann Taylor's *Address Unknown* (1939) is a short story which brilliantly exploits the 'functional' value of letter-writing: an American Jew writes to his former German partner, now a Nazi, first to maintain their friendship across the Atlantic, then as a desperate means of reassuring himself of his former friend's true character and of the fate of his sister, and finally as a means of vengeance to compromise the German traitor with his Nazi masters. The artistic idea of the tale crystallised in the author's mind after reading some authentic letters, according to the publisher's introduction.

One could also compare the *Lettres portugaises*, at least in respect of their artistic impact, with the series of love-letters in Colette's short story *Mitsou, ou comment l'esprit vient aux filles*. Mitsou, a star of the Parisian music-hall, writes seven letters to her 'Lieutenant Bleu' at the front during the First World War, and he writes seven back. Six from each side follow their first meeting ('love at first sight' for Mitsou) and the last ones follow a second meeting in which the lovers discover carnal love. Since the character of Mitsou is the focus of the reader's interest, the young woman's letters capture the reader's attention more: she also has the last word, as the story ends with her last letter. Letter-writing has here the same functional role as in the *Lettres portugaises*, since it is the only means of communication between the front line and the rear; we find the same reflections on the life-defining value of the letters: 'je voudrais vous faire bien comprendre que c'est un événement dans ma vie que de commencer à écrire des lettres', Colette, p. 162; 'tout à l'heure je croyais que je ne pouvais plus vous écrire. Et maintenant il me semble que cette lettre-ci ne suffira jamais' (p. 172). The letters here too are a 'means of spiritual perfection' for the 'girl' who acquires some 'wit': 'Au bout de quatre mois [de correspondance], est-ce que tu n'étais pas ému de me voir grandir?' (p. 211). The development of a 'girl' into a life companion is accomplished in the course of these letters which begin with a cold and stilted 'Monsieur', go on to a bantering 'mon lieutenant bleu', and end with 'mon chéri' and 'mon amour'. Of course the general tone and the direction of the internal movement of Colette's letter-novel is different from those of the *Lettres portugaises*. The tone is the one dictated by the *concrete* milieu in which the letter-writer lives (the music-hall milieu) and the general development is *optimistic*: love at first sight becomes love for life and gives new strength to the one who loves.

The genius of the author of the *Lettres portugaises*, on the other hand, was to invent as the basis of his epistolary novel (or rather drama) an imaginary correspondence, solicited by no one, and consequently having a functional value. In fact, the five letters do not *only* reflect faithfully the state of the writer's soul at the moment of writing, as became the custom in the many subsequent epistolary novels, but are themselves the *sole means* by which a love destined to decay can continue and then die. The letters even accelerate this development. Marianne had felt obliged to give the absent lover 'un compte exact de ses . . . mouvements [d'âme]' (letter 5, p. 177), and in the end she rebels against this self-imposed routine. Choderlos de Laclos's novel *Les Liaisons dangereuses* is written in the form of letters because the author wanted to write it that way, but in the *Portugaises* writing letters (*Briefe die ihn nicht erreichen*, 'Letters that do not reach him', as in the title of the twentieth-century epistolary novel by Baroness von Heyking) is the only activity left to the lonely soul whose love wanes through and by the fact of the letters, their words drowned by an essentially incommunicable emotion. Thus the meaning of the letters changes from one letter to the next and Marianne specifies this meaning at each point:

1. Je ne puis quitter ce papier, il tombera entre vos mains, je voudrais avoir le même bonheur. (1, p. 150)

2. Il me semble que je fais le plus grand tort du monde aux sentiments de mon cœur, de tâcher de vous les faire connaître en les écrivant. (2, p. 151)

3. Je ne sais pourquoi je vous écris, je vois bien que vous aurez seulement pitié de moi . . . je vous écris ces lettres trop longues, je n'ai pas assez d'égard pour vous . . . (3, pp. 157, 158)

4. J'avais résolu de l'écrire [cette lettre] d'une manière à vous la faire recevoir sans dégoût: mais elle est trop extravagante, il faut la finir. Hélas! il n'est pas en mon pouvoir de m'y résoudre, il me semble que je vous parle, quand je vous écris, et que vous m'êtes un peu plus présent. (4, p. 167)

J'écris plus pour moi que pour vous . . . (4, p. 168)

5. Je vous écris pour la dernière fois . . . Suis-je obligée de vous rendre un compte exact de tous mes mouvements? (5, pp. 169, 177)

The letter as such is to begin with a substitute for physical contact, then a manifestation overwhelmed by feeling and embarrassing to the addressee, a desperate means to make the absent being present, then grasped by the writer herself as a form of self-consolation – and finally it becomes useless because it ceases to be supported by feeling. At the end of letter 5 Marianne revolts against her self-imposed routine of reporting her feelings. In 4, she is aware of the solipsistic character of her passion which is, she declares in 5, more precious to her than the lover's person. (She does however 'perseverate' at the end of 4 in frenetic farewells, as if she did not yet have the strength to make a decisive break with him; our emotional attitudes do indeed often lag behind our intellectual development.) By using the word *extravagantes* of her own letters Marianne is looking at herself as a critic and from a normative standpoint. It is also in 3 that she realises the danger she is in of 'writing literature': 'mon désespoir n'est donc que dans mes lettres?' (p. 157). If the idea of suicide has occurred to her, could it not be because she has discovered a will to live (more explicit in 5)? The letters, which by their nature necessitate the subordination of passion to intellect, have perhaps helped to volatilise the substance of sentiment – or has a crumbling sentiment perhaps sought the words that will surely kill it?

Given the basic psychological problem of the gradual decline of a love unfed by its object, given also the use of letter-writing as the functional element permitting the problem to be converted into a work of art, the author had to find a setting appropriate to a woman pouring forth her feeling in 'pointless' letters. The optimal setting was obviously that of a convent, and a convent moreover in a southern country more austere in its catholicism than France, the land of 'pleasures'. (Note Marianne's exclamation at the end of 4 (p. 168), 'Que ne suis-je née en un autre pays?'.) Marianne could not have been anything other than a nun. The author does in fact let us glimpse his own reasons for choosing a monastic setting by putting in Marianne's mouth in letter 5 a rehearsal (in a feminine mode) of the medieval motif or *topos* of the superiority of the cleric over the layman as lover. [There are many studies of this recurrent topic of medieval debate; see Brinkmann, Walther.] Heloise is not the only instance of a medieval nun writing love-letters: the very first love-poetry in the German language, 'du bist mīn, ich bin dīn: des solt du gewis sīn'* (Sayce, p. 4), was written by a twelfth-century nun from Tegernsee who confessed in her Latin text, just like Marianne, 'a die qua te primum vidi cepi diligere te' ('from the day I first saw you I began to desire you', Brinkmann, p. 147). Medieval satire also presented nuns ruled exclusively by Cupid: 'Normas claustrenses postponit seva libido / Quas Venus atque suus natus regit ipse Cupido' ('Violent passion ignores the rules of the cloister; Venus and her own son Cupid rule them', quoted in Brinkmann, p. 7n).]

Obviously a nun in love is more able than any other woman to live for her feelings alone. The habits of internal life and constant self-examination permit Marianne to disentangle subtly the dialectic of passion. The outside world does not distract her from her love. Physical immobility is imposed by her style of life, and the monotony of everything around her allows her imagination to fly by contrast to dreams of escape and of life in France with her lover, to romantic aspirations reminiscent in letter 1 of the love-in-death of Iseut, in letter 5 of the medieval Nicolette who disguises herself as a minstrel to rejoin her lover (*Aucassin et Nicolette*), in letter 4 of Griselda as the servant of the woman who ousted her (*The Decameron*). Finally, the insurmountable obstacles in the way of a marriage between a Portuguese nun and a French officer stationed in Portugal, involved in a banal adventure legitimated so to speak by his profession, are cleverly exploited to underline the contrast between the emotional nullity of the lover who is 'aimable' and nothing more, and the 'majesty of human suffering'

* 'You are mine, I am yours, you can be sure of that.'

incarnated in Marianne. The author did not take much care to make the local colour of the cloister at all plausible. F. C. Green has already noticed that the city of Mértola cannot be seen from the balcony of the convent of Beja, especially as it is 54 kilometres distant; even more seriously implausible is the tolerance of love and amorous sensibility in the convent at a period when according to Marianne herself strict ecclesiastical laws were in force against sinning nuns. How, may we wonder, could the seducer have got as far as Marianne's room, almost every day over a period of at least six or seven months, with impunity? How could Marianne have been made 'doorkeeper' as if the task were a reward for her amorous escapades? She has the time to converse at length in her 'room' (the word for 'cell' is carefully avoided) with her lover's portrait which apparently hangs in the place of the crucifix; she talks freely of her love to the other nuns, who seem touched by what she tells them; one French officer talks to her for three hours about her lover, another waits for some time beside her whilst she finishes a letter. In letters 1–4 there is no trace of a serious conflict between religion and love as there is in e.g. the Goncourts' *Sœur Philomène* (1861). All we find in the *Portugaises* are weak and vague phrases, like 'je ne mets plus mon honneur, *et ma religion*, qu'à vous aimer' (letter 2, p. 153), 'quelques mouvements de dévotion' (3, p. 155), listed together with other factors which might help to heal the wounds of love but which overall are ineffective: 'je sens bien que mes remords ne sont pas véritables' (3, p. 157). In letter 5, however, Marianne awakes from her erotic hypnosis and writes without mincing her words:

> J'ai vécu longtemps dans un abandonnement et dans une idolâtrie qui me donne de l'horreur, et mon remords me persécute avec une rigueur insupportable, je sens vivement la honte des crimes que vous m'avez fait commettre, et je n'ai plus, hélas! la passion qui m'empêchait d'en connaître l'énormité. (p. 175)

Idolatrie, *remords*, *crime* – here at last is the theological vocabulary one might expect from a nun! And that is what Marianne means when she talks at the beginning of 5 of 'la différence des termes et de la manière de cette lettre'! The absence of religious reference from 1–4 could be intended to show how far all religious life has been ousted from Marianne's soul by her monomaniacal love – but one would still expect a real nun to make at least passing reference to prayer, to the sacrament and to services. We can surely see here the influence on our 'epistolary drama' of the principle, accepted in the seventeenth century, that the sacred should not be presented on the secular stage. Marianne is a woman in love who happens to be a nun – she is not a nun in love. The latter conflict is in itself unclassical and belongs to the age of Diderot. Thus Marianne speaks like the heroine of a novel or play: without giving a thought to leaving the convent (which is like a determining force not susceptible to reasoned argument) she can nonetheless imagine taking another lover to arouse the jealousy of the man who has betrayed her. This sovereignty over sentiment, at least in her self-expression, seems much more appropriate to a literary character of high comedy than to a humble sister doorkeeper: 'Je suis persuadée que je trouverais peut-être, en ce pays, un amant plus fidèle et mieux fait; mais, hélas! qui pourra me donner de l'amour? La passion d'un autre m'occuperait-elle?' (5, p. 172). The convent of Beja is thus an abstract or negative décor, realistic only in as much as it is needed to provide a stage setting, having no other function than to guarantee the optimal situation for the dreams and tears of a woman in love savouring her anguish.

When Marianne finally abandons her love and remains in the convent where she had indulged her amorous excess, she does not seek the succour of the christian religion. Despite the monastic environment, the problem of love is resolved on a strictly earthly level. Jesus does not take the place of the lover; no reparations seem to be owed to the divine lover who has been betrayed. The Princesse de Clèves, in Madame de la Fayette's novel, withdraws to an (entirely undescribed) 'house of religion' as an act of moral stoicism; in Marianne's case, the unity (or rather, continuity) of place constitutes an even more painful affirmation of stoicism: a life goes on though its mainspring is broken. The convent remains to the end a negative place, a place of abnegation: it is not envisaged as a convent in itself, just as earlier it had been the setting of a *crime passionnel* in a purely abstract way.

The nineteenth-century catholic Barbey d'Aurevilly was unable to accept the underlying psychological content of the *Lettres portugaises*, which he found shocking:

> On parle de passion sincère! Mais la passion d'une religieuse pour un homme, si elle est possible, doit être quelque chose de terrible, d'inouï, de tragique à faire pâlir Phèdre . . . Pensez-y donc! une religieuse! une épouse de Jésus-Christ! nourrie jusque-là du pain eucharistique, et tombée des hauteurs de la Pureté et de la Grâce dans les fanges de la passion humaine, et demandez-vous ce que doivent être l'amour et sa faute pour une pareille femme, sinon le plus grand des crimes, le plus affreux des adultères, l'infidélité à Dieu même, le sacrilège dans la trahison! (Barbey d'Aurevilly, pp. 46–7)

Since he can find no trace of moral doubt in the letters of the alleged nun, since there is nothing in them more than 'une femme qui pleure en se regardant pleurer, comme dans les romances', Barbey denies the historical authenticity of the texts:

> Non! Tout cela n'est pas vrai. Quelqu'un a menti! Nous ne savons pas le nom du menteur, mais qu'importe! . . . Nous avons nié la religieuse; un autre que nous a nié la femme, un autre qui se connaissait aux passions et à leur langage: 'Je

parierais que les lettres de la religieuse portugaise sont d'un homme!' écrivait Rousseau à d'Alembert.* (Barbey d'Aurevilly, pp. 49–50)

However, we do not follow Barbey's refusal to see in the *Lettres portugaises* anything other than 'absence radicale de talent, qui implique celle de l'âme'. ('Talent' and 'soul' are determined here by Barbey's *a priori* judgment as a catholic for whom Saint Theresa is the model both of writerly 'talent' and of 'soul'.) Nor do we accept his explanation of the work's popularity simply as the result of the anti-religious tendency of the seventeenth century: such an explanation would force us to minimise the value of seventeenth-century attitudes such as those of Madame de Sévigné and Saint-Simon, to whom we should also add Madame d'Aulnoy.

Another point that has not, I think, been explained before is that the internal development of Marianne, detached as she is from all external reality, is conditioned by the fundamental unreality of the image of the lover. We only see him through Marianne's eyes, and she describes him according to her internal needs, in scenes which are foregrounded by her memory, without any apparent consideration of the reader: but the various descriptions of the lovers' meetings are arranged, dosed and gradated by the author with consummate artistry so as to leave us only at the end of the work in full possession of the whole story of this love affair, rather as in those regressively structured stage plays where the last scene provides the key to the whole plot. Thus in letter 2 we learn the details of the meetings in Marianne's room through a nostalgic exclamation. 'Quoi! tous mes désirs seront donc inutiles, et je ne vous verrai jamais en ma chambre avec tout l'emportement que vous me faisiez voir?' (p. 152). Only in letters 4 and 5 do we learn of the circumstances of the start of the affair (in 4 its external circumstances, in 5 its psychological motivation) – because in the last two letters Marianne's memory, in a last-minute frenzy, seizes upon any detail which might rekindle the guttering flame. Now from all the pieces of information about the lover that are strewn through Marianne's letter one can hardly construct a picture of a living man. We have no illumination of his objective personality; Heloise (to whom Stendhal awarded the honour, alongside our Portuguese nun, of representing *amour-passion*) is very different in this respect, because she knows why she is in love: in fact, she loves the most brilliant man in the Europe of her day. Marianne only knows why she loves because she loves: she is in love with her own love. The French officer only provides a pretext for her passion: he is destined from first sight to be the loved one *en bloc*, Marianne's *homme fatal*, to be Man with respect to Marianne:

* The reference is to Rousseau, *Lettre*, p. 200n.

Vous me parûtes aimable, avant que vous m'eussiez dit que vous m'aimiez . . . (4, p. 161)

The epithet *aimable* has its etymological sense ('lovable') for Marianne, rather than its objective sense ('love-ly', 'agreeable'). He is the man who has, by choosing her, distinguished Marianne:

Il me sembla que *vous vouliez me plaire* . . . que *vous m'aviez remarquée* entre toutes celles qui étaient avec moi . . . vous étiez bien aise que je vous visse mieux . . . (4, p. 164)

Je n'avais jamais entendu les louanges que vous me donniez incessamment . . . (5, p. 176)

If Marianne admires the lover's horsemanship, though fearing for his safety, it is because she was 'secretly interested' in all his actions: 'je ne prenais pour moi tout ce que vous faisiez', she says with an unconsciously critical perception of her fatal *coup de foudre*. In 5, she is happy to hear him well spoken of ('tout le monde me parlait en votre faveur', p. 176) because that confirms the quality of 'lovableness' which she herself accords him. We never know what the officer *really* was like in himself. One can even wonder if some of Marianne's philippics are not intended to sketch, in a pale and fleeting light as it were, the objective image of a brilliant French officer, e.g. 'Quel sacrifice m'avez-vous fait? n'avez-vous pas cherché mille autre plaisirs? avez-vous renoncé au jeu et à la chasse? *n'êtes-vous pas parti le premier pour aller à l'armée? N'en êtes-vous pas revenu après tous les autres? Vous vous y êtes exposé* follement, quoique je vous eusse prié de vous ménager pour l'amour de moi' (p. 175). Marianne can turn some of the officer's qualities into insults: he is 'respected' in Portugal: why didn't he stay there with her? And do not his polite and anodyne replies to reproaches (the replies which precipitate the breaking-off of the affair) indicate a well-balanced, temperamentally agreeable and gentlemanly character, who cannot be impolite to a woman? He is a ladies' man: he had a relationship in France before meeting Marianne (who learnt of it by one of his 'fâcheuses confidences'), he will have others in France, Marianne foretells jealously. But what of it? Is it not natural that a young, turbulent, unmarried, agreeable officer of high birth should have affairs? Why should this perhaps calumnied lover not have the right to reply, like Gide's Robert replying to the attack of *L'Ecole des Femmes*? (Actually there were pendant-replies to the *Lettres portugaises* invented in the seventeenth century.) It is also very characteristic that Marianne never tells us her lover's name, though she presents herself under her name of Marianne; she does not wish herself to give him any reality beyond or outside of herself.

It is true, of course, that Marianne says in letter 2, 'je n'ai aucun plaisir qu'en nommant votre nom mille fois le jour', and in 4, 'Adieu, je n'ose vous donner mille noms de tendresse' (pp. 154, 168). Obviously the use of hypocoristic terms (pet names) would be proper only in comedy, and the negative stylistic trait of suggesting instead of naming names puts these letters in the tragic genre, which is equally indicated by the complete absence of humour. The classical separation of the genres is strictly maintained, and the atmosphere of the *Lettres portugaises* is the 'majestic sadness' of *Bérénice*. Note also the absence from our texts of any description of everyday life or even of the time of writing the letters themselves – was the sun setting, was the Angelus bell ringing when Marianne finished her letter? Only her soul speaks, and her memories are stylised as in high tragedy.

In the *Lettres portugaises* we are thus in the presence of a 'narcissistic' love, of that kind of 'psychic angina' or narrowing of attention which Ortega y Gasset found typical of the pathological side of love. The paleness and lack of picturesque description of the lover contrasts with Marianne's sharp vision of all that concerns her own sentimental life. It would probably not be wrong to attribute the ultimate fading of the passion to Marianne's lack of a precise mental picture of the person of her lover: the love had nothing to rely on outside itself, nothing from which to draw nourishment. The lover was already dead in Marianne when the correspondence began, and the passion had become autarchic already in the first letter. It was not the dull or infrequent replies of the lover that killed the passion but the exiguous image of the loved one. The five acts marked by the five letters really constitute a single last act – as in the tragedies of ancient Greece – of a tragedy that has been growing for a long time. In the case of Marianne, the tragedy began at the point the two lovers came together for the first time, and because of the imbalance between the two members of the pair: the lover was not objectively real! And that is perhaps what distinguishes human passionate love from love *tout court*: as the female of the spider *Galeodes kaspicus turkestanus* devours the male which aspires to its love, so passion destroys its own object. In passion of the *amabam amare* type ('in love with love') the partner exists only as the creation of the lover's solitary mind.

Marianne's love is, then, an example of Stendhalian love which consists of the 'crystallisation' of a passing experience, that is to say of endowing the object of love, from the very first meeting, with perfections that are not really present, with false perfections; and so the image adorned with beauties that do not belong to the original cannot last, and love dies. Ortega saw clearly that Stendhalian love of that kind is a 'false love', directed towards a false (or falsified) object and thus condemned to death: 'love dies because it was born of an error'. In the experience of Stendhal, 'a man who never loved nor ever was loved', the death of love is consubstantial with its birth; his theory of crystallisation derives from thinking of love from the point of view of its (necessary) ending. However, true love is based above all on a deep knowledge of the loved one and of his or her *true* qualities, and the greater the knowledge, the deeper and broader true love grows. It is in its most illustrious examples immortal, as in Dante's love for Beatrice: even if modern man can no longer equate a beloved woman with a theological virtue, he still knows Dante's device of equating a true perfection of the object of his love with absolute Perfection.

The *Lettres portugaises* thus contain a disillusioned critique of passionate or false love and are imbued with the pessimism of a La Rochefoucauld; they constitute a continuing demonstration of the monologic solipsism which travesties the dialogue of two souls which true love should be. And in the end the false dialogue discovers itself to be a monologue – and thereby finds itself superfluous. The letters cease when one soul, having poured out all its false contents, gains the courage to remain painfully alone and itself. 'It is enough to be.' The pained cries of the letters themselves form but a prologue to the great silence of disillusionment in a reluctantly accepted life without passion. Marianne will probably not die like her pendant, the unhappy Wilhelmine whose love at first sight for a very ordinary young captain is related by Stendhal in chapter XXIII of *De l'Amour*.

What gives our text an exemplary importance for the seventeenth century is the fact that the 'majesty of human suffering' is embodied not in a character of high rank but in a woman of 'mediocre' social status (Marianne herself grumbles at 'la médiocrité de [sa] condition', p. 174). The monastic setting, an invention of genius, gives Marianne the privilege of living her passion with all the aristocratic exclusivity and sovereignty of a Bérénice or a Princesse de Clèves. And so the expression of her feelings can draw on all the refined elegance which courtly life had given to the French language, on all the intellectual culture in the analysis of love which the salons had produced. A passionate soul emerging from the common people but ennobled by her passion writes the lucid and at the same time sensitive prose of a Madame de Sévigné or a Madame de la Fayette.

'Lucid' and 'sensitive' – with these two terms I mean to characterise the convergence of intellect and feeling which distinguishes the language and thought of the seventeenth century. I am thinking here of e.g. those sentences which appear to have a logical basis (stressed by parallel members and causal conjunctions) but which in reality only follow a logic of the heart:

> Je me défendis de revenir à une vie que je dois *perdre pour vous*, puisque je ne puis la *conserver pour vous* . . . (I, p. 148)

The highlighted phrases, linked by a causal conjunction, construct a kind of logical mirage before our eyes. Only the heart can indulge in the specious logic of 'if I cannot live for you, then I must die'. Another example:

. . . vous m'avez fait espérer que vous viendriez passer quelque temps avec moi. Hélas! pourquoi n'y voulez-vous pas passer toute votre vie? (1, p. 149)

Those are not the only two alternatives in reality: *hélas* gives the pained reply to the false logic suggested by the *pourquoi*.

Je ne mets mon honneur et ma religion qu'à vous *aimer* éperdument *toute ma vie*, puisque j'ai commencé à *vous aimer*. (2, p. 153)

Does one have to continue all one's life whatever one has begun to do?

Il faut que *vous ayez eu* pour moi de l'aversion naturelle, puisque *vous ne m'avez pas aimée* éperdument. (5, p. 174)

'Not loving' does not necessarily mean 'disliking'. This illogical ellipsis is much more like a cry of passion from the heart. The false causality opens out a perspective onto the *lacrimae rerum*.

There are also in our text many of those paired expressions which, whilst they introduce an intellectual element, also suggest by analogy a kind of fatal continuity:

Je connais trop bien mon destin pour tâcher à le surmonter; *je serai malheureuse toute ma vie*; ne *l'étais-je* pas vous voyant *tous les jours*? (5, p. 173)

Je vous aime *mille fois plus* que ma vie et *mille fois plus* que je ne pense . . . (4, p. 168)

One stylistic figure of intellectual origin which is particularly pronounced in the *Lettres portugaises* is what I shall call 'painful antithetical comparisons', where the nun's 'I' confronts the lover's 'thou':

Ne devais-je pas prévoir que *mes plaisirs finiraient plus tôt que mon amour*? . . . je ne connais que trop que tous les mouvements . . . n'étaient excités en vous que par quelques *plaisirs*, et qu'ils *finissaient aussi tôt qu'eux* . . . (2, pp. 151–2)

. . je sais bien que *vous* êtes aussi facile à *vous laisser persuader contre moi*, que *je* l'ai été à me *laisser persuader en votre faveur* . . . (4, p. 162)

Votre famille vous avait écrit? ne savez-vous pas toutes les persécutions que j'ai souffertes de *la mienne*? *Votre honneur* vous engageait à m'abandonner? ai-je pris quelque soin *du mien*? (4, p. 162)

. . *vous pouvez vous souvenir* de *ma* pudeur, de *ma* confusion et de *mon* désordre, *mais vous ne vous souvenez pas* de ce qui *vous engagerait à m'aimer* malgré vous. (4, p. 167)

Adieu, *j'ai plus de peine* à finir ma Lettre que *vous n'en avez eu* à me quitter, peut-être, pour toujours. (4, pp. 167–8)

Fundamentally, these polemical antitheses do no more than repeat the central motif of the whole work, namely the great antithesis 'I love you' / 'You do not love me'; and it is this basic motif which gives these expressions the poignancy of a despairing embrace.

Marianne's exclamations *ah*! and *hélas*! are the distinguished sighs of a French novelistic or theatrical heroine, they are stylised expressions replacing popular exclamations like *mon Dieu* which are absent from our text. A sentence such as 'je vous aime mille fois plus que ma vie et *mille* fois plus que je ne pense' (4, p. 168) is very close to the language of Racine:

> Cet amour est ardent, il le faut confesser.
> Plus ardent mille fois que tu ne peux penser . . .
>
> *Bérénice* II.ii, 421–2

And the tragically paradoxical closing of letter 1 is surely pure Racine: 'Adieu, aimez-moi toujours; et faites-moi souffrir encore plus de maux' (p. 150).

Who, apart from a lady of French high society, schooled in rhetoric, could let herself go in for subtly gradated pathetic declamations such as these?

> Vous m'avez consommée par vos assiduités, vous m'avez enflammée par vos transports, vous m'avez charmée par vos complaisances, vous m'avez assurée par vos serments, mon inclination violente m'a séduite . . . (4, p. 161)

> Mais avant de vous engager dans une grande passion, pensez bien à l'excès de mes douleurs, à l'incertitude de mes projets, à la diversité de mes mouvements, à l'extravagance de mes lettres, à mes confiances, à mes désespoirs, à mes souhaits, à ma jalousie! (4, p. 166)

Who, apart from a marchioness in her Parisian *salon*, would polish epigrams such as these?

> . . . je voudrais que toutes les femmes de France vous trouvassent aimable, qu'aucune ne vous aimât, et qu'aucune ne vous plût. (4, p. 165)

Who, apart from a society lady accustomed to analysing complex human situations, could draw up this list of disparate elements contributing to a single effect?

> Votre éloignement, quelques mouvements de dévotion, la crainte de ruiner entièrement le reste de ma santé . . . le peu d'apparence de votre retour, la froideur de votre passion et de vos derniers adieux, votre départ . . . et mille autre raisons . . . semblaient me promettre un secours assez assuré . . . (3, p. 155)

Larat claims that contemporary readers of the *Lettres portugaises* 'ont bien senti que ce qui fait leur charme, c'est leur spontanéité, le naturel de leur désordre et de leur forme sans apprêt' (?) and that Dorat, the eighteenth-century editor of a new edition of the *Lettres*, wrote in his gushing manner: 'tout y est vrai, naturel, de cette simplicité attachante, premier charme des écrits auxquels on revient et dont on ne se lasse jamais . . . Pour peu qu'on ait de la sensibilité, on relit six fois les *Portugaises* avant de s'apercevoir qu'elles sont mal écrites.' As late as 1832, Sainte-Beuve is still insisting on the non-literary nature of the *Lettres portugaises* which he groups together with the love-letters of Mlle de Lespinasse and Mlle Aïssé:

Ce sont des livres qui ne ressemblent pas à des livres, et qui quelquefois même n'en sont pas . . . Aussi les lettres écrites au moment de la passion . . . sont-elles inappréciables et d'un charme particulier dans leur désordre. On connaît celles d'une Portugaise, bien courtes malheureusement et tronquées . . . (Sainte-Beuve, 'Du Roman intime', pp. 1007–8, 1009)

I would like to believe that I have proved the opposite, that the *Lettres portugaises* form a complete and well-ordered book, written with skill by an author who knew his business, and that their stylistic disorder is more an artistic and intentional 'beau désordre' than a natural disorderliness.

It is far from certain that the *Lettres portugaises* 'subordinate logic and clarity to exclamatory vehemence' as has been claimed. There are two sources of this misapprehension. First, reading the exclamatory phrases *separately*, without taking into account the logical linkage between the ideas; second, reading excited *passages* without taking account of the *structure* of the letters seen as an artistic whole. Let me take for example a passage peppered with interjections, questions and exclamations:

Je vis, infidèle, que je suis, et je fais autant de choses pour conserver ma vie que pour la perdre. Ah! j'en meurs de honte: mon désespoir n'est donc que dans mes lettres? Si je vous aimais autant que je vous l'ai dit mille fois, ne serais-je pas morte il y a longtemps? . . . Hélas! pourquoi ne vous en plaignez-vous pas? . . . je vous ai trahi, je vous en demande pardon. Mais ne me l'accordez pas! Traitez-moi sévèrement! Ne trouvez point que mes sentiments soient assez violents! Soyez plus difficile à contenter! Mandez-moi que vous voulez que je meure d'amour pour vous! (3, pp. 157–8)

First of all, the first three sentences cohere logically between themselves, subordinated as they are to the epigrammatic idea 'je fais autant de choses . . .'; and so do the last six, subordinated as they are to 'Hélas! pourquoi ne vous en plaignez-vous pas?'. Secondly, these two main ideas are tightly linked to each other ('je ne fais rien pour perdre ma vie' – 'pourquoi ne vous en plaignez-vous pas?'). Certainly there is a fragmentation of the period into staccato exclamations, but certainly not the sort of chaotic expression that a modern novelist would give to a heroine assailed by the incoherent, contradictory and zigzagging impulses of her subconscious. Our passage is in fact rather stylised, and the last six exclamations even contain a kind of 'syntactic anaphora' of rhetorical origin. As for seeing the passage in the work as a whole, it has a rational place in the dialectic of 'the letter as substitute for life shared with the lover' and in the series of allusions to a lover's suicide (the death-in-love motif) which pervades the last letters of the correspondence.

The defiance of cartesian rationalism is not as total in the *Lettres portugaises* as has been made out. Although Marianne is herself an anti-cartesian sensibility, she judges her own character from a cartesian standpoint. Larat's very words on the spirit of the French seventeenth century (assaulted from the 'outside' by the influence of the *Portugaises*, which he believes to come from Portugal, by the English and by Rousseau the Swiss) provide an excellent description of our text:

> Le génie de Descartes est bien l'inspirateur des générations du grand siècle que semble organiser dans tous les domaines le *Discours de la Méthode pour bien connaître sa raison et trouver la vérité*. Socialement le 'généreux' en est le produit, qui trouve sa joie très pure à connaître sa passion, à en dénombrer les éléments, à les ramener à leur source et, par un renoncement aux contingences qui pourraient le troubler, se rend 'en quelque façon semblable à Dieu' et 's'estime au plus haut point qu'il se peut légitimement estimer'. (Larat, p. 637)

Does not Marianne judge her passion in the court of cartesianism? Does she not know her passion, does not she not enumerate its elements and reduce them to their origin? Does she not render herself 'alike unto God' by isolating her love – and killing it?

Marianne's love may well 'en rêvant descend dans ses entrailles . . . / Comme quelqu'un qui cherche en tenant une lampe', to quote Hugo's *Tristesse d'Olympio* (*Œuvres poétiques*, I.1098), and reach down 'jusqu'au fond désolé du gouffre intérieur', but there she finds no 'sacré souvenir' of Love, but only the nothingness of dead passion. The ending of the *Portugaises*, like that of *La Princesse de Clèves*, coincides with an internal 'end' as clear and firm as the action which it brings to a conclusion, as 'finished' as a mathematical demonstration. The romantic poet is more sentimental and, in search of the infinite and the vague, Hugo extends the sentiment beyond the end of his poem. The difference between the two inspirations is the difference between one full stop and three . . .

The miniature art-form of these five letters, with its concentrated unity of internal action, with its radical 'monologism' (a conversation not of several people placed 'beneath a single light' as in the classical theatre, but of a solitary soul with itself, beneath the lamp, so to speak, of psychological introspection) is the classical expression of passion abstracted from the context of life and subjected to rational analysis.

It is surprising that Pierre Trahard, in the first chapter of *Les Maîtres* *de la sensibilité française au XVIIIe siècle*, makes no mention of the *Lettres portugaises* alongside Fénelon, Pascal et al.; and surprising also that he dates 'the self-analysis of sensibility' only from 1718–25. What are the *Portugaises* if not a reflection of self-analysing sensibility? And do they not contain the term *sensible* in all the fullness of meaning it was to have in the eighteenth century? The seventeenth century no doubt was able to see in Marianne only an authentic heroine of sensibility, to hear only her *hélas*!, to perceive only the spontaneity of her heartfelt exclamations: but it seems to me that the twentieth-century critic has too much historical perspective to fail to recognise in the *Lettres portugaises* an author of genius. He gave his heroine abundant cartesian lucidity and a language which even if it heralds the preromantics from afar is nonetheless redolent with the literary nobility of French prose of the classical period.*

* A seven-page study of Rilke's German translation of the *Lettres portugaises* has been omitted.

LIST OF REFERENCES

The following list gives the publication details of all the works quoted and the principal works referred to in the chapters of this book which I have been able to identify and locate, with the exception of attributable Latin phrases for which references are given with the quotation, and with the further exception of the plays of Racine, which have been quoted according to the text of the current *Nouveaux Classiques Larousse* editions. Wherever possible, I have used recent editions of the texts involved rather than those Spitzer may have had access to, and for works in German I have used, where available, current English translations. Also included in this list, of course, are works referred to in the translator's footnotes and intercalations.

Anon. *La Vie de Saint Alexis*, ed. C. Storey. Oxford: Blackwell, 1968.

Auerbach, Erich. 'Racine und die Leidenschaften', *Germanisch–romanische Monatshefte*, 16 (1926).

Mimesis. The Representation of Reality in Western Literature (1946), transl. W. R. Trask. Princeton University Press, 1968.

Barbey d'Aurevilly, Jules. '*Lettres portugaises*' (1854) in *Femmes et moralistes* (1906). Geneva: Slatkine Reprints, 1968, pp. 41–51.

Batteux, l'abbé Charles. 'Observations sur l'*Hippolyte* d'Euripide et la *Phèdre* de Racine' (1776), quoted in Mesnard (q.v.) III.280–1.

Benjamin, Walter. *Ursprung des deutschen Trauerspiels* (1928), ed. Rolf Tiedemann. Frankfurt: Suhrkamp, 1963.

Bertram, Ernst. *Nietzsche. Versuch einer Mythologie*. Berlin, 1918.

Boileau-Despréaux, Nicolas. *Œuvres*, ed. M. Amar. Paris: Lefèvre, 1824.

Satires, ed. C.-H. Boudhors (1934). Paris: Les Belles Lettres, 1952.

'Lettre à Perrault' (1699) in *Dialogues, Réflexions critiques, Œuvres diverses*, ed. C.-H. Boudhors. Paris: Les Belles Lettres, 1942.

'Réflexions critiques sur quelques passages de Longin' (1710) in ibid., pp. 179–83.

Boislisle, A. de (ed.). Saint-Simon, *Mémoires,* vol. XXVIII (Grands Ecrivains de la France). Paris: Hachette, 1916.

Boulenger, Jacques, and Thérive, André. *Les Soirées du Grammaire-Club*. Paris: Plon, 1913.

Braunschvig, Marcel. *Notre Littérature étudiée dans les textes*, I (1924), 24th edn. Paris: A. Colin, 1962.
Brémond, Henri. *Prière et poésie*. Paris: Grasset, 1926.
Brinkmann, Hennig. *Entstehungsgeschichte des Minnesangs*. Halle: Niemeyer, 1926.
Brunetière, Ferdinand. *Etudes critiques sur l'histoire de la littérature française*. Paris: Hachette, 1888–1903.
Histoire de la littérature française classique (1515–1830), vol. II. Paris: Delagrave, 1912.
Brunot, Ferdinand. *Histoire de la langue française des origines à 1900*. Paris: A. Colin, 1913.
Charrier, Charlotte. *Héloïse dans l'histoire et la légende*. Paris: H. Champion, 1933.
Colette. *Mitsou, ou comment l'esprit vient aux filles* (1919) in *Œuvres complètes*, vol. V. Paris: Le Fleuron, 1949, pp. 125–212.
Commynes, Philippe de. *Mémoires*, ed. Gaston Calmette (CFMA). Paris: Les Belles Lettres, 1965.
Cordemann, M. *Der Umschwung der Kunst zwischen der ersten und der zweiten Fabelsammlung La Fontaines*. Munich, 1917.
Corneille, Pierre. *Polyeucte*, ed. R. Sayce. Oxford: Blackwell, 1973.
Des Hons, Gabriel. *Anatole France et Jean Racine, ou la clé de l'art francien*. Paris: Le Divan, 1925.
Diderot, Denis. 'Paradoxe sur le comédien' in *Œuvres complètes*, ed. Jules Assézat, vol. VIII. Paris: Garnier, 1875, pp. 361–423.
Droncke, E. M. 'Heloïse and Marianne: Some Reconsiderations', *Romanische Forschungen* 72 (1960) 223–56.
Faguet, Emile. *Dix-septième Siècle*. Paris: Lecène, 1890.
En lisant Corneille. Paris: Hachette, 1913.
Feise, Ernst. '*Cardenio und Celinde* und *Papinianus* von Andreas Gryphius', *Journal of English and Germanic Philology* 44 (1944) 181–93.
Fénelon, François de. *Lettre à l'Académie* (1714), ed. Ernesta Caldarini. Geneva: Droz, 1970.
France, Anatole. *La Révolte des Anges* (1914) in *Œuvres complètes illustrées*, vol. XXII. Paris: Calmann–Lévy, 1949.
Fubini, Mario. 'Umanesimo, Teatro, Poesia nell'opera di Jean Racine', *La Cultura* 4 (1924) 62–71.
Gide, André. *Incidences*. Paris: NRF, 1924.
Voyage au Congo in *Œuvres complètes*, vol. XIII. Paris: NRF, 1937.
Gilson, Etienne. *Les Idées et les lettres* (1932). Paris: Vrin, 1955.
Abelard and Héloïse (1938). London: Hollis and Carter, 1953.
Giraudoux, Jean. *Siegfried von Kleist* in *Le Théâtre complet de J.G.*, vol. IX. Neuchâtel: Ides et Calendes, 1947.
Gmelin, H. 'Zum Problem des Humors in der französischen Literatur', *Die Neueren Sprachen* 41 (1933) 12–25.
Goethe, Wolfgang von. *Wilhelm Meisters Lehrjahre* in *Werke* (Hamburger Ausgabe, 14 vols.), vol. VII. Munich: Beck, 1973.
Elective Affinities (1809), transl. R. J. Hollingdale. Harmondsworth: Penguin, 1971.

Green, F. C. 'Who was the author of the *Lettres portugaises*?', *Modern Language Review* 21 (1926) 156–67.

Gryphius, Andreas. *Cardenio und Celinde* (1657), ed. Powell. Leicester University Press, 1967.

Guilleragues, Gabriel de. *Lettres portugaises*, ed. F. Deloffre and J. Rougeot. Geneva: Droz, 1972.

Correspondance, ed. F. Deloffre and J. Rougeot. Paris: Droz, 1976.

Hadamard, J. 'Science et monde moderne', *Renaissance* 1 (1943) 550ff.

Heer, Friedrich. *Aufgang Europas. Eine Studie zu den Zusammanhängen zwischen politischer Religiosität, Frömmigkeit und dem Werden Europas im 12. Jahrhundert.* Vienna–Zurich, 1949.

Heidegger, Martin. *Was ist Metaphysik?* (1929). Frankfurt: Klostermann, 1955.

Heiss, Hans. 'Die Kunst Molières', *Neue Jahrbücher für Wissenschaft und Jugendbildung* 4 (1928) 663–72.

[Review of Spitzer, B13], *Literaturblatt für germanische und romanische Philologie*, 1931, col. 121.

Hofmannsthal, Hugo von. *Das Buch der Freunde* (1922). Frankfurt: Insel-Verlag, 1965.

'Das Schrifttum als geistiger Raum der Nation', *Neue Deutsche Rundschau*, 1927.

Hugo, Victor. *Œuvres poétiques*, ed. Pierre Albouy. Paris: Gallimard, 1964.

La Légende des siècles, ed. Jacques Truchet. Paris: Gallimard, 1962.

Cromwell, ed. Annie Ubersfeld. Paris: Garnier–Flammarion, 1968.

Jolles, Andre. *Einfache Formen* (1929). Tübingen: Niemeyer, 1974.

Keyserling, Hermann Alexander. *Das Spektrum Europas.* Heidelberg, 1928.

Klemperer, Victor. [Review of Cordemann, q.v.], *Literaturblatt für germanische und romanische Philologie*, 1920, cols. 41–5.

Pierre Corneille. Munich: Hueber, 1933.

Knoche, Ulrich. 'Betrachtungen über Horazens Kunst der satirischen Gesprächsführung', *Philologus* 90 (1936) 373ff.

Köster, Albert, *Schiller als Dramaturg. Beiträge zur deutschen Literaturgeschichte des XVIII. Jahrhunderts.* Berlin: W. Hertz, 1891.

Kuttner, Hans. [Review of Spitzer, B13], *Zeitschrift für französische Sprache und Literatur* 53 (1929) 332.

La Fontaine, Jean de. *Fables*, ed. with introduction and notes by Georges Couton. Paris: Classiques Garnier, 1962.

La Motte, Antoine Houdar de. 'Discours sur la poésie en général et sur l'ode en particulier' (1707) in *Œuvres complètes* (1754). Geneva: Slatkine Reprints, 1970.

Lancaster, H. Carrington. *A History of French Dramatic Literature in the Seventeenth Century.* Baltimore: The Johns Hopkins Press, 1929–42.

'The Horse in French Plays of the Seventeenth Century' in H. Peyre (ed.), *Essays in Honor of Albert Feuillerat.* New Haven: Yale University Press, 1943, pp. 103–14.

[Replies to Lynes, q.v.], *Modern Language Notes* 59 (1944) 391, 586.

Lanson, Gustave. *Choix de lettres du XVIIe siècle.* Paris: Hachette, 1891.

Boileau. Paris: Hachette, 1892.

Etudes d'histoire littéraire. Paris: Champion, 1929.

Larat, P., and Larat, J. 'Les *Lettres d'une religieuse portugaise* et la sensibilité française', *Revue de littérature comparée* 8 (1928) 627ff.

Laurand, Louis. *Etudes sur le style des 'Discours' de Cicéron* (1907). Paris: Les Belles Lettres, 1926.

Lemaître, Jules. *Impressions de Théâtre.* Paris: Lecène et Oudin, 1888–1900.

Lerch, Eugen. '"C'est son rêve accompli"', *Zeitschrift für romanische Philologie*, Beiheft 42, 1912.

Prädikative Partizipia für Verbalsubstantiva im Französischen. Halle, 1912.

[Review of K. Arnholdt, *Die Stellung des attributiven Adjektivs im Italienischen und Spanischen*], *Archiv für das Studium der neueren Sprachen* 139 (1919) 242–56.

Lessing, Gotthold Ephraim. *Hamburgische Dramaturgie*, ed. Otto Mann. Stuttgart: Kröner, 1963.

Lips, Marguerite. *Le Style indirect libre.* Paris: Payot, 1926.

Ludwig, A. [Article on Spitzer], *Vossische Zeitung*, 31 August 1929.

Lynes, Carlos J., Jr. 'A Defense of the *Récit de Théramène*', *Modern Language Notes* 59 (1944) 387–91.

'The Récit de Théramène once more', ibid. 584–5.

Marmontel, Jean-François. *Poétique française* (1763). New York: Johnson Reprints, 1972.

Martin du Gard, Roger. *Les Thibault.* Paris: NRF, 1922–8.

Marty-Laveaux, Charles. *Lexique de la langue de Jean Racine* (1873) = Mesnard, vol. VIII.

Mauriac, François. *La Vie de Jean Racine.* Paris: Plon, 1928.

Maurras, Charles. *Pages littéraires choisies.* Paris: Champion, 1922.

Meillet, Antoine. *Esquisse d'une histoire de la langue latine.* Paris: Hachette, 1928.

[Review of Spitzer, B13], *Bulletin de la Société de Linguistique de Paris* 30 (1929) 145.

Menéndez y Pelayo, Marcelino. *Estudios sobre el teatro de Lope de Vega* in *Obras completas*, vol. XXXIII. Santander: CSIC, 1949, pp. 171–82.

Mesnard, P. (ed.). *Œuvres complètes de Jean Racine*, 8 vols. (Grands Ecrivains de la France). Paris: Hachette, 1873.

Mornet, Daniel. *Histoire générale de la littérature française exposée selon une méthode nouvelle.* Paris: Larousse, 1930.

Müller, Günther. 'Die Form der Legende und Karl Borromäus Heinrich', *Euphorion* 31 (1930) 454–68.

Neubert, Fritz. 'Zur Wort- und Begriffskunst der französischen Klassik' in *Philologisch–philosophische Studien. Festschrift für E. Wechssler.* Jena–Leipzig: Gronau, 1929, pp. 153–77.

Norden, E. *Die Antike Kunstprosa.* Leipzig: Teubner, 1909.

P. Vergilius Maro Aeneis Buch 6. Leipzig: Teubner, 1916.

Olschki, Leonardo. *Die Romanischen Literaturen des Mittelalters.* Potsdam: Athenaion, 1928.

Paléologue, Maurice. 'Les Lettres d'amour de la religieuse portugaise', *Revue des Deux Mondes* 95 (1889) 914–28.

Péguy, Charles. 'Victor Marie, comte Hugo' (1910) in *Œuvres en prose 1909–1914.* Paris: Gallimard, 1957.

Peyre, Henri. [Review of A. F. B. Clark, *Jean Racine*], *Romanic Review* 31 (1940) 296–8.

Pfandl, Ludwig. 'Der Narzissbegriff. Versuch einer neuen Deutung', *Imago* 21 (1935) 279–310.

Pourtalès, Guy de. 'Annotations aux marges d'un La Fontaine' in *De Hamlet à Swann*. Paris: Crès, 1924.

Proust, Marcel. *Contre Sainte-Beuve*, ed. M. Regard. Paris: Gallimard, 1954.

Rabelais, François. *Le Quart Livre*, ed. Jean Plattard. Paris: Les Belles Lettres, 1946.

Radice, Betty. 'Introduction' to *The Letters of Abelard and Heloise*. Harmondsworth: Penguin, 1974.

Raynouard, F. J. M. *Lexique roman*. Paris: Sylvestre, 1838–44.

Régnier, H. (ed.). *Œuvres de La Fontaine*, 11 vols. (Grands Ecrivains de la France), new edn. Paris: Hachette, 1929.

Rilke, Rainer Maria. *Briefe aus den Jahren 1906–1907*. Leipzig, 1930.

Ronsard, Pierre de. *Œuvres poétiques*, ed. Marcel Cohen. Paris: Gallimard, 1965.

Rousseau, Jean-Jacques. *La Nouvelle Héloïse*, in *Œuvres complètes*, ed. Raymond Gagnebin and Marcel Raymond, vol. II. Paris: Gallimard, 1961.

Lettre à M. d'Alembert sur son article 'Genève' (1758), ed. Michel Launay. Paris: Garnier–Flammarion, 1967.

Roustan, Mario. *Précis d'explication française (méthode et applications)*. Paris: Delaplane, 1911.

(ed.). La Fontaine, *Fables et œuvres choisies*. Paris: Didier/Privat, 1935.

Rudler, Gustave. *L'Explication française, principes et applications*. Paris: A. Colin, 1902.

Sainte-Beuve, Charles-Augustin. 'Du roman intime, ou Mademoiselle de Liron' (1832) in *Œuvres*, ed. Maxime Leroy, vol. II. Paris: Gallimard, 1960, pp. 1007–24.

Port-Royal (1840), ed. Jean Pommier. Paris: Droz, 1937.

Saint-Evremond, Charles de. 'De la tragédie ancienne et moderne' (1692) in *Œuvres en prose*, ed. René Ternois, vol. IV. Paris: Didier, 1969, pp. 170–84.

Saint-Marc Girardin. *La Fontaine et les fabulistes*. Paris: Calmann–Lévy, 1886.

Saint-Simon, Louis de Rouvroy. *Mémoires*. Paris: Gallimard, 1953.

Sayce, Olive. *Poets of the Minnesang*. Oxford: Clarendon Press, 1967.

Schiller, Friedrich. *Gedichte*, ed. Klaus L. Bergahn. Königstein: Athenäum, 1980.

Schlegel, August Wilhelm von. *Comparaison entre la 'Phèdre' d'Euripide et celle de Racine*. Paris, 1807.

Schmeidler, B. 'Der Breifwechsel zwischen Abelard und Heloise: eine Fälschung?', *Archiv für Kulturgeschichte* 11 (1930) 1–30.

Schmidt, Julius. [Review of Spitzer, B13], *Zeitschrift für französische Sprache und Literatur* 53 (1929) 332.

Schröder, Rudolf Alexander. 'Zur deutschen Würdigung Racines', *Corona* 2 (1932) 536–9.

Spitzer, Leo. 'Zur Entstehung der sog. *erlebten Rede*', *Germanisch–romanische Monatshefte* 16 (1928) 327–32.

'Zum französischen historischen Infinitiv', *Zeitschrift für romanische Philologie* 50 (1930) 533–47.

Stengel, E. *Das Ross in den altfranzösischen Artus- und Abenteuerromanen.* Munich, 1888.

Strachey, Lytton. *Books and Characters.* London: Chatto & Windus, 1922.

Taine, Hippolyte. *La Fontaine et ses fables* (1860). Paris: Hachette, 1907.

Taylor, Kressmann. *Address Unknown. A Tale.* London: Hamish Hamilton, 1939.

Thérive, André. *Le Français, langue morte?* Paris: Plon, 1923.

Thibaudet, Albert. 'Réflexions sur la politique', *Nouvelle Revue française* 30 (1928) 433–45.

'Boileau', *Nouvelle Revue française* 47 (1936) 141–58.

Trahard, Pierre. *Les Maîtres de la sensibilité française au XVIIIe siècle (1715–1789).* Paris: Boivin, 1931–3.

Truc, Gonzague. *Le Cas Racine.* Paris: Garnier, 1921.

Valéry, Paul. 'Au sujet d'Adonis' (1920) in *Variété.* Paris: NRF, 1924, pp. 51–88.

'Discours de la diction des vers' (1926) in *Œuvres*, ed. Jean Hytier, vol. II. Paris: Gallimard, 1960, pp. 1253–9.

Voltaire. 'Remarques sur *Polyeucte*' in *Œuvres complètes*, ed. A. J. Q. Beuchot, vol. XXXI. Paris: Garnier, 1880, pp. 370–418.

Vossler, Karl. *Sprache als Schöpfung und Entwicklung.* Heidelberg: Winter, 1905.

La Fontaine und sein Fabelwerk. Heidelberg: Winter, 1919.

Frankreichs Kultur im Spiegel seiner Sprachentwicklung. Heidelberg: Winter, 1921.

Jean Racine (1926). Bühl: Roland, 1948.

Wackernagel, Jacob. *Vorlesungen über Syntax*, vols. I–II. Basel: Birkhauser, 1920 and 1928.

Walther, H. *Das Streitgedicht in der lateinischen Literatur des Mittelalters.* Munich, 1920.

Walzel, Oskar. *Geschichte der deutschen Literatur*, 3rd edn. Berlin: Akademischer Verlag, 1921.

Weisbach, Werner. *Die Kunst des Barock in Italien, Frankreich, Deutschland und Spanien.* Berlin: Propyläen, 1924.

Winkler, Emil. 'Von der Kunst des Alexiusdichters', *Zeitschrift für romanische Philologie* 47 (1927) 588–97.

Grundlegung der Stilistik. Bielefeld: Velhagen und Klasing, 1929.

Wölfflin, Heinrich. *Renaissance und Barock: eine Untersuchung über Wesen und Entstehung des Barockstils in Italien*, 7th edn. Basel: Schwabe, 1968.

INDEX OF NAMES

INDEX OF RHETORICAL AND SPECIAL TERMS

23484903R00199

Printed in Great Britain
by Amazon